I AM Brother Oji

Roots, Rock, Revolution of a Modern Nomad
A Biography

Mello Ayo

Also by Mello Ayo

Love Rhapsodies and Blues

Good Morning, Afrika! A Photo-Journey Home

I AM

Brother Oji

Roots, Rock, Revolution of a Modern Nomad

Copyright © 2022 by Mello Ayo. 836981

All rights reserved. No part of this book may be reproduced or transmitted in any form or by any means, electronic or mechanical, including photocopying, recording, or by any information storage and retrieval system, without permission in writing from the copyright owner.

To order additional copies of this book, contact:
Xlibris
844-714-8691
www.Xlibris.com
Orders@Xlibris.com

ISBN:	Softcover	978-1-6698-0937-1
	Hardcover	978-1-6698-0936-4
	EBook	978-1-6698-0935-7

Library of Congress Control Number: 2022902135

Print information available on the last page

Rev. date: 03/31/2022

Copyright © 2022 Mello Ayo

All rights reserved. No part of this publication may be reproduced, distributed, or transmitted in any form or by any means, including photocopying, recording, or other electronic or mechanical methods without the prior written permission of the author except in the case of brief quotations embodied in critical reviews and for academic or noncommercial purposes permitted by copyright law.

Unless otherwise attributed, all photo images including lead headshots are used with permission courtesy of Brother Oji, who has generously opened his extensive archives and MACPRI collection to the author.

"Young and old protesting at the ROM March 1990" provided courtesy of Neville White Jr. Photo of Brother Oji standing outside ROM in 2018, provided courtesy of Eryck B.

Brochure cover image of Into the Heart of Africa used with the express permission of the copyright holder courtesy of the Royal Ontario Museum. *Lord Beresford encounter with Zulu warrior* attributed to *Illustrated London News*, 1879. *Negro World* clipping of the "Declaration of Rights of Negro Peoples of the World" attributed to Marcus Garvey and Amy Ashwood, 1926. Other news clippings are used under paid licensed permission from their respective sources. "Ugly Court Display Mocks Justice" republished with the express permission of *Toronto Sun*, a division of Postmedia Network Inc. "Demonstrators Clash with Police" used with express permission of the Toronto Star Newspapers Limited. All rights reserved.

Quotations cited are directly from Brother Oji's speeches and writings or from interviews recorded by the author. Quotes from his poems are from a yet to be named collection of unpublished poems and are used with his written and expressed permission. All rights reserved.

Front and back cover design by Mello Ayo in collaboration with Xlibris design team. Front cover image sourced from the Oji Archives featuring a poster originally designed by Minister Faust and used by the Coalition for the Truth About Africa. Quote is attributed to Fred Hampton. Rear cover image also sourced from the Oji Archives.

Dedicated to

Maia and Joie; Nana Akpaabe Adessa, RA Ndemelle, Naa Shika Isaga,
Naa Joomo and Akos, and to all the children of the world.

Mello Ayo
Toronto, Ontario
www.melloayo.com

I was not intended to be a footnote on the pages of history. I am meant to be a full story of new possibilities and potential as a testament to my ancestral lineage.

Brother Adisa S. Oji

Contents

Acknowledgements xv

Preface.. xvii

Chapter 1
ENTER THE MWALIMU.. 2

Chapter 2
ADISA S. OJI V. REGINA 9

Chapter 3
WHO I AM 37

Chapter 4
WHAT A BAM! BAM! 49

Chapter 5
OH CANADA! 66

Chapter 6
OUR HOME ON NATIVE LAND 79

Chapter 7
YOUNG POETS OF THE REVOLUTION 108

Chapter 8
LOOK FOR ME IN THE WHIRLWIND 132

Chapter 9
MARRONAGE 159

Chapter 10
THE NEW REVOLUTION 172

Chapter 11
FAMILY 211

Chapter 12
REPAIRING OLD WOUNDS / SMALL AXE BIG TREE 221

EPILOGUE... 252

APPENDIX 269

Bibliography 299

Index 301

Acknowledgements

First, please allow me to acknowledge the individuals, families, and organizations whose collective contribution led to the Royal Ontario Museum protest in 1991. The outcome was a result of interplay between a cast of strong characters who selflessly came together to organize and agitate for change. Their unwavering dedication, commitment, and sacrifice deserve more credit than I alone can offer. For those among you who confided in me, including Silbert Barrett, I hope this book in some small way gives you a measure of validation.

To the original people of Canada, thank you for allowing me the opportunity to live and work in your traditional territory. Your inexhaustible faith is inspiring. Your tradition, culture, and long history have kinship with the lived experience of people of African ancestry and are part of a shared tapestry. May we continue to draw empowerment from each other. Thanks also to all Canadians, particularly those contributing significantly to traditions of equality, justice, and anti-racism, and who continue to uphold values integral to peace and human rights.

This biography has been in the making since 2010 with initial drafts completed by 2015. During the intervening years, and up until now, I have had the good fortune of meeting and speaking with many people—too numerous to mention all by name—who were unbelievably generous with their time and insights. Whether our conversation was casual or more in-depth, I thank you.

I wish to thank Dan Rahimi, former director of collections and vice president of programming at the Royal Ontario Museum. Dan was one of the first third-party sources I interviewed for this project. His thoughtful forthcoming recollections of his encounter with Oji following the ROM incident further convinced me that this was an important story worthwhile sharing. Similarly, Professor Edward Chamberlin's account of his relationship with Oji helped in better understanding Oji's evolution. The professor's perspective along with his generosity of time enriched my experience as well as the content of this narrative. I owe him a debt of gratitude, even as I do Dr. Afua Cooper, who granted permission to reference her work, and to Minister Faust, for his recollections of the Young Poets of the Revolution.

Special mention goes to the management and staff of the Multicultural History Society of Ontario (MHSO), including Ms. Elizabeth Price and executive director Mr. Carl Thorpe. Mr. Thorpe and the MHSO helped me to better appreciate the nuanced historical complexities of the African Canadian experience. Mr. Thorpe was also kind to offer valuable insights based on his many years of public service. Thanks goes to Professor Lorne Foster for introducing me to the MHSO and to Mr. Thorpe.

Gratitude to Ahmad Saidullah and Ewart Walters, both of whom provided exceptional critique and timely invaluable suggestions. Ahmad and Ewart were two of my strongest literary supporters. As fellow writers, they understood the challenges I faced. Their strong support helped push me forward. To Sarah Margles and Sheri Golberg, who took valuable time to read early drafts and give invaluable feedback, and to Haile Mika'el and Rosemary Sadlier, for their fact-checking, thank you. To the management and staff of the Royal Ontario Museum including

CEO Josh Basseches, Silvia Forni, and Swarupa Anila, and to Rita Shelton Deverell, member of the Board of Trustees, thank you for embracing the opportunity to engage in constructive conversations regarding the ROM's past, present, and future. Our positive interactions were tremendously valuable.

Singled out for special recognition is my high school English literature teacher, Mrs. Georgie Kennedy, who fortuitously resurfaced some forty years later at an opportune time for me to benefit from her tutelage once more on how to write and tell stories. Her pointers were invaluable. Her suggestions helped with clarity and structure while emboldening my relentless efforts to get this right.

To all the many people who interacted with me on social media and who offered encouragement, advice, and guidance, thank you. Thanks for being more than a bystander.

Speaking of bystanders, Ms. Yvonne Grant refused to be one. She played a special role in Brother Oji's life. I thank her for her humble account, which added texture and drama to the narrative. Aside from operating a great Caribbean corner store, she is a light to many.

Special heartfelt thanks to Donna Johnson-Huggins, my spiritual partner, my biggest cheerleader and inspiration. From early on, her eagle vision latched on to the essence of what I was doing and wanted to accomplish. Her acute understanding inspired me; her positive enthusiasm kept me on purpose and on point. Donna, I thank you.

Above all, thanks to Brother Oji for giving me a ringside seat to his life and work. He kept faith, never wavered. He remains an inspiration to me and no doubt to many others. Gratitude also to his immediate and extended family for allowing me a seat at their kitchen table, whether in Toronto, in Jamaica, or in Ghana. Brother Oji, may your family and your many ancestors, as well as mine, be blessed by the words of my mouth and the meditation of my heart as rendered here in this book.

Grateful acknowledgement to the Toronto Arts Council for their generous support. And thanks to the Xlibris Team for enabling my artistic vision.

Finally, I reserve special thanks to all who have supported my creative, artistic, professional endeavours over the years. I am, because of you. There is nothing new under the sun. Although I have been inventive by experimenting with how I have presented this story, some of the details shared herein have been documented and told in one form or other by many who preceded me. If I have brought any new insights or added anything unique to this conversation, it's solely due to fleeting moments of inspiration. To my many teachers and guides, to the many forerunners whose steps I follow while attempting to create my own unorthodox footprints, my sincerest gratitude for paving the way. Many influences have helped to shape this book. If, however, there are any blunders or omissions, I take sole responsibility. Stay inspired.

Mello Ayo

Toronto, Ontario
January 2022

Preface

Mi Bibini

Obroni aba
The old woman said
As the traveller approached her gate How did she know?
Could one deny her wisdom of age?
For without even seeing the traveller's face
She repeated
Again and again
Obroni aba
"The white man has come."
Identity not determined by pigment
The wise does not identify belonging
By you standing in her face
But by scent
Your fragrance
Smell connecting you to environment
The posture with which you carry yourself
Character displayed
Loyalties
Temporal and spiritual
Geographic home base
These are all part of who you are
And even deeper than the other skin
That has corrupted
The spirit (surface wise) that lie within
The language you speak
The culture and traditions you practice
Make you up
No pleading for understanding
Or explaining
To the wise old woman
Could change her position
For skin is just a cover if the true essence
Does not lie within
You are Obroni she says
Your nose be flat like mine
Is true

> Your skin be dark like mine
> Even darker
> Is true
> You eat the same foods
> I do
> Is true
> The preparation is different
> But is same food
> So in some way a little better
> Not enough to wipe away
> The white paint that stains
> The dark canvas
> And the old woman continued
> With sadness on her face
> And a small grin on the left side of her mouth
> She explains with heart and passion
> "I thought you were like The other Black Americans …"
> Who come here?
> Thinking they better than us
> You not like them I see
> So I am sorry to say
> But
> You still be Obroni
> You must come home
> And learn to become Bibini again …
>
> —Brother Oji[1]

Racism and injustice occur on urban streets as well in corporate white-collar boardrooms. Racism also occurs in academic and intellectual institutions. Spanning the late 1980s to the early '90s, Toronto experienced a groundswell of race-based grievances. One of those watershed moments was the student-led protest against the Royal Ontario Museum's mounting of a controversial exhibit ominously entitled Into the Heart of Africa. Demonstrators were so disturbed they derisively referred to the museum as the Racist Ontario Museum. Opened in November 1989, the landmark exhibition was to be the first of its kind in the institution's seventy-seven-year history. It turned out to be phenomenal, but for the wrong reasons. The ill-fated exhibit and the catastrophe that followed altered the course of museums worldwide and proved to be a monumental life-changing experience for everyone involved. What began as a ripple in a small pond widened to become a wave of local, national, and international significance. In addition to disturbing Ontario's placid but delicate race-relations, upsetting the

---

[1] From an unpublished collection of poems. Used with permission.

province's cosmopolitan image of itself, the entire episode became a global landmark lesson for museums in how *not* to mount, curate, and stage exhibits. So profound was the impact on archival institutions around the world that, for the first time, conservative administrators were compelled to rethink and transform how they conducted their business.

As a result of his contentious role in the upheaval, one of the protagonists was arrested, criminally convicted, then imprisoned. He was the only one among the demonstrators to have met this fate. Three decades later, this is his story. While the ROM affair is an intriguing starting point, this biography is not intended to be an exhaustive account of the museum's catastrophic exhibit. The ROM incident is but a chapter in a more far-reaching, captivating memoir serving only to pinpoint one of many defining moments in one person's heroic journey.

The erasure of the ROM incident from public memory is a loss. There are major lessons to be learned from this under-publicized episode, lessons which are still applicable today. In the case of Brother Oji, the aim is not to restore his legacy to popular public consciousness. For it was never there to begin with. This is an attempt, for the first time, to record his contributions to the many other national and international landmarks in the web of life. When weaved, this web places Brother Oji within the long tradition of social and political activism for Black liberation. When distilled, the primary lesson of this tradition becomes clear. Racism—principally the anti-Black variety, the most redolent, enduring crime against humanity—may be reformed, transformed, even dismantled. But in the end, it ultimately must be toppled if *justice is to roll down like water and righteous like a mighty stream*; meaning, nothing short of revolution will do.

Poet. A quiet storm. An uncorked bottle of homemade wine. Vinegar too. He is a gourd of excellent palm oil. Tough as kola nut. He can be soft like shea butter. Irascible from time to time, but mostly affable. He is serious, a lightning rod with a wry sense of humour. He is a high-stepper to Afro beats and reggae rhythms. He is loved; he is reviled. Loved by family and friends; reviled by those who least understand him, or care to. He is a beloved son, a close-knit brother, a loving uncle. He is a husband, a proud father, a self-determined man, an intellectual, an entrepreneur, a community activist and Pan-Africanist. He lives by the dictum: "If you have no confidence in self, you are twice defeated in the race of life. With confidence, you have won even before you have started."[2] He is infused with the spirit of Marcus Mosiah Garvey, his self-assured attitude easily mistaken for arrogance. As he continues to evolve, the full extent

---

2 Quote attributed to Marcus Mosiah Garvey Jr., a Jamaican national hero and champion of Pan-Africanist thought and action, a Black empowerment activist, an avant-garde independent publisher, journalist, entrepreneur, orator, and visionary founder and first president-general of the Universal Negro Improvement Association, popularly known as the UNIA. For more on Garvey, see chapter 7: "Look for Me in the Whirlwind."

of his self-confidence is yet undetermined. He continues to live, proudly running his race with a rare panache as if it is no one else's business but his own. As a provocateur and evocateur, he is nowhere done. His name is Brother Adisa S. Oji, and I am honoured to be entrusted with the assignment of uncovering his story.

This is not *his* autobiography. This is his story as told by me, not him. Any subjective interpretation offered here is mine, not his; I am certain he would have told it differently. For that is who he is—independent, autonomous, self-determined. He is opinionated, self-reliant, yet he is not an isolationist. He remains rooted in community. This narrative is my interpretation of Brother Oji's life and work—a biographical account I believe is worthy of being told. Anchored in Jamaica, Canada, and West Africa, *I AM Brother Oji* is a sweeping, broad historical overview covering a wide array of human experiences seen through the prism of one person's life story. What this narrative may teach us, only each of us can decide. Perhaps, *I AM Brother Oji* holds important lessons for all of us.

Brother Oji often cites me as his personal biographer. While I smile at his designation, I know he is sincere. By all accounts, we should take him seriously. Over the many years of working on this project, whenever I wavered, it was his fire that spurred me on. Anyone who knows him well will tell you he is not to be taken lightly. So I pressed on knowing better not to be derelict in duty. And I am glad I did. For when Brother Oji's story completely unfolds, when he has fully lived his life's purpose to the very end, many will rush to say, "We knew him when ..."

This is more than simply a personal interest non-fictional account of one person's pilgrimage. Our personal histories are never only our own. Each life unfolds as part of a bigger picture—a web of interpenetrating crisscrossing narratives. For as long as I have known Brother Oji, his life has been a rich tapestry—a portrait of converging visible and invisible threads, intertwining influences stretching backward and forward through time in ways obvious and in other ways beyond that which we can dream or imagine. Brother Oji's life is a beautiful spectrum through which many shards of light reflect. His behaviour, his outlook, his attitude collectively encapsulate an important era in modern human history, exemplifying the web of bisecting currents that continue to affect all of us. His life, as it turns out, can be likened to a kente cloth—a colourful, magnificent fabric of intricately woven threads running over and under each other to create unique interconnecting patterns. These patterns, seemingly arbitrary, reveal much deeper serendipitous connections and associations when examined closely. As a result of this complexity, the narrative voice of this memoir fluctuates between that of a biographer and that of a social historian making for a cinematic multilayered story that zooms in and out.

In preparing this biography on and off for a number of years, many would ask, Why is a biography of this individual important? Why should anyone want to read about his life and work? It is as if we need to justify each other's story. The need to validate our worthiness before we can claim entitlement to wider public acclaim and be celebrated or acknowledged in today's popular culture is so strong it verges on obsession. It is as if we have to be dead before we can truly be celebrated or honoured. All *our* stories are important; and this memoir—Brother Oji's first act, if you will—certainly is.

Primarily, this biography celebrates the life of an exemplary Jamaican Canadian of African descent, his migration and displacement, and his discovery of self-empowerment. The chronology spans his youthful years from birth through to his thirties when he stood on the brink of manhood holding a light ahead for other youthful enthusiasts. The path he took is informative.

The landscape he traversed is instructive, tempestuous, and is remarkably beautiful. To observe his passion for self-determination, to recapture the thrill of his youthful enthusiastic vigour is to be reminded of the fire in our belly and how flames of hope can once again be rekindled, how they can burn regardless of circumstance, or even because of it. At a time when many young people are becoming disenchanted, slumping into alienation and learned helplessness or collapsing into subcultures of violence, a look at how one young man kept his youthful optimism alive and how he refused to become a victim while making a positive difference is deserving of our attention.

As we peer into the life of Brother Oji, we may also wonder at his multiple identities. Christened Fitzroy Anderson at birth by his parents, he is an African Canadian born in Jamaica, a trifecta with its own blessings and complexities. Coupled with his African Jamaican background are minor strains of German, with Arawak Indian roots thrown in. He embodies the Jamaican motto: "Out of many, one people." Since 1974, he has made his home in Canada, a nation proud of its unique and rich diversity. As we hone in even closer, questions may arise regarding his Canadian citizenship and where that status sits in relation to his place of birth and to his place of origin. Are all three identities compatible? Or do they collide? Where does his loyalty rest in relation to all three aspects of his personhood? How do you hold on to roots that are already partially severed while becoming immersed in a new culture that tends to contradict or deny those very same roots? Where is home? Who defines and interprets who or what we should be in a pluralistic multicultural milieu? The question of identity is a puzzle. *I AM Brother Oji* provides an opportunity to learn how one individual navigated this perplexing terrain.

At every turn on Brother Oji's journey, he was faced with someone or something trying to define him. Two questions relentlessly reappeared: Who am I? How did I get here? In his poem "Mi Bibini," he confronts piercing questions of identity as he stood within the sneering gaze of an old African grandmother who at first greets him disparagingly. Through her eyes and voice, he is called on to verify or validate his identity. She, by her manner, compels him to critically unpack his self-knowledge. In response, he had to define his place of belonging. Somewhere in this stirring encounter, he learns that in order to (re)discover or uncover himself, he will first need to "come home."

However, the complimentary philosophical questions confronting him, and many others who share his pedigree, are: *Where is home exactly*? And *what is my purpose*? In response to these questions, Brother Oji provides a resounding answer. While his response may not be to our liking, it is his answer. And this is the point. He has chosen to define himself. He refused to accept the conventional expectations imposed by his upbringing and the neocolonial education he was offered. Instead, he insisted on interrogating it, and by so doing, he embarked on a journey to re-establish himself and to realize his purpose. And he has done so in keeping with his right (some may even go so far as to say his responsibility) to cultivate his own destiny. For those who continue to explore questions of identity and belonging, an enchanting trip with Brother Oji is worthwhile taking.

This biography is intended to benefit anyone having difficulty defining home. This story makes for a good travelling companion for anyone journeying home, especially if they are doing so for the very first time. It is a story of multiple explorations. For this reason, this book applies to all Canadians and others interested in taking an Africentric excursion through the Canadian mosaic. It is dedicated to all, but to Canadians in particular who are hopeful; to those who have an interest in Canada's ability to truthfully confront its history while acknowledging and transcending differences to become a model of nationhood where equity, justice, and peace are enshrined. It is also dedicated to all immigrants in North America who arrive in search of a *better life*, especially those of African and Caribbean descent who are seeking to secure a safe place of belonging in the North American cultural matrix.

Running deep within the Canadian cultural psyche is a discomfort with conflict, a fear of disagreement, a penchant for denial, which prohibits any meaningful progressive discussion on topics related to race and racism. One of the aims of this biography is to uncover the raw impact of colonialism so as to provoke a healthy discourse on these matters. *I AM Brother Oji* is an instructive springboard case study for academics, scholars, university and college students in social sciences and the humanities who are interested in examining the impact of enslavement, colonialization, and racism on contemporary society.

Community workers and activists interested in social justice and human rights should also find this narrative valuable as well as political decision-makers responsible for overseeing and implementing social policy.

Undoubtedly, the subject is uncomfortable and may easily trigger negative and traumatic responses for some. Conversations about the harsh legacy of colonization and the oppression that ensued is unlike conversations about the Toronto Maple Leafs or the Montréal Canadiens or the Canadian Football League or maple syrup. The accounting of colonialism is a tough history that includes cultural genocide, racism, violence, physical, emotional and sexual abuse, and the unconscionable use of power to control and to inflict lethal harm on untold millions of people. Indeed, the long arc of history suggests that colonialism and racism is a borderless global phenomenon affecting North and Latin America, African, Caribbean, and Asian Pacific countries, engineered by and exploited for the benefit of primarily a powerful privileged White elite who would prefer to have this history sanitized or swept under a rug.

The unwritten history of Canada—the history that is rarely taught—is a disturbing one. From the point of view of people of African ancestry, beyond romantic myths and fairy tales, this history is generally one of dehumanization and exclusion; of being deliberately kept out, barred from privilege and power; and of being left behind the development curve in neglected decadent communities where children grope in the white smog of an inferiority complex. It is a history of hopes built and destroyed untold times then rebuilt and destroyed yet again in a continual dance of two steps forward and three steps backward; of hopes dashed by racial inequality, of meagre progress made by a people despite their best efforts to rise above a pernicious violent system which postures as a democracy for all, but which on closer examination is not far removed from apartheid. To be Black in Canada, certainly in any part of the world where colonialism has left its ugly stain, is to be ceaselessly in a struggle for recognition as a *human being*, a persistent fight, day and night, for equality, for freedom, for equitable justice, and for peace of mind.

To find his way through this quagmire, Brother Oji used an Africentric personal map. He refused to sleepwalk his way through the stifling rules dictated by postcolonialism. He instead broke free from its conventional constrictions to dedicate himself to what he called the African Image Revolution. In so doing, he cultivated an autonomous, distinctive, and dignified profile. How he did this is instructive and can help to contribute to and deepen our understanding. As a by-product, we gain a better appreciation of the historical dynamics of Canadian anti-Black racism and a more fulsome understanding of how justice can cave in under the heavy weight of exclusionary discriminatory policies. The role of Africa and the place Jamaica—or any Third World postcolonial plantation society for that matter—occupies in the global scheme of colonialism will also come into focus. Brother Oji's story offers an alternative to narratives advanced by the dominant culture, and represents an experience not usually adequately featured in literary mainstream publications. *I AM Brother Oji* is an invitation for Canada, and for postcolonial societies in general, to reestablish a new authentic relationship with its past, present, and future. This invitation, by extension, applies likewise to the Royal Ontario Museum, which, since 2013, has been publicly making attempts to rebrand itself as an ally of equity and racial justice.

Most countries (and institutions) with an unsavoury past find novel ways to forget, to move on, to escape responsibility, and to remain blameless. They mythologize, sanitize, or whitewash their histories or simply remain silent on the subject. A cursory apology may be offered; the saying of "sorry" may come at long last, but often falls short of full admission of guilt or the giving of full restitution.

Is there a conspiracy of silence? Is Canada and North America generally prepared to confront this history, or will we continue to turn away, preferring to hide this unsavoury part of our politics beneath the rug of untruth? Who should be and can be held responsible? What will it take to bring this issue to centre stage? Or is there no interest? Or should we, as some have suggested, "Forget about it?" While discussions of these questions are out of the scope of this biography, the narrative will be a helpful launch pad to further insight.

Erna Paris, author of *Long Shadows: Truth, Lies and History,* had this to say: "Perhaps lies and inventions about history are inevitably exposed because the leaders who propagate such fables fail to understand something visceral and primary: that ordinary people will remember, even when they are ordered not to; that the victims—including their children and even their grandchildren—will not disappear, although they may be traumatized and cowed for years."

This biography serves as a remembering. In this memorializing, Brother Oji is an unlikely hero. The wider nation may not be familiar with him or his work, making his story that more poignant during times of growing conflict and racial strife. The remembering or historical memory coursing through his life story is worth unpacking because the question of mutual respect and tolerance in a healthy pluralistic society remains a challenge in our time. Everywhere, Western democracies are struggling to find the balance between conformity and diversity. Everywhere, Western democracies are struggling to find an agreed upon ideal, an amicable set of common values to which everyone can equitably lay claim. Today, we find ourselves teeter-tottering between the need to belong and the need to be different. Where Brother Oji has chosen to be on this teeter-totter is deeply complex. His story will help to fill out some of the currently blank spaces and lead to a better global understanding of the varied consequences of racial injustice and inequality. Through this, we may begin to see new and different possibilities of how a nation can best heal the most disconcerting parts of its history. By understanding the profound love that drove Adisa Oji, it may be possible to learn from his example of how to transform negativity into a powerful source of upliftment and healing.

Over and above any discussion of race and narrow-minded adversarial politics, this biography is significant because of the humanity flowing through its narrative. Oji's story is a call to become more open, more compassionate, an invocation to check assumptions and irrational judgements. It is an invitation to find more mature life-affirming ways to confront injustice and to make space for greater equitable liberation of human potential. For a man who considers himself to be the *Mwalimu*—the teacher—this may be his greatest lesson yet.

One caveat. Throughout certain sections, notably in reference to Canada, I have made remarks about the lived experience of Indigenous people. To be clear, I do not, and cannot meaningfully, speak on their behalf. I am exercising judgement based on my years of learning and exposure acquired professionally during my practice in the field of diversity, inclusion, equity, and human rights. In addition, I have had the privilege—if I may be so bold as to make such a claim—of partnering and fostering friendships with informed individuals from the Indigenous community, who have taught me a great deal. While my opinions may be shared widely by them and others, the views expressed here are my own. I have highlighted Indigenous concerns—and hopefully I have done so respectfully—only to illustrate the pervasive, persistent, and consistent nature of colonial exploitation relative to Black and Indigenous populations. I also wish to express solidarity and to underscore the affinity between Black and Indigenous people of colour. I hope I may be forgiven for taking such liberties. I do so sensitively with the Truth and Reconciliation Commission of Canada's call to action as my touchstone, specifically as it relates to justice and education goals, including the developing of culturally appropriate curricula and the enabling of greater cultural understanding pertaining to the history of social injustice and the legacy and history of colonialism.

A note on language. As a practice, I do not routinely use racially derogatory terms. However, during the course of this text, certain racial descriptors, which may be considered offensive, are intentionally cited in the form of quotations. It is not my intent to perpetuate the use of these terms. There is also no intent to sugar-coat history. These expressions are sensitively inserted as a means of authentically highlighting the shocking character of racial injustice and abuse. I regret any harm or hurt caused by the usage of crude racial epithets. I hope your encounter with these degrading designations will be sobering and will be offset by the narrative's inherent dignity.

One other word of caution. As I write, I am acutely aware and must make you, the reader, beware of the danger of a single story. The story of one man is not the story of the whole. Should you find resonance and are able to relate to this chronicle, I hope you will find echoes of your own voice reverberating on these pages. In so doing, I hope you will become empowered to join in Brother Oji's revolution or, if you have not already done so, to initiate a complementary justice movement of your own. If on the other hand you find this account new to you and outside of your domain of immediate lived experience, I invite you to lend open-minded attention. At first blush, complex accounts of race and racism may appear foreign or irrelevant to you. You may feel you are not affected directly. So why care? Please consider making this part of your menu of stories to help inform you on how to make the world a more inhabitable place for all and aid in the realization that, in spite of our varied life encounters, we are all inextricably connected.

Finally, Brother Oji's story is an appropriate way to mark the Decade of People of African Descent. The 2015–2024 International Decade for People of African Descent was proclaimed by the UN General Assembly on December 23, 2013. The theme selected by the UN is "People of African descent: recognition, justice, and development." Two of the objectives of the proclamation are to promote respect, protection, and fulfilment of all human rights and fundamental freedoms by people of African descent *and* to promote a greater knowledge of and respect for the diverse heritage, culture, and contribution of people of African descent to the development of societies.

Brother Oji is a worthy champion and cultural ambassador for Africa and for people of African descent. His story, while singular, is relevant to the objectives laid out by the UN General Assembly and contributes greatly to a better collective understanding of the experiences of people of African descent.

Further to that, it is my ardent desire that this biography will contribute to the building of mutual recognition, mutual respect, and underline the shared responsibility we all have for peace, justice, and human rights and to positively engage in ongoing public dialogue and actions to support this vision.

In addition, this biographical account is relevant as we consider Ghana's 2019 Year of Return, an effort by the Ghanaian government to encourage people of African ancestry to return to the continent of Africa generally and to Ghana specifically. Although 2019 will be in the history books by the time you read this, the narrative of *I AM Brother Oji* symbolically commemorates the ongoing call for repatriation and is emblematic of the diasporic journey back to Africa. Known as *Sankofa*, there is currently a growing movement of historically displaced Africans who are intent on restoring their sense of identity and belonging and who are doing so with remarkable personal sacrifice and success. *I AM Brother Oji* is a celebration of this resilience, a theme worthwhile exploring particularly today when many African Canadians and African Americans are striving to better understand their place in an ever-changing contemporary global landscape. By drawing attention to the value and meaning of roots and to the deep human need for belonging, *I AM Brother Oji* makes an extraordinary gift to anyone interested in observing these initiatives and commemorative events.

This is a story for all time. Intended to be a literary as well as a visual experience (a picture speaks a thousand words), this book serves as a teaching aid for adults and children alike. May this book be a source of enlightenment for all; particularly, may it reinvigorate those who love peace, whose goal it is to creatively engender a better world by recognizing the inherent greatness in each of us.

We are more than footnotes on the pages of history. We are, in fact, the authors.

Before I was born, there was a thought of me. I feel that. And, in the process of my mother bringing me into this world, she is a great mother and a well-chosen vessel to bring me into existence. And I believe in the work of the Ancestors. It is said that two sets of people know the most about the afterlife—those who are closest to death and those who have just been born. And sometimes, you don't ever break out of that cycle. You are born and you have a chronological age, but you still have an age that is beyond chronology. So, I felt, and I feel to this day, from the age of three to now, that I don't really live a true, chronological existence.

Brother Adisa S. Oji

Chapter 1

ENTER THE MWALIMU

They roam the open spaces of our conscience. For them, time has no meaning. They awaken us from our restless slumber. Like antidotes to commercially injected hypodermic stupor, they spur us to reach higher, dig deeper, walk taller. Their words have wings. When uttered, such words hang suspended as if forever, spanning generations, a bridge from one to the other. They show us how to move like poetry on a page; how to be magnificent, magnanimous; how to spread our own wings across the sky of history and fly. They are table turners, game changers. Like guiding stars, they lead us into promised lands where all things seem possible. Acting as midwives, they help us give birth to new and improved editions of ourselves. Leaving behind redemptive legacies, they are forerunners who spawn revolutions within and without. More than dreamers, they are real, aiding and abetting our eternal quest to be wise, wonderful, and free, adding texture and tone to our lives, raising our hopes, heightening our expectations, exemplifying for us the best of who we are while showing the way to what we could be and need to become. They light a candle in our darkest moments, reminding us that our liberation is most at hand in dire moments when we think we are lost. When our captive chains eventually fall shattered at our feet, they are the ones who inspire us to persevere, frequently reminding us to hold on, keep faith; reminding us to never give up when the chips are down. They inspire us to stay motivated, to persist in our pursuit of that which is wise, loving, and right, even in the face of unyielding wrong, hate, and peril.

During some of our worst times, they point us to better days. They make us stronger than we thought we ever could be, teaching us how to face our foes with grace, revealing that even though all is broken, we can still rise; for there is resurrection after death, and death before resurrection. They bring healing, and although impoverishment may fill our streets, flooding our humble homes with its barren emptiness, they continue to empower our flagging zeal. They allow us to see stormy weather for what it is—a prelude to brighter days.

Protected by the unseen, they withstand fire without crumpling in the engulfing flames. They dare the impossible, forcing iniquitous systems to back up, back off, pivot, turn, or topple. They are our heroes. We answer when they call. We rise when they beckon. We mourn when they are gone, martyrs for a cause. We respond when they exhort us with their refrain, "Up you mighty people; you can what you will!" Heroes are not without flaws. They are not unlike us mere mortals. Perfect or not, without our *heroes* and *sheroes*, our world would be less ennobled, woefully less enriched.

The popular profound presence of contemporary heroes of African ancestry—leaders with courage, intellect, and moxie are slowly disappearing into the mist of history, rapidly becoming extinct, forgotten. And yet, Black heroes are all around us, living, breathing daily, quietly adding extraordinary richness to our lives. Everywhere, every day, oftentimes unbeknown to us, we are surrounded by them, whether they be artists, artisans, activists, community workers, teachers, preachers, entrepreneurs, or everyday ordinary people who breathe extraordinary life into the earth, who stand like light on a hill, if only for a select few to see. Even so, they remain seemingly hidden beneath a bushel or behind a screen, invisible to the public eye.

Each Black History Month, there is an offering of Black historical figures who are modelled on parade for us to acknowledge and to celebrate. The accomplishments of noteworthy elderly people of colour, although largely unrecognized for the remainder of the year, are also spotlighted and so, it should be.[3] We stand on their shoulders. It is appropriate to salute them. But where are today's present contemporary heroic icons? Isn't it time we broaden and deepen our knowledge of present-day narratives? Isn't it time to include newer and fresh faces of individuals who possess the potential to renew our sense of purpose while adding contemporary meaning and relevance? Isn't it time to widen public awareness to include memories that are unfolding currently? Isn't time to denounce the scarcity of positive Black images as a deliberate obfuscation of the truth? Isn't it time to refute and dispel the simplistic commercialized Black stereotypes that presently prevail in today's pop culture media platforms?

Certainly, the time has come; it is time to pull back the veil of misrepresentation and under-representation, pull back the curtain that shrouds the greatness of amazing Black African individuals who are right now moving us forward with passion, commitment, and vision, and are actively doing so with fearless determination. In documenting unwritten history-in-the-making (some would say *our-story*-in-the-making), we will ultimately bring light to the profound contributions of genius, imagination and creativity made by young people of African ancestry presently among us. In telling narratives that are happening now, we will reveal the interconnectedness between past, present, and future, bearing witness to the deep forces that have shaped the exquisite beauty, strength, and profound sense of pride that flow through the human family.

It was for this reason that I sat with a man who is swiftly and startlingly approaching his own milestone. He spoke freely, his words flowing like a river in the fullness of spring, meandering powerfully through the myriad of ideas flooding his intellect or emanating from his spirit. He spoke animatedly without wincing or cowering from tough questions, ever conscious of his responsibility to re-image himself, to uplift *his* people beyond and above the low grade to which he and others like himself have been maliciously assigned.

Across timelines, he moved in lockstep with his ancestral past, drawing upon their suffering, tenacity, and wisdom. Imbued with knowledge of self and love for his family, he conveyed a

---

[3] Black History Month while recognized globally, is a distinctly First World event. Founded by African American Historian Carter G. Woodson as Negro History Week in 1926 to celebrate and honour the lives and contributions of people of African ancestry, the February remembrance was initially seven days long. By 1976, the occasion mushroomed into a month-long event. Through the groundwork of the Ontario Black History Society (OBHS) and the efforts of its founders, Dr. Daniel Hill and Wilson Brooks, February was proclaimed Black History Month in the city of Toronto in 1979. Today, Canadian Black History Month has become a formal institutionalized event, thanks to the advocacy of Rosemary Sadlier, former president of the OBHS, and the political leadership of the Honourable Jean Augustine and Senator Donald Oliver. Those who aspire to go beyond mere celebration have adopted African Liberation Month as an alternative, giving greater emphasis to activism and African revolutionary traditions.

passion for freedom, justice, and redemption. He spoke about his life and ideals thoughtfully with a heady complicated compound of hip, hubris and humility.

Brother Adisa Sadiki Oji spoke of his ancestors often as if they were here in the present; he spoke as someone honoured to walk in their footsteps, humbled to be part of their lineage. He courts, invokes, even craves their presence as if they were treasured mentors, his spiritual fountainhead.

From the cavern of his basement on late evenings, we sat and talked for a few weeks, mind-travelling through his life's journey, exploring his guiding stars as he summoned up his story with mire and mirth. His reflections conjured images of a colourful kente cloth. The iconographic motif, his own historical quilt, unfurled as he spoke. Beautifully, passionately, his kente cloth unfolded like a gift of grace, with patches of turbulence, defiance, and hope. To listen was illuminating; to hear was to be inspired. To understand was to be jolted into a retrospective glance to places and times when it all began. And while he did not speak in minutiae about everything, you could hear it, see it; you could sense the birth of a new, yet ancient, radicalism throughout his personal narrative. He was gracious. Without restraint or condescension, he imparted his own *akwantu*, his own journey.[4] He is a living story, here and now, not a calcified relic dead or gone. This is a book of heroes, and Brother Oji is emerging to be one of them.

Toronto, Ontario, September 2010. We are sitting in the basement of his home, which doubled as his private office, located at the time in the northwest section of the city. The lateness of the hour did not perturb him. He remained lucid, erudite throughout, when suddenly his phone rang. Jarringly, the ringing ruckus pierced the moment like an unwelcome alarm clock at daybreak, except it was not daybreak. It was 10:30 p.m., time rapidly approaching midnight. Seated, bespectacled, with eyes closed, head cocked back as if in a deep trance, but not too deep as to be unfathomable, his flow of thought was momentarily interrupted. Alerted now, the then forty-four-year-old man—tall, lean, dressed completely in black from his head to his sandal-clad feet—composed himself as he reached for the cordless phone resting among the tumult of miscellany that congested his cluttered desk. Pausing apologetically, he took the call. It was a business associate.

His office was a jumble of meaning. Papers, books, gadgetry haphazardly strewn, overran his desk like a brainstorm in progress, making for a colourful landscape of things past, present, and of things to come. Perched between and upon his computer's keyboard were faded photographs standing stoic-like, some with faces gazing intently, others smiling peacefully. Aging and slightly

---

4 "Ah-quent-two-oh"—meaning "the journey." Also refers to the title of a feature documentary: *Akwantu: The Journey*, which recounts the story of the Maroons of Jamaica, who fled plantations and slave ships to form self-governing communities in the island's interior. More details in chapter 9.

askew, the photographs wilted at their edges, signifying the passage of time. Despite the toll, the images revealed faces of relatives, children and adults, and heroes proudly portrayed. His wife and budding family who remained in Ghana were among the ensemble.

Occasionally a photo toppled, shifting out of place as we huddled or fiddled around the busy table, dislodging pictures from their delicate position of prominence. As they fell, they would be returned to their perches, serving as iconic sentinels, calm inducers, sources of inspiration, reminding their owner of his loves, his passions.

Everywhere beamed with meaning in his basement office. What seemed to be a wall was but a window into another world. Over on one side was an image of his grandfather; on the other was his grandmother. On another wall was his uncle. "Mother God," one of his signature photographs, was also mounted—an image of an old woman whose intensive, deep gaze calmly penetrated and watched over the room. On each wall encircling the room, brown eyes flickered, holding within their gaze untold allegories inviting many interpretations. Others invited an embrace. Every eye glowing in the room seemed like a window through which a whole other world could be envisioned, a world some may consider foreign or exotic. But here in this place, nothing seemed foreign at all. Everything seemed to be at home, inhabiting the dwelling like communal ancestral spirits from long ago and present day, living as if they were one and without end.

Resting on the floor were artifacts, crafts, and carvings. We were surrounded by all things African in a room of many journeys—journeys that had no straight lines, journeys that ran the way of a Langston Hughes poem, not smooth or as the crow flies. It was the way of no crystal stair, the way of tacks and splinters, the way of many meandering rivers to cross, mountains to climb, burdens to bear. The way of the weary blues.

It was a journey powered by liberation, allowing for full self-expression, discovery, and the realization of purpose. It was the way of personal freedom, vindication, the way of wonderment. It was the way of a warrior, of an activist walking the way of revolution, a revolution of consciousness, of sound, of image, and of spirit indomitable. It was the way of one of Mother Africa's lost children returning home, unvanquished. It was the way of destiny chosen. It was the way to which this tall man was called, a path only few choose to walk; the way to which many are called, but for which only a few are ultimately selected.

After bidding farewell to his caller, the man known as Brother Oji slowly placed the phone back among the muddle, then eased back into his chair to continue his reflections as round midnight made its surreptitious approach ahead of morning.

There are some who, citing his youth, would hastily scoff and laugh at the idea of designating Brother Oji a hero. He is fifty-five years old in this moment, eleven years since we first began discussing his biography. Some may also cite his lack of extensively lived experience or the absence of a legacy or body of exemplary works; others may choose to point to his underachievement and other perceived deficiencies.

Brother Oji, just as well, is unlikely to consider himself a hero, but for different reasons. He is more likely to consider himself a servant. Keenly aware of his destined responsibility, he sees himself as the custodian of an ancient mandate to lead a life of significance. His declared highest goal is to one day join the ranks of his ancestors. His chosen purpose is to become worthy of being called on as one of the honoured ones, to be a shoulder upon which others may one day stand. To achieve this designation, he must first lay claim to a life of meaningful consequence.

In this regard, he is living his life with the end in mind; living as he sees fit, purposefully, with distinction, passion, with love.

One disclaimer: If you are looking here for the usual glorified role model, then look elsewhere. You will not find Oji's image sprawled on the front pages of weekly news magazines or elite journals. One day perhaps, but as of now, he is not the primary subject of topical political discourses, current events, or popular culture. Chances are, he has never made, and probably never will make, the top ten lists of people critically acclaimed for this or that. You likely won't find him in the spotlight of primetime. He will not be the subject of praise based on popular preoccupations, nor will he likely be embraced as the latest fad or fetish. For after all, he has, as some have derisively declared, *wasted* his life.

Brother Oji was affectionately given the name *Mwalimu*, a Swahili word meaning "teacher," by someone who knew him well. He has lived up to that name, continuing to teach formally and informally. His personal journey recorded here is itself a life lesson. Significant as his achievements are, his attainments only represent the external trappings of an individual whose real worth lies much deeper. His potential is yet to be fully realized. If you are looking for more profound treasures that rest deeper and have loftier meaning, then look here in this literary portrait where you will find a snapshot of a living testimony, an enigma, a peculiar and strange man preparing himself for entry into immortality. In so doing, you will also be inspired to build bigger dreams and to live life more purposefully.

There is a quote Brother Oji often recites as if it is his own mantra: "If you love your people, you will want to work for your people. And the more you work for your people the more you love your people. And the more you love your people the more you want to work for your people … get the message?" So said the late Kwame Ture (Stokely Carmichael), civil rights leader and Pan-Africanist. So, too, says Oji.

Herein lays a brief life sketch of a man—his roots, his rock, his revolution—a man who when he speaks often begins and closes with the words: "I AM Brother Oji."

I do not let anyone bother me. Not even the police anymore—who brutalized in connection with my protest against the ROM exhibits. I do not like colonizers or oppressors of any stripe or colour. But I do not let them worry me because ... I AM Brother Oji!

—Brother Adisa S. Oji

Chapter 2

ADISA S. OJI V. REGINA

March 25, 1992. Ontario Court of Justice, Old City Hall, 60 Queen St. W., Toronto. Typed on the docket in bold print was "***Her Majesty the Queen Against Devon Johnson and Adisa Oji.***" In other related criminal proceedings, documents made reference to *R. v. Devon Johnson and Adisa Oji*. The *R* stood for "Regina," the Latin word for *Queen*; or "Rex," the Latin word for *King*. In this instance, the reference was to Queen Elizabeth II, the monarch sitting on the British throne since 1953. A photograph of her sits prominently at the head of every Canadian criminal courtroom. In Canadian criminal court proceedings, at her majesty's pleasure, she is represented by a Crown Counsel who, together with a presiding judge, administer the law according to rules that are professed to be fair and unbiased.

"All rise. Court is now in session, His Honour Judge M. Martin presiding!" As everyone stood in the hallowed chamber of justice waiting for the judge to be seated, a stale, stuffy, strange musk enveloped the courtroom. It was not a mustiness that came by way of the nasal passage. Rather, it came through understanding of what stood behind and beyond the pompous regalia. Buried somewhere deep in the antechamber was a seldom remembered legacy, the slowly decomposing remains of the many fatal victims of colonialism mixed with the malodour of a long-embedded history of imperial rough justice stretching as far back as the fifteenth century overseen by the Queen and her long line of royal predecessors.

Over the long course of civilization, humans have arisen to soaring heights of achievement, bringing great and lasting value to the benefit of all. Over the course of this same journey, we have also witnessed abysmal lows of deliberate harm leading to wanton human destruction. The onset of such a period in human history began in the fifteenth century onwards when Europeans nations including Britain, Spain, Portugal, France, Germany, Italy, and Belgium set out on a competitive rivalry to establish colonial empires. The lynchpin that held these empires together was racism. British imperialism in particular engendered a pseudoscientific mythology of racial superiority, an ethos that proved to be an especially important ingredient for all the so-called colonial "powers." This ethos formed the foundation upon which vast colonial empires were constructed. In so doing, a virulent toxic sludge of racism, xenophobia, and injustice was set in motion, triggering a cycle of violence that continues to proliferate even now, occupying visible and invisible spaces, known and unknown, producing immeasurable grief worldwide. Instead of joy and goodwill, war and genocide expanded on a global scale, irreversibly fracturing humanity into mind-boggling blocs of oppressed and oppressors, of "us" and "them," of "haves" and "have-nots." With this, the history of "the other" formally began. It was the beginning of divide and conquer, the onset of chattel slavery on a scale of cruelty never before witnessed in human history, the internationalization of peonage and peasantry, and the initiation of persistent poverty and intergenerational misery to last well into the twenty-first century. There is a great deal of unaccounted criminal injustice here, the toll of which is yet to be fully assessed, the loss yet to be fully recompensed. Colonial establishments were proficient in embedding their philosophy in organizational and institutional structures wherever they went. To the extent that they were successful, archaic remnants of colonialism, the removal of which today seems unattainable, still remain in many current institutions, including law enforcement, justice, and penal systems.

That one set of individuals and or group could and should exercise power over others on the basis of "race"—a social construct—was transformed from a mere idea into a living, breathing system with rules and norms. The rule dictated, either explicitly or implicitly, that one so-called race would be inherently superior to another—power and privilege becoming the exclusive preserve of the dominant race; submission and obedience being the lot of the lesser. The purveyors of this concept were not interested in racial slurs, jokes, or hate crimes. These would come later as by-products, incidentally, vicariously, or as collateral drama in a larger complicated tragedy. The purpose of the hypothesis of racial superiority was to secure entitlement to sovereignty. By this means, European social, economic, cultural, political, and institutional power and control could be justified, codified, maintained, and legitimized. With weaponized concentrated force, the self-proclaimed superior race, on the premise that they were "better than," went on to plunder and rout. With impunity, they proceeded to direct, dominate, and dictate others throughout the world, enforcing various forms of slave and wage labour to enrich themselves while impoverishing untold millions around the globe.[5] Wherever they went, the purveyors of this power destroyed, disrupted, or slowly dismantled the natural and social life support systems of every indigenous culture they came into contact. That which they did not destroy, they expropriated or set about recreating in their own image. Methodically, like concrete, they poured their toxicity onto any culture that resisted, poisoning, strangling them to death, or burying them alive, making local environments impossible to inhabit with any degree of human dignity. They created language, expressions, and rituals designed specifically to sustain the mental and physical illusion of their proclaimed dominance, claiming dignity only for themselves, while on the other hand creating language, expressions, and rituals to lock their victims in a perpetual state of mental slavery and physical submission. For example, look no further than the simple act of labelling using such English words as *black* or *white* associatively, one generally having devilish associations, the other divine.

To further propagate their philosophy, they employed a process of socialization, using various tools of cultural encoding such as the mass media apparatus, schools, religious doctrine, and a range of subtle and not-so-subtle mechanisms, including tradition, music, literature, natural and social sciences, and the practice of law. Wherever they went, they erected life-size monuments and images to themselves, situating them prominently in central locations for all to see. These emblems served to constantly remind onlookers who had elevated if not godlike status. Over time, the policy and habituation of racism would globally become a deep-seated part of commonly held values and beliefs. In this way, racism needed minimal enforcement or reinforcement; it became naturalized, internalized, a self-automated system requiring very little or no external influence. Racism became similar to the air we breathe—invisible with no readily identifiable source, a necessary social function accepted as a truism. Should anyone

---

5 Human slavery as a practice has been part of human existence for thousands of years, showing up in African, Persian, Greek, Roman civilizations, and in antiquity. Black African enslavement engineered by European countries in the fifteenth century onwards, and later practiced in North and South America and the Caribbean for close to four hundred years, however, took on a fundamentally different character by virtue of its rapid explosion, scale, dimension, intensity, and magnitude of violence. It was globally the most widespread, most concentrated in its focus and also by far the most profitable. Although human slavery has continued in many varied forms, Black African enslavement has cast the longest shadow and has had no equal in tragedy.

enlightened enough, bold enough, step outside of this norm to challenge its tenets, they are either "neutralized "or made to mysteriously "disappear."

The most virulent form of racism found its earliest and most devastating expression in colonialism and neocolonialism. (It is also possible to say colonialism and neocolonialism found its most devastating and lasting expression in racism, illustrating how policy and practice are intertwined.) When industrialization began to breathe new life into colonial aspirations between 1881 and 1914, the table was set for the rise of a new brand of race-based imperialism. The gluttonous fledging economies of Europe needed fresh blood, leading them to make vampire-like raids on Africa, a phase in history aptly described as the Scramble for Africa. The Partitioning of Africa soon followed. This new round of conquest involved the Europeans powers of Britain, Germany, France, Italy, Portugal, Spain, and Belgium as they unleashed a fresh wave of redesigned imperialist agendas. A lot was at stake as European nations engaged in power struggles that inevitably spilled over into foreign territory. The primary contestants were arch-rivals Britain and France, one an empire, the other a republic, both vulnerable to the growing influence of Germany, Russia, and the United States. Threatened also was Portugal, an old colonial power, which after decimating Brazil was trying desperately to hang on to Angola and Mozambique, even as the Belgians were attempting to hold on to the Congo while the Germans took a chokehold on Namibia. Led by Prince Otto von Bismarck, Germany convened a "world" conference. Like harbour sharks, the delegates—a cabal of White patriarchy—gathered at the Berlin Conference in 1884 to salivate over African spoils. To avoid a warlike feeding frenzy, they worked out an agreement in which they committed to maintain a peaceful balance of power among themselves. Together, they laid claims to coastlines, rivers, lakes, plains and mountains they had never seen, offering territories to each other without regard for the millions of indigenous people who lived there. It was an arrogant land grab on a monumental scale, the intent of which was to rob, plunder and exploit Africa's natural resources under the disguise of spreading Christianity, commerce, and civilization. As it turned out, the ulterior motive was ultimately the extraction and transfer of wealth from Africa through conquest for the benefit of European industrialization. Great Britain, in particular, the so called "bread basket" of the world, would become a major beneficiary.

With renewed fervour, they then proceeded to artificially carve up the continent, expropriating a significant amount of Africa's natural wealth to the detriment of its people.[6] As if they were gods, the delegates looked at all they had done and said it was very good. It was so good that on the proverbial seventh day, instead of resting, they continued unabated with impunity their insatiable plunder, undeterred and determined. To justify their conquest, they employed a variety of mythologies including the *White man's burden*—a self-proclaimed responsibility to advance civilization derived from their self-ordained divine authority to convert African masses to Christianity. They subscribed to, and promoted, pseudoscientific rationalizations based on eugenics—the genetic reproduction of supposedly superior traits—as a means of bolstering their self-anointed superiority. To further their agendas, they recruited an assortment

---

6 The Berlin Conference was not the first occasion of world superpowers sitting down to split the known world between them. The Treaty of Tordesillas between Spain and Portugal signed in 1494 also allowed these two countries to share the spoils of global conquest. Spain claimed any new lands discovered outside of Europe west of an imaginary line in the Atlantic Ocean while Portugal commanded lands east of it.

of anthropologists, explorers, armies, missionaries, mercenaries, and mercantile barons to execute their mission, while institutions such as churches and museums were employed to reinforce and perpetuate their ideologies. In less than thirty years, only Liberia and Ethiopia would remain independent of European control. And British colonialism in West, East, and South Africa (and the Caribbean) would continue to thrive.

The net result of this toxic mix of racism and colonialism has been more than overwhelming. Out of the magnitude of this sludge, many have gone from poverty to prosperity. Many continue to derive wild blessings and extravagant benefits from it, living in ease and idle contentment. In their smug indifference, the beneficiaries of racial injustice are apparently clueless as to the exploitative and oppressive methods used to enable their grand affluence and unearned power and privilege.

While many gained, many more lost and bled and continue to lose and suffer from the countless after-effects. Generations of individuals—men, women, and children—have had their lives and livelihood ruined, unable to completely escape, recover from, or transcend the toxic effects of this racial pill. Unable to remain whole, or to live without injury when touched by racism's long grungy reach, many have died resisting. Some have succumbed to this catastrophe, spiralling downward in post-traumatic grief, while others have cursed, raging against it with righteous indignation, hoping somehow the calamity will cease. To a great extent, this grief is unacknowledged, an extreme injury conveniently forgotten without recompense or reparations.

Meanwhile, there are others whose goal is to illuminate. They are unafraid to face off with the untidy truth of history. In the case of colonialism and slavery, they know they are up against longstanding strongholds of abuse. The aim of these game-changers is to find creative ways to transform this sludge into pathways to liberation. Against all odds, they are converting the dreadful outcomes of racial oppression into a way forward. They are the ones who, if they are successful, will help redeem us and help humanity rise again to soaring heights of achievement.

"All rise. Court is now in session, His Honour Judge M. Martin presiding!" As everyone stood in the courtroom waiting for the judge to be seated, and as the accused, both of whom were conspicuously Black—Devon Johnson and Adisa Oji—stood for their respective arraignment in the predominant presence of White court officials, what may have first appeared to be *Regina v. Devon Johnson and Adisa Oji* was in fact the reverse. This was *Devon Johnson and Adisa Oji v. Regina*.

"Not guilty at all," said Johnson in answer to charges of assault and obstruction of justice.

"Not guilty," said Oji in answer to two counts of assault and one count of unlawful escape of custody. Nine accused individuals had originally been involved in this matter, collectively charged with some twenty offences under the Criminal Code of Canada. Now only two remained standing. They refused to yield, refused to admit criminal wrongdoing for confronting the unjust racist philosophy and practices wrought by generations of British colonial domination. This brings us to March 10, 1990.

In downtown Toronto, a small crowd of demonstrators, young and old, gathered to picket on the sidewalk facing the main entrance of a museum located at 100 Queens Park. Each week as word spread, the crowd grew, sometimes forty, sometimes seventy people, many travelling from distances away. Gathering to march in protest before the Royal Ontario Museum, familiarly known as the ROM, their objective was the closure of an exhibit, which opened months earlier in November 1989. They gathered dutifully on Saturdays, sometimes on Sundays, to demonstrate, starting usually at noon, rallying to the cause of a group calling itself the CFTA: Coalition for the Truth about Africa. Among their demands were that the ROM dismantle the exhibition, that the ROM acknowledge the racist nature of their exhibit and apologize to the community, that the ROM consult and gain prior approval on the form and content of any future exhibitions about Africa and Blacks in general, and that the ROM hire more Black consultants and staff, including having more Blacks on the ROM's board of directors.

Young and old protesting at the ROM March 1990
(Photo by Neville White, Jr.)

The CFTA was a loosely held group of forty organizations.
(Source: CFTA Brochure/Oji Archives)

The coalition was a loosely held group of forty organizations and activist groups within the African Canadian community from the Greater Toronto Area. It was led and facilitated by the African Caribbean Students Association (ACSA), a student organization based at the University of Toronto. It had come to this after much discourse and discord. The Black community, heterogeneous in origin and outlook, could not arrive at a united front. Fractured as it was by an increasing generation gap, class differences, and ideology, the community seemed to have developed divergent attitudes and approaches to the Royal Ontario Museum's controversial exhibit. Organizations such as the Black Action Defence Committee, the Urban Alliance on Race Relations, and the Black Professional Business Association, among others, had their own strategies that varied from the CFTA, which was primarily a youth movement. Although individual members from each group rallied to the cause of the other, attempts to streamline and strategize a common approach met with mediocre success. Nevertheless, the young activists cobbled together an alliance, the magnitude of which was no mean accomplishment.

As the protest gathered momentum, members within the coalition—a core of eleven provocateurs—would distinguish themselves as the ROM 11, so called because they gained the reputation of being the only ones to be charged and arrested for their involvement after a clash with the jagged edge of law enforcement. Members of the CFTA, who were for the most part of African descent, shared a common passion. Allied with them were a handful of White students who espoused a social justice agenda. During the day and on many late nights, key members of the group met regularly to plan and plot strategy. They compiled lengthy mailing lists and orchestrated a self-propelled organic media campaign to get their message out on the streets and to the high and mighty. The core protagonists were young like-minded activists who held Africa close to heart. They regarded Africa as Mother Earth, embracing the continent not as an artificially fragmented entity partitioned by the whims of colonialism but as a whole. They regarded Africa as the source of their lineage, the original home of civilization, and made no academic distinction between East, West, North, or South, preferring to see Africa as united, not as fragmented by the rules of divide and conquer. Africa represented the wellspring from which they drew inspiration. For this reason, they took issue with the *"Racist Ontario Museum"* for its persistence in mounting and promoting an exhibit entitled, *Into the Heart of Africa*. According to the coalition, the exhibit was a celebration of the plundering rape of Africa—sub-Saharan Africa—an exploitative, self-serving spectacle showcasing expropriated artifacts stolen from the continent. In the view of CFTA, the exhibit was trite, condescending, deceitful, and misleading. Further, it tarnished the image of Africa and its people. It was as if someone had publicly insulted or, worse, gravely wounded their mother, then afterwards invited them and others to celebrate the spectacle. *Into the Heart of Africa* was akin to a kick in the teeth, a spit in the face. The exhibit was considered a provocation to all African Canadians. As far as the CFTA were concerned, they were "sick and tired" of the long history of mistreatment meted out to Black African humanity and of having their human rights—the rights of African Canadian people—routinely despised and ignored.

In the words of one demonstrator, "We want African experts and scholars to be consulted as to the mounting of any exhibit on Africa. This is the first exhibit on Africa in the seventy-seven-year history of the ROM and look at the mess they have made. We want a formal apology specifically to the African community and to all the people and citizens of this province."

Mostly peaceful, the orderly demonstrations ran for a few months into the spring of 1990 under the disinterested gaze of police officers. Demonstrators walked in circles carrying homemade signs, chanting slogans over a megaphone. They blew whistles and handed out flyers explaining their case to anyone who cared to listen. *Would the ROM mount an exhibit of the Jewish holocaust from a Nazi perspective? Of course not!* One picketer, his face earnest with conviction, carried a sign declaring "THE ROM ENDORSEMENT: OVER ONE MILLION AFRICANS MURDERED BY THE EUROPEANS." Flyers in circulation called for a Black mass rally demanding an end to the exhibit.

While the demonstrations were the most visible dramatic expression of protest, the CFTA had a menu of tactics. Part of their movement called on supporters to participate in a phone and letter campaign, imploring the public to lobby the ROM's corporate sponsors. Donating funds to support the cause was also encouraged.

Initially, ROM security and demonstrators had amicable interactions. A peaceful coexistence developed as the more gregarious demonstrators occasionally exchanged pleasantries and jokes. Providing protestors stayed curbside, both parties appeared to have gotten on well, each getting to know the other each week as the protest progressed.

On Thursdays when entrance to the ROM was free, CFTA members entered the museum's exhibit space, taking with them interested parties to conduct guided tours of their own. This enabled them to explain their position. At first, this caused no official concern. Demonstrators were generally peaceful, even professional. They were diplomatic, focused with a businesslike manner, clear about why they were there, causing no disruption. Soon, however, matters turned for the worse as it became evident that the ROM had no intentions of heeding their entreaties. In all social movements, there are twist and turns, and a shift occurred here, subtle but real. If initially the protestors were tolerated as an annoying nuisance, by this time, they would attract negative critical attention from the authorities. On the surface, this appeared to be a setback. In the dialectic of protest, however, this shift proved to be a momentum changer for the CFTA. As the push and pull of their struggle intensified, the demonstrators escalated their agitation. As their upheaval became increasingly dramatic, so, too, the negative publicity associated with the landmark exhibit. With negative publicity came repression.

Disconcerting problems with the ROM's exhibit surfaced long before the demonstrations began, indeed, even before the exhibit opened. Originally entitled *Into the Heart of Darkness,* it was later renamed *Into the Heart of Africa.* The change was prompted after the ROM received feedback from well-meaning sources. The exhibit, branded as a "celebration of the rich cultural heritage of African religious, social, and economic life between the years 1875 and 1925," was curated by anthropologist Jeanne Cannizzo. Prior to the exhibit's unveiling on November 16, 1989, a consultative group consisting of a few noteworthy representatives from the African

Canadian community were invited to preview the exhibit. This step might have been easily missed. No one among the curatorial team seem to have initially thought of it until someone gave them a friendly tip recommending that they speak with people within the Black intelligentsia.

The late Charles Roach, lawyer, justice activist, and elder in the Black community, was among the distinguished group of twelve invited to the screening. According to Roach, while four endured, eight were so disturbed they left before the tour ended, unable to stomach what they had seen. In a public statement, Roach said, "We were chilled from the very beginning. What we saw was a glorification of imperialism. What we saw in it was the roots of apartheid and the genocide that has gone on in Africa. We would have no objections if they labelled it as such, but they do not." What Roach and the group witnessed, and what others would soon come to discover, is that African culture when seen through the eyes of enslavers, colonizer, and White missionaries is *not* a pretty thing when you look into it too much.[7]

As early as October 1989, Clem Marshall also participated in early meetings with the ROM. Marshall, a renowned Black Canadian educator and writer specializing in race studies, language, culture, and ancestry, immediately raised red flags. Together with other community representatives, Marshall endorsed a letter to the ROM outlining essentially the same critique brought forward by the CFTA. According to Marshall, "The cumulative tone of the exhibit was paternalistic, and paternalism is the form of racism we encounter most often in Canadian society."

Although disagreement about the exhibit may have appeared split along racial lines, not everyone who criticized it was of African Canadian descent. Gary James in a letter to the editor of a community weekly was emphatic: "I feel great shame and embarrassment of what my people have done to Africans in the past. The R.O.M.'s show in my belief was a deliberate attack on Africans, and I hope that this museum will open discussions with the appropriate representatives of this community."

Meanwhile, the ROM had staunch defenders. A professor of history at Wilfrid Laurier, Terry Copp, who visited the exhibition, saw nothing wrong. In his view, the "curator should be praised for her efforts" to "promote respect for African culture without expressing contempt for those who saw it through nineteenth century eyes."

One man from Brantford, Ontario, applauded the exhibit as an accurate view of Africa. "It is one of the most educational and complete African displays I have seen in a long time ... I'd encourage everyone to see the display at the ROM and get a true, accurate portrayal of Africa and its people," he declared. Those in favour of the exhibit dismissed opposing views as merely gripe about "political correctness."

While critics argued that the exhibit presented Africans as barbaric and primitive, Cuyler Young, then director of the ROM vigorously defended it. "It is a historical examination of Canada's involvement in Africa. It has to tell a story that is historically true," said Cuyler. A ROM spokesperson, Linda Thomas, reiterated this view by saying the exhibit was presented from the perspective of missionaries and soldiers and as such was "historically accurate and

---

7 Line made famous by Joseph Conrad in *Heart of Darkness*. The full quote reads, "The conquest of the earth, which mostly means the taking it away from those who have a different complexion or slightly flatter nose than ourselves, is not a pretty thing when you look into it too much."

historically based." Every effort, she said, was made to check for "stereotypical language" and to guard against "false representation."

But then came the retort from Molefi Kete Asante, an African American professor and philosopher specializing in African studies: "This is the defence of the indefensible. The defence of the Museum is the same arrogance the missionaries had."

As the dispute went back and forth, and as the ROM hovered on the brink of making an appalling error, they still had a chance to change course. Although the ROM's decision-makers exercised poor judgement by consulting *after* their plans were well underway, they still had an opportunity to reformulate their approach and did not.

ROM administrators were selective in who they listened to. In a clear case of confirmation bias, instead of heeding dissenting voices, they opted to listen to favourable reviews from members of the African Canadian intelligentsia who *gave them a pass*. Community consultations were part of the CFTA's demands, however the coalition considered these initial consultations disappointing, sketchy, even suspect. From their perspective, the role of the on-side consultants was to help "*sell*" the exhibit to the Black public rather than to offer critical feedback on context and positioning. Notable individuals such as educator Elizabeth Parchment and the aforementioned Charles Roach, who outrightly objected to the exhibit and who requested an entire rewrite of much of the text, were ignored. Stubbornly, the ROM refused to heed their advice, leading Afua Cooper, one of the lead voices among the protestors, to remark: "This was a classic example of White people not listening to what Black people were saying, of knowing what's best for Black people."

The museum never anticipated what followed. Ignoring naysayers, the ROM administration proceeded full tilt with their exhibit. It was expected to run until August 6, 1990, with scheduled appearances in Ottawa, Vancouver, Los Angeles, and Albuquerque. A year after opening, the exhibition and tour were cancelled. Ultimately, the ROM, an agency of Ontario's Ministry of Culture and Communication having financial assistance from the Ministry of Citizenship and sponsorship from Imperial Oil and Nabisco, at long last would apologize for its indiscretion. The museum would under duress eventually concede that it was wrong to ignore CFTA concerns. However, before yielding, they first saw fit to put up stiff-necked resistance by engaging in a costly protracted public battle with a group of young protagonists they clearly underestimated, protagonists who themselves would pay an exorbitant price.

What the ROM leadership missed in their rush to exhibit was the big picture. Toronto, and the province of Ontario, was proving to be a divided jurisdiction, one of gross inequities. Toronto's paradox was that it was a city in which the celebration of the history of one community could be the source of agony for another. The ROM exhibit may be likened to a curtain, which when raised revealed an unexamined tumult of grievances, a gaping hole in the heart of one of Canada's most diverse cities. In this stark unfolding historical drama, the burgeoning anti-apartheid movement, cresting at the time, served as a backdrop, while the unreasonable police shootings of Black citizens in the Greater Toronto Area served as the foreground. This was made all the more explosive by the growing revelation of rampant anti-Black racism in the province's workplaces.[8] It was in this troubled sociopolitical cocktail that the ROM insensitively unveiled its exhibit. *Into the Heart of Africa* was akin to lobbing a grenade into a gas tank.

The demonstration by the CFTA rapidly became a rallying point for multiple irritations. Finding common ground with the ROM demonstrators were protests related to cruise missile testing, Inuit or Indigenous rights, the abusive use of police powers against Africa Canadian citizens—all found voice at the Queens Park demonstration. Fervent passion rose even further to an all-time pitch as the apartheid system in South Africa was finally becoming unhinged, adding to the long list of race-based grievances bubbling up globally. When Nelson Mandela was released from prison on February 11, 1990, the protestors became even more emboldened. With confidence in the righteousness of their campaign renewed, they approached the demonstration with even greater fervour.

Meanwhile, across town in the east-end community of Scarborough, the Black Action Defence Committee, during the month of May, would hold its own demonstration with close to three hundred protestors marching in opposition to police brutality chanting repeatedly, "Who are we? Africans! Africans! African people must harmonize. African people must organize." The timing for *Into the Heart of Africa* could not have been worse.

South of the border, the racial chasm was also widening. In August 1989, Yusef Hawkins was shot and killed in Brooklyn, New York. By the spring of 1990, the trial of the two men held responsible for his killing was rapidly approaching, providing a provocative parallel to Toronto's increasingly racialized landscape. Hawkins, an African American youth had been walking with friends in Bensonhurst, a predominantly White neighbourhood, when they were attacked by a mob, one of whom pulled a gun and shot the sixteen-year-old twice in the chest. Hawkins's death was the third mob-killing of a Black man by White vigilantes in New York City during the 1980s. As the trial approached, protest demonstrations led by Reverend Al Sharpton erupted in New York City. On May 17, 1990, Hawkins's killer was convicted of second-degree murder. The second defendant, acquitted of murder, was convicted on lesser charges. This was no consolation to the protestors who continued to demonstrate throughout Bensonhurst. In the spring of 1990, the air had become a boiling cauldron supercharged with racial tension. Tensions would cross the border northward as many African Canadians began to realize that racial brutality had no boundary; that racism had an uncanny universal face.

Closer to Toronto, in London, Ontario, another racial controversy began to dominate mainstream and academic media. According to the much-disputed pseudoscientific research of Professor Philippe Rushton of the University of Western Ontario, Blacks were at the lower end of the ladder of human intelligence. He made his revelation regarding racial differences at a major American science conference in 1989. In simple terms, Rushton's study was a recycling

---

8 Racism's durability is extraordinary. Thirty-one years later in 2021, an external review would reveal that discrimination and harassment within the Ontario Public Service (OPS) continue to be "persistent and unyielding." Investigation uncovered that OPS Black employees work in a culture of fear of their White managers and co-workers who face little to no consequences for bad behaviour. For details see CBC article posted June 7, 2021 (www.cbc.ca/news/canada/toronto/anti-black-racismops-report).

of nineteenth-century anthropological concepts of racial classification based on eugenics in which European races were deemed to be the highest expression of human civilization, while darker-skinned races were relegated to the bottom. Aside from the suggestion that race is a scientific concept rather than a social construct, implicit also in this ideology was the need to control and supervise people of colour, who were held to be inherently childlike or primitive. Many denounced, derided, debunked, or booed the professor; others came to his defence. The university failed to repudiate him, leaving him free to continue expounding his White supremacist ideas through his lectures. Intended or not, Professor Rushton fuelled a new wave of justification for Eurocentric White power and privilege. Attended by hordes of undergrads, including Black students, the professor, knowingly or unknowingly, adversely impacted a new class of educated Black professionals who, if not guarded, stood the risk of internalizing self-contempt when learning of his race theory. Not long after, Black students at Western University would experience psychological abuse in the form of sinister pranks carried out by White students who gloated in their self-supposed superiority.[9]

With this development in London, Ontario, an entire community was appalled yet again. They were offended that a professor with a platform in one of the country's premier institutions of higher learning would be allowed to promote White supremacist values based on false science. Stunned, African Canadians were left wondering why in the twentieth century they were continuing to be pierced with the same damaging end of a sharp nineteenth-century sword.

The sword said it all. On entering the ROM's exhibit, the viewer's line of vision was immediately drawn to the larger-than-life image of a violent encounter in which a colonial soldier, Lord Beresford, resplendent in uniform and helmet, mounted high on his stallion, is seen attacking a Zulu warrior dressed in loincloth. The outstanding mythical image depicts the colonial soldier piercing a long sword through the chest of a Zulu defending his homeland, implying dominance of the former, the latter surrendering to the power of his conqueror. Draped across the ceiling for visual effect was the Union Jack, unfurled in a manner to psychologically suggest who commanded the space. It is at this point that the exhibit's theme is established—the conqueror vanquishing the conquered, half-naked savages being civilized by onward European Christian soldiers fighting for the cross. In this depiction, the choices open to Africans become clear—convert or die; equally clear are the winners and losers. Although South Africa's apartheid system was in effect many thousands of miles away and was about to be toppled, it was as if this system of violent White supremacy was being graphically re-enacted here in a Toronto museum.

---

9 I was a student at Western during the time of Professor Rushton. While I was not a student of the professor, it was difficult to escape the repercussive effects of the controversy.

The content and presentation was so troubling the Toronto Board of Education declared the exhibit unsuitable for elementary-age students.

The major criticism of the exhibit was its glorification of colonialism coupled with what seemed like a celebration of the dehumanization of Africans. In addition, it reinforced negative stereotypes about Africans by using scripted terms such as "barbarous people" and "savage customs." The exhibit was also criticized for its condescending tone. In one pictorial, a group of African women was seen on their knees performing laundry while a White woman looked on approvingly. In another installation, a running slideshow simulated a narration by an English missionary who recounted his benevolent work in Africa with the "natives."

ROM curators took the initial furor for granted. Much ado about nothing sums up their initial attitude to the criticisms. They had no foresight or insight about the connection between their exhibit and the upheaval bubbling up outside their doors. When opposition came, they were unmoved, some might say thickheaded. ROM administrators showed very little sign of having any inkling as to what all the fuss was about. Leading museum staff—director Cuyler Young; his successor, John McNeill; associate director, Robert Howard; and guest curator, Jeanne Cannizzo—showed no initial hint of penitence or willingness to understand. They jointly defended their exhibit. "If we thought [the exhibit] was racist, we never would have mounted it," said Howard in May 1990.

The museum's stated intention was to showcase a collection of images and artifacts "brought back" from Africa by Canadian missionaries and soldiers during the height of colonialism, a collection mostly misbegotten according to some critics. In the now-infamous catalogue accompanying the exhibit, curator Jeanne Cannizo was prescient when in her epilogue she concluded:

> By studying the museum as an artifact, reading collections as cultural texts, and discovering the life histories of objects, it has become possible to understand something of the complexities of cross-cultural encounters. In the same process, the intricacies of different cultural configurations are revealed in objects through which various African peoples have expressed not only their individual artistry but also their deepest communal concerns. Finally, by placing in context the relationships, however brief, problematic, and painful, that developed as Canadian soldiers and missionaries travelled into the heart of Africa, *it has become clear that the past is part of the present.* (Italics mine)

The curators insisted they had no ill intent. They nonetheless displayed a lack of judgement when it came to understanding the *impact* of their behaviour and decision-making. (The promotional brochure for the exhibit, which portrayed a bare-breasted African woman in a grass skirt, illustrated their myopic view.) The exhibit was decidedly pitched from the point of view of the colonizers, and ostensibly the ROM's intent was *honesty*; they wanted to present the undiluted truth by remaining true to the meaning of the items on display. However, their decision-making was foolhardy. If they meant for the exhibit to be a critical deconstruction of colonialism and race, they failed. And if they thought the exhibit would be entertaining and uplifting to all their constituents, they were wrong. Anyone aware of the dynamic of oppression, or acutely aware of the current surrounding or prevailing social climate, would have been dumbstruck by the naive public relations risks taken by the ROM when it showcased *Into the Heart of Africa*—375 highly politicized African artifacts seen through the lens of White imperialists. It is said that there is no one as blind as someone who refuses to see. As for the Royal Ontario Museum, they had an unacknowledged blatant blind spot, making it almost impossible for them to grasp the gravity of their undertaking. Jeanne Cannizo may have been the handmaiden publicly blamed (and shamed) for this fiasco. But she did not act alone. She was part of—indeed trapped in—a complex diseased anatomy infected by institutionalized racism. *Into the Heart of Africa* was but a mere symptom of a deeper more malignant affliction.

The ROM's failure to manage the public relations fallout was epic. In the wake of this failure, four other museums planning on mounting the exhibit—the Canadian Museum of Civilization, Vancouver Museum, the Natural History Museum of Los Angeles County, and the Albuquerque Museum—all cancelled in advance after hearing of the ROM's fiasco. More immediately, because of this failure, a growing number of demonstrators were now at the museum's doors waiting to offer their unsolicited advice. As the ROM's obstinacy grew inside, so did the demonstration solidify outside. Trouble brewing outside would soon infiltrate the doors of the venerable museum. What may have initially begun as a fairly amicable affair would deteriorate, thereafter very rapidly taking on a more heightened sinister character.[10]

Attempts by the coalition to have formal meetings with ROM officials failed to yield positive results. Although the ROM offered to meet, they refused to shut down the exhibit as a precondition. In response, the CFTA refused to meet as long as the exhibition continued. The impasse continued unabated as attempts to break the deadlock failed. Search to find a mediator satisfactory to both sides proved difficult leading to an overall sense of futility, which further paralyzed the process. With each party locked into its position, each accusing the other of stalling and or cancelling, there were no obvious off-ramps on the road to conflict. According to the CFTA, they were willing to continue negotiating; however, the museum, in their opinion, was stonewalling and refusing to meet. The CFTA claimed that ROM's representatives were responding in ways ranging from patronizing to insulting, leading them to conclude the ROM's attitude was one of arrogance and disrespect. From the point of view of the CFTA—and they were unwavering

---

10 The ROM had a precedent from which to learn. After D. W. Griffith's release of the Academy Award winning *The Birth of a Nation* in 1915—America's first blockbuster—a landmark silent film lionizing White supremacy and representing people of African ancestry as violent subhumans, the Museum of Modern Art (MoMA) in 1946 temporarily shelved the film because of "the potency of its anti-negro bias," and opted not to screen it on the grounds that "exhibiting it at this time of heightened social tensions cannot be justified." MoMA, a repository of Griffith's work and memorabilia, has over the years attempted to walk a fine line between scholarly celebration of the filmmaker's masterpiece and distancing itself from the anti-Black racism inherent in the 1915 cinematic spectacle. See for example MoMA's June 2009 presentation of D. J. Spooky's "Rebirth of a Nation."

about this—they were being belittled, treated as if they were a group without status. They felt as if they were being handled like misbehaving children, as if they were nothing but a bunch of Black unprofessional rabble rousers intent on upending the grand exhibit. In short, they felt as if they were not taken seriously.

Catalogue cover of the ROM's Into the Heart of Africa
exhibition, mounted November 1989.
(Photo by Reverend A. W. Banfield. Used with permission. © ROM)

The demonstrations continued each week, running into the month of May, mainly on Saturdays between 12:00 p.m. and 3:00 p.m., with interest and crowds continuing to grow with each passing week. The atmosphere became increasingly tense as demonstrators pushed forward with their efforts to force the ROM to shut down the exhibit. As demonstrators stepped up their opposition, they were joined by even more sympathetic community groups. Police reinforcements were also brought in to control the crowd. The presence of law enforcement added further fuel to the fire by perpetuating a stereotypical power dynamic in which the protestors, mostly Black, were perceived as potential criminals. According to the ROM, the protestors were preventing the museum from operating business as usual. Whatever goodwill there may have been between the ROM and the CFTA thereafter collapsed.

Following the rising unrest, steps were taken to prevent the demonstrators from entering the museum. Authorities now insisted protestors were no longer welcomed inside the building, that they would be regarded as trespassers if they were to enter. After months of protest with no signs that the ROM had any intentions of closing down the exhibit or to constructively engage, a few members of the coalition became eager to push their agenda by defying the lock-out. On May 5, they breached the doors and entered the museum, and everything changed. An ensuing melee broke out involving a clash between onsite paid duty police officers and a number of protestors. Criminal charges were laid. Lives and fortunes were changed forever.

One member of the CFTA who was counted among the ROM 11 was Adisa Oji, then acting president of the University of Toronto's African Canadian Students Association. On March 21, 1990, eleven days after the demonstrations formally began, he would celebrate his twenty-fourth birthday. March 21 is a special day for him in many unbelievable ways. It is the first day of spring, marking the equinox when day and night are of equal duration. March 21 also marks the International Day for the Elimination of Racial Discrimination in memory of March 21, 1960, when South African police opened fire in Sharpeville, killing innocent demonstrators who were peacefully protesting the inequality of apartheid. As such, March 21 was in perfect symmetry for Adisa Oji as he moved into the public spotlight at a decisive stage in his personal history, during which he, too, would eventually have his clash with police agents.

When he and his comrades stepped out in front of the museum on that beautiful spring day in May, Adisa Oji quickly realized the full weight of his calling. Other members of the ROM 11 such as Andre Bratu, Jennifer Isaac (now deceased), Devon Johnson (Yaw Akyeaw), Sandra McKenzie, Ras Rico, and Kwabena Yafeu also confronted their own destinies that day, each in their own way. Sandra was no more than eighteen. Bratu was White. There was one elder among the eleven young activists. He, too, stood up. A few in the group suffered job losses after their reputation was sullied. Others were forced to flee the city after having been blacklisted.

Silbert Barrett, a CFTA spokesperson and then president of the Ryerson Anti-Apartheid Movement, was also arrested that day. He would have his criminal matter dealt with separately. Although he was not strictly speaking one of the eleven, he, too, would face unusual and unwarranted tribulation as he pursued a career in corporate Canada. A few members of the group prefer to remain anonymous. They continue to be apprehensive.

There are multiple perspectives on what occurred at the ROM's east-facing entrance on May 5, 1990. According to sources close to the protestors, they were victims of an unprovoked attack. In accordance with this view, demonstrators were peacefully protesting on the front steps when they were madly rushed by a squadron of extra-large, strong-armed policemen intent on provoking trouble. Police and security had reportedly been secretly filming the group from a remote location across the street, recording in detail the demonstration's patterns and habits while gathering intelligence on their leadership. According to this version of events, police, after identifying the main protagonists, stormed in to intimidate and viciously attack the ringleaders with the objective of putting an end to the demonstration by removing the heads of the movement. The brute force with which the police attacked suggested they were intent on doing lethal harm to the ringleaders. As leaders fell under the cruel beating, other protestors jumped in to help. In news reports, it was said, "Demonstrators clash with police." However, according to inside sources, it was the police who initiated the attack.

Court documents indicate that the protestors were attempting to enter the museum despite the order to stay out. Other media reports suggest demonstrators had "blocked" the entrance before being removed by police. Metro police detective claimed, "They charged at the museum. The security staff called for help." However, the situation may have been more nuanced. Demonstrators were peacefully, but forcibly, enquiring why Black patrons who had nothing to do with the demonstration were not allowed to legally enter the museum. The discussion as to who could and who could not enter seemed to have veered off into sharp animated disagreements, which then triggered a reaction from security and police. What happened next also depends on who is telling the story. Police and mainstream media reveal there was a "scuffle" or "clash," with three officers receiving minor injuries. Demonstrators would have a more dramatic version.

Leading the vanguard on Saturday, May 5, was Adisa Oji, who decided to challenge the exclusion by exercising his taxpayer's right by entering the publicly funded institution. Sinewy, tall, standing over six feet, he stood out in any crowd. He could not easily escape attention, even if he wished to. He was the Zulu warrior returning to set the record straight. Determined to defend the honour of his people, he attempted to enter the building whereupon he was immediately identified as a "trouble-maker." After he was stopped by security guards, he was forced back outside the vestibule. Security personnel made it clear they were intent on barring all the demonstrators, most of whom were Black, from entering the museum. Oji would be no exception. He was promptly turned back numerous times after persistently attempting to enter. Black patrons who had nothing to do with the protest were also being refused entry. This created an added layer to the skirmish. *How do you differentiate Black patrons from Black demonstrators?* This seemed like a clear case of racial discrimination, at least to Ras Rico. For him and others, this was an added source of provocation. Said Ras Rico, "Since our demonstration started, a lot of Black people from out of town, and others who are in no way connected to us, have been turned away from the museum because the guards are afraid they might be members of the coalition who want to destroy the exhibit." As far as the CTFA were concerned, this reeked of racism, adding further to their list of grievances.

Continuing to force the issue, the predominantly Black demonstrators began to use their numbers to ripple up from street level to the steps of the building. Eager to make their point, they went face to face with the wall of security personnel assigned to keeping them out. Tensions mounted. Sensing a threat, security and paid duty police employed by the ROM became hypervigilant as hostility heightened. As demonstrators continued their movement unrelentingly, moving forward like waves up from the street onto the stairs, attempting to force their way into the building, security stood jittery but firm. Meanwhile, as Oji continued his undeterred attempts to enter through several different doors, he was repeatedly escorted out on each occasion. Wearing a white T-shirt, an army fatigue cap perched atop his crown, he blew his whistle as he, along with others, continued to forcefully pry their way into the ROM's rotunda.

If Oji was hoping for a confrontation, it came to a head on his next effort. Whereas first, there was a bubbling tension, on this occasion, the bubble erupted into pandemonium. According to news report, the confrontation is said to have involved as many as thirty-five police officers and fifty demonstrators. In chaotic situations like these where events unfold at lightning speed, no one can be sure what happened next. On this fateful attempt as he was being escorted out, Oji broke free before they could get him completely outside. With Oji at large, the ROM's entry was now breached. A scuffle followed as he was tackled by four or five paid duty officers who shoved him up against the wall, ultimately dragging him to the ground in a headlock, his feet spreadeagled, his glasses knocked from his angular face. It is alleged that during the fracas, Oji turned to push one of the officers, forcibly knocking the man's hat to the ground. It is here that he allegedly sustained his first criminal assault charge.

Demonstrators claim that for every protestor there were five police officers. Outnumbered in the chaos, they scrambled for safety, shouting, "Don't shoot! Don't shoot!" "We weren't fighting them. We were trying to get away," said Ras Rico. Bystanders watching were aghast by the brutality. Appalled, some tried to interfere but were cautioned by police to "f——off and mind their own business."

Meanwhile, on seeing Oji physically hurt, colleagues came to his aid. Devon Johnson (Yaw Akyeaw) was also under attack. One demonstrator who jumped to help was Silbert Barrett. He was convinced police had murderous intent given the violent way they lunged for the demonstrator's throats. Silbert was eventually manhandled and dragged downstairs as he yelled "Murder! Murder!" for all to hear. He was the first to be charged and arrested. Next came eighteen-year-old Sandra McKenzie. Both Barrett and McKenzie were charged with assaulting a police officer and assault with intent to resist arrest.

With Oji on the ground, and demonstrators rushing to his aid, they were successful enough to pull police away from him or at least to distract them. Others meanwhile created a shield or a human tunnel to help usher him back outside. The maneuver somehow worked. Sensing impending physical danger, fellow demonstrators urged Oji to immediately leave the scene through the screen they had set for him, which he did. In the confusing bedlam, Oji soon found himself outside, dazed, disoriented, but free. This stunt would earn him the criminal charge of escaping lawful custody.

Before the day was done, the demonstrators marched to the police station where Barrett and McKenzie were held to chant and push for their release. Hours later, the two emerged to loud cheers, the demonstrators more convinced of their cause despite the brutality meted out to them.

The sword said it all. Lead image of the exhibit featured Lord Beresford's violent encounter with a Zulu warrior. (Cover of *Illustrated London News Vol. LXXX, No. 2099*, Saturday, September 6, 1879, as displayed by the ROM.)

The past is part of the present. Police clash with protestors outside 100 Queens Park at the Royal Ontario Museum. (*Toronto Star* ©, June 3, 1990)

Following this incident, the ROM successfully sought and obtained an injunction to prevent the demonstrators from entering or picketing directly in front of the building. It was an interlocutory injunction, meaning the prohibition had no expiry date, and demonstrators were required to remain from within fifty feet of the building. As a result, demonstrators subsequently moved their protest north to Bloor Street to avoid violation of the injunction.

Weeks later on June 2, 1990, Oji would have a second eventful contact with the long arm of the law. He had returned to the ROM fearlessly with the usual plan of demonstrating. Like others, he observed the limits of the injunction by maintaining a safe distance. However, while walking with another demonstrator on his way back to the subway not far from the ROM at about 1:30 p.m., two plain-clothes officers in an unmarked police car—a red Ford Taurus—jumped out to apprehend him. They had continued their surveillance of him, waiting for an opportune time to make an arrest for the May 5 incident. Now that Oji was relatively alone, isolated from the crowd, the men dressed in suits jumped out of their vehicle for a surprise ambush, attempting to corral him. If they expected him to submit passively like a lamb, they miscalculated. Startled, Oji had the presence of mind to inquire as to why he was being apprehended. They instructed him to shut up, to get into their vehicle. Instead, Oji delivered a primal scream as if calling on the aid of invisible forces.

June 2, 1990. As he was under police attack, Oji delivered a primal scream as if calling on the aid of invisible forces. (Photo by Gerry Cromwell on behalf of MACPRI/Oji Archive.)

The possibility of a Black person getting shot, killed, or wounded by White Toronto police officers in 1990 was not far-fetched. During the early tenure of Toronto police Chief Bill McCormack (1989–1995)—a lifetime police officer whose policing career began as a constable with the British Colonial Police in Bermuda and who came from a multigenerational family of police officers (four of his five children were police officers, one of whom later became president of the Toronto Police Association in 2009)—trigger-happy policing was frequently in the news, particularly when law enforcement guns were pointed squarely at people of African ancestry. A Black teenager, Marlon Neil, was gunned down, wounded by Toronto police only weeks before on May 14, 1990. He was shot by a White constable who attempted to stop the unarmed sixteen-year-old after he allegedly drove through a speed trap. The officer proceeded to fire three shots from his .38 calibre revolver as Neil drove away. Two shots pierced the door of Neil's vehicle. The third zipped through the window, landing in the young man's upper left shoulder, causing him to lose control of the vehicle, which subsequently crashed to a near-deadly halt, leaving the youth in a pool of his own blood. This was the fourth shooting of a Black citizen by Metro-area police over the previous six months, setting off another protest of about five hundred demonstrators who on May 19, marched from Queen's Park to police headquarters on College Street, the women carrying hand-written banners listing eleven recent victims of police violence with the caption: We Won't Forget!

Listed among the names was Sophia Cook, twenty-four, who the previous October 1989, months after McCormack was appointed, was shot in the back and wounded by police while she was a passenger in a car. She was left paralyzed. Listed also was Lester Donaldson, who in August 1988 made the mistake of allegedly grabbing a knife when confronted by five police officers in his rooming house apartment. He, too, was shot and killed. Lester Donaldson was mentally ill. Identified on the list also was Michael Wade-Lawson, a Mississauga teenager, who in December 1988, in a neighbouring jurisdiction west of Toronto, was shot and killed by Peel Regional Police for allegedly driving a stolen car.

In the opinion of segments within the Black community, police accountability for the use of excessive lethal force in these occurrences was unsatisfactory. Despite outcry from the Black Action Defence Committee (BADC) and other outspoken police critics, attempts to hold police liable for inappropriate use of force were never successful. In police parlance, these were justifiable police homicides, a permissible use of force in the line of duty. The typical police response as exemplified by Chief McCormack was that police acted properly according to protocol, that these shootings were "by the book," necessary for purposes of "self-defence" or "in defence of public safety." Any suggestions that these killings were race-based were vociferously dismissed as nonsense. In rare instances where police personnel were charged and where the matter went to criminal court, there were no findings of guilt. Police were ultimately exonerated.[11]

In this context, Oji screamed for his life. He could not tell if the men attacking him were police or not. Either way, he felt his life was threatened. His yell attracted the attention of fellow demonstrators who were within earshot. As the White males, presumably police officers, tugged at him, he continued to resist, pulling himself away from the car to which they had him pinned. A tug-o-war of sorts followed between Oji and the out-of-uniform officers as they tried to ram him up against the vehicle. It was during this fracas that one of them allegedly flashed a badge. As Oji continued his screaming, his companion blew a whistle to draw even more public attention. Soon crowds of demonstrators rushed to the scene. About forty to fifty protestors surrounded the officers in an attempt to create a wall to protect Oji from the small army of men who were struggling to arrest him.

Police reinforcements arrived and a fierce struggle ensued, lasting almost twenty-minutes. In the end, the officers prevailed. This time, Oji could not be rescued. Through brute force and numbers, officers twisted his hands, squeezed his fingers, eventually manhandling him against their car. Overpowered with handcuffs on his wrist, Oji was whisked away to Toronto Police 52 Division.

On this occasion, nine people, including Oji and Johnson (Yaw Akyeaw) were arrested with a total of twenty criminal charges. Oji now faced two assault charges and one for unlawful escape. One of the assault charges stemmed from an allegation that he had bitten an officer on his left thumb during the street arrest. No one witnessed the bite. The officer is said to have had no visible injuries to show for it. Oji claimed they tried to shut him up by stuffing something down his throat to prevent him from screaming. "Two big white men in business suits jumped out of a car and grabbed me," he said. "They never identified themselves as police officers and they never answered my question about why they were grabbing me. I thought I was being abducted."

---

11 Up until the time of the ROM exhibit, beginning in 1978, there were five fatal Toronto police shootings of Black citizens under questionable circumstances. These included the deaths of Buddy Evans in 1978, Albert Johnson and Michael Sargeant in 1979, Leander Savoury in 1985, and as mentioned, Lester Donaldson in 1988. Two other police incidents, the shooting of Sophia Cook in 1989 and Marlon Neil in 1990 resulted in severe injuries. The Black Action Defence Committee was formed in 1988 to address what was considered the systemic erasure of Black lives by law enforcement. To the horror of many in the African Canadian community, while this seemingly targeted violence against people of African ancestry was happening on Toronto streets, the museum was content with exhibiting similar historical degrading scenes of violation of African life and culture. (See ohrc.on.ca: *"Timeline of racial discrimination and racial profiling of Black persons by the Toronto Police Service, and Ontario Human Rights Commission (OHRC) initiatives related to the Toronto Police"* for more details.)

Charges were eventually withdrawn for some of the accused after they agreed to a peace bond, a compromise provision in the Criminal Code that allows the crown to waive prosecution. This allowed the defendants to walk away from their charges without sustaining a criminal record in exchange for agreeing to "keep the peace" for a period of six months. By agreeing to a peace bond, there was no implicit admission on their part that a crime had been committed. However, any violation of the law or of the terms of the peace bond could lead to further criminal proceedings against them.

Depending on who you ask, this development was due to strong political pressure exerted by members of the African Canadian community who regarded the charges as politically motivated. Groups within the legal community such as the Nelson Mandela Law Society of Osgoode Law School at York University and the Concerned African Students of Osgoode Law School regarded the trial of the ROM 11 as a political trial. Said Joma Nyakorema Nkombe, chair and founder of the Pan African Law Society of York University, "The 11 politically accused were out there risking their lives in order to restore the dignity of the African heritage, plundered by over 400 years of racism, which in conjunction with colonialism contributed to freezing our heritage in a particular time and space." According to newspaper reports, others including the Crown prosecutor, regarded the peace bonds as purely prosecutorial in nature, an outcome free from political interference.

Oji and Johnson (Yaw Akyeaw) refused to entertain the idea of a peace bond. They deemed themselves innocent. From their perspective, it was the systems of oppression and anti-Black racism that were guilty. As for Oji, he was in no mood to cut a deal with what he regarded as an unjust system. He was prepared to go the distance, to expose "the oppressive, lascivious, and brutal manner in which police handled the arrested demonstrators." He felt the ROM could have prevented the brutality by acting responsibly, and they did not. Instead, they stubbornly stood by in complicity, allowing violence to occur on their doorsteps, all for the sake of doing "business as usual."

"What's wrong with this picture?"—CFTA flyer offering a counterpoint to image displayed by the ROM. (Oji Archives)

CFTA supporters including some of the ROM 11 outside Ontario Court of Justice at Old City Hall, 60 Queen St. W., Toronto. (Oji Archives)

For Oji, the entire ordeal turned something inside him. He had read about this level of repression, but now he had seen and experienced police abuse of power firsthand. It would shape his views, strengthen his resolve, and help to refine his purpose. Over time, this experience would enliven his political consciousness. His involvement with the CFTA deepened his understanding of himself, allowing him to develop a greater appreciation of and connection with other historical revolutionary figures such as Sam Sharpe, Paul Bogle, and Marcus Garvey. Likewise, Kwame Ture (Stokely Carmichael), Rosa Parks, Martin Luther King Jr., Viola Desmond, Dudley Laws, and others.[12] The prison release of Nelson Mandela—anti-apartheid revolutionary and freedom fighter who exited imprisonment with a raised fist—was still fresh in his and everyone's mind. While he would not claim to be part of this distinguished lineage of icons who were arrested for challenging the status quo of their time, he, too, would end up in criminal detention for a cause he believed was just.

All is quiet on the east entrance to the Hilary and Galen Weston Wing of the ROM in 2021, a distinct difference from the mayhem on May 5, 1990.

(Photo by Mello Ayo)

---

12 Sharpe and Bogle, less known internationally, are also Jamaican national heroes. Read more about them in chapter 4. The late Dudley Laws was one of the leading voices of the Black Action Defence Committee (BADC), a Toronto-based activist group advocating for racial justice in policing and law enforcement. More on Viola Desmond in chapter 6.

My story and how I am, begins with how I have lived to elevate the name of my mother's mother and father.

—Brother Adisa S. Oji

Chapter 3

WHO I AM

In a land of contradictions where it can feel like summer all year-round, it was the night of the first day of spring in 1966 when a Black boy-child sprang into the world. The third child of his parents, he would spend his first eight years on the Alfred Rowe family farm located in Ridge Pen, a district located in the parish of St. Elizabeth in Jamaica's southwest. His birth was inauspicious, without pomp or ceremony. His parents named him Fitzroy Anderson. In years to come, he would rename himself.

It was an easy birth in a land known to be hard, especially for citizens of African descent. The morning following the boy's birth, life unfolded ordinarily—an ordinary day of nothing much, everything *irie*, an ordinary Jamaican day blessed with an extraordinary gift. Morning dew glistened on the mottled green grass, giving the appearance of diamond crystals sparkling throughout the undulating yard that surrounded the family's homestead situated in the middle of an agrarian countryside. At a guarded distance, the distinct green rolling slopes of Malvern stood stately towering over the wisps of mist hovering along the blue-and-white horizon. It was the dawning of a new day blessed with serenity, a solitary morning star twinkling brightly in the great beyond. A pool of water from yesterday's rain rippled placidly in the yard as a gentle breeze fanned over the pastoral landscape. A solitary turkey vulture flew above gracefully in circles. Locally known as *John Crow*, the not-so-pretty bird with its black plumage and red bald head performed early reconnaissance flights before eventually landing with wings outstretched to scratch indiscriminately by the standing pool of idle water, wading and waiting. Such was Ridge Pen early in the morning. And for most of the day, the village moved in a lazy rhythm in harmony with life and death, unhurried, dreamlike.

In the meantime, a mongrel dog, the family pet endearingly known as Tricksy, sauntered about the yard with a languid gait. Oblivious to the sound of other canines barking beyond, Tricksy wagged her tail carelessly as she went about her dog-like business, slowly and without anxiety. She walked contentedly at ease, a dog's life, which she lived effortlessly, freely, feigning self-sufficiency, running wild whenever, wherever she wanted. She barked at the ominous looking *John Crow*, chasing it away easily from the yard, the buzzard flapping away disinterestedly as it returned skyward to resume its encirclement, scanning for other yards, trees, and housetops on which to perch.

Such was the happenings of another day in this rustic landscape where the scorching sun in its brilliance sometimes can be unforgiving, where only the longsuffering thrive and where the longsuffering are many. A village of folk tied together by the earth, bonded by a history of shared tradition pulsating for generations. Here under the gaze of the Santa Cruz Mountains, cows, donkeys, goats, cats, and other domesticated animals enjoy a leisurely existence, each day promising to be a repetition of the other. Except for the birth of a newborn child on March 21, 1966, it was an ordinary day in Ridge Pen. At least, so it seemed.

The moment of true birth occurs long before a child comes from their mother's womb. In certain West African traditions, it is said that the moment of true birth comes when a child first enters their mother's thought. According to this belief, long before the child known as Fitzroy became flesh and blood with mind, body, and spirit, he had already existed as a thought in his mother's imagination. He was first a prayer in her God-filled soul. Expressed as a longing in her heart as she went about her daily concerns, tending to her chores, her rituals, and other labours, the boy was already with her in spirit before he arrived in flesh. Perhaps this is why he would seem to be much older than his years suggested, old in the sense of being mature, endowed with an uncommon ancient disposition, possessed with a striking sense of purpose. Before he was conceived in his mother's womb, the boy known as Fitzroy was already born of spirit, a gift from faraway. *Where did he come from? What is he doing here?* These questions would perpetually confront him as he made his way from boyhood to manhood. While these questions would confound others, the answers would eventually become crystal clear to him, deepening his knowledge of self, his passion, his sense of direction.

Geraldine Anderson, the boy's mother, a devout Christian woman, has elusive memories of the day her son first arrived in her thoughts. She cannot remember vivid details of where or when he first entered her imagination. She only remembers having the thought, the thought of having a boy as her third child. She had previously given birth to a son followed by a daughter, both of whom were precious and close to her heart. Now the thought of a son was again calling out to her. The call came not very clear at first, but obscure, like a faint whisper, a vibration—a vibration mothers sometimes hear and feel in the depths of their hearts as they listen to the heartbeat of their children waiting to be born. It is a vibration she still hears today. With the passing of many years, more has since been revealed to her, the vibration comes now with even greater clarity, richer, stronger. It is the same vibration that piloted her son into the world, the same vibration that now uniquely moves him. The same vibration that piloted him through his rites of passage to manhood and has accompanied his struggles, his setbacks. It is the same vibration that would become his rallying cry, his freedom. It is the same vibration that led him to eventually reclaim himself and to rediscover his roots. A person, after all, can't help but move in the direction of their vibrations, and Oji's mother couldn't help but hear his, whether she liked it or not. Geraldine Anderson, throughout the years, would hear the vibrations of all her children as they made their way through life. She would hear their vibrations particularly as she made her soft whispering supplications during her daily prayers on early mornings and late evenings. But the vibration generated by the boy named Fitzroy had a different ambience and tone, a different tenor, an ambience that became even more pronounced as he grew into manhood, an ambience that would become cause for misgiving as well as joy.

Fitzroy's mother remembers getting back to full strength the day after giving childbirth. There would be no midwife or medical help. The following day, a nurse dropped by to make sure all was well; and it was. That was it. At the time of birth, Theophilus Anderson, the child's father, a police constable and an independent entrepreneur, was away on business. He operated a sound system, a mobile music disc jockey set-up designed for street dances and parties. The couple had met years before at the village square where each respectively had a sister who managed a store. It was love at first sight. Because of his official status as a police constable, Theo, as he was affectionately known, commanded immediate respect. He instilled fear in some. He was known to be stern, causing many to act in deference. Many preferred to be quiet around him. Somehow, however, Geraldine broke through his guard to become his wife. As it turned out, when Geraldine lay poised to have their third child in a little room, she was to bring their second son into the world in Theo's absence. It was her own father, Alfred Rowe, who was there by her side to offer comfort. And so, Fitzroy was born not in the presence of his father but under the watchful gaze of his maternal grandfather. As it also turned out, Geraldine's mother was also away taking care of *her* own mother. Such was the family fraternity. Each generation taking turns to care for the other.

Fitzroy's mother and father would successfully go on to have one more child together, a third boy, Winston. There would have been a fifth child; however, the baby girl, delicate at birth, failed to live a full life. She could not breathe well, exiting the world as quickly as she came. An appalling lingering grief, one hard to bear, weighed heavily on the family. The boy known as Fitzroy remembers his father weeping, a man known to be rugged, proud, suddenly brought low. Laden with heartache, the police constable often escaped into the toilet to sob, locking himself away. Tricksy, who followed broken-heartedly behind, was his only company. Even the dog mourned.

So it was that Roy, Suzette, Fitzroy, and Winston became children in a nucleated family, part of a larger extended family network on the Rowe compound located in Ridge Pen where they would take the first tentative steps that would begin to shape and define their future.

In later years, the Rowe compound has been subdivided into smaller parcels of land dedicated to multiple dwellings and family plots. But in 1966, there was only one house, the place where it all began, a place now referred to as *Bottom Yaad*. And in that house, grandparents Alfred and Geraldine Rowe were the patriarch and matriarch of the Rowe family household.

Fitzroy's mother (also named Geraldine) and father did what they could to make a livelihood to support theirs, but it was Alfred and Geraldine Rowe who raised all the children in the Rowe compound. And there were many, making the compound feel like a small village, a multigenerational community of kinfolk. Alfred's brothers, Louis and Ivan, had several offspring. They in turn had their own children. Fitzroy's mother also had ten siblings, and each in turn had their own children. Grandma Rowe, while she didn't live in a shoe (and she definitely knew what to do), had a hand in rearing all, if not most, of the children present. She was living proof that while it may take a village to raise a child, it takes a grandmother to raise a village. Grandma Rowe was a stalwart, as steadfast in her presence as she was unshakable. She was a fixture on the compound, as common place as the rising and setting sun, and no less magnificent in presence, reach, and influence.

For a small child growing up in Ridge Pen, it must have appeared as if there were children everywhere, swarming like ants running about, each one related to the other. In the childlike mind of Fitzroy, there must have been at least fifty children gallivanting freely in the yard on any given day without care or woe. Children were prohibited from going inside the house during the daytime. At sundown, they flocked inside. Come bedtime, each carved out a spot to sleep—under the bed, on the bed, around the bed, making do with whatever space available. Everybody was taken care of. It was a miraculous feat and demonstration of love, care, and patience by Grandma Rowe, who took charge of orchestrating the entire affair from sunup to sunset.

The Rowe family's connection to the land runs deep. Joseph Rowe was the first to inherit the property. He in turn received the property from Edward Rowe who was the first to acquire it when he came to Ridge Pen. Joseph Rowe would pass the property on to his son, Alfred, so that by the time Fitzroy was born, the Ridge Pen property had been in the family for at least three generations.

It is a strange irony that despite land ownership, the Rowes were relatively poor, with no readily visible exit from the cycle of poverty that entrapped them except through hard labour. The livestock they owned and the cash crops they farmed never generated a surplus, at least not sufficient enough for reinvestment or expansion. It was good enough for subsistence survival. To sustain their livelihood, parcels of land were sporadically sold off in exchange for yam and cassava or to purchase medicine and other necessities or to meet some other pressing, critical, unforeseen need. Often transactions were made between extended family members. One such sale took place at or about the time Fitzroy was born. The sale was made to Theophilus, who was offered a parcel of land on the property. This common law land title continues to sit in the Rowe's family legacy.

Although the family owned their property, money was scarce. There was never enough to buy clothing, shoes, schoolbooks, or medicine. Alfred Rowe planted tobacco; his wife planted corn. Grandma Rowe also had goats. Regularly, she shepherded them up and down and around the property. Her goats were her best friends. Every now and then, she achingly had to part with one or two as they were sold in exchange for money to pay for school fees and various other supplies. Even so, liquid cash was difficult to come by.

The beauty of childhood is a child's ability to make poverty inconsequential. While children are negatively impacted by deprivation, they are not always readily conscious of it. Through this blissful ignorance, the children on the Ridge Pen property found joy in their circumstances. Living in a little homestead with only three rooms made them closer. As a child, Fitzroy was predisposed to introspection. He was often alone in the nearby banana walk or sitting by himself under one of the many trees dotting the compound, tinkering with a relic or artifact such as a pot or drum or homemade toy. You could say he was at play, but the way in which he passed his time suggests there was more to this than simply self-amusement.

From anywhere in the compound, Fitzroy and his many companions would see banana trees. They could stare all day at large green fronds willowing in the breeze. The greenery around them was so commonplace they likely took it for granted. Not so much the smell—the odour of rotting plums; the rich, unmistakable hit to the nose of the many mango-bearing trees with *stringy, number 11,* and other common varieties. The hit was pervasive and awesome.

When Grandfather Rowe was not out in the field working, the old man could be seen sitting on his veranda smoking tobacco, a pipe hanging from his thick lips, smoke billowing over his head and down his weathered face, the fragrant smell migrating throughout the yard. Grandma Rowe also smoked tobacco, but she most likely did so privately among the banana grove where she frequented. Both grandparents were industrious and hardworking. On early mornings, Fitzroy observed his grandpa getting up at dawn to tend to his plots of yam, dasheen, coco, cassava, and tobacco; or he would observe the old man walking his cows out to pasture. Grandma, meanwhile, had her goats, which she tended with great care. Before her mind left her later in life and she became frail in advanced age, she was known not to lose a single goat except when they had to be reluctantly sold off. If one became lost (and she knew each by sight), she would, in her determined attempts to rescue her missing flock, stop at nothing until she found it, returning home afterwards tattered and torn, owing to her having to fight relentlessly through thickets of bush and barbwire fences.

When not under a tree contemplating, Fitzroy loved rainy days, the flooded yard with its mud puddles, the excitement of the children stripping down to go outside to play in the tropical downpour. Too much rain was either a bane or a blessing for farmers, but for the children of Ridge Pen, rain was heaven-sent. They romped and laughed, their black feet ashen, their brown eyes bright with laughter, mischief, and hope, overjoyed at being able to bathe and soak in the deluge, the cool hot wetness beating down on their dark glistening skin, shining like polished bronze. Fitzroy often heard stern instructions issued to him and the children urging them to "come out of the rain before you catch a cold," a warning they mostly ignored, warranting yet another ominous threat, "If you don't hear, you will feel."

"Come out of the rain before you catch a cold," a warning mostly ignored. (Family album/Oji Archives)

Fitzroy recalls outhouses in the yard, quaint, non-flushing, do-it-yourself amenities otherwise known as pit toilets or shithouses. These, too, possessed a not-so-amiable odour, the experience of which was so commonplace as to be familiar, normal, as normal as the pungent smell of Mass (Mister) Oswald's pigsty located up the road, which produced its own unmistakable whiff that travelled downwind to the Rowe compound.

Of a more pleasing nature, the young boy also experienced the congenial fragrance of hibiscus flowers, which would flare up as hummingbirds, or doctor birds as they are locally known, made their house calls, stirring up flowers, awakening their sweet nectar, the fragrance punctuating the fresh country air. Small, colourful, and eccentric, the birds with their long tails frequented the arbour, attracted as they were to the many flowering plants surrounding the little homestead.

The sweetest aroma of all was the aroma of cooking coming from outdoor pots in makeshift outdoor kitchens, smoke meandering skyward, signaling *"pot a boil"* or *"food soon come."* With many children to feed, food was of great importance in the Rowe compound. Grandma Rowe had a cabinet in which she hid her provisions for safekeeping, an insurance against theft from rats, cats, dogs, and other pests. This was no guarantee, of course, as there was always someone who thought they were clever enough to break in to scrounge for provisions, whether it be flour, rice, sugar, or fish.

Once, Fitzroy's older brother, Roy, showing an early talent for stunts, orchestrated a plot. One night, he successfully drained sweet condensed milk from a can located in the buttery by poking a hole in the can and sucking it out through a straw, much to the children's delight as they satiated their sweet tooth. Fitzroy also recalls how he and his bosom buddy and partner in crime, a cousin by the name of Sam, concocted a scheme to break into grandma's cabinet to steal her seasoned fried fish, which they gleefully devoured. Later, when leftover bones were discovered and the deed uncovered, Sam vanished from the yard, leaving poor little Fitzroy alone to take licks, the no-nonsense spanking that was bound to come, and come hard, because of their selfish greed. Fitzroy took the licks well, but he would never forget the lesson. Grandma was not mean. She was proficient. She knew the thin line between full belly and starvation. Her frugal management made sure there was enough food for everyone. At mealtimes, there usually was one pot of food to feed adults and children, each flour dumpling accounted for as it entered the pot and accounted for again when it exited. To ensure all had equal share, Grandma lined up the plates, serving each openly with an even hand. As far as Grandma was concerned, making sure children were fed was her way to let them know they were loved and cherished.

The buttery was not the only source of food. Mango trees were everywhere in the neighbourhood and beyond. During mango season, which ran from April through to July, nobody starved. On long walks to and from school, and during the summer, Fitzroy and the other children regularly cut through bush and barbwire fences to feast on ripe mangoes. They would eat *till dem belly full*, proving true an old Jamaican expression that during mango season, *"no pot ah fi cook"* (no need to cook during mango season). During mango season, whenever the children arrived home from school or wherever, it was understood that the children were already satisfied. In such situations, Grandma Rowe did not need to worry about feeding them.

For nutrition, there were also a variety of plums, including hog plums, and pears, guava, peanuts, and also cherries added to the mix. Further afield were tamarind trees up at Mass Gussy. Across Mass George, they could pick two greenskins and eat raw beans, and up at Mass Wilbur, there was jam belly full. Out at the Junction, some quarter mile away, there were other treats to be had on the way while fetching water. These adventures were naturally done on foot and on bare feet. Walking barefooted was commonplace, not the exception, but the rule. Bare feet, seen through the eyes of children in Ridge Pen, were not a mark of poverty. It was a matter of nature, not unlike the sun rising then walking across the sky to set on the other side. No shoes necessary. No one questioned it. It was the way things were. Whether going to school at Geneva Basic School located three to four miles walk away or fetching water or playing marbles—no shoes. To Fitzroy, the distance from home to anywhere seemed like forever. But like everyone else in the village, he, too, walked bare feet. Years later, he would walk long enough to eventually find his own pair of shoes and walk in them proudly. And he would soon learn that the places he needed to get to were in fact not that far at all.

Located on the property not very far from the homestead was the family burial ground. The Rowe family in the sixties and early seventies by all measure were *dirt poor*, but those who died, died well; those who lived, also lived well. Fitzroy remembers an enchanting time, content without want. His family was short of nothing but did not have enough for somethings. In the midst of abundance, there was need. They had the ability to plant but not the capacity to accumulate wealth, their socio-economic status held in check, their existence held in abeyance. The "socialist" government of the day implemented food welfare programs allowing low-income families access to rice, bulgur flour, and other cheap staples. Fitzroy remembers joining in line to receive such handouts, never missing a day when the government food truck rolled into the village. Yet he cannot recall this as a mark of poverty. Despite having no access to good medicine, shoes or school uniforms, or books to read, and being a recipient of government handouts, Fitzroy recalls his childhood as being happy. He and his companions lived in an innocent dreamlike paradise where fun in the sun and rain were fair and square, where childlike playful ways held their own complex *secrets* yet unknown.

It was under these conditions, and in this compound, under the watchful gaze and care of grandparents, from birth to the age of eight, that Fitzroy found his ground. Here he learned the lessons of life that shaped the person he would eventually become. It was from his grandparents that he learned the value of industry and hard work. He remembers all three Rowe brothers being hard workers. They often walked long distances, sixty miles or more, accompanied by hampered donkeys in search of piecework or any type of employment possible. Any honest work would do. They were jack-of-all-trades, master of all. They made personal sacrifices to find work to make a living to support their families. Strong as an ox, and equally durable, they worked hard long days into the night to the extent that they oftentimes developed advanced stages of hernia. Even hernias were commonplace.

From his grandparents, he learned the value of providing for family. *If there is one corn grain, everyone must eat.* In the Rowe's family compound, rice or a side of meat in gungo peas soup, even *sweetie* or one banana went a far way. This personal commitment to family and to community left an indelible imprint on the young boy. The extended family circle on the Rowe compound lived at or below the poverty line. Nonetheless, they held life and limb together through ingenuity, through their natural instinct for survival. Their communal living and their depth of spirit, coupled with their religious faith, kept them afloat.

In the larger context, their existential conditions were inextricably linked to deep historical forces tied to a set of entrenched, exploitative socio-economic relations. These socio-economic relations were based on principles of inequality designed to enable a few, while disabling many others. The Rowe family was in the latter category. Despite their herculean efforts, they were hamstrung by an onerous socio-economic order governed by forces beyond their immediate control. For the little boy named Fitzroy, this would be of no apparent immediate consequence. But as he advanced into manhood, he would soon come to discover a new appreciation of this bigger, more complex picture as more *secrets* began to reveal themselves.

As Fitzroy Anderson grew into manhood, he continued to learn from his grandparents. From them, he heard repetitive themes that, like a refrain, were reinforced daily. In 1995, he heard it again when he approached his grandfather for the last time prior to the old man's passing. Alfred Rowe, aged and elderly, was extremely ill by then. As if consulting a wise sage and with much affection, the boy once called Fitzroy, now a man, posed a question to his grandfather while he was on his sick bed. "What message do you have to give young people, Grandpa?" Enlivened, the old man sat up and replied without hesitation, "Manners, *mi pickini*, manners is great. Have manners. It will carry you through the world."

This advice carried a paradox. Not that there was anything wrong with it. The advice was sound. It sank deep into the boy's consciousness to become an enduring connection between him and his grandfather, the man under whose watchful eye he had entered the world and who had welcomed him into the family. Politeness, decency, respect, and honour would be the glue holding the family together. These values provided the benchmark for how the boy would eventually live his life.

The advice, however, had a flip side. When he became a man, this flip side would cause Fitzroy to disconnect from the systems of oppression that shaped his grandfather. By this time, the boy known as Fitzroy would be known as Adisa Oji, and in the sincere counsel received from the old man, he could now hear echoes harkening back to colonialism. He now understood, better than he ever could before, how colonialism had wrapped its tight grip around Alfred Rowe and others of his generation, how it had taught them to be submissive, compliant, and obedient. He could sense in their humble penitence a conditioned behaviour that discouraged them from aspiring beyond their designated status as hewers of wood and carriers of water. Oppression had become internalized, self-automated, part of a colonial dehumanizing paradigm that programmed Black Jamaicans to remain humble, to accept their condition, and to never question or challenge the status quo, a status quo requiring absolute loyalty; otherwise, it would react brutishly to those who objected to it. The message of *manners* was more than just about having a good code of conduct; it was a matter of survival, an advice given "for your own good." The old man meant well. But in his exhortation could also be heard the need for *surrender*, a tendency toward internalized self-devaluation—a lesson that would be passed on to Oji's parents who in turn would pass it on to him and his siblings, a learned submissiveness handed down from generation to generation.

As these *secrets* began to be revealed, and as anti-Black ideologies began to be exposed, Fitzroy Anderson the boy would become Adisa Oji the man. The internalized cycle of self-depreciation, which normally is on auto-pilot, would come to a halt. With this newfound attitude, he took the concept of *manners* and converted it into a powerful lesson about self-liberation based foremost on self-respect, self-determination, and autonomy. By embarking on this approach, Adisa Oji would build on, rather than erase, his grandfather's legacy. Whereas that legacy was previously at risk, that birthright could now be snatched from the system of oppression that had once imprisoned it. Now the gift received from his grandfather could be liberated, decolonized, and repurposed, safeguarded and sustained into a brighter, more progressive future, one more in keeping with the highest hopes and best dreams of those who came before him.

Grandma Nana Geraldine Rowe. Making sure the children were well fed was her way of letting them know they were loved and cherished. (Family album/Oji Archives)

"Manners, *mi pickini*, manners is great. Have Manners. It will carry you through the world." Oji with Grandpa Alfred Rowe. (Family album/Oji Archives)

At this point in my life, I believe everything has happened to me for a reason. All the choices I have made were necessary. The path that I am on, although difficult, it is the right one for me.

—Brother Adisa S. Oji

Chapter 4

WHAT A BAM! BAM!

Fitzroy Anderson's first time on an airplane was in 1974. He was eight years old and a reluctant traveller.

It was June, when he, along with his two brothers and sister, left the island where they were born to go to a continent where people of their kind are made to feel as if they don't completely belong. He would not have intellectually known this in advance, yet the young boy Fitzroy experienced a profound mix of excitement and foreboding. The anxiety was more than he could bear. It would be his first time away from home. The prospect of leaving the comforting circle of extended family and friends, the free, open, sunny fields of Ridge Pen where he romped and found his legs, was inconceivable. He was just about to settle into his grade 2 schooling when word came that it was time to go overseas to be with his parents. Jolted by the news, it was as if someone pushed him over a cliff's edge.

His destination abroad had promise. A few years earlier, in hope of making a better life for the family in general, but more specifically for the children, his mother and father left for Toronto, Canada. Now, a long-awaited reunion with his parents had finally arrived. He wanted to reunite with his parents, but the thought of leaving his grandparents, who raised him, and letting go of all the things he had grown to love caused him deep anguish. He had not been in his parent's company for some time. He looked forward to being with them again even though in an entirely foreign strange place, a thought that left him with great uncertainty. Torn, overwhelmed with confusion, overcome by torment, the boy lost his usual composure and went into hiding. He was unwilling to leave the home he had known all his life. When he heard it was time to go, he went to a familiar place of refuge. He hid under his bed and refused to budge.

Over the previous year in preparation for the trip, his mother had begun to groom all her children for this moment. Subtly, she prepared the young boy and his siblings for travel to the "great white north." She shared with them anecdotal stories in an attempt to get them acquainted with the idea of travelling overseas. She sent ahead an assortment of clothing from Honest Ed's, the one-of-a-kind discount bargain department store frequented by immigrants and anyone on a shoestring budget. Foreign clothes had a certain smell, feel, and look. It was important for the children to get used to this early. Maybe they would become enticed, get the taste of foreign life, dressing and looking the part. The little boy's first ever pair of shoes was from Honest Ed's, given to him in 1973 when the orientation first began. Getting a brand-new pair of shoes from *foreign* was a big deal. Walking around barefooted in Canada was not the norm, and fitting in was important. In his parent's mind, the boy needed to get used to the idea of wearing shoes. Nevertheless, dress or no dress, shoes or no shoes, the little boy Fitzroy could not bring himself to leave. He still would not budge.

It took a cunning ruse cooked up between his mother and his aunt to get Fitzroy out from under the bed; something about going to visit so-and-so. Even then, the boy still resisted. He was inconsolable. His caretakers had to haul and pull him outside to the waiting vehicle. Dressed up wearing an unaccustomed pair of shoes that felt as if they were a size too big, the boy cried in the car all the way to the local airport. He cried on the flight all the way to Toronto. With head shaking, he sobbed, sighing as he entered Canada, unaware of the life awaiting him and his family.

On arrival, the young boy noticed how much cooler it felt. For the next few years as he settled into his new home, Fitzroy would go deeper inside, his introverted nature bordering on that of a recluse. During these few frozen years, warmth escaped him. He would eventually come out of himself, but only when he began to discover who he truly was. Only then would he begin to slowly defrost to regain his footing to walk the land that his family had chosen.

It is difficult to say what exactly lurked in little Fitzroy's mind as he sat solitarily under the trees in Ridge Pen with his assortment of pots and pans. It is hard to say what deep fears plagued him when he was forced abruptly to migrate to Canada with the hope of assimilating into Toronto life. We will never completely know the deep thoughts of his subconscious or know whether or not he had prescient visions of protests, riots, marches, and massacres. We will never fully appreciate if he had a foreknowledge of matters related to race, colour, culture, or identity. What we do know is that at the time of his coming of age, the world was a troubled place, particularly for people of African ancestry, who were facing hostilities almost everywhere.

On March 21, 1960, six years to the day before Fitzroy Anderson was born, in a place geographically far removed from Jamaica, miles beyond the tranquility of Ridge Pen, lethal bullets were flying. Sixty-nine innocent Black people were killed that day when in Sharpeville, South Africa, police unleashed gunfire on a group of unarmed Black Africans who were peacefully protesting against apartheid. One hundred and eighty others were wounded. In the aftermath, a state of emergency was declared. The African National Congress (ANC) and the Pan-African Congress were banned. A day begotten by hate, March 21, 1960, is not easily forgotten by those who lived through it. And so, while the boy Fitzroy Anderson was peaceably coming into the seemingly ordinary world of Ridge Pen on March 21, 1966, tortuous memories, far from ordinary, were being relived in Sharpeville, South Africa.

Through this fortuitous twist of history, Fitzroy's birthday became forever linked with what would eventually become the International Day for the Elimination of Racism. The United Nations General Assembly, knowing that the time for change had come, readied itself to give birth to a proclamation of its own on the very same day and in the very same year that Fitzroy Anderson arrived. The 1966 proclamation issued a worldwide call for the redoubling of efforts to eliminate racism and discrimination.

This mystery of marriage between birth and destiny continued to deepen for Fitzroy Anderson when in 1965, one year prior to his birth, also on March 21, a man named Martin Luther King Jr. led over three thousand people on one of several civil rights marches from Selma to Montgomery, Alabama, USA. A groundswell of student-led sit-ins, stand-ins, marches and Freedom Rides—forms of non-violent resistance—were already rapidly rising in the deep American South as a means of ending anti-Black racism. Alabama, known for its severe Jim Crow laws, legislated Black Americans to a life of endless humiliations, gross disadvantages, and subhuman cruelty. The marches were intended to draw critical attention to these injustices with the hope of triggering change in the consciousness of the racialized American South. By the time the protest march led by Dr. King occurred, a new social awakening would begin to peak, laying the foundation of what would become the model for modern-day youth movements for justice, civil and human rights, with widespread student participation. Among the march was a young man from Trinidad, twenty-three year old Stokely Carmichael, who would go on to stoke the fire of what would become known as Black power, and whose legacy would captivate the imagination of a generation of young people yet unborn, including Fitzroy Anderson.

Days before King joined the march, on March 7, 1965, the world came to know Bloody Sunday. On this day, six hundred civil rights marchers—men, women, and children—moving in double file formation, were swarmed and beaten by Alabama State troopers. A crowd of close to a hundred White people stood by laughing and shouting, proudly waving confederate flags. Under the hooves of horses, enveloped by tear gas, the marchers fell, stumbled, and ran gasping for breath, fearing for their lives while they were jeered and cajoled. It was an ugly scene, reminiscence of many others in which violent White mobs attacked peaceful, defenseless Black citizens. John Lewis walked in both marches. In his memoir, *Walking With The Wind*, he described a similar scene in Montgomery during the 1961 Freedom Rides, labelling it as a "wilding," a kind of "madness," typified by a White angry crowd "screaming and reaching out and hitting and spitting ... like animals." Years later, on March 7, 1965, there would be plenty more bloodshed and weeping as a nation known globally for liberty and democracy suddenly became exposed for its own inhumanity and hypocrisy.

Unrelenting in their courage and resistance to oppression, the protestors returned on March 21, 1965, this time with Martin Luther King Jr. leading the procession. "Segregation is on its deathbed," he told the people gathered in front of the offices of Alabama governor, George Wallace. "I know you are asking today, 'How long will it take?'... I come to say to you this afternoon, however difficult the moment, however frustrating the hour, it will not be long because truth pressed down to the earth will rise again," King intoned. Despite Martin Luther King's lofty vision of non-violence and powerful entreaty, many wondered, especially young Black idealists, how much more violence Black people could tolerate before they retaliated and took matters into their own hands, particularly when the laws and safeguards in place to protect citizens repeatedly failed to protect them.

As if to say truth pressed down had risen again, a year later to the day, Fitzroy Anderson was born. But change can be long in coming. The realization of Dr. King's dream was still a far way off. The truth of which he spoke still had trouble rising; truth would still be pressed down to the earth. On April 4, 1968, three years after making his remarks in Alabama, Dr. Martin Luther King Jr was assassinated on the balcony of a Memphis motel. And while this was America, not Canada, truth was pressed down here in 1974 just the same even as Fitzroy made his agonizing trip toward a Toronto airport.

In spite of that, March 21 remains a day of multiple anniversaries commemorating epic struggles. In many ways, March 21, the dawn of spring, is extraordinary in its significance. Although he did not choose his name or his moment of birth, the timing of Fitzroy Anderson's arrival in the world was a promise of things to come. Some describe this as *destiny*; others call it *synchronicity*. The seemingly inexplicable thread connecting Fitzroy Anderson to his future was already beginning to unravel even at the moment of birth, stretching like a lengthy kente cloth billowing in the tropical wind from then until now. It would take the young boy some time before he would come to terms with his destiny. But from early on, it was clear that a part of him already knew that he was but one link in a very long chain.

As the plane lifted then circled, pointing its nose in a northerly direction toward Canada, the little boy cast his watery eyes below as he watched the island slowly fading fast. Afraid to watch, he closed his eyes, hoping the whole ordeal would end. It didn't. As the plane rose to cruising altitude, his heart sank. He was not able to put a name to it then, but as the island below became visibly smaller with each passing second, he became increasingly homesick. He had sung "Jamaica, Jamaica, Jamaica land we love," the national anthem, several times. Now, he suddenly realized how much and what it meant to him.

Jamaica, land of wood and water, is rich in soil, yet the masses are poor. The vibe here is hauntingly frightening and happy-go-lucky. Beautiful and beguiling, dark and mysterious in places, exuberant and bold, tantalizing to the senses, such is the nature of this place once inhabited by Amerindians—Indigenous Arawak and Taino communities. It is the third largest island in the Greater Antilles, the fourth largest in the Caribbean Sea.

For some, Jamaica is a place from which to rob red dirt for export and to reap where others sow. For others, Jamaica is nothing but a beach, a tourist paradise, a place to escape to for hedonistic and other pleasures, a place to run to and then leave. But for those unable to leave, Jamaican life has more profound meaning. Whether they choose to call it "ya'ad," "jamdown," or "the rock," those with deep attachments to the country understand that beneath its sunny skies, embedded between the island's shoreline of white sandy beaches with its iridescent emerald-turquoise sea and the lofty mountainous interior is a history of injustice and the quest for its opposite, a history of blood and fire, hurricanes, and earthquakes, natural and unnatural disasters, and much wailing and gnashing of teeth. Anyone born here is familiar with the urge to leave, explaining why Jamaicans are scattered far and wide across the globe. However, the island folkways die hard, cutting so deep it is impossible to run away completely.[13]

Jamaica—235 kilometres from end to end, and 84 kilometres wide—is not that big. It is a small island with a big heart, a little Caribbean Island whose worldwide reputation dwarfs its physical size. It is a place bathed by sunshine where many aspire to greatness, while others continue to dwell in a metaphorical shadow with little or no shade from the scorching heat of a blistering past in which Africans were enslaved, sugar was crowned king, and a British imperial monarch sat on a distant throne while having the island's wealth for a treasure chest and the people as one of many footstools.

---

[13] As the popular Jamaican saying goes, "Yuh can tek a Jamaican outta Jamaica but you can't take Jamaica outta him."

Jamaica *land we love*—a former settler-colony founded as a plantation slave society—is a place where vast amounts of profits have been generated based particularly on the violent exploitation of people of African ancestry. As such, the island is a uniquely perverse place plagued by danger and filled with deadly intrigue. Within this miasma of institutionalized oppression where extreme social and economic inequality prevail, then and now, and where the majority of inhabitants, Black and poor, live in deprivation, Jamaica has long been fertile ground for all sorts of trouble. Rebellion and revolt punctuate Jamaica's history. A colourful cast of individuals have chosen to rebel and confront systems of racial injustice. From the two Juans—de Bolas and de Serras—warrior Maroons from the seventeenth century who tormented Spanish and English militias, to the legendary Three Finger Jack, who established one of several refugee colonies of freed Africans in the eastern sections of the Blue Mountains. From Cudjoe, Cuffee, Nanny, Quao, and Tacky, who each took turns to challenge British imperialism, to Sam Sharpe, who in 1831 led a Christmas rebellion that almost toppled the plantation system and who said prior to his execution, "I would rather die on yonder gallows than die a slave." To Paul Bogle, the Black Baptist deacon who initiated a protest march for justice and equality by leading a grassroots movement for civil rights that culminated in what became known as the Morant Bay Rebellion in 1865. And to untold numbers of workers who, in 1938, participated in a wave of strikes throughout the island, ultimately leading to a full-blown riot calling for better working and living conditions for the mostly Black working class. In response to these efforts, reprisals from British imperialism came swift and without mercy, often resulting in executions, indiscriminate slaughter, and increased repression. Occasionally, there would be a commission of enquiry. In the words of a revered but militant Jamaican son known for his unflinching critique of the social order and his fierce calls for *equal rights*, "Everyone is crying out for peace, yes / None is crying out for justice."[14]

Jamaica is a catastrophic intersection where race, class, and gender collide, resulting in significant carnage and trauma; a place where unwritten colour-coded caste arrangements have tied experience to skin tone—if you are dark, so may be your future; if light, there may be less of a fight. Here, prejudice and animosity run long and deep like silent subterranean rivers, which on occasion can and do erupt. Jamaica is a land where love and hate have blurred lines and where racialized division into *haves* and *have-nots* struggle in an epic give-and-take for dominance and survival.

Looming alongside the verdant hills and rugged grandeur of the mountainous interiors of Jamaica is a long tussle with the well-worn legacy of colonialism, a struggle belied by beautiful imageries of a land awash in hot rhythmic sounds and warm colours evoking everlasting sunsets. Blessed by nature, cursed by the deeds of a few less-than-noble characters, this country has lived long and hard through many trials and tribulations. It is a place where the term *"Dread"* refers not to the haunting horrors of history but to the knotty locks confronting it; a place where many are quick to bemoan due to its many desperate ills, and where, just as quickly, many will

---

14 From the album of the same name, "Equal Rights," released in 1977, the second studio album by Peter Tosh (October 19, 1944–September 11, 1987). Before establishing himself as a solo artist, Tosh was an original core member of the Wailers (1963–1976) together with Bob Marley and Bunny Wailer. He was murdered, September 11, 1987, after gunmen broke into his home in Kingston, Jamaica. He was posthumously honoured with Jamaica's Order of Merit on October 15, 2012. With the passing of Bunny Wailer in Kingston on March 2, 2021, at the age of seventy-three, came the end of an era.

serenade with praise for its devilish beauty, playfulness, and enchantment. Loud and musical in laughter and speech, the people dance in a romantic tryst with joy and suffering, their cadence driven by the beat of persistent poverty, their feet, hands, and lips moving in unison with sounds of misplaced gaiety. Here, you are likely to find men, women, and children dancing on flaming rocks while making the world dance with them, each day saying "Good morning" with a smile as they pass each other on dusty country roads. On peaceful evenings, you can find common folk mingling with *peenie wallie* fireflies that dart about doing a dance of their own to a cacophony of chirping crickets and toads wooing their lovers in a tropical night. Such is the life here; at least, for some.

Jamaica is where "*Carry mi ackee go a Linstead Market, not a quattie wut sell*" is real life and where "*Come missa tally man, tally mi banana. Day dah light an' mi waa'h go home*" is more than calypso. Here, the soul of the masses and that of the island is that of a survivor-nation caught up within the throes of a grand historical *pocomania*—a small madness—buried deep within the psyche, causing much travail even as the people struggle to liberate themselves and remain warm and true. Resiliently, they carry on in this *bam-bam*, often exchanging stories in the glow of *Home Sweet Home* kerosene lamps, counting what little blessings they have one by one, while some in rags with nothing to count only dream, even as some who have no dreams continue to scavenge, their dreams long dead and gone as they drag themselves day to day, place to place, begging bread and seeking solace where none can be found.

Never short on notoriety or alternate realities sitting side by side, Jamaica, reputed to have the most rum bars and taverns per square mile, is also reputed to have the most concentration of churches; it is a land where many strains of religion—predominantly in the Judeo-Christian tradition—compete for souls in a loud spiritual marketplace, coveting and competing for the minds and hearts of men, women, and children even while many continue to stagger off course into inebriation, insanity, and bedlam. Gathered to worship on any given day—all dogmatically dedicated to their sectarian view of biblical scripture, the seen and unseen and the afterlife, each faithful to their own theology—are Catholics, Anglicans, Methodists, Protestants, Pentecostals, Church of God, Sabbath Day Adventist, Jehovah Witnesses, and other splinter groups and fractions of faith such as the Christian Brethren Assembly, the home church of the Andersons, located a three-mile walk away from Ridge Pen.

In this gumbo, staunch and orthodox segments of the faith community have taken legalistic umbrage with each other. They have, in the course of history, sat on opposite sides. Baptists have been emancipators. Anglicans have been slave owners. Both have built and supported institutions of learning. As a rule, Eurocentric-informed theologies have shared a common disdain for non-Christian ideologies and have condemned with united scorn any practice involving Witch Doctors, Obeah, Spiritualists, or Voodoo, all of which have their own adherents in this religiously diverse nation boasting a motto proclaiming "Out of many, one people."

Coming out of this stew of "isms and schisms," another celebrated revered son and an international superstar, in his song *Talkin' Blues,* candidly professed, "I feel like bombing a church, now / Now that you know the preacher is lying."[15] Known for his impassioned idealism, Bob Marley was wailing on behalf of those who rest nightly on cold ground with rocks for pillows and an open sky for a ceiling, *sufferers* permanently disfigured from prolonged browbeating, those who the "White man's" religion have failed to reach or rescue.

Yes, Jamaican life can be hard and soft. Here, rural peasants lead a life of meagre subsistence in the presence of surrounding wealth. Here, palaces on hillsides overlook multitudes of urban poor, who live and die in haphazard shack-filled overpopulated slums in gullies and areas known locally as *dungle* or *back-o-wall*, otherwise sometimes referred to as *shanty town*.[16] Here, the privileged and the exploited exist in juxtaposition, one on top, the other below, reminiscent of the days of Great Houses and slave quarters—wealth and poverty coexisting in precarious uneasiness. Here, it is not unusual for the rich to be cocooned in secluded majestic bubbles perched on green hills overlooking parched plains, bedecked in satin or silk and luxurious linens, sipping martini with pinkies pointing skyward to crystal chandeliers set in great big halls, laughing frivolously to the din of silver spoons dipped in buttered bread while debating why the poor are getting poorer and what should be done. This, too, is Jamaica, where contradictions are plentiful, where justice is scarce, and where oppression refuses to die.

Nevertheless, from this grim life can be found gold and diamonds in the rough; the seemingly old, yet ageless; the free, yet bound; the bold and brave, yet meek. Here, you will meet African descendants with calloused hands going about their daily business completely unaware of their special legacy, seemingly oblivious to their place in the historical drama of human life. Agrarian souls, primarily tied to the land, their hands are hard due to working the soil sunup to sundown. Here, those who cannot find a job will seek to make one; if the work isn't close by or available within the limits of the village or town, they will walk miles or ride further on bicycles or donkeys, armed with tools of trade, ready to work. Some peddle whatever can be bartered, bought, or sold. Here, men risk life and limb to fearlessly climb tall coconut trees without a harness, legs wrapped around slender cylindrical trunks, hoisting themselves upward, leap frogging in vertical clamber to dizzying heights; later you will see them husking coconuts with a few swings of a machete, transforming them into jugs of coconut water to drink and quench thirst or a bowl of jelly to eat. Here, women work double duty to hold life and limb together. They work at home and away on farms, in fields, and at factories; as hawkers in marketplaces or on the streets; or as domestic workers—child-rearing, cooking, ironing, and cleaning in other people's homes—sometimes single-handedly raising multigenerational families either as mothers or as grandmothers in an unending battle with intergenerational poverty. Through their efforts, sons and daughters attend school. With hard work, a few lucky ones may enter university, locally or overseas.

---

15 "*Talkin' Blues*," from the album *Natty Dread* by Robert Nesta Marley (February 6, 1945–May 11, 1981), released October 1974. In 1977, Marley was diagnosed with a melanoma. In February 1981, he was awarded one of Jamaica's highest honours, the Order of Merit.

16 "Tenement Yard" is another common term used to describe government-sponsored multifamily housing schemes built initially with the intention of creating housing for the urban working class. Following Jamaica's post-independence years, these "yards" have deteriorated into ghettos consisting of densely populated substandard dwellings with shared amenities. Some have become "garrison" communities, a hotbed for political tribal wars.

Hard work notwithstanding, and even though the land is prosperous, many here like the Rowe family remain deprived. Still, they continue to worship, play, and laugh as if the little they have is enough. For the most part, they remain generous and gregarious, never letting poverty interfere with simple pleasure. Whether mixing mortar, building infrastructure, tilling the soil or fishing, they carry on just the same; whether raising animals or tending to landscapes or *chilling* by the roadside, sitting on a wall watching, waiting … waiting for nothing, waiting for everything. With everything scheduled to arrive no time soon, it is all the same. Here, time is elastic.

Jamaica is a place where a mass murdering *White Witch* who lived in a Great House is a celebrated attraction. It is home to song and dance and circumlocution, of this and that, horse dead and cow fat; home to *Ginnals*—devious characters aiming to outsmart friends and enemies by making sense out of nonsense—playing fool to catch the wise, as they say. It is home to folkloric tales of *duppies* and roaming mythical apparitions; home to hipsters, rude boys and tricksters; home to the spider *Anancy*—the sky god—a throwback to West African culture, a controversial humorous diminutive larger-than-life archetypal character symbolizing human empowerment, transformation, guile, and acuity. It is home to Gran' Market, held every weekend before Christmas and on Christmas Eve, sometimes on Christmas Day, when marketplaces in villages and towns come alive with the sound of vendors, firecrackers, popping balloons, and *sweetie* (candy); the gurgling sound of poured rum and sorrel; and the munching of grater cakes. It gets louder with Christmas carols as choirs compete with street revellers dancing to reggae music blaring from dusk until dawn on avenues lined with larger-than-life audio speakers. It gets even more raucous with *Jonkonnu*—men and women prancing in public dressed in colourful outfits, masquerading to the sound of fifes, rattle and bass drums, and other makeshift instruments, much to the amusement of children and adults. While some shun this masquerade out of fear or scorn, this creolized parade has served to keep the African spirit alive.

Yes, the African spirit has remained unyielding, finding various ways to reassert itself through electrifying personalities. Alexander Bedward (1848–1930) and Marcus Garvey (1887–1940) were two of the first to decisively break the psychological stranglehold of racial oppression by boldly postulating and interpreting life, religion, freedom, and social justice through a Pan-African lens. In an era when White and Brown people were esteemed and being African was reviled, Bedward and Garvey were two of the first Jamaicans to publicly articulate Black pride on a nationwide scale.

Although the fullness of this history and unique way of life, rich with stories of philosophers, warrior-kings and queens, and freedom fighters—a legacy abounding with puzzling contradictions, legends and myths, messiahs and music, dance, and unfathomable beauty—although this knowledge may not have been readily available to Fitzroy Anderson's conscious mind at eight years old, this was part of his inalienable birthright, part of the *collective consciousness* he shared with many others. And he would miss it.

During the 1960s, Jamaica was enthralling and compelling as the rest of the world. In 1962, following the example of other former colonies, the country gained its independence, politically unshackling itself from Britain, long regarded as the mother country.[17] With this decision, Jamaica presumably broke away from 307 years of British colonial stranglehold. For the duration of three centuries, starting with the 1655 British invasion led by Admirals Robert Venables and William Penn, Jamaica yielded to the colonial domination and imperial wishes of the British Empire.

The British Empire, which lasted some three hundred years, at its peak had sovereign control over one third of the world's known population. This encompassed a vast amount of territory stretching from North America to Australia—including notably Ghana and Nigeria in West Africa, Kenya in East Africa, and the sub-continent of India— with Jamaica and an assortment of other islands and archipelagos thrown into the mix. The British Empire had an enormous boot-print.

While development was officially stifled in colonial outposts such as Jamaica, these possessions ensured the dynamic industrial development of Britain, a pattern that was accompanied in many cases by White racial domination and racial segregation. Prior to that, the island was held by the Spanish who named it Santiago. Italian explorer Christopher Columbus, then on contract to the monarchs of Spain, is said to have "discovered" the island in 1492, this despite the fact that an Indigenous community welcomed him and his sea-weary crew. In the name of God, monarchy, and gold, the Spanish took no time in mercilessly subduing and destroying the local Arawak and Taino communities, thereby giving themselves free reign to do whatever they wanted until the British came along and did the same to them.

When Britain acquired the island, they quickly moved to exploit its strategic and economic value. In order to militarily defend the island from their enemies, they entered into alliances with a coalition of outlaws and bandits—pirates and privateers (Henry Morgan and the Buccaneers being the most famous)—to police and protect the colony. Headquartered in Port Royal on the island's southeast, the swashbuckling seamen had open license to plunder the Caribbean and terrorize Spanish and other foreign outposts. This led Port Royal to develop a late seventeenth-century reputation of being the wickedest city on earth. Garrisons and tribal conflict in Jamaica are nothing new, nor is the practice of hiring outlaws to conduct "official" clandestine state business. Jamaica, since the arrival of the Europeans, has long been accustomed to war and strife and dirty inhumane business. Take a long backward glance on the trajectory of this beautiful paradise and the historical evidence will reveal that someone is always battling for spoils; someone is always forced to defend what they have for fear of losing it to someone else who is preparing to forcibly seize it. Violent power politics and exploitation, a direct legacy of colonialism, started here long before independence.

Jamaica's history suggests that this country has been designed to be an appendage, a lackey satellite, existing for and at the behest of a ruling power located someplace else. In their time of empire, England did what it could to exploit the island for its own benefit, frequently stifling local budding expressions of grassroot democracy and freedom. This was particularly pronounced in

---

17 Several other Caribbean countries gained their independence from Britain during this period, including Trinidad and Tobago (August 1962), Guyana (May 1966), and Barbados (November 1966), signaling an apparent shift in the global distribution of power away from the former colonial empire.

the treatment of Black African workers and peasants who faced persistent oppressive working conditions across the island, the majority relegated to the bottom of the social hierarchy. This relegated status first began with the British mass importation of enslaved Africans. It continued when slavery was abolished (August 1, 1834) and persisted when Britain followed up by importing masses of indentured Indian and Chinese labourers to stack the labour force. After this phase of social engineering ran its course, colonial administrators continued to bring in an assortment of anybody from anywhere for mistreatment and exploitation, including Germans. By this means, they were able to control the labour market, stocking the colony with an oversupply of workers with the specific intent of providing plantations and factories with free or cheap labour. More insidiously, the social policy of the day allowed for a tiered social formation in which the labouring classes were further fractured into gradations of access and privilege—haves and have-nots—with the African Jamaican community being the least favoured. The "first come" would be the "last served." Historically, injustice is no stranger to Jamaica. And Jamaica is no stranger to injustice.

Prior to Jamaica's independence, the imperial British overlords reigned over the island with a sense of supremacy, instilling in the governed an internalized sense of inferiority. When in 1774, Edward Long, a so-called historian and British colonial administrator who owned and operated a slave plantation on the island, wrote *History of Jamaica*, he was not alone in arguing that Black African people were innately inferior to White folks. This was a widely held view among European colonizers, a view that was as widespread as it is persistent. At various times during the course of colonial occupation, the English ruling class regarded the local non-White or non-European population as heathens to be converted; as slaves to be exploited; as serfs to be kept in a state of perpetual dependency; as troublemakers to be kept under lock and key, contained, or worse, terminated through hanging or execution; or as subordinates or subjects to be kept humble and subservient. Never during the era of British colonialism did the idea of *equality and justice for all* enter into the political equation, except of course in moments of enlightened self-interest when justice was deemed to be theirs and theirs alone. Equality, if considered, only narrowly and selfishly applied to the White English governing class. During the Morant Bay Rebellion in 1866 for instance, freed Blacks demanded equal political and economic rights and representation from the White-dominated House of Assembly—a self-governing quasi-local democratic body. Rather than agree with such a demand, the White planter class decided to squash the assembly rather than share political power with their ex-slaves. Rather than sharing equal political rights with Black citizens in a democratic local assembly, the White colonialists sacrificed their own sovereign freedom in favour of direct rule from Britain.

British colonial rule in Jamaica was typified by economic exploitation, the destruction of meaningful equitable democracy, and the systematic denial of opportunities for people of African ancestry. African cultural identity was often stifled or belittled. It is interesting that even after its independence, Jamaica continued to regard itself as part of the British Commonwealth with Her Royal Highness, Her Majesty Queen Elizabeth II continuing to be the acknowledged official head of state.[18] A colonial mindset continued to be a part of the country's DNA, persisting long

---

18 In the eleventh hour (announced in 2020 but voted on in October 2021) as this book was being finalized, Barbados declared that it would be removing the Queen as its head of state and will appoint in place its first president as a republic. "The time has come to fully leave our colonial past behind," said then president-elect and governor general Dame Sandra Mason, who was inaugurated on November 29, 2021, on the occasion of Barbados' fifty-fifth year of independence from colonial rule.

beyond independence. The belief that the English is superior (and Africa is inferior) was ingrained in those they governed. The refusal to question this belief largely explains its perpetuity. Indeed, although the golden age of empire was over and "London bridge" was falling down, the age of racism knew no boundary. Racist ideology would continue on its not so merry way.

With the arrival of independence, Jamaica stood poised to shed its colonial past, poised to embark on the creation of a new social order with forward-looking possibilities. It could, if it so choose, begin to fashion its own model of nationhood by exercising to the fullest its new sovereign autonomy to move forward in an albeit complicated postcolonial world. Its new leaders now had the burdensome task of building a new nation, of creating a new day within a new world, one fully reflecting the nation's self-determined aspirations, culture, and natural potential. If successful, independence for this small country could usher in a new reality, one that went beyond the symbolism of a national flag emblazoned with the colours black, green, and gold, and beyond a rousing national anthem. Multitudes of ordinary Jamaican people previously disengaged from national life could now expect their voices to matter, to be heard. Masses of unemployed men and women could now look forward in hopeful anticipation of meaningful employment in a modern dispensation. Malnourished children could now expect to eat well; many barred from certain privileges, living as if they were third-class citizens due to being born poor and out of wedlock, could now have some hope of redress or relief. So, too, the hordes of functionally illiterate adults throughout the country for whom getting an education was an unreachable luxury; so, too, the many chronically ill, the elderly, and so on. Indeed, Jamaica's independence brought great expectations. The land was rich with possibilities. It was a time of immense excitement and anticipation.

Ten years into Jamaica's independence, in 1972, a new governing party, the People's National Party (PNP), under the leadership of Michael Manley, galloped into political power. Riding in on waves of heaving hysteria, the new government heightened public expectations with a political platform offering *"Power to the People"* and promising *"Better Must Come."*[19] Daringly, the new regime immediately on assuming power began to dismantle what they believed were some of the country's most unfair socio-economic systemic structures. By so doing, the PNP administration pushed the boundary of Jamaica's embryonic independence by decolonizing and testing limits that had never been vigorously challenged before. Convinced that Jamaica was being milked and short-changed by unfair international balance of power and payment

---

19 The slogan (and PNP campaign anthem) was adopted from a song made popular by reggae artist Delroy Wilson (October 5, 1948–March 6, 1995) in his 1971 album of the same name, *Better Must Come*. "I've been trying a long, long time still I didn't make it / Everything I try to do seems to go wrong / It seems I have done something wrong / But they're trying to keep me down / Who God bless, no one curse / Thank God I'm not the worst / Better must come one day."

arrangements, the new regime decided to curtail the free rein foreign investments once enjoyed. Foreign investments now had to cooperate within parameters consistent with Jamaica's best national interest. Important public utility functions were to be nationalized, as were other industries such as the two major planks of the economy—sugar and bauxite—which would now come under more public scrutiny and control. The decision to impose a bauxite levy in 1974 was tantamount to a daring offensive against a powerful platoon of foreign multinationals—Reynolds, Kaiser, Alcoa, Alcan, Revere, and Anaconda—six companies with significant global, political, and economic clout stacked against a Third World government on a small Caribbean Island. The retaliatory consequences would be far-reaching.

Undeterred and steadfast in its commitment, the new administration stridently bucked the international monetary system by wading into the commercial banking sector, which was previously jealously guarded as the exclusive preserve of private ownership. Major land reform programs were initiated to encourage small farmers to engage in productive economic activity. While the expropriation of property was not expressly intended, it was evident from the government's maneuvers that it wanted to extend popular participation in the nation's economy while reducing dependency on vicarious external forces. *"Tun yuh han an mek fashion"* (be innovative and creative) became the maxim of the period encouraging the use of local resources through local ingenuity and initiative. These were, to say the least, very ambitious undertakings, which if successful would greatly disturb the distribution of wealth and power in a country where wealth and power were known to be concentrated in the hands of a few rather than widely spread among many.

Every Jamaican at the time would have been aware of at least some of these initiatives or be touched by them. Fitzroy Anderson, his brothers and sister, and his cousins and family would have been no exception. Young Fitzroy, for example, was familiar with Manley's Project Land Lease. The program was fully in effect in the Ridge Pen District. It was well known, even if perversely, that the Manley government was providing land plots to people who had none, five acres there, ten acres here, and so on. This created a buzz in the community, inciting extra interest in land ownership and in farming. In exchange for leasing land for x period of time at no or low cost, owners were required to plant and produce viable cash crops for the commercial market. These were heady times. Children and youth in Ridge Pen were not immune to it. The prospect of owning land, and of farming, or getting free higher education to escape poverty, to have social mobility, and to rise to a life of worth were compelling reasons to be Jamaican. It was also a compelling reason to resist the lure of migration. Young Fitzroy may not have completely understood, but his reluctance to leave Jamaica in 1974 made perfect sense.

From an existential standpoint, many poor people took solace in the coming of this new day. An example cited by Rachael Manley in her remembrance of her father's life and work, *Slipstream: A Daughter Remembers*, is the experience of a woman named Sylvia. It is said that before 1972 when Sylvia walked down the streets in her own country, she always felt she was walking in borrowed shoes, a pair that was not her own. Since 1972, however, every step she took, Sylvia had a new and empowering awareness that her shoes now belonged to her. The Manley experiment with egalitarianism, if it could be called that, was a brave one worthy of pursuit. Given the internal and external pressures, as it turned out, it became a rather costly endeavour. A mere flirt with the idea took hell to achieve. Despite the Jamaican adage of "no problem," there were significant and problematic consequences, even if unintended.

During their second term in the 1980s as the political philosophy of the Manley regime crystallized into one of Democratic Socialism (announced as party policy in 1974), the Western world, particularly the US, balked as if unable to stomach the possibility of another Cuban model minutes from its doorstep afloat in the Caribbean Sea. The clash of contending forces that resulted rose to such an intensity that by the end of the decade, Jamaica had nose-dived into a deep, dark abyss typified by political bedlam, social catastrophe, violence, and near economic collapse. Manley, his policies, and his supporters were depicted as foolhardy, misguided, and reckless. The opposition, the Jamaica Labour Party (JLP) led by Edward Seaga, having support from outside foreign interests, was cast as guardians of the status quo. The resulting decay stemming from this intractable conflict between the two rival perspectives was calamitous for the country and its people. Public faith in the nation's basic institutions of law and governance was undermined, leading to such a deterioration of morale that citizens were said to be leaving the island in droves. But not everybody left. Not everybody could leave or wanted to leave. "Nuh wey nuh betta dan yard" (Nowhere is better than home) remained a strong sentiment among a core of Jamaican die-hards. Infuriated that their stranglehold on the economy was threatened, the Jamaican business elite consisting mostly of people of Asian, European, and light-skinned background took flight. Those who remained—largely Black businesspeople, the working and poorer classes—began thereafter seizing whatever slivers of opportunity that were left behind.

Jamaica's attempts to transform the colonial-era oppressive structures of race and class, while not a complete failure, ultimately fell short. Social and economic inequality remained firmly entrenched. Despite the mayhem and destruction that followed, the Manley era of the early seventies was arguably the most provocative expression of Jamaican grassroots conviction and gregariousness. During their term in office, the local popular culture—specifically, African Jamaican—once muzzled and alienated, found new freedom of expression, giving vent to deeply held yearnings. The outburst and blossoming of local culture in dress, speech, music, and art was like that never seen before, making the island a larger-than-life player on the international stage.

The local language, scoffed at as a *dialect*, or more commonly derided as *patois*, now gained mainstream acceptance as an effective tool of communication. Previously regarded as broken English (as opposed to the Queen's English) spoken primarily by the poor and uneducated, the Creole lingua franca assumed new respectability. Linguistic scholars attracted to the veracity of the speech form began to regard it as a language worthy of recognition in its own right. Former professor of Caribbean culture and social history at the University of the West Indies, the late Edward Kamau Braithwaite, called it a "nation-language," suggesting that there should be no shame or loathing associated with speaking it or applying its rhythmic lilt. Everywhere during this pivotal period in Jamaica's social history, there was the sense that a new Jamaican psyche, once damaged by the ravages of enslavement and colonialism, was now gaining energy. It was a time of new possibilities, of free education; a time when *"no bastard nuh de again,"* meaning children formerly branded as illegitimate could now have the same rights and privileges as those born in wedlock. It was a time when previously illiterate men and women could come *"into the light"* via a national literacy program. And into the light they came, willingly in great numbers.

In a country where over 90 percent of the population are of African descent, devoted attention soon shifted to Africa. Certainly not for all but for a significant number of people, Africa became the new standard bearer, the new ideal, the mother country of choice, finally displacing Britain and eclipsing the looming *Big Brother*—the USA superpower hovering nearby. On April 21, 1966, exactly one month after Fitzroy Anderson was born, His Imperial Majesty Haile Selassie of Ethiopia visited Jamaica to great fanfare with over one hundred thousand Rastafarians from all over the country flocking to meet him at the Norman Manley International Airport. According to Rastafarian doctrine, the emperor was/is the prophetic manifestation of God, a coming prediction made by yet another messianic figure, Marcus Mosiah Garvey.[20] Marcus Garvey, head of the Universal Negro Improvement Association, the father of the Back to Africa Movement and Jamaica's first national hero, was long gone by the time of Haile Selassie's visit. However, the spirit of the two men and the thread connecting them would figure prominently as Jamaica began to lay claim to its African roots.[21] Twenty-four years later, as Fitzroy began to restore his own ties to Africa, he too would come to acknowledge Rastafarianism intellectually as a form of resistance, a stirring attempt to reclaim an African persona decimated by colonialism.

Marcus Garvey invoked biblical images of Ethiopia stretching forth her hand like a bereaved mother in an effort to encourage Africans in exile to return home. The exhortation viscerally inspired many to return to their African roots, either in body or in spirit. During the vibrant years of the seventies, these ideas took on new life and meaning. The infectious mood was picked up by a new generation of Jamaicans calling for a new kind of revolution, cultural in nature, one spearheaded by reggae music created by musicians such as U-Roy, Jimmy Cliff, the Melodians, Burning Spear, Dennis Brown, the Wailers and others. The growing Rastafarian movement became the symbolic face of this new era. Collectively, they co-created a hallmark island philosophy encapsulated in such expressions as *"Roots" "Irie"* and *"Ital,"* and called for a movement dedicated to the unification of Africa and the restoration of Black consciousness, pride, and power. According to Dennis Forsythe, quoted in a 1980 edition of *Caribbean Quarterly*, "Rastafarianism is the first mass movement among West Indians preoccupied with the tasks

---

20 After returning to Ethiopia from Jamaica, the emperor, while gracious during his visit, was reportedly concerned with the godlike divine status attributed to him by Rastafarians. In conjunction with the Holy Synod of the Ethiopian Orthodox Tewahedo Church (EOTC), and in fulfilment of a request made by numerous Jamaicans, the emperor subsequently established a Jamaican branch of the EOTC in May 1970. Today, schisms continue to exist between and within the Rastafarian community as to the significance and role of the Ethiopian Orthodox Church, which is not to be confused with the Ethiopian Zion Coptic Church, another offshoot of the Rasta worldview.

21 Leonard P. Howell (June 16, 1898–February 25, 1981), a Jamaican Garveyite, is credited as the founder of Rastafarianism in Jamaica. After returning to Jamaica in 1932 from his travels abroad, including Ethiopia, he began advocating loyalty to the emperor of Ethiopia as opposed to the king of England, thereby challenging the foundation of British colonialism and initiating a new wave of cultural resistance to imperial control. Lowell was eventually jailed and placed in a mental asylum. He is remembered as one of the early pioneers of Pan-African thought and practice.

of looking into themselves and asking the fundamental question, Who am I? or What am I? As such it reflects the spirit of Garveyism ... it is an alternative call for a counter-culture more suited to the needs of black people."

This was the land of Fitzroy Anderson's birth, and these were the prevailing conditions slowly unfolding at the time of his departure as a young child. The cultural exuberance, the bitter struggles plaguing the young independent nation would make a remarkable impression on him. While embracing Jamaica's cultural motif, he, too, would soon have to confront the struggles that afflicted many of his compatriots, and this he would do by embodying a strong African identity.

Consistent with the impeccable timing of Fitzroy Anderson's birth, the first Jamaican Independence Festival Song Competition was held in 1966. When the winning original song was announced, the words and spirit of the lyrics—"Bam! Bam! What a bam, bam!"—could be likened to a foretelling of the boy's emerging potential.

"Bam! Bam! What a bam, bam!" The sound of Toots and the Maytals' singing was guttural yet melodious.[22] Supported by a strong reggae-driven harmony flowing through the rhythm section, the melody echoed over a lilting syncopated beat reverberating like a chant floating above the accompanying percussions and a *Nyabinghi* drum line. When listened to carefully, "Bam! Bam! What a bam, bam!" plays like a warning alerting many that a young warrior was born. By 1974, as the young boy made his way to Canada, these cryptic lyrics served as a forecast of what was to come for the young boy christened Fitzroy: "I want you to know that I am the man who / Fight for the right, not for the wrong / Going there, I'm growing there / Helping the weak against the strong / Soon you will find out the man I'm supposed to be / Help this man, don't trouble no man / But if you trouble that man it will bring a bam, bam! What a bam, bam! Bam, bam!"

---

22 The initial core members of Toots and the Maytals included lead singer/songwriter Fredrick "Toots" Hibbert and backing vocalists Henry Gordon and Nathaniel Mathias. Toots died while the manuscript for this book was being finalized. He passed away in August 2020 at the University Hospital of the West Indies, Kingston, Jamaica. He was seventy-seven.

One time I didn't want to be in Canada any more ... back in the early 90's ... and I packed up and went home.

—Brother Adisa S. Oji

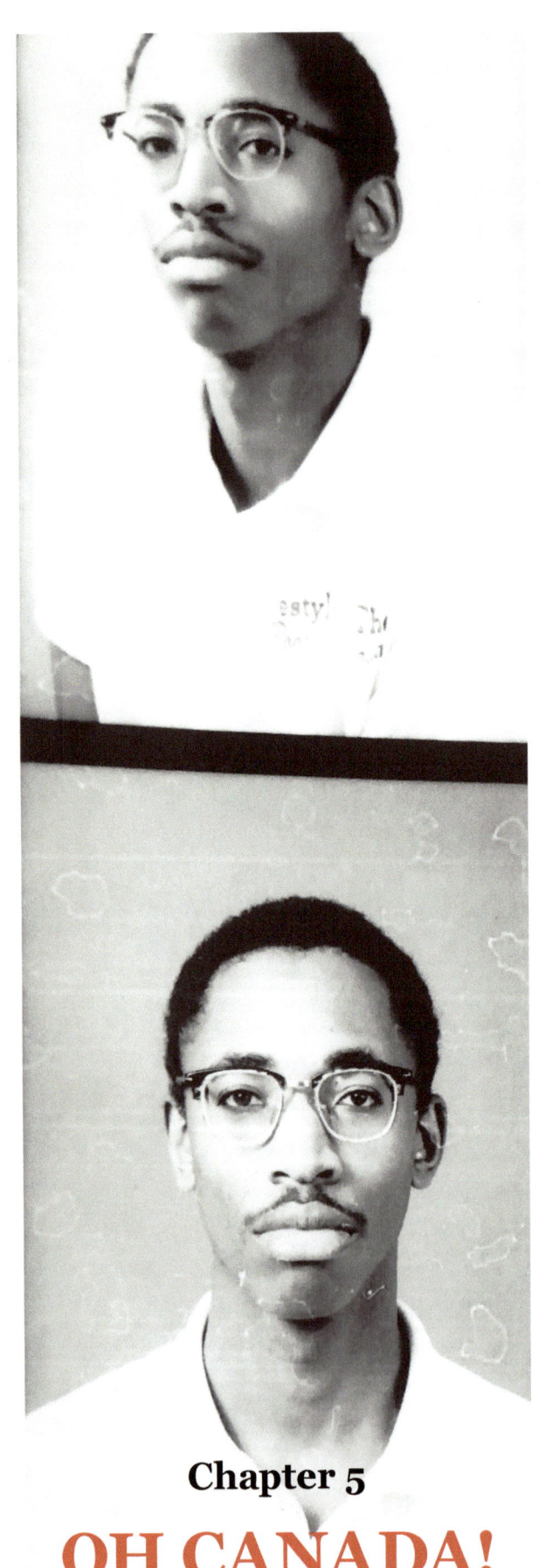

Chapter 5
OH CANADA!

Nothing is as it appears. He may not have known it, nor would Canadians immediately realize, but when Fitzroy Anderson entered Canada with his family, it was a perfect choice. When Canada accepted the Andersons within its borders, the family would become a perfect disturbance, a superb fit within a profoundly powerful but troubled tapestry. This is an impenetrable mystery not easily understood, neither at the moment when it happens or as time unfolds. For the hero's journey runs contrary, tending to suggest imperfection as it surges, slips, sputters, and spurts, winding and twisting its glitchy way along challenging pathways difficult to follow or comprehend. In this chronicle, weak becomes strong, the blind becomes sighted, and the downtrodden rise to great heights of achievement. Here, wounds convert to strength, dormant dreams come alive, and those who are marginalized, against all odds, arise to uplift themselves, contributing much value to the sum total of Canadian sociopolitical life, art, and culture. Through their arrival and presence, the Anderson family would make the African Canadian tapestry a little greater, less bleak, allowing it to radiate with a kind of nobility that at times has been denied full and unqualified respect.

As far as appearances go, "O Canada! Our home and native land" is home to polite, orderly revolutions and bittersweet pills. Revolutions—not the violent transformative variety, but the kind more akin to maypole dancing in which participants jig repeatedly around a central pole, in this case a centrepiece defined by "whiteness," the goal of which is to make complex twisting patterns with multicoloured ribbons only to then dance in reverse direction to untwist the knotty entanglement. As compensation for participating, sweet-bitter pills are dispensed—a sweet carrot, maybe a bitter stick, an award or penalty, depending.

Analogies aside, the Canadian national anthem triggers deep emotions for those who believe in its sentiment. The euphoria of patriotic fervour makes it is easy to become elated with the anthem's lofty ideals. Many newcomers flock to this country. Unlike its neighbour to the south, Canada does not have a statue of liberty to symbolize the welcome intended for those entering its borders; no Ellis Island as such. Still, the "True North strong and free" have attracted many just the same, many who came with *glowing hearts* in search of a new home. They come from far and wide throughout the world seeking possibilities—for peace, freedom, prosperity—hoping to find that which eluded or had been denied them in their home country. Immigrants not only receive. They also give. They fill positions, occupying empty spaces no one else is prepared or willing to abide. They extend the tax base while contributing to the nation's GDP. They stem the tide of labour shortage and can, if allowed, become model citizens, leaders in their field. Through this means, Canada—and Toronto in particular, its most populated city—has earned the worldwide reputation of being an enriched cultural ethnic mosaic. In this mix of multicultural communities, everyone is supposedly engaged as equal partners in a social democratic dance. This was and remains the public hype; except this has never been the whole truth.

The private truth is that Canada is a European settler colonial state where the dance floor is uneven, divided into unequal parts. There are parts exclusively reserved for some where others are shut out. Parts are tilted downward to the detriment of many who slip off the edge into oblivion, while the up-end carries clear advantages for a few who remain tall, growing ever taller on account of their entitlements. Another truth, no longer as private, is that Toronto, the heart of multicultural Canada, is a fractured city, estranged along racialized socio-economic lines, with the chasm between rich and poor becoming increasingly wider in each generation. The 2020 COVID-19 pandemic's revelation of ethnic disparities in exposure, hospitalization, and mortality rate comes as no surprise to those who for years have been calling attention to the unequal racial distribution of positive determinants of health. In Toronto and other Canadian cities, the intergenerational racialization of poverty makes for a good case study.

When at age eight Fitzroy Anderson entered this multicultural dance where "whiteness" is central, assimilation would be perplexing. He was unsure if he was invited to the dance or not. He would show up anyway, soon to find himself not on the dance floor but at its precipitous edge. Here, he would stare in wonder, looking in from the outside; wondering if, how, and when he could assert his presence; wondering whether or not he could dance to the prevailing uncomfortable monotone neocolonial rhythms. Assimilation seemed impossible, even undesirable.

One open secret was that Black immigrant boys such as Fitzroy were never really allowed to flourish on the Canadian dance floor. Whereas they entered normal, healthy, and strong, speaking a lyrical form of English, here, in this setting, they are declared incompetent. Stunted by a perceived language barrier, they are delegated to "special needs." By this and other means, they are pushed from the centre, edged out dangerously close toward the turbulence of an awaiting whirlpool. Here, before long, they become trapped in the downward tug of a negative current, causing them to drift out or to detach even further, before disappearing into the subterranean night of a deep abyss filled with fear, despair, and unbearable self-hate.

Fitzroy, like his peers, would soon enough come to understand the grind. They, sooner or later, would encounter face-to-face the undeniable reality that comes with living in a land of false promises, one that find subtle ways to devalue and diminish those it considers to be outsiders; a place cleverly capable of embracing then alienating them, pressing and beating them down and out while labelling them as "the other," sliding them craftily, slowly, to the fringes where other detained misfits await. He would come to know that being labelled a "visible minority" meant you were not visible after all, that you were never seen or heard except when screaming loud with discord, and only then maybe. He would come to know, as others before him, that being too loud, too contrary could bring swift, severe punishment; that holding on to the immigrant's dream was like grasping at straws and drowning, except worse—like entering into a long Halloween night full of ghouls wearing fake masks and faded overworn costumes, a night with more tricks than treats, more horror than happiness, lots of gore for sure with very little or no childhood glee. Confronted by systemic barriers preventing entry to the mainstream's dance floor of conventional success, young Fitzroy Anderson would be faced with a choice similar to that of many of his contemporaries. What path should he take? Many of his cohorts came to Canada looking for the good life. Only few really truly found it. For most, the good life was flirtatious, wispy, ephemeral, full of promise never fully realized; those who found it or made it, enjoyed the outward material trappings but lacked true inner fulfillment. Most on arrival were naive in thinking the streets were lined with golden opportunities, unprepared for the wreckage they were about to walk into. Many did not realize they would be narrowly boxed into a corner. Nor would they know how to constructively navigate their way out. In 1974, Fitzroy Anderson may have had a premonition before arriving. His intuition may have been correct. For as he began his initiation, as he reluctantly commenced his hero's journey, he would have little knowledge of what he was about to face, no conscious awareness of whose footsteps he might have been following.

Caribbean Islands, as well as parts of mainland Guyana, were initially inhabited by Arawak, Caribs, or Taino Indians before the arrival of Europeans. Many Caribbean people have Indigenous roots. Taino images, male and female, adorn the Jamaican coat of arms. Maroon warriors, Juan de Bolas, and Juan de Serras were said to be descendants of escaped Africans who cohabited with Tainos in free independent villages snugly situated in Jamaica's mountainous interior. Fitzroy's maternal great-great-grandmother was of Taino/Arawak extract. Despite this background, emigrants from the Caribbean to Canada may be forgiven for overlooking the fact that for generations, Canada has long been the traditional home and, in some territories, the sacred gathering place of many Indigenous people. New immigrants to Canada may be forgiven for not knowing the meaning of Six Nations or who or what was the Iroquois Confederacy or the Haudenosaunee. They may be forgiven for not knowing that the Six Nations (also referred to as the Iroquois Confederacy or the Haudenosaunee) was an allied group of First Nations people with a long and legendary history, including the Mohawks, Oneidas, Onondagas, Cayugas, Senecas, and Tuscarora. They may also be forgiven for not knowing that Indigenous communities are situated throughout urban, rural, and remote areas across Canada, or that the name *Ontario* is of Indigenous origin, a reference to the glittering waters of Ontario's numerous lakes. New Canadian immigrants are more likely to know of, let's say, the CN Tower, Niagara Falls, or Casa Loma, places of interest that, in the popular imagination, far overshadow Indigenous presence and contribution. Largely excluded from orientation packages given to Canada's new arrivals, the first people of Canada, more than one million of them who self-identify as Aboriginal (according to census figures), have been made invisible, presented only as nostalgic cultural relics of a distant past. It is as if an entire culture has been made to disappear.

Nor would emigrants entering Canada from the Caribbean be readily aware that they were walking into unfinished dirty business, that the land they were entering was appropriated through foul play by European settlers who had a "finders, keepers, losers, weepers" mentality. Nor would they immediately realize that land rights and ownership in Canada, massive acreage of Indigenous territory, remain tied up in legal dispute stemming from the Canadian government's legacy of questionable land seizures. A true understanding of this history is apparently not essential for citizenship, nor does it appear to have been an important part of Canadian grade school education.

Emigrants from the Caribbean to Canada are more likely to gain their knowledge of Aboriginal culture through hearsay or through written diluted sources laden with polite self-serving delusions or derogatory stereotypes, or both. On arriving to Canada, Fitzroy Anderson and his family would not have readily known that Toronto sits on ancestral territory belonging to the Wendat, the Haudenosaunee, and the Anishinabek Nation, including the Mississaugas of the Credit, or that the territory is covered by Treaty 13, which allows for shared partnerships between numerous allied nations such as the Iroquois, Ojibwe, Cree, and Mohawk, who collectively agreed to be peaceful custodians of the resources in and around the Great Lakes. They were more likely to hear that the native people, the Indians, were part of a community of idle individuals who were exempt from paying taxes. When Fitzroy Anderson (who was also brought up in a communal culture with close ties to the land) entered Canada, he would not have known that he would be following a long history established by the First Nation, Inuit, and the Métis people, three distinct groups, each with their own proud and unique history, language, culture, and core beliefs. He would not have known that he would be following the footsteps of someone like Louis Riel, the Métis rebel-hero portrayed as a Canadian champion on the one hand and labelled as a Canadian lunatic on the other. (More about Louis Riel and the Indigenous experience later.)

There would be other footsteps too that Fitzroy would follow but likely not have known. Footsteps such as that of Mathieu Da Costa, African explorer and linguist; the footsteps of Harriet Tubman, the liberator; and the footsteps of Josiah Henson, the community builder and lover of freedom known for his acute moral compass. Fitzroy also would be following the path of the Underground Railroad, but likely not have realized it immediately. Additionally, he would not have likely known that he was following in the footsteps of Maroons, who were trans-shipped from Jamaica to Nova Scotia because of their resistance to British colonial rule. Authentic awakening would come later as he pried open a new world to reveal the remarkable footprints of other Black African Canadians—Lincoln Alexander, Bromley Armstrong, Zanana Akande, Jean Augustine, Akua Benjamin, Carrie Best, Rosemary Brown, Hugh Burnett, Rubin Carter, Anne Cools, Alvin Curling, Lennox Farrell, Hedy Fry, Harry Gairey, Marlene Green, Stanley Grizzle, Wilson Head, Daniel G. Hill, Leonard (Len) O. and Gwendolyn Johnston, Winston LaRose, William Peyton Hubbard, Michaëlle Jean, Ken Jeffers, Spider Jones, Denham Jolly, Dudley Laws, Donald Moore, Norman Otis Richmond, and Charles Roach, to name a few of the many that they are—a host of trailblazers—the list goes on—whose bright light still shines. Although not consciously aware at the time, Fitzroy would walk through terrain taken by these pioneers.

He would also follow a path cut by six Caribbean undergraduate students—Terrence Ballantyne, Allan Brown, Kennedy Fredericks, Wendal Goodin, Rodney John, and Douglas Mossop. Believing they were each deliberately singled out for failure by a White faculty member, the six initiated a protest against racial discrimination at Montreal's George Williams University in December '68, early 1969. They, along with other students, notably Ann Cools and Rosie Douglas, occupied a computer lab on the university's ninth floor in an effort to draw attention to their cause, only to be trapped by a suspicious fire before they were brutally arrested by riot police. During the furor, Montrealers clamoured in the streets below, chanting, "Let the niggers burn!" and "Send the niggers back home!"

As if ignoring the haters, the arrival of the Andersons in Canada in '74, together with droves of other Caribbean people looking for a better life, would only be five years removed from this frightful chapter in Canadian race relations. When the family arrived in Toronto, who was to say if antagonistic racial sentiments were any less rife here than in Montreal? No matter. They came just the same. Though not immediately clear, Fitzroy would move in the direction of some who had preceded him. He would become part of a link in a long chain of Black and Indigenous people of colour, individuals who were worthy of respect and recognition but who were not always extended the worthiness, respect, and recognition they unquestionably deserved. Even so, Fitzroy would stride toward his destiny. He would make his unique mark, leaving behind his own unforgettable impressive footprints while *mashing some bunions* along the way.

For the moment though, the eight-year-old boy would have far less lofty preoccupations. Rather than getting ahead of himself, the most he could do was to sob during the almost four-hour flight from Montego Bay airport to Toronto. Fitzroy Anderson's world was about to take a sudden turn; he was about to hear a different tune. As "Jamaica, Land We Love" faded, "O Canada" began to take its place. The white noise of an urban hum with its busy-ness soon replaced tranquil green pastures. The crowing of roosters would no longer be heard in the morning. In an instant, hummingbirds flitting about during the daytime went missing, so too dogs barking at night. The cacophony of insects twittering or shrilling at eventide went silent. At daybreak, his eyes greeted concrete and steel instead of trees and open fields; glass replaced greenery. A distant lake now sat still where once there was an ocean; no more sun-drenched seasides to idly roam or run. There would be no more rolling hillsides, only subways and streetcars, paved roadways with white lines bordering multiple lanes bearing heavy rushing traffic. Gone was the rural languid pace, the gravel, semi-paved roads where animal life mingled easily, moving unhurriedly alongside cars, buses, trucks, motorbikes, and pedestrians. What prevailed now was a dreadful organized tangled web of concrete, wood, and steel stretching distances over a grey, flat, unbroken urban landscape.

Buildings seemed larger, much closer, too close for comfort. Claustrophobic. The family home situated at Lansdowne and Bloor was the furthest thing from the country homestead Fitzroy had been accustomed to. Most of his life, he had spent outdoors. Now, most of his time was spent indoor; and while outdoor, the comfort of bare feet was replaced by the wearing of shoes. Very soon, heavy jackets, winter boots, toques, gloves, and scarfs would become necessary. Gone was the minimum bare essentials. One season became four, each requiring its own wardrobe.

As Fitzroy Anderson's external world shifted, so did his inner life. Caught between things longed for and the anticipation of things hoped for, the young boy inhabited his sorrow, wearing it like a garment. He ached with longing for his grandparents. People in his new home country seemed different. They went about their business as if no one else mattered or existed, averting their eyes, never saying good morning or offering so much as an acknowledgement. He sensed his own difference. It had never crossed his mind before—this bugging question rudely asserting itself into consciousness—this question about skin and complexion. Whereas before it hardly mattered much, speech, dress, and behavior, even the look of his hair, now took on greater significance. Suddenly, there were lots of room for awkward mistakes, *faux pas* as they were known in these parts. There was little room for risk-taking, almost no room for the life he had left behind. Every move, every step now mattered more than ever, or so it seemed. Each move, each gesture or expression now affected his sense of belonging, determining whether or not he would be part of the in-group or the out-group. For any child, this meant a great deal. For an immigrant Black child, and a sensitive one at that, this was even more acute.

Fortunately, life has a way of balancing itself out, offering sweet to go with bitter. Following his first Toronto summer, autumn blossomed into variegated warm colours, spellbinding young Fitzroy's eyes with wonderment as he watched with enchantment as nature unfolded its charm. Elm, maple, chestnuts—trees shedding nuts and other things he was not sure could be consumed—their green leaves erupting into shades of gold, yellow, and brown, a splash of earth tones ... raking and romping in it. The first sighting of snow elicited wows—a mesmerizing fascination, albeit short-lived, as white, dusty, featherlike fluff fell from the sky, landing softly on rooftops, settling gently on parched ground ... shovelling and romping in it ... the making of a first snowman. It was amazing to behold, enticing for a while. Here, the stuff of Christmas cards as seen in Jamaica—a country where it never snowed and where there were no such thing as snow people, reindeers, or a White Santa Clause—finally became real. For the first time, Fitzroy began to understand the meaning of "wash me and I will be whiter than snow," a refrain he often heard sang in his church accompanied by shouts of "Hallelujah!" and "Amen!" Wonderment, however, would soon change to dread when hats, boots, thick socks, scarfs, and mittens became necessary attire against stinging frostbite. From wearing a minimum of clothing to suddenly having to wear multiple heavy layers was a changeover Fitzroy and his siblings could never relish. The feeling of desolation was made worse by stretches of dark, long, grey, overcast days with little or no sunshine. *Jesus! Have mercy!*

Culture shock and all, for the first few months, the Anderson children acclimatized themselves as all immigrant children must, one way or another. Their new social environment was beguilingly filled as it was with an assortment of fresh adventures—human-size metal boxes called elevators going up and down within the bowels of buildings, sprawling stores with moving staircases called escalators—a joyride on hard metal steps—and shopping centres otherwise known as malls. Not to mention the ubiquitous television set with its unrelenting ability to project popular culture into the house, a distraction that would eventually influence Roy to enter Hollywood. And then there were foods that were fast, fast like Kentucky Fried Chicken or McDonald's, which made cooking at home no longer necessary. With both parents working, Colonel Sanders helped out more than a few times. The colonel was no match for grandma's cooking, though. *No way.* Certainly, waiting in line for Grandma Rowe's one-pot cooking was far more engaging. But to have instant food on demand was like a dream. An odd one, but a dream, the stuff of fantasy. Truth was that Fitzroy Anderson's parents were far too busy working to keep up. Fast food was convenient.

Family life for a while became the buffer from misery. Cocooned in a warm God-fearing home, at least for a time, Fitzroy's three siblings made for great companionship. They took comfort from each other. Each paved the way for the other as they made their way through school and their new life. The elder brother, Roy, was the pacesetter. The youngest, Winston, trailed behind Suzette and Fitzroy, who were sandwiched in between. In this way, they insulated each other from the harsher realities afflicting immigrants in broken family homes separated by time and space.

It was Theophilus who first made his way to Canada. He had abandoned the idea of policing to work his way into Ontario's ever-expanding construction industry as a labourer—a construction demolitionist. He worked diligently, dedicating himself to sponsoring and supporting his wife, eventually bringing her to Toronto in 1972. As was the practice for many immigrants, the children were left "back home" in the care of grandparents while the parents hustled to put away money, laying the foundation for what they hoped would be a better future and a happy family reunion. Geraldine, shortly after arrival, took employment as a factory worker as a full-time machine operator. She worked as hard as she could, keeping pace with her husband. When the time was right, she eventually returned to Jamaica to chaperone her children back to Canada. With the children's arrival, it was the first time in many years that the family would be together again. With *each one helping one*, uncles and aunts soon followed, thanks to the sponsorship of the hardworking Theo. Through his diligence, their family was able to live in a detached home, not an apartment. With everybody living together as a unit, the children thrived in a sheltered, protected world based on strict devotion to church life at Davenport Gospel Hall, and later at Ossington Avenue Baptist Church. Anchored in a home culture insisting on respect for authority, Fitzroy and his siblings learned strong family values—the importance of hard work, discipline, service, and personal commitment. On this footing, the Anderson household began to sink their roots into African Caribbean Canadian life.

Theophilus Anderson was the first to make his way to Canada. His diligence allowed him to sponsor immediate and extended family members. (Family album/Oji Archives)

The safety of home notwithstanding, it was outside the home where the sensitive Fitzroy was most vulnerable. Moving from Jamaica to Canada had shaken his sense of self up from the roots. Regaining his bearings was tough, sometimes awkward. While this demanding adjustment proved to be his pain, it also proved to be his opportunity. As he advanced through youth following the lead of his elder brother and sister, he acquitted himself well, showing early signs of industry as he ran paper routes and secured temporary summer employment at the annually held *Canadian National Exhibition*—the CNE. He picked up assignments with Dickie Dee Ice Cream where, in addition to doing counter duty, he pedalled a tricycle around the city selling ice creams, Fudgsicles, and ice lollies out of a mobile freezer. He made rounds in downtown Toronto at hot spots such as the Eaton Centre, Toronto City Hall, and the roadside entrance to the Centre Island ferry, which stood at the foot of Bay and Queen's Quay adjacent to the Harbour Castle Hotel. Ringing his tricycle bell to alert one and all, young and old, he was the new cat in town. Through this means, he oriented himself to the wiles of city life, slowly overcoming his initial shock as he began adjusting tentatively to Toronto's urban rhythms.

He discovered helpful guides, made a few friends, and learned from a few good teachers. Sometimes and somehow, they found him. In the fourth grade, which can sometimes be mean, insecure, and competitive, Dale, a peer student, once pummelled him in full view of schoolmates. The beating was painful, the embarrassment even more so. With time, Dale, once a foe, became one of his best friends.

Fitzroy's sixth grade teacher Ms. Donna Whitmore, a White woman, was one of the first person outside of his immediate family to make an impact on his life. Like a godsend, she reached out to the insulated boy-child, helping him to gradually come out of his shell. She encouraged him to find his own voice, to be himself. As he grew, he settled into his new life, becoming better adjusted in the largely Italian community where his family initially settled. With time, he learned to lower his guard, soon becoming "one of them," counting among his friends, characters such as Peppi, Joseppi, and John Carlos, with whom he often shared meals of spaghetti. When the announcement came that their favourite singer, Elvis, was dead, the boys cried together.

In 1979, five years after his arrival in Canada, Fitzroy's mother and father separated. It was painful; so painful he felt numb. This was far from what he and his siblings ever expected or wanted. They nonetheless had to *deal with it*. Tensions had been simmering in the home, eventually boiling over. The pressure of migration and resettlement, the dislocation, the heavy toll of conflicting expectations, and the confusing incompatible roles and responsibility each person was called on to play, at times this can be too much of a strain for one family to bear. And for the Andersons, things snapped, hitting a point of no return.

Theo, at first flush, seems to have been the source of the family's troubles. His command-and-control style rubbed his family the wrong way, which led to discomfort within the home. A man known for having a strong sense of personal pride, Theo in Canada found himself subordinated in a new social order where he was not in full command. He ached under the weight he carried. As a Black male in Toronto in the 1970s, the full sum of indignities he had to face we may never know. For he carried it silently, even though he may not have carried it well. For a man accustomed to being in charge, the loss of entitlement in his diminished social status in a foreign country was insufferable. No longer the man in charge outside the home, Theo at home insisted on having a heavy hand, enforcing what he knew best—hard work, discipline, obedience. His dictatorial demands came at a great price. As time passed, respect for his authoritarianism begun to unravel.

Returning home after partying late one night, Roy had surreptitiously slipped in through their basement widow. Upon finding out, Father Anderson gave the young teen a severe beating. Fitzroy, as if he had been sitting on edge nursing a grudge, exploded. Brazenly, he challenged his father. He was barely thirteen. This do-or-die confrontation with the head of the family was never ever done, at least not in the Anderson's household. Unrelenting, in desperate rage, Fitzroy threatened to kill his father if he ever attempted to physically harm any of them again. On these matters, the family is understandably reticent. From 1979 on, Theo lost his moral command in the home. With it, he lost his role as head of the household and chief breadwinner. Geraldine assumed sole responsibility for the care of her four children while assisting with the care of her own parents who remained in Jamaica. It was a heavy burden for her to bear. Geraldine, however, like most mothers who love their children, didn't think much of it. She carried on; she did what she had to do. No questions asked. She found a way. As for Fitzroy, he found his voice.

After the marital breakdown, Fitzroy and his now single-parent family struggled to stay positive. With the family's sense of security threatened, the weight of family disintegration became increasingly heavier. By 1982, the turmoil began to visibly affect Fitzroy. His performance in school suffered; his grades plummeted. It was here that a well-meaning guidance counsellor directed him to transfer from the level 5 program at Central Technical High to Brockton Vocational school.

While at Brockton, Fitzroy wandered into the school's choir. He also joined their drama club, slowly expanding his range of interest, gradually emerging from his well-guarded shell. He would later return to Central Tech for grades 12 and 13. It was during this time that he met Olivia Chow, herself an immigrant who came to Canada in the 1970s. Ms. Chow, years later, would enter municipal and provincial politics to make an impact as a justice advocate and community activist. But here, early in her civic career, she must have seen great potential in young Fitzroy. She invited him to be a part of her Bridging the Gap Peer Career Counselling Program, which subsequently led him to represent his school at deputations called "School Works." Through this means, he became directly known to the Toronto District School Board. It is during this period that he made his debut television appearance on TVOntario, a publicly funded educational television broadcaster, soon followed by radio interviews on CKLN and CBC Radio networks. He was later interviewed by *Maclean's* magazine for a feature on Martin Luther King Jr. Progressively, Fitzroy Anderson's voice began to mature as he steadily began to discover his stride. It is here that his tutelage in leadership earnestly began. He was about to learn that no one builds a house without first counting the cost, that no one builds without first considering the foundation of rock or sand.

Fitzroy, his two brothers and sister, were groomed in the Christian church. A natural leader, Fitzroy soon became a Sunday school teacher. The church to which he and his family belonged boasted a sizeable congregation largely made up of people of African Caribbean background. On the other hand, the pastors and administrators of the church were predominantly of European extraction, Anglophones—more specifically, White men. Within the kingdom of God, this may be of little consequence. However, in the emerging world of Fitzroy Anderson, this represented a glaring discrepancy, one requiring resolution. *Why? Why the racial divide between leaders and followers? Why is White supervision required for Black worship and devotion to God?*

"*Why?*" is a question often posed by youth, supposedly out of curiosity. At other times, the intention is to challenge. For Fitzroy Anderson, "*why*" was a means to his awakening. Why this? Why that? Some would have preferred if he wasn't as inquisitive. Curiosity killed the cat, remember? Still, he persisted. "Why in a church of 95 percent African people, all the pastors and administrators are White? Why did *Maclean's* choose to exclude me from their feature print article?" Persistently the *whys* flooded his overactive mind, first about school, then about church, then about all the missing pieces and places where he could not see himself and others reflected. Soon his exploration expanded to include more explosive questions regarding history: "Why did I not know more about MLK? Why did I not know about Malcolm X, Sojourner Truth, Harriett Tubman, and the other great contributors to our people's progress? How come no one told me?"

There was a lot Fitzroy Anderson did not know. There is a lot he had not been told in school or church. Both school and church appeared to have propagated a particular kind of sterilized knowledge, one that was deficient by design. What if Fitzroy Anderson and others were to know the truth of their history and place in the world? Once Fitzroy became aware of this knowledge, he would never remain the Fitzroy Anderson many had come to know and admire.

A budding draftsman in school. Once the youth called Fitzroy understood how a house was constructed, he would never be the same. (Family album/Oji Archive)

ROM 11 Set an Example

Long time ago in a city called Toronto
Whitey say blacky cannot determine
Any whitey African show
So when we stand up and revealed our plan
We not taking any more white
Racist indoctrination

(Excerpt from a poem by Brother Adisa S. Oji)

Chapter 6

OUR HOME ON NATIVE LAND

When the Andersons emigrated from Jamaica to Canada in the 1970s, they were following the footsteps of other Jamaicans who had come years prior in search of a better life. In the early stages of this recent modern migration, many Caribbean people came in response to North America's demand for cheap labour. As early as the First World War, Jamaicans and other West Indians, as they were often referred to, were recruited to work in the coal mines of Sydney and in the shipyards of Halifax, Nova Scotia. During the fifties and sixties, as Canada experienced economic growth, scores more arrived to fill the increasing demand for labour, primarily for low-paying jobs including domestic work, jobs local White Canadian citizens either refused or were unwilling to do. Between 1955 and 1967, the only legal way for Caribbean people to enter Canada was under the Domestic Worker Program—no Canadian experience required. It was assumed that Caribbean nationals made good maids and servants. As a result, many qualified Jamaican and Caribbean nurses, teachers, and other professional women were compelled to become housemaids in White Canadian households. More than a few African Caribbean families can trace their Canadian presence back to this humble beginning. Of distinction, Jean Augustine, Member of the Order of Canada, originally from Grenada, is known to have emigrated to Canada in 1960 under the West Indian Domestic Scheme. From this humble entry into Canada, she was able in thirty-three years, to become in 1993 the nation's first African Canadian woman to be elected to the House of Commons and to serve in a federal cabinet.

Upon arrival, many Jamaicans found life not better, but bitter. Still, they came, making the best of it. Between 1973 and 1977, Jamaican migration to Canada peaked in response to favourable immigration policy changes. Most moved to live in Toronto, Ontario, concentrating themselves in and around the areas of Bathurst, Eglinton, Kensington Market, Cabbage Town, Jane-Finch, and the Bloor-Danforth corridors.[23] They choose (or were likely forced by circumstances) to move and live side by side with other marginalized groups including Italians, Jews, and Irish with whom they found common ground. As Black folks from across the diaspora assembled in these settings, they quickly established families, set up businesses and communities, and joined or created church networks in which to worship and have fellowship.

One of the individuals who made it possible for Jean Augustine and others to break through racial barriers and gain access was Donald Willard Moore. Himself an immigrant from Barbados, a one-time a sleeping car porter and an avowed Garveyite, Moore was instrumental in helping to reverse Canada's racist immigration policies. He openly challenged the official bias toward people of Caribbean origin. In 1954, he led a coalition of equity-seeking groups to Ottawa to pressure the Canadian government to become more inclusive. (Who knew Canada had its own version of a March on Washington?) Although, hardly successful, Moore and his allies, including Bromley Armstrong, made their stand. Unrelentingly, they continued to advocate, doing whatever they could to open doors and create opportunities for Afro Caribbean people and families in Canada. The Domestic Worker Program can be traced back to these grassroots efforts. Moore's advocacy was not partial; immigrants from other non-white countries also benefitted from Black activism. In years to come, Canadian immigration policy would begin to diversify under Prime Minister Pierre Elliot Trudeau.

---

23 As early as the 1960s, a strip of a few blocks along Eglinton West was on its way to becoming Little Jamaica, a cultural business destination with numerous vendors, barber and haircare shops, reggae music outlets, and stores. By 2020, the once vibrant epicentre of Jamaican Caribbean culture would suffocate due to gentrification and the massive construction of a new cross-town subway line.

In pursuit of pleasure, purpose, and belonging Caribbean people gathered in bookstores such as *Third World* on Bathurst just north of Bloor, or at *Burkes* on St. Clair, or at *A Different Booklist* in Mirvish Village, finding affinity in each place, and above all, knowledge. For safety and wellbeing, they created a new wave of community institutions such as the Harriet Tubman Community Organization (1972) and the Black Business and Professional Association (1983). To shield themselves from the dreary wasteland and to weather the storm, they bonded in Caribbean affiliations like the Jamaican Canadian Association (1962) where collective action blossomed, and folkways thrived even as it was grafted into a strange cold country.

Music became another pillar of faith, an escape, an avenue for expression, and a salvation of sorts. Canadian mainstream airways and television stations neglected or routinely shunned Afro Caribbean culture, leaving many to flock underground. Starving for Black cultural experiences, Caribbean people in Toronto attended after-hours joints. They watched and listened to American Black TV programs and Black American radio whenever they could pick up the temperamental wave frequencies coming out of Buffalo and or Detroit. More often than not, their dials were tuned to off-beat Canadian community or university radio stations in a desperate attempt to enjoy the colourful, spiced, and syncopated beats that moved them. DJs, musicians, artists, and radio show hosts who were purveyors of Black artistic consciousness, while they struggled to get major air play or to develop a mass audience, they would, over time, bring an essence to Canadian culture that was previously missing, livening it up somewhat, leaving behind a rhythmic catalogue of ground breaking Black music many would later capitalize on. But on the whole, in the early days, the Caribbean Black community occupied a marginalized cultural backwater, making do with what little they had in order to make up for what they didn't.

To keep Caribbean tradition and culture alive, basement parties and organized fetes became popular, the biggest of which evolved into *Caribana,* a festival held every summer since 1967. The event grew to become known as North America's biggest street party, each island—Trinidad and Tobago in particular—bringing its own flavour to the celebrations. Energetic and colourful, the festival gave Caribbean people an identity—something they could call their own—and a chance to escape the bitter edge. As the celebrants were jumping up, the festival during its peak was generating unprecedented economic activity in the form of tax and other revenue flowing from travel, tourism, and hospitality.[24]

With each cascading generation as the community gained foothold, it grew to become more diverse, making room for other festivals to fill the Black cultural void—*Rastafest* (1977), *Afrofest* (1989), *Reggaebana* (1993), *Jerkfest* (2001), and the *Irie Music Festival* (2002)—all crammed into the fleeting months of summer.[25] Not quite so, but it was as if the community lapsed into

---

24 There is a sense that the festival—a cultural asset—has since lost touch with its roots. Due to ineptitude, infighting, and greed for monetary gain, *Caribana* has lost some of its initial cache. The name *Caribana* has been auctioned off and the festival has adopted a new name: the Toronto Caribbean Carnival.

25 During the course of finalizing the manuscript for this book in 2020, news of the death of individuals related to the narrative continued to surface, signalling the urgency and importance of memorializing this history. On December 3, 2020, Denise Jones, president and co-founder of Jones & Jones Production passed away at age sixty-four. Founded in 1987 by Allan and Denise Jones, the music promotion company was popularly known for preserving and supporting Jamaican arts and culture in Canada. In addition to *Reggaebana*, Jones and Jones were also responsible for *Jambana-One World Festival*.

hibernation each winter to recall with exuberance the preceding summer's frolic in the sun while waiting longingly to come alive again the following year to enjoy another summer of bacchanal.

In a place where belonging and connections were hard to come by, Caribbean people embraced whatever they could to satisfy their thirst for community. They played dominoes or played mass; gathered outdoors to eat, jam, or jump up; played cricket or soccer (known to them preferably as football); or otherwise hustled to make a dollar. When they were not doing that, so-called West Indians gathered in their community stores to shop, to reminisce, to muse, and to feel at home. Caribbean Corner, a notable Jamaican-style grocery food store, established in Kensington Market in the early 1970s, became a community hub for homesick Caribbean people, including the Andersons who, at one time, lived nearby. The proprietor, Ms. Yvonne, would later figure positively in Fitzroy's life, albeit in a small but remarkable way.

Remarkably, years later when Canadian crime rates ballooned, particularly in urban centres such as metropolitan Toronto, Black crime would be blamed as the culprit. More specifically, the driving force would be identified as a "Jamaican crime problem." This prompted Canada in the late 1990s to launch a series of mass "criminal removals" in which significant number of criminally convicted persons without citizenship were routinely deported to Jamaica. For the most part, these individuals were raised and schooled in Canada. To a great extent, their criminality was incubated in Canadian urban settings. Indeed, those who were being literally dropped off in Jamaica without any supports were individuals for whom Canada had become home, and who had no real remaining roots left on the island.

Ironically, these persons, mostly young men, had no secure roots in Canada either. If they did, such roots were tenuous. In a psychological sense, they were "homeless," living in a "no man's land" with no sense of real belonging. Immigrant Black boys slipped from or were pushed off Canada's multicultural dance floor, often much too early in their tender childhood. Socialized through powerful mass media images, through harsh negative experiences in schools, and through Eurocentric religious doctrine, traditions, music, literature, science and the practice of law, they could not find themselves reflected or included in any positive way. Finding themselves under the gravitation pull toward alienation, (their parents dealing with similar or worse constraints were unable to stop them), they became inevitably trapped in a vortex from which escape became near impossible. Displaced, many young men shifted deep into the shadows, rapidly internalizing an acute bitterness, and a self-affirming negative stigmatization. After being shut out of mainstream society for so long, they reinforced their outsider status by opting to self-eliminate themselves. As an alternative to disempowerment, youth immersed themselves in what they considered to be a more empowering sub-culture, albeit costly and no less punishing, but one that brought a greater sense of belonging, instantaneous respect, and recognition, not to mention momentary material gain. Marginalized and excluded from access to constructive information, right knowledge, meaningful connections, valuable experience and expertise, resources, and the ability to positively shape their own destiny, this beautiful cohort of once innocent young talent became lost in a whirlpool, unable to unlock their greatest potential and capacity for good. When they became undone, they were deemed persona non grata, then ejected.

As it turned out, the Andersons (and many other Black Jamaican families) would never be caught up in this wave of deportation. For one, the Andersons were bona fide Canadian citizens. Secondly, as law abiding citizens, they were far removed from a criminal lifestyle. As Christians, they were taught to be in the world but not of it. However, when Oji incurred criminal charges, it was a predicament causing no end of anxiety for him and his family. Had it not been for the moral righteousness of his cause, his conviction would have been a big blemish on an otherwise wholesome family reputation.

At the time of the Anderson's arrival in Canada, the most outstanding Canadian public figure was Prime Minister Pierre Elliot Trudeau. (Bill Davis was premier of Ontario, 1971–1985, the sixth in a long consecutive line of Conservative Ontario premiers since 1943.) During his long tenure in office (1968 to 1979 and 1980 to 1994), Trudeau made it his business to launch his country on a path of social and cultural transformation. With his hallmark ideas of "participatory democracy" and "a just society," he advanced the cause of Canadian bilingualism and multiculturalism. He furthermore endeared himself to Caribbean people and to Caribbean leaders such as Michael Manley when he openly showed support for Third World development. In the case of Trudeau and Manley, they had a personal friendship stretching back to their time as students at the London School of Economics, a relationship that had more than a passing interest to the US administration. Both men had shown friendly tendencies to Castro and Cuba; and any threat to US hegemony, or shadow or turn in the Caribbean suggesting a rise in socialism or that promoted liberation movements or Black revolutionary thought was deemed by the US power bloc to be akin to an unpardonable sin.

Trudeau was a controversial figure, an enigmatic intellectual with a flair for statesmanship. His media projected image, in part, was that of a playboy, and while he attracted harsh criticism from numerous quarters, he won praise and gained admiration from countless individuals who embraced their Canadian identity precisely because Trudeau called on Canadians to embrace them. Whereas in the 1950s, the influx of immigrants came primarily from so-called developed countries such as Britain, Ireland, Italy, and wider Europe, by the 1970s, Trudeau, building on the immigration policy of his predecessor Lester B. Pearson (and heeding the calls of early visionaries such as Donald Moore and others), encouraged immigration increasingly from India, China, Vietnam, Africa, and the Caribbean. Many from the Jamaican Caribbean Canadian community proudly trace their first arrival to Canada back to this period when immigration legislative restrictions were relaxed, thereby allowing for a massive inflow of Black citizenry into the Canadian urban centres of Toronto, Montreal, and Western Canada. Among the many arrivals would be the Andersons.

It is a small wonder that Fitzroy Anderson should leave one country for another when both countries had leaders who shared similar qualities. Both Manley and Trudeau were known to be fiercely independent and vocal, each having strong personal beliefs about justice and equality, qualities that Fitzroy would later emulate as he entered manhood.

While it may appear that Black presence in Canada is recent, the history of African presence in Canada predates the 1970s by far. African influence predates the Confederation of Canada, and it wasn't always about bacchanal or merrymaking. Black presence has been an integral part of the Canadian historical experience for a long time, with people of African ancestry participating in the building of many early Canadian settlements, towns, and cities. More significantly, from early on, they have made and continue to make remarkable contributions to Canada by injecting the body politic with the practice and principles of freedom, equality, and justice, compelling the system to accord more respect, more dignity to all its citizens. Although African presence stretches over four hundred years of Canadian history, this knowledge remains uncommon, largely untold, finding existence only in the periphery of the Canadian imagination or in the nation's blind spot.

As far back as the founding of this nation, Africans have participated in its creation and evolution, interfacing, not always, but primarily through the dehumanizing experience of enslavement and the long struggle for freedom. The dominant legacy left by these forerunners is embodied in their determined persistent crusade for desegregation and the advancement of human and civil rights, a struggle for which they have yet to earn full recognition. Although they were pioneers who contributed to the modernization of Canada, they currently occupy a rank in the nation's consciousness similar to that of a footnote; either that or their role is made to look dubious or questionable. It took Viola Desmond, who experienced and resisted racial discrimination in 1946, seventy-two years (1946–2018) before she was popularly and formally recognized by the posthumous honour of appearing on the $10 Canadian bank note. Viola Desmond, born in 1914, died in February 1965, too soon for her to get the news. It took fifty-three years after her death before she finally gained national acclaim for being a Canadian civil rights activist and businesswoman. She had a rich full life, one that was so much more; she had as full a life as one could have in 1946 during the era of White supremacist culture in New Glasgow, Nova Scotia. All the same, the most she will be remembered for is having refused to leave a Whites-only area of the Roseland Theatre when ordered to do so, and subsequently fighting for the right to equal treatment. (As if she was not allowed to rest peacefully even in death, Viola Desmond's headstone in Halifax was vandalized in 2020 with racial slurs.)

Frenchman, Samuel de Champlain is credited to be the de facto founding father of Canada. His leadership contribution is well-documented in history books. His efforts are lauded in the role he played in "discovering" what would eventually become known as Canada. What may be less known is that Canada under the French also began with the introduction of African enslavement, an institution that would become legally entrenched under British rule. Who knew that Africans were legally enslaved in Canada, first by the French then by the British—Black men, women, and children bought and sold on auction blocks like commodities to be used in homes, farms, and public works as "free" labour between circa 1600 and August 1, 1834? When it comes to comparing British Canadian slavery with the US version, views vary in favour of British Canadian benevolence. However, the fact remains that Canadian paternalistic slavery was just as bitter and no less racist, prompting someone to remark that "Canadian Negro Hate is incomparably meaner than the Yankee article." Who knew? Like a well-kept Canadian family secret, not much is said about the British and French enslavement of Black and Indigenous people in colonial Canada and the widespread acceptance of this practice.

Although abolished in 1833 throughout the British colonies, slavery's momentum remained powerful; its racist sentiments and norms continued to be a prevalent part of the collective consciousness of Anglophone and Francophone North America (Canada), filtering from one generation to the next like an unyielding addiction, replenishing its hold at every turn. (The Slavery Abolition Act attempted to extend oppressive arrangements as long as possible. Although passed in 1833, the Act came into effect August 1, 1834, with ex-slaves declared apprentices—half-free—until full freedom in 1838.)

Africans, enslaved as well as free, therefore have been longstanding participants in Canadian historical memory. They have been a part of the fabric of Canada since inception, facing squarely the exploitative maneuvers of *downpressors* at every juncture. Africans accompanied de Champlain in the early 1600s during his first exploratory voyages. They were present when he established the first permanent settlements in Port Royal and Quebec City, which in turn led to the creation of New France and other French settlements along the St. Lawrence River, the Acadia (Maritimes), and the Great Lakes. But who knew? Who knew that African presence in Canada predates the Seven Years' War (1756–1763) during which Britain and France battled for supremacy in Canada and after which Britain gained control? Whoever heard of Mathieu Da Costa, a freeman, linguist, and explorer who acted as an interpreter and guide for the European fur traders and explorers? As early as 1608, Da Costa is known to have been an active diplomat mediating between Indigenous people and the Europeans in and around what eventually became known as the Maritimes. He is said to be the first person of African descent to reach Canada. Who knew, and why have we not heard of others?

Many have heard of Harriet Beecher Stowe's *Uncle Tom's Cabin*, her best-known novel about the injustices of American slavery. But who knew that the idea for her story might have originated in Canada based on Josiah Henson's memoir entitled *The Life of Josiah Henson, Formerly a Slave, Now an Inhabitant of Canada*? And who knew that he was one of the earliest champions of nonviolence? Who knew Canada had its own Booker T. Washington? A born leader, a Methodist preacher, and a community builder, Josiah Henson is known for his principled idealism. He is a noteworthy person of African ancestry who ought to have an honoured place in the annals of Canadian history. Yet it is difficult to locate him in the nation's self-identity or to establish with any great significance his role in the country's historical memory. Josiah Henson, born into enslavement June 15, 1789, in Maryland, USA, was sold numerous times during childhood. In his mind, heart, and soul, he was however free. He came to believe that it was better to buy his freedom (manumission), rather than risk escaping. He was not interested in becoming a fugitive, always on the run. He had integrity, was principled, law abiding, and remained relentless in his pursuit of freedom, eventually earning enough to buy his and his family's emancipation. He was however betrayed by those who "sold" him his freedom, and eventually, he was sold back into enslavement. Possessing a heightened sense of integrity, Henson refused to hate his captors or to use violence against those who deceived him, this despite being a victim of their duplicity and irrational brutality. Undaunted, in due time, Henson did escape from the antebellum south and, in 1830, escorted his wife and children to freedom via the Underground Railroad. The perilous six-week journey took them to Upper Canada (now Ontario). Looking to be of service beyond himself, Henson, using his organizational and community building skills, became a leader in the Underground Railroad community. By 1842, he collaborated with others to organize an independent community near Dresden, Ontario, a community made up of other refugees in search of freedom. The Black settlement, appropriately called Dawn, was open to all people regardless of colour. Henson welcomed kindred spirits and like-minded men and women who wanted to build community, communities that were independent, self-sustaining; communities where education and various industries could grow and thrive. To this end, he led in the creation of a vocational school aimed at providing training and education for Black residents, often excluded from White Eurocentric schools. An inspiring and industrious man who radiated self-respect, Henson authored his biography, using the proceeds from the sale of his book to support the Dawn settlement. In 2010, Canada Post dedicated a stamp in Henson's memory. His cabin still stands in Dresden, yet few Canadians are aware of Henson's significance.[26]

It is unlikely that when young Fitzroy Anderson made his way through the Toronto public school system (whether attending Brock, Regal Road, or Winona public schools) that he would have learned of this inspiring history lesson dating from the eighteenth and nineteenth century, one illustrative of a strong Black leader, a dignified freedom fighter who was selfless, industrious, ingenious, and broadminded. Fitzroy's entry into high schools such as Central Technical, Brockton, and Western Technical High would equally yield little of this knowledge; and he would be no more the wiser of the proud history from which he and others originated.

Fitzroy Anderson, were he to rely on his public-school education or on his attendance at church, would also unlikely have heard of the Black Loyalists—enslaved Africans fighting for the British in the war of the American Revolution between 1775 and 1783. During the war, Africans used the opportunity to escape American enslavement by taking sides with the British who lured them with a variety of dubious incentives. During this time, and after the war, many evacuated to destinations under British control, including Canada and to places within the British Caribbean. Some used the opportunity to return to Africa. Identified as Black Loyalists because of their dedication to the British Crown, these men and women became an important part of the fabric of Canadian life, a fact unearthed for mass consumption in Lawrence Hill's popularly acclaimed novel (and later television series) *The Book of Negroes*. The original *Book of Negroes*, an archival document held by the British containing information and descriptions of the Africans who fought on their side, had been in existence for over two hundred years. Who knew? And who knew that some of the promised incentives made by the British such as land grants were never always honoured? Who knew that the land, if provided, was likely infertile and useless for farming? Or that laws and regulations would be passed to disenfranchise Black Loyalists of the property they had been promised? There is a term for this practice: Legislated racism. Traces of legalized racism still exists today—Jim Crow in camouflage.

---

26 The Dresden settlement thrived for a time before tensions developed. Disagreement between Henson and other administrators of the community caused some dissension. To add to their trouble, many returned to the American South to fight for the Union Army during the American Civil War. With a dwindling population, the vocational school eventually closed its doors in 1868; and Dawn, as an organized settlement, disappeared. Henson remained in Dresden until his death in 1883.

Black Loyalists are deep in Canada's distant past. But what about more modern-day Black Canadians? What would Fitzroy Anderson's public school education have to say regarding Sam Agee, Herb Carnegie, Delos Davis, George Dixon, Harry Jerome, Fergie Jenkins, Sam Langford, Ray Lewis, William Oliver, Willie O'Ree, or John Arthur Robinson and the many other unsung heroes whose names are unknown? To list the many names would require volumes, to call their names would require more than each day in the month of February. And yet, the mentioning of their stories is akin to an afterthought in the annals of Canadian folkloric history; so very little currency given, so much general acclaim and recognition of value withheld, denied, or deferred. Why is African Canadian leadership and contribution always muted? As Fitzroy Anderson made his way through school and as he began to sink into Canadian life, what disturbed him most was not the narratives he was being told. It was the ones that were concealed.

Who knew that on February 28, 1956, a restaurant in Chatham, Ontario, was fined fifty dollars for refusing to serve two Black students? Who knew this was an intentional protest action staged by students who wanted to draw attention to segregationist practices in Ontario's places of business? Who knew that during the 1950s and '60s anti-Black discrimination remained widespread in vast sections of South Western Ontario—the same region known to be the gateway to Canada's Underground Railroad—including Chatham, Windsor, and Dresden, where Josiah Henson once found freedom and made his home? Who knew that in Merlin, a town close to Chatham, the last segregated Black school in Ontario was finally closed in 1965? Who knew that up until the sixties, many areas throughout Ontario continued to condone racial segregation not only in education but across a wide range of business and services, including restaurants and bars? Who knew that elsewhere in Canada, segregated schools were phased out around the same time, with the last segregated Canadian school located in Nova Scotia shutting its doors as recently as 1983? Who knew that these unjust inhumane practices were legislated out of practice because of the refusal of members of the Black community to accept inequality? Who knew that change came because of their rugged determination to stand up in alliance with religious associations, organize labour, civil rights advocates, and other equity-seeking groups, and demand political/legal action?

Who knew that Ontario's Fair Employment Practices Act (1951) and Fair Accommodation Practices Act (1954) would never had been passed had there not been an uproar? Who knew that even after the law was passed, race continued to be a silent qualifier in all walks of life? Who knew a vibrant chapter of the KKK was active in Ontario in the first half of the twentieth century, openly parading in southwestern parts of the province, promoting, and in some cases enforcing its White supremacist views, the maple leaf logo clearly affixed to their coveralls?

Young Fitzroy Anderson and his extended family, on entering Canada, had no knowledge of this history and would have no awareness during those initial years. Canada appeared to be a land of well-kept family secrets—well-guarded classified information, guarded knowledge that was not part of the required orientation for entering the country. Nor, apparently, was it required knowledge for Canadian born citizens. As Fitzroy Anderson made his way through the Ontario school system, he would become increasingly aware of how little he knew, that there was a deep reservoir of untapped history he was not being told but slowly beginning to discover through his own self-education. The cover-up would offend him to the point of disgust.

As a schoolboy, he was never told of Nova Scotia's link with Jamaica and Africa. In 1796, following the second of two Maroon wars in Jamaica fought against British armed forces, approximately six hundred African Maroons were captured and then transported from Jamaica to Nova Scotia where they were "released." As was their practice, the local British officials assigned the African Maroons to perform manual labour. (The modern Seasonal Agricultural Worker Program for migrant workers from the Caribbean could be seen as a modern, updated version of this practice.)

While in Nova Scotia, the Maroons did the best they could to survive. As if still in Jamaica's hilly interior, they made every effort to replicate their free independent lifestyle. But odds were stacked against them. Consistent with another typical colonial pattern, the British provided the Maroons with infertile land, making it difficult for them to maintain their independence as farmers. With imperfect soil and poor farming conditions, the prospect of Maroon autonomy was as poor as the land they were provided, forcing them to work for others in order to make a living. Stubbornly, they tried, but the land demanded too great an effort. The soil yielded little. Accustomed to heat and sunshine, the Maroons found the harsh cold weather of Nova Scotia unforgiving. The climate prohibited them from cultivating their preferred tropical food crops such as bananas, yams, pineapples, and cocoa. While some died from the extreme conditions for which they were unprepared, others moved to other locations in Nova Scotia where they settled, but with not much more success. By 1800, most of the Maroons were relocated—trans-shipped—to Sierra Leone, Africa. Gone but not forgotten, the legacy of the Jamaican Maroons who were forced to migrate to Nova Scotia remains. Some of their descendants lived in Africville. Some remain in North Preston. When Fitzroy and his family arrived in Toronto in 1974, they might not have known it, but they were following in the footsteps of ancestors. The full significance of this *Akwantu*, or journey, would not come into focus until much later.[27]

As previously mentioned, people of African ancestry also entered Canada via what became known as the Underground Railroad. This fact is sometimes highlighted as inflated proof of Canada's reputation as a safe haven from the grim racist conditions of American slavery. A highly secretive ad hoc network of routes and safe houses, the Underground Railroad was used

---

27 For more details about the Maroons and their relationship with British colonialism, as well as the Anderson's ancestral ties with the Maroons, please see "Maroonage," chapter 9.

by enslaved Africans in the nineteenth century to escape the US Fugitive Slave Act. Searching for freedom, self-liberated Africans fled to Canada, Mexico, and beyond. Instrumental in these efforts were figures such as Harriet Tubman, Sojourner Truth, Fredrick Douglass, and many other freedom fighters and humanitarians who with the aid of White abolitionists helped to facilitate the movement. Over a period leading up until 1860, the Underground Railroad rapidly became the way out for many American enslaved Africans. Estimates suggest that thirty thousand made their way into Canada by as early as 1850. Settling in such places as Upper Canada (Ontario), they congregated in and around the Ontario horseshoe area, including Toronto, Niagara Falls, and Windsor, and migrated as far north as Owen Sound. Some settlements of freed African people also appeared in Quebec (Lower Canada) with traces stretching west as far as Alberta, Saskatchewan, and Vancouver. Perhaps the most significant early Black settlements were those located in Nova Scotia, particularly Africville, where a strong and vibrant Black community established itself.

However, as self-liberated Africans escaped across the US border, they stretched out over the vast territory known as Canada, extending east, west and north. They strategically congregated around nearby streams, creeks and isolated wooded areas to create safe havens for their families, the heart and soul of which are only now being unearthed by their descendants.[28]

But freedom has its price. The men and women (and sometimes children) who escaped endured an arduous ordeal. Running scared, constantly in hiding, dodging bullets, and eluding armed bounty hunters accompanied by man-hunting dogs became a matter of course. Often they went without food or shelter for days, frequently exposed to the harsh elements of cold, rain, and heat, fleeing night and day without rest. Many did not make it. For those who did, there were existential questions to confront once they arrived at their destination, the most nagging of which was "Are we really any better off?" Although free, they were still considered fugitives from the law and were deemed "wanted" or escapees, refugees-at-large subject to recapture, certainly torture. Many who were fortunate to avoid recapture before entering Canadian borders often became disappointed in their new home. Although they were free, they were still subject to discrimination and anti-Black racism, rampant features of British North American (Canadian) life. History records, for example, that in 1784, race riots occurred in towns such as Shelburne and Birchtown, Nova Scotia, in which White mobs pillaged Black-owned properties, ultimately driving the free Black residents out of the townships. All across Canada, it was not uncommon for Blacks families to be constantly on the move in search of safe havens, desperately attempting to flee White terrorism or oppression, an exodus back and forth in search of freedom, peace of mind, and meaningful livelihood.

On realizing the growing number of Blacks migrating into Canada, attempts were made by government officials to restrict or discourage Black entry. Intent on maintaining Canada as a "white man's country" (a phrase used by Prime Minister Mackenzie King), a variety of legislative steps were introduced in the early 1900s to prohibit entry to immigrants belonging to any "race deemed unsuited to the climate or requirements of Canada." Laws were designed to "ban races

---

28 In one of my first road trips to Collingwood, Owen Sound, and Tobermory in Ontario (Grey Bruce County), I almost drove off the roadway when to my surprise I spotted an inconspicuous road sign denoting *Negro Creek Road,* one of the many clues of historical Black presence throughout the area.

with peculiar habits" or, more blatantly, to prohibit the landing in Canada of any "immigrant belonging to the Negro race." When legal exclusion failed, practical exclusion through informal, indirect, unwritten rules proved to be more successful. Preferred and non-preferred lists of countries from which immigrants would be accepted were compiled with preference given to British and White Europeans. In many areas of life—social, commercial, political—Blacks were belittled or frequently barred from meaningful participation. Many were forced to take a back seat or no seat at all in areas of employment, housing, business, and a range of social amenities. Even in the most sacred of places—the church—Black exclusion was normalized. If and when Black religious participation was permitted, it was restrictive. Worship was confined to formats exclusively based on strict Eurocentric norms.

On arrival to the earthly "Beulah Land" of Canada, American Black refugees attempted to attend established Canadian churches hoping to be embraced in Christian brotherhood and love. However, they encountered innumerable barriers to inclusion. In the case of Toronto's White congregations, Black refugees desirous of becoming members of these church communities were required to have papers certifying their "release" as well as proof of payment to their former slave masters. (What part of *escape* couldn't they understand?) Forced to worship among themselves, refugees from the Underground Railroad formed their own congregations, leading to the formation of what would become the seed of Toronto's First Baptist Church. Given the hate of the many against the few, religious racial segregation amounted to a necessity. Nevertheless, in cases where integrated worship did occur, racial stratification and White superiority continued to permeate church culture, with few exceptions.

While this history is rich in content, this inhospitable aspect of Canadian life is rarely communicated. The practice of slave auction blocks, the benefits derived from the international commerce of Black bodies have been whitewashed or erased. That Canada was a prime destination of the Underground Railroad is the extent to which knowledge is promoted by well-meaning mainstream sources. Even supposedly well-informed Canadian leaders appear to be limited in their exposure to this sinister side of Canadiana. That many Black refugees came to Canada, then took a U-turn, choosing to return south because of Jim Crow experiences is not very well advertised. Fact is, Africans escaped or moved in both directions across the border, a touchy bit of detail largely hidden from Canadian popular imagination. While some argue that Canadian slavery was a more benign form of bondage given the absence of a plantation system, and given the fact that nannies, housemaids, butlers and indentured slaves were oftentimes regarded as "part of the family," Canadian enslaved Black people were no less abused than their American counterpart. They were regarded as property and dehumanized just the same, subject to strict supervision, surveillance and punishment. For ease and convenience, it is best that this history—the full breadth of Black Canadian experience—be buried or forgotten. Even liberated Blacks who chose to remain in Canada have had their names erased from the archives, their presence or contribution unaccounted for, made ghostlike or insubstantial. Museums and galleries assigned to memorialize the annals of Canadian social history have either buried or lost their names, preferring instead to denote and highlight White benefactors and founding fathers, some of whom where themselves slave owners.

Despite altering profoundly the socio-economic and cultural soil of their adopted home, refugees from American enslavement and their progeny are buried in inauspicious graves across

Canada, unequal in death as they were in life. They died with an undying faith in the distant promise that one day their new home would embrace them and their descendants as equals.

Undaunted while facing wide-ranging sociopolitical and economic discrimination, Canadian Black families continued to thrive as best they could under adverse conditions. Forced as they were to segregate into churches, clubs, and civic groups, Black Canadians continued to faithfully volunteer their services to country and crown, perhaps under the mistaken belief that altruistic community or military service would win social respect or political inclusion. As it turned out, racism does not work this way. Many Black Canadian men who stepped forward to enlist in the First World War, for example, faced rejection because of race. Those who were eventually admitted into the Canadian Armed Forces, as eager as they were to serve, were not entrusted to bear arms. Instead, they were ghettoized and segregated into a so-called No. 2 Construction Battalion, where they were relegated to building ditches and roads and where they endured unending racial indignities during and after their tour of duty. One hundred years plus later, in March 2021, the Canadian government expressed its intentions to formally apologize to the country's first and only segregated military unit for the racism they endured. As was the case with Viola Desmond, none of the six hundred members of the unit will be alive when this formal public apology is issued. Only their descendants will receive it, some learning of the extent of the injustice maybe for the very first time.[29] How do you continue to love a country that does not love you back? By World War II, conditions for Black Canadian enlisted soldiers had changed little. Most were treated like maids in uniform. On their return to civilian life, the reward they received for enlisting during wartime was more rejection during peacetime. Still, they pressed on, protesting here, resisting there, attempting to keep dignity and hope alive wherever and however possible.

Fitzroy, an inquisitive young man dissatisfied with the trivial Eurocentric clichés fed to him at school and in church, persisted in questioning *why*. His inquiries met with resistance, and not surprisingly. When unrevealed Canadian history is peeled back, found beneath the surface is a multitude of sins. Thereunder lies a collected debris of broken hearts and dead bodies buried beneath thick veneers of a beautifully crafted Canadian narrative of peace, justice, and goodwill. Embedded within this historical narrative of a gentler, more polite nation is the mockery of justice. Buried there alongside are the many scattered souls of those who have been aggrieved or demonized.

Throughout Canada's history are blots concealing instances of government-endorsed exclusionary and racist discriminatory practices, acts that today would be considered multiple

---

29 Calvin Woodrow Ruck, a former member of the Construction Battalion, can be credited for bringing the battalion's story to public attention in his book, *The Black Battalion 1916–1920: Canada's Best Kept Military Secret*, published in 1987.

human rights violations. These misdeeds, some of which were barbaric, have targeted native Indigenous people, and at various times, Jews, Chinese, Japanese, South Asians, African Caribbean Canadians, and other immigrant groups, including Irish and Italians, illustrating that although anti-Black racism may be considered to be the most enduring or deep rooted, racism isn't always a "Black thing." Even the Quebecois and Francophones, descendants of French colonists, have had their share of unequal treatment in the Canadian body politic, a condition that has led to acute animosity between French and English Canada. This bone of contention is so deep, its origins so remotely far back in time, that this schism continues to be an explosive national controversy with seemingly no end.

In this multicultural soup, racism has been viciously violent, targeting with terror those who dare to challenges its ethos. Take the account of Louis Riel for example. Part of a community of mixed Cree, Ojibwa, French, and Scottish ancestry collectively known as Métis, Riel and his people were considered outliers, a community excluded from the definition of who is British North American. In the early days when Canada first began to envision itself as a nation, it projected itself primarily and unmistakably as an Anglophone society dominated by heterosexual White men—primarily English, Scot, and Irish. Within this montage, even White women were excluded from positions of power. Women were not in frame except as possessions, trophies, or appendages treasured primarily for their reproductive value—precious "guardians of the race" who, in due course, would fight for their own liberation from White patriarchy. Cliques dominated by Anglo-Saxon White males were the order of the day, the A-listers, the preferred in-group, the preeminent core of Canadian society who shared in the main spoils of citizenship, the cabal deciding who else, if anyone, would share in the benefits. This was the nascent narrow definition of Canadian national identity, and it was exclusive, not inclusive.

While Riel and his community embraced their outsider status, they considered themselves equally entitled to just and fair treatment; they wanted to have the right to self-government, and they wanted it on their own terms. In the late 1800, Riel led his community in a bid to secure their political autonomy. They resisted Anglo-Saxon imperialist control and demanded equal sovereign participation in a democratic Canada. In so doing, they threw a wrench into Canada's pristine image of itself. For challenging the status quo, for daring to set up an independent Métis provisional government and proceeding to militarily defend it, Riel was ultimately hanged on an order issued by Prime Minister John A. Macdonald. Louis Riel was only forty-one when he died on November 16, 1885. Today, on the third Monday of each February, Louis Riel Day is celebrated as he is remembered for his fight for justice, his defence of minority rights, and for his role in establishing Manitoba as a Canadian province. His official recognition was long in coming. The first Louis Riel Day was celebrated February 18, 2008.

Preferring to be regarded as civilized and congenial, the Canadian mind aspires to perpetuate the myth of national harmony. In this state of mind, the Anglo-Saxon Protestant defenders of this idealized image are reluctant to speak of, or to admit responsibility for, infamous acts of injustice. If and when confronted, a quick and ready denial is likely. Should there be an admission of responsibility, it will likely come slinking in many generations after the fact or when incontrovertibly found out.

The most poignant episode illustrating the Black experience in Canada is the account of Africville, Nova Scotia, which in its prime had four hundred residents of African descent accounting for over eighty families. Located at the northern tip of the Halifax peninsula, Africville is said to have begun "where the pavement ended," and ended "where the city dump began," meaning that the community was the brunt of scorn by Halifax City officials who consistently failed to provide suitable amenities for residents, deliberately neglecting the area, leaving it to succumb to decay and decline. These conscious acts of racist urban planning caused much suffering for the families residing there.

Prior to Black Harlem, New York, there was Africville, considered to be one of the earliest concentrations of Black life and culture in North America. George Dixon, who in 1890 became the first Black Canadian world boxing champion, was from there. Strands of American jazz can be traced back to Africville. In-laws of Duke Ellington lived there. He and other jazz greats often visited, as did heavy weight champion Joe Louis. ("Take Me to Africville" was a request often made by visiting African Americans.) Member of the Order of Canada jazz pianist Joe Sealy is a descendant of Africville. His father, Joseph Maurice Sealy, hails from there. Joe's Juno Award–winning *Africville Suite* is a dedication to that history and to his dad. And Portia White, the first African Canadian classical performer to gain international fame, once taught in Africville.

Africville established itself between the mid-eighteenth and early nineteenth century (circa 1749 to 1815) as Africans who came through the Underground Railroad, and Black Loyalists and Jamaican Maroons began to populate the area, creating in essence an African village. Over two hundred years plus up until 1969, descendants consolidated themselves into a dynamic caring community centred on family, church, and legacy. Although their ancestors—enslaved and free—helped to build the city of Halifax, the practice of segregation pushed people of African descent outside the city core to an isolated area along the Bedford Basin along the Atlantic coast. Many in Africville were property owners who paid taxes, this despite the fact that the municipality failed to provide clean running water, sewer, or infrastructure for human safety and comfort. Even so, for those who lived there, Africville was not a slum. It was *home sweet home*, their *New Jerusalem*. Despite deprivations, Africville enjoyed a vibrant, close-knit social communal lifestyle until it was cut short by the horror of urban planning racism. Powerful White city interests, with deliberate precision, frequently located undesirable amenities in and around the thriving Black neighbourhood. A prison, a disposal pit, and an infectious disease hospital were typical of the kind of activities located there, a reflection of the official jaundiced attitude toward the inhabitants. A series of these discriminatory public policy decisions eventually led to Africville's displacement and dissolution. After years of municipal neglect, the city of Halifax in the 1960s, under the guise of urban renewal, decided to evict the citizens of Africville. Homes were bulldozed to the ground without notice, oftentimes in the dead of night, a community's vision of itself destroyed, their shared sense of togetherness levelled without ceremony, their hopes shattered by an ugly unforgettable nightmare—and all because of a bridge.

The city's stated motive for evicting the residents and for expropriating the land on which Africville stood was based on the need to construct a bridge. Named after A. Murray MacKay (who at the time of the opening of the bridge was chairman of the Board of Commissioners and chief executive officer of Maritime Tel & Tel), the bridge became Africville's death knell. That the bridge would be named after a member of the White corporate elite was never questioned. It seemed naturally befitting that the bridge be named after one of their own, a prominent stalwart and community leader. The interest of Africville citizens was subordinate to all other considerations.

The opening of the A. Murray MacKay Bridge on July 10, 1970, should have been celebrated as the bridge that racism built. Instead, the occasion was marked as a major historical event for the city, excitement fuelled by international media attention. The leading-edge design of the bridge with its impressive engineering features was exploited for good measure, pundits touting it as a remarkable landmark. The erection of the bridge and the accompanying hoopla overshadowed any and all injustice. That there had to be the wholesale destruction of a Black community was seen as a small price to pay. Africville with its own historical bridge to a strong African past was regarded as dispensable. Illustrative of White privilege, this episode also reveals how powerful oligarchs build and maintain empires. In the end, Africville and its citizens became fodder for power, its residents treated as historical footnotes. For an asterisk, the remaining land space where Africville once stood was converted into Seaview Memorial Park.

"Why? How come? When did this happen? How come I didn't know about this?" There were very few honest answers, if any, to these questions, especially when posed by young inquiring minds attending local Canadian schools or churches, young minds such as Fitzroy who were beginning to detect discrepancies in the tales that were being spun. With each bit of interrogation, weaknesses began to show in the prevailing overarching master narrative of European dominance. For Fitzroy and others, this narrative was beginning to appear suspect—incomplete, illegitimate. Fitzroy, for one, developed an increased antipathy, forcing him to reject the account of history he was being fed, an account apparently afflicted by selective memory. In Canadian history (as with the history of powerful oppressive nations), the more unsavory parts are either filtered out or forgotten.

Brother Oji in 2017 with Crazy Eddie, the hermit of Africville, the longest protestor in Canadian history (MACPRI/Oji Archive).

Brother Oji teaching the game of Oware in North Preston, Dartmouth, Nova Scotia, in 2011. (MACPRI/Oji Archive)

In concluding: Who knew that one man—Eddie Carvery—never gave up the fight for Africville, staging what was to become Canada's longest running protest? He squatted in the park in protest for twenty-five years before the world took notice. Carvery's demands included a public enquiry and compensation for residents. Halifax City tried to evict him soon after his vigil began in 1970. He was finally removed in November 2019. He is probably still there somewhere in spirit, if not in body.[30]

Finally, forty years after the inauguration of the A. Murray MacKay Bridge, in February 2010, the City of Halifax made a formal apology to the bereaved citizens of what used to be Africville.

Undaunted, the African presence in Nova Scotia remains intact. Less than twenty kilometres away from where Africville once stood is North Preston, a rural suburb in Dartmouth, Nova Scotia, the largest Black community presently in modern Canada. Strong, upstanding, proud, religious, and independent, the community is reminiscent of Africville, having strong ties, memories, and relationships with the history of the liberation of African people. Similar to Africville, North Preston has had to contend with Nova Scotia's hostile racial environment of systemic racism and municipal neglect. However, in what appears to be an ironic twist in historical fate, North Preston remains unmoved. As if ghosts of the past have returned to haunt, the community has become the incubator for an underbelly of vice. Violent fragments

---

30 What brought Carvery recognition was the media hoopla surrounding the Group of Seven (G7) summit held in Halifax, June 1995. The G7 (you could say it is a modern-day version of the Berlin Conference of 1884) is a multinational economic body consisting of the past beneficiaries of slavery and colonialism and the current advocates of global capitalism—United Kingdom, France, United States, Germany, Italy, and Canada. All, including Japan, are considered to be the world's most advanced economies. Japan has its own history of imperial conquest and occupation, the most recent of which took place in 1937 during what's known as the Nanjing Massacre where imperial Japanese troops mass murdered and raped Chinese citizens. For more on the life of Eddie Carvery, see Jon Tattrie's *The Hermit of Africville*, published 2020 by Pottersfield Press.

of an angry youth subculture have emerged. Largely masculine in character, this contingent of strong, beautiful, animated young adulthood in the springtime of life has struck a dissonant chord by posturing as modern-day gun-toting hip-hop warriors alienated from the dominant culture. They have proven to be a harm to themselves and others. It is accurate to say these young men are in some ways misunderstood. They are difficult to grasp or comprehend by outsiders who have typecast them in the roles of pimps and drug dealers. What is clear is that North Preston will not go the way of Africville, especially if this youthful turbulence can be transmuted, repurposed, to serve a new and alternate, less banal, more noble existential truth.

What is also clear is that North Preston is much more than its vices. When Oji visited there in the summer of 2011 to participate in the Seventh Annual Leadership and Management Summer Institute for Educators sponsored by the Council on African Canadian Education (CASE), he knew he was witnessing the unfolding of a powerful, vibrant, impactful, and unforgettable revolution. (Consistently represented by a White member of the Legislative Assembly [MLA] in years past, unless something drastically changes, the riding of Preston will, for the first time in its history, be represented by a person of colour as all the 2021 declared political candidates are people of African ancestry. This will no doubt open up new frontiers of opportunity as well as create the usual complications.)

(In a moment of reverie while writing this passage, I wildly imagined the people of Africville returning to the A. Murray MacKay Bridge each year on July 10 to march and to reclaim the bridge as their own, renaming it the Africville Bridge!)

Arguably, the most abhorrent historical wrong is that inflicted on the original people of Canada, a history that is both tragic and triumphant. Tragic because of the long-lasting enormity of the calamitous consequences of pain, loss, and suffering endured by Indigenous people. Triumphant because after all their trials and tribulations, First Nations people remain standing as the undeniable founding inhabitants of North America.

While others who occupy this land are considered immigrants or descendants of immigrants, the Indigenous peoples are neither; they have no other homeland to return to. Whereas others who migrate to Canada may seek to integrate, Indigenous people were never so inclined. For eons, they considered themselves a sovereign nation having their own customs and traditions, their own definition of rights and obligations to each other, and to the land and natural resources. When the Europeans began to arrive during the sixteenth and seventeenth century—the Jacques Cartiers, the Étienne Brûlés, the Samuel de Champlains, and other explorers, adventurers, later to be followed by emissaries, missionaries, and a multitude of settlers—they would be harbingers of doom. Unintended, inadvertent or not, in the wake of European arrival, Indigenous people progressively became unwilling victims of kidnapping, torture, murder, genocide, enslavement, racism, and an array of unimaginable suffering. The notion of "discovering" a "new world," which is in fact not new, is uniquely Eurocentric. What indigenous people would soon discover is that the White man's heaven can be a living hell.

Misinformed new immigrants to Canada, sometimes grudgingly, often admit to hearing reports (usually from anonymous sources) of Indians getting a free ride—that is, Native people are exempt from paying taxes and are presumed to be lazy, living off government coffers. What is lost in this popular stereotype is that the *Indian Act* is the source of many ills; it is a tool of control and oppression. What perhaps is also lost is that all immigrants in Canada, including the Anderson family, have made their home, for good or for ill, on traditional Native land and consequently are unwitting beneficiaries of a what could be described as state-sanctioned violent expropriation of assets.

(A brief account of Canadian Indigenous history is relevant here because of the intersection of the Black African and Indigenous experience. As oppressed communities, they frequently found solidarity in their shared circumstance. In addition, the European colonization of North America—in this case by British and French settlers—provides stark, horrific examples of how institutionalized racism led to the plunder of Indigenous culture with lasting devastating effects. By any measure, British and French empire building in Canada shatters the myth of White racial superiority. This history demonstrates instead the detestable degenerate conduct of European colonizers who spared no terror when dealing with others unlike themselves. When honestly told, the history of European contact with Indigenous people provides the backdrop for Brother Oji's emergence as a vanguard for racial justice.[31] When he and others stood before the ROM, they had a long list of historical grievances to contend with. *Into the Heart of Africa* was but a nasty straw tucked in among truckloads of bales of hay, hay Europeans made during colonial heydays when their imperial sun was still shining.)

Canada secured its independence from Britain after the Second World War and thereafter chartered a course best described as bipolar. National political life appeared to experience extreme mood swings, the body polity vacillating, like a pendulum swinging back and forth. While forcibly removing Indigenous children from their homes, Canada as we know it was also beginning to enter the world stage, branding itself as a modern, cosmopolitan, and enlightened nation-state. In 1965, to signal its coming of age, Canada adopted the maple leaf flag as its symbol of nationhood, the same maple leaf that adorned KKK robes. Two years later, Canada opened its arms to the world in the form of the World's Fair—Expo 67—which brought international spotlight on the city of Montreal, Quebec, a city where, two years later, a number of its citizen

---

31 For a very brief history of European contact with indigenous people in Canada, see a reprise of this chapter in the appendix. Please also refer to chapter 7, "Young Poets of the Revolution," in which Afua Cooper shares her reflections on the European colonization of Indigenous culture.

would call for *niggers* to go home. Nine years later in 1976, two years after the arrival of the Anderson family, the games of the XXI Olympiad was held in Montreal, further enhancing Canada's growing reputation as a world-class destination, a power-player on the world stage, this in defiance of widespread calls for a boycott due to the participation of New Zealand whose rugby team had competed in apartheid South Africa earlier that year.[32]

As Canada advanced its world standing, progressive legislative tools such as the Canadian Bill of Rights (1960) and the Canadian Human Rights Act were introduced. Enacted in 1977, the Human Rights Act was intended to ensure fair and equal treatment while providing protection against discriminatory practices based on specific prohibited grounds including race. In 1982, the Constitution Act would be proclaimed, finally granting Canada the sovereign right to govern itself, a political maneuver engineered by Pierre Trudeau. Entrenched within this constitution was the Canadian Charter of Rights and Freedom, which guaranteed citizens civil and political rights. In 1986, the federal government further enhanced Canada's reputation as a progressive destination by enacting the Employment Equity Act, which required federally regulated employers to identify and eliminate barriers to employment faced by historically marginalized groups such as racialized and Indigenous people and women. It was an exciting, if not bewildering, period of nation-building, even as Black Caribbean people with high hopes began to assert themselves in Canadian life, attempting to understand as best they could the manic-depressive mood swings of a society, one which seemed just and egalitarian on one hand, and unequal and discriminatory on the other.

The Montreal Summer Olympic games were symbolic of Canada's growing global prestige. Those entering Canada during the giddy seventies will recall how memorable it was. While the Montreal games would leave the city with a scandalous debt, the heightened excitement overshadowed everything else, giving Canada cause to be proud and loud. The games, with its accompanying media hype, intensified Canada's profile, leading to an infectious patriotic love for the maple leaf. Despite a number of African nations electing to boycott this Olympiad (the boycott was declared while African athletes were already in the village), Canada pressed forward. A few Caribbean nations, including Trinidad and Tobago, Guyana and Jamaica, also participated.

Canada failed to win a gold medal.

Aside from the politics, the intensity of athletic competition made the Montreal games intriguing. A fourteen-year-old, Nadia Comaneci of Romania, became the first gymnast to score a perfect ten; Bruce Jenner of the USA set a world record in the decathlon to earn a place on Wheaties cereal boxes. In the pool, American men dominated, as did the German women. The German female team won all but two gold medals, raising suspicions about their illegal use of injected testosterone, an issue that would again bring Canada into the spotlight twelve years later. In weightlifting, Vasiliy Alexseyev, a Russian super heavyweight, asserted himself over his German competitors to win one of the seven gold medals won in that event by the

---

32 The affinity between Canada and South Africa's minority White racist regime goes back to the 1940s–'50s when apartheid was officially instituted. The idea of setting up "homelands" for Black South Africans gained support when South African officials visited Canada to study the reserves. The segregation of indigenous peoples on reservations became a template for the adoption of apartheid.

Soviet Union. And in boxing, the Spinks brothers, Michael and Leon, emerged as America's new boxing hopefuls.

Of all the competitive excitement, none was more highly anticipated than the marquee event that captured the Anderson's family attention and that of all Caribbean Canadian homes. When sprinters Donald Quarrie of Jamaica and Haseley Crawford of Trinidad and Tobago faced off for a head-to-head showdown in the 100 m and 200 m, it would be the ultimate unforgettable confrontation. It was an exceedingly promising time to be in Canada and to be Canadian, and the world took notice. Both men shared the spoils. Crawford became the first Caribbean sprinter to ace the 100 m and the first Olympic champion for his country, while Quarrie took top prize in the 200 m, establishing himself as a Jamaican legend. It was electrifying to watch and to be a part of. The Anderson family had arrived in Canada just in time to be part of the thrill.

Sporting distractions aside, all was not well in Quebec, Canada's second largest province, a residual leftover fragment from France's failed North American imperial conquest. Quebec nationalists had long insisted on having a distinct identity from English Canada—a case of two colonial offspring in a postcolonial squabble. In Quebec, an archaic political structure founded on the theocratic authority of the Roman Catholic Archdiocese was giving way to secular forms of governance. During the 1960s, this theocratic form of politics eventually collapsed, making room for a modern civic socio-economic governance framework in which church and state were held at arm's length.

As if sensing their moment had come, Quebecois nationalists used the opportunity to make a thrust for independence and sovereign recognition. The movement created mayhem climaxing in the 1970 October crisis when FLQ (*Front de liberation du Quebec*) activists, in the name of an independent Quebec, kidnapped two prominent government officials—British trade commissioner James Cross and Quebec labour minister Pierre Laporte, who tragically died in the ensuing skirmish. Trudeau, in response, called out the armed forces and police. He invoked the War Measures Act, a decision that continues today to be a flashpoint. During this crisis, Canada appeared to be a nation in civil war rather than the idyllic peaceful nation it purported to be. Canada's self-image was punctured by violent scenes and images in Quebec, highlighting cracks under the tranquil facade. As a result of this episode, the Quebecois' aspirations for sovereignty attracted sharp and critical attention from English Canada where White Anglo-Saxon dominance was held as the norm. A country known for peace and civility was forced to contend with crucial questions regarding the value of violence and the use of armed struggle in the pursuit of political diversity, autonomy, and independence. Old colonial chickens had come home to roost as the descendants of British and French colonists continued to battle for the leftover spoils of imperialism.

By 1976, the Parti Quebecois, for the first time, became the elected power in Quebec, marking a new respectability for the Francophone nationalist movement. This also signified a considerable shift in the Canadian political landscape. French linguistic rights and Quebec sovereignty henceforth became standard topics for discourse and referenda, overshadowing, although not entirely eclipsing, parallel debates about the rights and freedoms of other groups making up the Canadian mosaic.

Anyone perusing Canadian history can be forgiven if on first look they were to conclude that the French and the English were the only two founding nations, the only ones that mattered. The debate regarding Francophone nationalism versus the English idea of a confederate

Canada has assumed such prominence in the nation's political discourse that everyone and everything else is shrouded in obscurity or made to appear as a sideshow. While English and French Canadians continue to compete for dominance, they both seemed to have forgotten whose territory they are on and the Africans who contributed to nation-building. No doubt, there are other colonial-related chickens waiting to come home to roost, and when they do, the landscape will likely change again even further.

***

This was the current sociopolitical backdrop unfolding when the Anderson's arrived in Canada from Jamaica in June 1974. They were leaving one commonwealth country for another, exchanging one liberal parliamentary democracy for the next; one built on an island, the other continental. Jamaica was regarded as a developing Third World nation, whereas Canada was seen as one of the most advanced economies in the Western world. Held in common was their membership in the Commonwealth of Nations. More pointedly was their shared legacies as settler-nations steeped in the political culture of empire, imperial monarchy, British colonialism, racism, and slavery.

What the Andersons may not have known was that they were jumping from the frying pan into the fire, that they were walking into a historical hot bed covered by a blanket known as the "good life," an illusion beneath which hid a nasty underbelly of unfinished business. Little did they know they were entering a quirky culture with the tendency of giving with one hand and taking with the other, an alluring culture adorned with smile-like smirks ready to hit back when least expected, or worse. Little did they know that they would be making their new home in a land where political correctness was rapidly becoming an art form, a form behind which firmly stood well-guarded imbalanced structures of disproportionate concentration of power and privilege. Although they would find out soon enough, little did they know that here where everyone is presumably colour-blind, the facade would occasionally crack, pierced by the probing question, "So where are you from?"

On entering Canada fresh off the plane from Jamaica hoping to find a land of equal opportunity, the Andersons would not have immediately been aware that opportunities were not equally granted or enjoyed here, that multiculturalism was a policy position, not a long-standing practiced tradition. These tidbits did not appear in travel guides. Nor would they immediately comprehend the degree to which being Black in Canada meant being judged frequently and foremost by skin colour, not by content of character or by capability. Here, people with dark skin aim to blend in rather than stand out. Who knew? Who knew that to survive here you had to dim your lights? (An actor friend of mine facetiously told me this is how the phrase "fade to black"—film speak for disappear—was first conceived. Essentially, stay quiet or invisible in the background; if seen, smile a lot, be a team player, be agreeable, inoffensive, don't rock the boat, don't draw too much attention to yourself, etc.) Little did the Andersons know that they could be held responsible for their own racial victimization if it came to that or be accused of "stirring up trouble" or "playing the race card" should they complain. Little did they know that any demand for replacement of the dominant rule of White entitlement would elicit accusations of reverse racism. When they went to pick up their visas at the Canadian embassy, this advice was not offered. As new Black Canadians entering the country, it is unlikely they were told anti-Black racism is a thing to consider or provided with any special advice on how to properly acclimate to this requirement. Nor was this noted in fine prints on travel documents. They may have missed it. What the Andersons may also have missed is the unwritten basic rule: Here "bullshit baffles brains." Above all, as was the case with most immigrants to Canada, little did they know they would be making their new home on somebody else's native land.

The Andersons had come looking for a better life, and like many immigrants before them, they found it. The weather wasn't always great, but Toronto streets were clean, as was the water supply, readily available at the twist of a tap. Heat, electricity, or hydro were reliably available when needed, all utilities smoothly accessible as long as they could afford to pay the bill; and they could. But even if they couldn't, there were support systems and income safety nets to help.

Thankfully, they didn't require social assistance. Employment was easy to find. Canada's economy was flexing; its agriculture, mining, manufacturing, construction, banking, and public sectors were rich with opportunities for work. Construction of the CN Tower and other Toronto landmark projects were underway. Ontario Place, a sprawling multi-complex entertainment venue by the waterfront, had only recently been opened. Low- and mid-rise buildings still dominated the Toronto landscape, but soon high-rise structures would puncture the city's skyline. In this beehive, as the city grew in geographical size and population, there were many marginal, manual, or menial jobs for the taking even if no one else wanted them. New immigrants could pick up part-time work if they wanted to. It was possible to work two jobs at a time, sometimes three. It became almost a mark of pride to be able to hustle day and night.

If they became sick, a social insurance number and health card could get the Anderson's access to a range of services, including "free" health care. For this they were grateful. "Toronto the good" felt relatively safe. Walking or using public transport, the family moved about freely in a city that appeared organized with infrastructural amenities laid out in communities populated by people of mixed backgrounds, all of whom for the most part got along harmoniously. Access to public schools, colleges, and universities held great appeal. If there was one experience an immigrant family wanted to offer their children, it was an education—a pathway to future success, a way out of poverty. After all, this was the point of moving the children overseas. To be outstanding or prosperous in Canada meant having an education; at least, that was the outlook. And in Toronto, Canada, it was here for the taking if you could get it.

Fitzroy Anderson would receive his; only, his education, or more precisely his self-education, would take him in a somewhat different direction than expected. Within fourteen years of his arrival in Canada, he would pull back the lid of White supremacy and take a peek. He would see through the veil. What he discovered transformed him. Fitzroy Anderson the boy would be transformed into Brother Adisa Sadiki Oji the man. *Adisa*—a name of Yoruba origin, identified him as one who makes his meaning clear. *Sadiki*, a Swahili name, referred to his faithfulness. *Oji*, also of Nigerian origin, identified him as Black. Adisa Sadiki Oji would become the "Faithful Black one who makes his meaning clear." In the fiery crucible of a postcolonial settler-nation founded on White supremacist values, Adisa S. Oji discovered himself.

His parent's separation in 1979 had propelled him into early manhood. He loved his mother dearly. He had watched her as she single-handedly supported the family, and he was moved to find meaningful ways to help. He wished nothing more than to please her. But he wanted to do so in ways he also could be proud. He needed to find his own path, answer his own calling. When the maturing Fitzroy Anderson could not find answers to his questions, he opted to leave the Christian church that nurtured him and set about seeking answers elsewhere. In an eleven-page letter, he respectfully tendered his member resignation from the congregation. As if *born again*, Adisa S. Oji soon emerged.

Out of a need to refuel and to regain perspective, he returned to Jamaica twice during this period. In 1986, twelve years after arrival in Canada, he returned to Jamaica for the first time. He spent two weeks during which he had a lovely memorable reunion visit with his grandparents, who were amazed at how much he had grown. He took time to soak up not only the sunshine but also their wisdom. He returned again in 1988 and, on this occasion, spent a year attending the University of the West Indies, Mona campus, as a student in the University of Toronto's Study Elsewhere Program. During his studies at Mona, he met other aspiring new-world thinkers who were keen on challenging old-world models and practices, students and faculty who were passionately exploring alternate pathways to decolonization. Professor Edward Kamau Brathwaite, under whose tutelage he fell, became a major influence. Overall, the experience shaped the intellectual that Adisa Oji would become, adding new insights to his philosophy and way of being. His renewed awareness was transformative on many levels.

Throughout this visit to Jamaica, the evolving Adisa Oji also revisited the Ridge Pen family farm where he again spent valuable time with his grandparents as they edged closer to their afterlife. By the close of his trip, he would edge closer to affirming his new identity and embodying it in every way.

In light of all he had come to discover about himself, the history of his family and of his ancestors; in light of all he had come to learn about Canada, Africa, Jamaica, and the world in general—he could no longer be the same. He could no longer co-sign his own oppression or be complicit in the oppression of others. His name change was a reflection of this transformation. The *slave* name of Irish and Scottish origin that he had been given no longer suited him. It had become meaningless. In fact, he found it unpalatable. The boy, Fitzroy Anderson, born 1966, in the Ridge Pen District of St. Elizabeth, whose birth name translates as "Bastard son of a king," had outgrown the limits imposed on him. He would change his name to reflect his liberation and expanded sense of self, a definition of self that had a strong African identity at its core. More than merely symbolic, a rightly restored identity also changed his reality. No longer was he comfortable with the idea of being *owned* or being defined by others. With this recognition, he made a choice to *reclaim* his ancestry by accepting a name more accurately reflecting his true essence, one that affirmed the dignity of his lineage. In so doing, he triggered a series of events that would change his life trajectory.

While at the University of Toronto, Adisa Oji met the late David Maltby, a photographer who introduced him to the world of photography. Maltby saw in Adisa Oji a compelling photo subject, perhaps because of Oji's stature. But more importantly, it was Oji's standing as a student activist that caught Maltby's eye. Together, the two arranged for a photo shoot entitled "One day in the life of Oji." During the session, Oji got a glimpse of what was possible. It was then that the idea of MACPRI was conceived, thereby setting the stage for him to become a documentary photographer. He was twenty years old. (More on Maltby's profound influence later.)

Adisa S. Oji, with eyes wide open, became a documentary photographer at age twenty. (Family album/Oji Archives)

Not long afterwards, his path would lead him head-on into a radical public controversy of profound significance, one that would put him on a collision course with British colonialism and anti-African racism. The event for a brief moment would define him. However, the incident would also help to redefine his chartered course through the miasma of masked discontent that permeated the maze of Canada's so-called multiculturalism. Plunging into what seemingly was a one-dimensional cause in which he confronted a major cultural bastion of colonial memory—the

Royal Ontario Museum—he would emerge at the other end to become a multifaceted character crusading for the restoration of African pride and dignity and the re-establishment of economic self-sufficiency. And this he would do in his own indomitable unique way.

While Canada may have had its so-called quiet revolution, the African Canadian community would have a not-so-quiet revolution of its own. This revolution, at least it's most magnificent and celebrated form, although not televised by the mainstream, would be captured by the pen and in the words of an Oji-inspired group of young poets. This revolution would also be superbly envisioned through Oji's eyes and through the lens of a panning Polaroid camera he now constantly hung around his neck or held in his hands. The discovery of photography allowed him to further transcend his inhibitions to finally overcome the reticence that had overtaken him when he first arrived in Canada. The art of photography allowed him to create his own dance, tell his own story, in due time setting him free to be on the path that would decisively lead him to discover even more answers to his many crucial questions.

MACPRI, or Mother Africa's Children Photographic Reproductions International, founded circa 1987, was modelled on the self-reliance philosophy of the Honourable Marcus Mosiah Garvey. (Oji Archives)

This revolution is not about guns. This revolution is not about bombs. This revolution is not about knives. This revolution is about changing the minds of our people into a positive direction.

—Brother Adisa S. Oji

Chapter 7

YOUNG POETS OF THE REVOLUTION

Historical record as well as lived experiences reveal that Canada has not always been kind to those with dark skin. Put that in a poem and spit *it*. No matter how you spit *it*, everyone knew *it*. *It* was no secret. The older generation whispered *it*. They spoke of *it* in hushed tones as if *it* were a private matter rather than a public sin. They told *it* in stories, anecdotally, allegorically, and made abstract references to *the man* or *the system,* never exactly saying who *the man* was; for it was secretly understood. The system, well, this was nebulous ... undefined ... just out there somewhere but understood nonetheless to be an all-encompassing source of affliction for those who are ... ah ... well, you know ... At this point the older generation would give a casual gesture, a swipe of the hand along the forearm. For *it* could never be spoken. *It* was coded in silence or sign language. *It* showed in myopic eyes, glancing over slumped shoulders, hoping no one was listening. *It* showed in the stoic lines of creased faces, wrinkled from too much code-switching: grinning and bearing it in public, then griping and bellyaching privately. Still, no one dared pout publicly, dared not shout openly. You could hear *it* in their trembling voices as they sang gospel music or hymns converted into disguised protest anthems—such as "We Shall Overcome"—their anger muted by a well-practiced civility. But they need not whisper or pretend. The younger generation was already stirred up. They already heard of *it*. They heard *it* from Dr. Martin Luther King Jr., Malcolm X; they heard *it* when they listened to Stokely Carmichael and the voices of the Black Power Movement saying with raised fist, "All power to the people!" And they knew just as much and more—Canada has not always been kind to those with dark skin. Anti-Black racism, after all, is a multi-intergenerational thing.

Canada has not always been kind to those with dark skin—those whose origins flow from Africa, Asian, Caribbean, and Latin American roots. Canada has not been particularly kind to people of dark skin, whether they were born within or outside its borders. A chronology of Canadian racial injustice reveals a tendency to only hire so-called people of colour during wartime or other national disasters. In peacetime, demand for Black labour *dried up like a raisin in the sun*. In this chilly atmosphere, people of colour instinctively knew they would be the last hired and first fired—always on a short term contract or leash. Through it all, Black people remained courageous, pressing forward, taking what they were given, making the most of it. It was never much; the pickings were slim to none. Not too many places employed them. They accepted the jobs they were offered and waited; they waited until they got what they wanted knowing full well waiting could be in vain. For generations, families of African ancestry in Canada struggled to transcend the poverty line. Only a remarkable few were able to scale the barricaded walls and escape from the underclass. During pre- and post-Confederation Canada (1885 onward), Black women were maids, and Black men were porters, door men or bell hops; not always of course, but a pattern repeated often enough to appear commonplace. These specialty areas in the service industry appeared to be the only options available. Even then, the door would only open so far and no further. If it wasn't a glass ceiling, it was a steel door. If not a steel door, then multiple hoops to jump through, barriers to get over or get around—a labyrinth of dead ends with lots of *Whites Only* or *No Entry* signs. Even when signs came down, everyone knew little had changed.

To be Black and wealthy in Canada during any phase of Canadian history was not improbable; however, this was a notable distinction, an exception spoken in celebration as "the first this" or "the first that" or "the only this" or "the only that"—as if there can only be one, two, or three at any given time. Wealth did not insulate the *ones* or *twos* or *threes* from the stab of racial discrimination. Racism in Canada has been inescapable, an affliction for all people of colour, regardless of class, creed, or level of education. Wherever there were signs of promise, White backlash was not far behind—as was the case when Queens University passed a motion in 1918 to ban qualified Black students from entering their School of Medicine. Never or rarely credited for their achievements, people of a darker skin were never allowed to rise too far into public prominence unless on the negative end of the hierarchy, yet they soldiered on trusting and obeying, telling themselves the best was yet to come, if only grudgingly. Given the long history of Black people in Canada, their amazing achievements and contributions, it is mind-blowing that many more people of colour are not further ahead, safe and secure in their place as members of a vibrant, viable community. In this climate of White supremacy, life has remained stingy in its generosity.

In the old days, Black mothers—bright, beautiful, and well groomed—gained entry into the workforce primarily through side or back doors of well-to-do homes. They entered as domestic nannies or servant-maids, leaving their own children behind to the capricious impulses of life or in the care of extended family, usually a grandparent. Black women attended diligently to the care of other people's children in other people's homes. This they did with pride and great care in exchange for a pittance on which to get by, while trying to imagine a better way out for their own children who were often barred from higher learning.

At night, Black men were away from their families. They worked long hours, travelled far and wide as attendants in sleeping or parlour cars. They served food, shined shoes, pressed clothes, and waited hand and feet to clean up after others in hope of earning a good tip. Masters of the waiting game, they waited at doors and at elevators, waited anywhere they could, waiting wherever and whenever they were told to. Collectively, they elevated the act of servitude into a sophisticated art form. Interestingly, they and their kin are still waiting, except this time they are waiting for the proverbial breakthrough, so long in coming.

Working mostly night shifts, men became night owls, the working bohemians of the railroad. This was not by choice; it was through necessity. Better shifts were exclusively reserved for White men who held the long end of the stick. Largely excluded from White labour unions, Black men who held the short end were left to form or join their own collective bargaining units. Even so, they dared not complain or retaliate. No complaining about pay scales, working conditions, or anything. "*Shut up or shuffle on,*" "*Grin and bear it,*" "*Don't bite the hand that feeds you.*" A good porter or doorman knew his place, held it well. Docility was the game, a skill acutely developed to avoid ill-fated consequences. Being fired, harsh discipline, physical endangerment, or threats were part of the benefit package should any Black person step out of line or be so brazen as to stare or talk back. Should they complain, their job could vanish or end up in someone else's eagerly waiting hand. Old Black men are experts at walking fine lines.

Called *George* when that was not their given name, Black men with eyes cast downward often answered, "Yes, suh," shuffling on with elegant dignity just the same. After all, this was the porter's life and livelihood, the means by which he supported his family and provided for his children's education. There were few other employment options aside from the railway, a doorway or an elevator; other forms of employment were slim to none. If you were lucky, you could become a tradesman, maybe a blacksmith, but even this had its risks. Black independent success attracted its own scrutiny, envy, and White rage.

When in 1945, inspired by the leadership of American A. Philip Randolph, a Canadian branch of the Brotherhood of Sleeping Car Porters was formed, a new Black manhood emerged. Prior, Black porters had to organize clandestinely. In 1917, when the Order of Sleeping Car Porters was formed under the leadership of John Robinson of Winnipeg and others, many were dismissed due to suspicion of union activities. A later alliance with the Brotherhood of Sleeping Car Porters however added strength to their bargaining power, leading to better pay, somewhat improved working conditions, and greater solidarity. With greater leverage, Black men began to move with greater sway. The brotherhood gave them a voice as they went up against one of Canada's top exploiters of Black men at the time—the Canadian Pacific Railway. For the first time, Canadian Black men experienced the power of united action as they engaged in collective activism, networking with other people of African ancestry throughout Canada and across the US and with Black men from the Caribbean, many of whom were inspired by the philosophy of a man named Marcus Garvey. By extension, the Black community became more energized. The union became the cradle from which Black leadership grew. Still, inequalities persisted.[33]

Forced to subsist in the worst parts of Canadian cities, Black families lived in public housing in disproportionately higher numbers. They had the highest unemployment rates. On aggregate, they were among the lowest of all income groups. To reside in an owner-occupied home was a privilege, a worthy goal to aspire to. Life was precarious. Those who lived in proud self-established communities would, without being consulted, have roads and railways plough through their neighbourhood. Black communities, as was the case with Africville, were vulnerable sites for garbage dumps, prisons, unappealing amenities, and other less-than-desirable forms of socio-economic endeavours. Left to perish, even deteriorate, these communities, Black and beloved, disappeared with little trace. Over time, Black communities became petrified or gentrified. Lost to the history books, these humble abodes were often coveted by condominium corporations with deep pockets and shallow consciences. Displaced and dispossessed, Black families were forced to move on with their most valuable possession: their dignity. Packed away in their suitcases were dreams mixed together with a random miscellany of conflicting emotions.

In spite of this, Black Canadian communities showed exemplary courage in the face of adversity. As a buffer against dehumanizing mistreatment, they cultivated an enriching social and civic life. They fostered mutual support and created self-help organizations. Black men enrolled in wars they did not initiate. Some died in service to their country. Those who returned faced the same terror they were asked to fight against overseas; on returning, they discovered that their *home and native land* was not as embracing as they hoped it would be. Still, when called on to fight and volunteer, they did so just the same, rendering service as missionaries and signing up for a variety of humanitarian causes.

---

33 A. Phillip Randolph is regarded as one of the architects of the March on Washington Movement, an early initiative that would spawn the March on Washington in 1963, and later the Million Man March in 1995. Also, for more on Black Canadian life in general but especially for what it was like as a sleeping car porter during this era, see Stanley Grizzle's 1998 memoir, *My Name Is Not George*.

Black families made good *citizens*. They sang in churches. They sang the Canadian national anthem. Their children also sang the anthem in schools, schools that housed books bearing images of black *Sambo*; yet they sang with *glowing hearts*. And while the children sang, their parents played and danced to the blues; they played and danced in city bars or dimly lit nightclubs. They played and danced in the few places allowing them entry, sometimes through a back entrance. Passed over, humiliated, degraded, and disenfranchised, astonishingly Black families still kept faith. To endure, adults adopted a variety of psychosocial coping habits, including the wearing of social masks, playing double roles—one outside the home when among White people, another at home among their own, living a double life to make good or to get by, a sometimes bewildering double consciousness, oftentimes unwittingly passed on to their young.

Confronted with the reality of everyday anti-Black racism in Canadian life, Black communities organized as best they could around shared values and common interests. They did so informally and formally as a means of survival, caring for each other, loving one another with the enduring hope that one day their children would thrive. Recognizing their inherent right to dignity and self-respect, they exercised what agency they had, organizing themselves in alliance with other justice seekers. Collectively they exerted pressure on the White men who governed, hoping they would act in good conscience by enacting and enforcing fair practices consistent with the liberal democratic principles they claim to represent. Black families raised their children with this cardinal faith, tutoring them to conform, to be respectful, encouraging them to get an education and to work hard. Education was the key; employment, the doorway. They all knew. Canada has not always been kind to those with dark skin, but an education offered a sliver of hope. Occasionally, a few bright stars would overcome the odds and rise up, breaking through with their intellect or creative talent. Men like Oscar Peterson, who wooed audiences with his artistry, or like Harry Jerome, Herb Carnegie, Fergie Jenkins, Willie O'Ree, and Ray Lewis who, with their athleticism, performed triumphant thrills in the complicated world of competitive sports with its tormented struggles. These were but tips of an iceberg representing many more unseen unsung heroes—trailblazers who paved the way, raised hopes, drawing attention to what was possible when you are young, gifted, and Black.

Gifted or not, the waters didn't always part. When Jordan River failed to allow free passage, Black people expressed their disappointments, fears, hopes, and dreams in profound ways. Forced to be quiet about their grief, they hid it in their worship services, blended it into their prayers, masked it in their music. You could see it in the way they walked, the way they talked, the way they made love or made peace; you could hear it in the way they performed, tell stories, or composed and recited poetry. They shared this knowledge tacitly with one another, strengthening their lifeblood with the hope that one day in the distant future, they would all overcome. In this and other ways, they kept their sanity, nourished their souls, and cultivated their voices, laying the foundation for other voices to follow.

During the closing decade of the twentieth century, one group of voices to emerge was the Young Poets of the Revolution, a literary collective of young writers who were also performer-poets. Labelled as Generation Xers—the children of Baby Boomers—they fulfilled their parent's dream by getting an education. They had done almost everything their parents asked of them. Although they realized their parent's educational hopes, this younger generation faced a new reality—a Black Canadian existence that seemed far more unjust, more brutal, grittier, and less forgiving. Life hadn't become better. Instead, it had become wretched. Like their parents, they knew Canada had not always been kind to those with dark skin. But unlike their parents, this new generation, born in the 1960s, '70s, and early '80s, knew there was a different and worsening emerging existential reality—one that was increasingly disturbing. As far as this young cohort was concerned, the situation was begging for a confrontation. Docility and denial be damned.

The singing of "We Shall Overcome" or waiting on others no longer satisfied; falling for the deceptive smoke screens created by an indifferent, self-righteous, White power structure was no longer going to cut it. The young had witnessed their parents' growing disillusionment, watched them as they proudly shuffled along, wearing their despondency like an ill-fitting winter coat sewn together by the flimsy thread of a guarded optimism. The young had seen enough of taunting half-empty cups, heard enough of the call to wait, to be patient. "Wait, things will get better," they were told. Well, things did not get better. This new generation no longer wished to wait in vain for love that was promised but was long in coming. They were tired of waiting the way their parents had done. They had seen their parents' struggle for equal status and economic wellbeing and heard their parents' muted scream for racial and social justice and watched in horror as those cries were ignored. If and when their parents did exert their legal rights, they were severely punished for it. How could this be? Despite legislative changes and numerous petitions to the power structure, racism and racist violence waxed instead of waned. How was this possible?

With each passing incident, the young became increasingly indignant. Instead of Black youth thriving, large numbers were dying violently on urban streets. Instead of Black youth rising to levels of success beyond that achieved by their parents, they were sinking fast through distressingly high rates of school dropout. Those who did not drop out were being miseducated with misinformation and disinformation. They were provided with a false knowledge of themselves and of their history, and or were told they had no history at all. Routinely, they were devalued into lower technical or vocational streams. Somewhere along the length of this cruel path of systemic discrimination lasting from womb to the tomb, young Black people, males in particular, were being incarcerated at terrifyingly unprecedented rates. When parents plant a tree, children should enjoy the shade. However, in the case of the Young Poets, their parents had eaten a bitter fruit. Now the children's belly ached, leaving them with no choice but to *spit it out*. Instead of cleaning spittoons, they would be filling them with spit-full of lyrical brimstone and fire.

In urban centres across Canada in cities such as Edmonton, Ottawa, Montreal, Toronto, and Halifax, the *hating* of people of African ancestry had solidified. Crossing generation to generation, the hatred spawned a new batch of young standard-bearers who could no longer make peace with injustice. These *new jacks*, if nothing else, were in love with being Black. They had no to low tolerance for racial abuse. No longer would they sit and be silent. Instead of fading to black, they rose up in true Black African selfhood insisting on being heard. They were going to speak their truth to the powers that be *by any means necessary.* In this aspect, they were truly members of the Generation X, referring to Malcolm X, who many of them admired and were inspired by. The hate you give would return multiplied, not in the form of guns, bombs, or knives. Rather, the reply would be in *spoken words* designed to chant down Babylon, triggering a new revolutionary consciousness for a people who were accustomed to being spoken down to. Now the children of the oppressed would speak up and speak out, uttering words as if they were "bullets from a gun." They would speak out in a manner loud and clear to anyone who had ears to hear and dared to listen. Disinterested in shining the shoes of others, they polished their own boots before hip-hopping, readying themselves to crush in defeat the horror of racial abuse beneath their stomping feet to the beat of radical verses and rhymes unfit for nurseries.

Held at the Bickford Centre, Toronto, in September 1992, the second annual became a marquee event. (Poster produced on behalf of MACPRI/Oji Archives.)

I am Andre Rowe
I am Jah
I am Denise
We are students of Mwalimu Oji
In St. Elizabeth, Jamaica
Inviting all CIUT 89 Listeners
To support the annual Young Poets of the Revolution presentation in Canada.

Melodious, young, confident voices rang out over the airwaves of a local community radio station situated on the University of Toronto city campus. Rarely heard on Canadian mainstream radio, the children's voices were promoting an upcoming poetry event featuring the Young Poets of the Revolution, their first public performance scheduled for September 1991 on the university's campus.

After kicking off their September 1991 performance, the poetry collective went on to stage at least four more in as many years: in 1992 and 1993 at the Bickford Centre and in 1994 and 1995 at Ryerson University. Gaining momentum by dropping what they termed *science* and *beats*, they held press conferences throughout the city of Toronto at strategic locations such as at *Timbucktu*, an African fashion clothing store in Kensington Market. For a number of years, they issued a publication under their group name and were featured occasionally on CIUT and CKLN, two local community radio stations that were hip to the new vibe.

The young wordsmiths rose to become the new voice of forgotten everyday people. Looking under the surface of things, they relied on their creativity and imagination to challenge the establishment by lifting the "we are not racist" rug to expose the underlying dirt. Using their intellect coupled with forceful lyrics, they filled a void, invoking visions of radical change, ranting and calling for liberation from all forms of oppression. They regarded themselves to be more than poets; they represented a movement. Their key message could be likened to a public service alert calling attention to a public health crisis, namely that racism was alive and well in Canada. They were intent on *calling it out*. Their resolve was to expose, as best as they could, the full spectrum of racism in all its forms, whether expressed through overt or covert exclusionary practices; through the slow, systematic marginalization of racialized people; through oppressive socio-economic measures; or by the more extreme targeted violence associated with over-policing, unreasonable arrest, police brutality, and the illegal use of lethal force.

Consisting of young people of African ancestry, the Young Poets collectively shared a common belief that racism in Canada was not an aberration, not a one-off practiced by *a few bad eggs*. For the Young Poets, Canadian racism was not a benign anomaly. Rather, the practice was embedded systematically in Canadian values, covertly weaved into various tools of socialization and control. Even the education to which they were privileged was contrived to instill Black inferiority while reinforcing the superiority of all things White. Although they did not initially know each other, they would become united in one purpose: to use original poetry—rap, dub, jazz, or reggae—to awaken and enliven their listeners to the ugly reality they had come to know.

Before the uprising of Black Lives Matter, the Young Poets of the Revolution had been lyrically chanting. Seems like as long as anyone can remember, people of African descent have been victims of violence, beaten down black and blue, or shot dead. The Generation Xers knew Canada has not always been kind to those with dark skin, but what they were now facing seemed more malicious. Abusive policing was now the contemporary urban face of chronic systematic racist violence resulting in the too often wounding or killing of unarmed Black people, mostly men, with little or no accountability. Long before the state-side weariness flowing from the acquittal of George Zimmerman in the 2013 shooting death of unarmed seventeen-year-old Trayvon Martin—shot dead because he looked suspicious and threatening; long before the dreary days when volatile race relations overtook the twenty-first century; long before the lofty sounding but empty platitudes and long conversations following the life-and-death encounters between police and citizens of African descent became mainstream; long before the untimely deaths of Michael Brown, Tamir Rice, Eric Garner, Freddie Grey, Breonna Taylor, or George Floyd in Minneapolis, now household names recited in condemnation of racial brutality; long before the death of Daniel Prude in Rochester, New York, a mentally ailing Black man who died of asphyxiation on March 30, 2020, a week after Rochester police put a bag over his head and pressed his face into the pavement for two minutes—long before this litany of woe, the Young Poets were already calling attention to this senseless carnage.[34] Even before Andrew Loku, forty-five—shot and killed by Toronto police on July 5, 2015, after refusing to drop a hammer; before the killing of Jermaine Carby, thirty-three—shot three times in September 2014 by Peel Regional Police in Brampton, Ontario, when police claimed a routine traffic stop escalated into a heated encounter; or before the October 2007 death of Quilem Registre, thirty-nine—tasered by Montreal police six times in less than a minute.

During the era of the Young Poets, there was the Rodney King incident in 1992. Prior to that was Yusef Hawkins—shot and killed by White vigilantes in Brooklyn, New York, August 1989. While these incidents were in the US, it didn't seem to make a difference; in Canada, Toronto in particular, the possibility of a Black person getting shot, killed, or wounded especially by White Toronto police officers was alive and well just the same. Remember Marlon Neil—the teen gunned down, wounded by Toronto police on May 14, 1990. Remember Sophia Cook, twenty-four—shot in the back and wounded by police October 1989 while she was an innocent passenger in a car. Remember, December 1988, when Michael Wade-Lawson—a Mississauga teenager was shot and killed by police for driving a stolen car. Remember, August 1988, when mentally ill Lester Donaldson was shot and killed by police in his rooming house apartment. If the ad nauseam recitation of these incidents seems excessively repetitive, that's because it is. Regrettably, history repeats itself. Black African communities have been *here* before, many times. Caught in a ceaseless and rapid crossfire, the Young Poets many years ago used their creativity to convert this experience into poetry, dropping beats, spitting about this deadly danger. Even then, it seemed not too many of us were paying attention.

---

34 Shortly before this book went into publication, in a precedent setting case, Minneapolis police officer Derek Michael Chauvin was charged with second and third-degree murder and second-degree manslaughter in relation to Floyd's death. He was convicted by a jury on all three charges on April 20, 2021. As if open season was declared in the US, a spate of questionable police killings of Black people occurred about the same time as Chauvin's trial concluded. The names of Daunte Wright, Ma'Khiah Bryant, and Andrew Brown Jr. can be added to the growing list of dead, a list too long to be included here. Although in Canada there were no reported incidents of similar fatal police killings over the same time period, "carding" and police racial profiling of Black and Indigenous people continue to be a concern, aggravated by the reluctance or refusal of the federal government to legislate nationwide anti-racism policing standards. In the meantime, racism persists across a range of areas, including housing and real estate, banking, commerce, employment, education, and in the arts. Notwithstanding that anti-Black racism has become a popular topic of discussion, and it is currently fashionable for Canadian organizations and institutions to support (at least in words and pronouncements), diversity and inclusion initiatives, institutionalized and systemic racism continue to prevail in high and low places under the leadership of paternalistic liberal sounding decision-makers (the majority of whom are part of a White male patriarchy) who are keen on perpetuating the mythology of a "raceless" colour-blind Canada.

Young Poets of the Revolution in Kensington Market spitting rhymes and dropping beats. (YPOTR photo on behalf of MACPRI/Oji Archives.)

One of the visionary organizers within the group, Minister Faust, was himself a featured poet. With an outspoken voice, he identified himself as the defence minister of the Militant Rap Party. He first met Brother Oji in the summer of 1991 while in Ottawa, when both were attending an event held by the African Canadian Cultural and Educational Services (ACCES) and where both were scheduled to speak. Present also were other poets including the Original One, ONI, and AKWM. On hearing Minister Faust deliver his spoken word performance, Oji was impressed enough to invite him to perform at an upcoming Toronto event. Minister Faust agreed, as did the others, and a partnership ensued. Together they organized participants from across Canada, extending from Alberta in the west to Nova Scotia in the east, to form a new generation of performer-poets. Their stage performances were compelling; their print publications, fiery.

In addition to speaking at related press conferences, Minister Faust performed twice as a member of the collective. An Edmontonian from Alberta, he went on to pursue a career as a writer, eventually becoming a communications consultant providing a range of services. He also blossomed into a playwright, a journalist, and an author of several books, including *War & Mir* and *The Alchemists of Kush*, a fictional hip-hop epic. "He is an outstanding, dedicated, and selfless brother whom I admire greatly," Minister Faust said in reference to Oji, who is credited for launching the collective. According to the Minister, "What we are doing as poets as young people is to kick reality on what is being done to us, and it is that point when people wake up from their dream." Not one to mince words, Minster Faust was known as a closer who, when he marched on stage, would shoot poetry for thirty-five minutes, enflaming the crowd with his incendiary lyrical phrases with lines such as the following:

> Africa unite! The only thing we have to loose is our handcuffs
> An' our appointment with the coroner
> But I won't say "Sorry, sir"
> If there won't be justice, I swear it won't be just us
> Cuz their hour of power is sour
> But it'll soon be over
> As soon as you an' me yell "Black Power!"

The concept of a poetry collective came to Brother Oji following his involvement with the Royal Ontario Museum demonstrations. In the aftermath of the ROM protest, he quietly began to rebuild his public profile. He had become more emboldened, persuaded that he needed to act with even greater vigour. Despite facing criminal charges related to his involvement with the ROM 11 and the CFTA, he continued to approach life with an ever-increasing sense of purpose. Undaunted, he seized the creative challenge of telling a different story from that told by *Into the Heart of Africa*. His goal was to re-image Africa and African people through the creative use of words and images, to challenge stereotypes and to debunk racist mythologies. As his standing in the community began to rapidly evolve, he realized he had a bigger platform with greater reach from which to teach. Previously seen as a strident student and community activist, he now earnestly began to inhabit the role of the *Mwalimu*.

Oji's chosen area of specialty is African culture. It has become popular to construct Black history around the experiences of enslavement, emancipation, the civil rights movement, and narratives about the first Black person or persons to break through this or that barrier. Implicit in this narrative is that Black history began in the fifteenth century with the advent of slavery, consequently misleading some to adopt the false notion that Black history is anchored entirely within the struggle against dehumanizing injustice. However, ancient and advanced Black civilizations inhabited the world long before the advent of the mass enslavement of Africans. Predating the Greek, Roman, and British Empires were vibrant Black African communities, which ultimately became the root of all modern human civilization. The Black African origin of human progress as illustrated by Egyptian or Kemetic culture and empire is but one example of this lasting influence. Timbuktu, famous city of the ancient Mali Empire led by Mansa Musa, known for its scholarly libraries with magnificent literary works, though now lost, also has a prominent place in human history; similarly, the kingdoms of Songhay in the west and Kush in the ancient kingdom of Nubia to the east. As Oji began to learn more, he would come to know that a true history of Black Africa is critical to understanding the origins of human achievements in astronomy, mathematics, medicine, architecture, and science in general. This would become an important part of his historiography.

Based on his understanding that West Africa has been the primary ancestral source of diasporic Africans in the Caribbean, he elected to specifically focus his attention on sub-Saharan Africa, particularly West African peoples, chiefly Ghanaians. His mission was to acquire and impart a true *knowledge of self* as it related to people of West African ancestry. This was intended to serve as a counterpoint to racist ideology and practice, the perpetuation of which has led to pervasive self-ignorance within the Black African diaspora. With this in mind, he embarked first on redefining his public image. While he celebrated Jamaica as his place of birth, and acknowledged Toronto, Canada, as his place of citizenship and where he was raised, he deliberately began to make it clear that his ancestry was preeminently African. His brand, MACPRI, became an expression of his philosophy. Motivated by his love of Africa and its people, he began to embark on creating artistic and business enterprises to convey and promote a Black African worldview, or more specifically what he described as the *African Image Revolution.*

MACPRI, or Mother Africa's Children Primarily or, by extension, Mother Africa's Children First International Association, was unquestionably modelled on the self-reliance philosophy of the Honourable Marcus Mosiah Garvey. "If we allow other people to feed us, one day we will go hungry," said Garvey. Taking this to heart, Oji embraced this philosophy, embodying it in whatever form he could. He led by example by embarking on independent economic development models that allowed him to support himself and his family while contributing to the growth of the wider African community. According to him, "It is the responsibility of all of us to nurture all the young fruits in our gardens. But we cannot claim the fruits if we have not planted the seed but abandon it and allow another farmer to tend to the crop."

Self-reliant and independent, the MACPRI initiative gained increasing strength throughout the early 1990s based primarily on Oji's work as a photo-documentarian. Resistant to promoting art for art's sake, his images projected a distinctive look. His photographs were not driven by a need to be spectacular, sensational, or aesthetically charming, although in some ways they were. His main goal was to shift and uplift the representation and reputation of Africa and to reflect the radiance of African people everywhere. (We will revisit this in a later chapter.) By elevating an African-centered aesthetic in a predominantly Eurocentric environment, Oji's efforts were paradigm-shifting. Through his creative intellectual endeavours, he encouraged a refocusing of attention on narratives that were either previously denied, misunderstood, or misrepresented. By so doing, he began making history while also retelling it differently through the use of words and images, rendering the Black African experience in a positive, life-affirming way. According to his prospectus, the African Image Revolution was about "radical change in the way we see and organize ourselves as a people ... because the missionaries saw us one way and they were presenting their racist, white supremacist perspective, we need to present a perspective of us that is liberating. It is about reciprocity ... To build something that lasts forever, that our young people, our children, our progeny, will always be able to benefit from."

The Young Poets of the Revolution was part of MACPRI's overall vision of nurturing *young fruits* and bringing new voices into the mainstream discourse on racial politics, identity, and justice—modern-day griots rooted in Africa's oral tradition who could spin new narratives in creative, innovative ways. The urban streets of Toronto and Canada had its own poetry and originality. Largely ignored in mainstream literary canon, these voices yearned for an outlet, one with a platform befitting of their experience. Out of this need, the collective was born.

And so, as the children spoke over the Toronto airwaves, they were lending their voices to the revolution—the African Image Revolution and, by extension, to the Young Poets.

MACPRI flyer promoting second annual of the Young Poets of the Revolution. (Poster produced on behalf of MACPRI/Oji Archives.)

This is not to say that the Young Poets were the first Canadian Black poets to call things out or to speak about the Black Canadian experience. They were following in the footsteps of others who paved the way. During the 1970s when Oji and his family arrived in Toronto, Harold Head, author, editor, and publisher, was vigorously working to promote Black literature and poetry. In 1974, he authored one of the first collection of poems by an African Canadian entitled *Bushman's Brew*; and in 1976, he edited the first anthology of African Canadian poems and prose—*Canada in Us Now*—which included entries from the late Austin Clarke and Charles Roach and Dionne Brand, among others. Although tutored in the colonial tradition of Shakespeare, Wordsworth, Blake, Byron, Shelly, Keats, and the like, this early cohort of Black Canadian writer-poets began to shape a different brand of poetry. Their style, content, and approach were primarily informed by Third World life and influenced by Afro-Caribbean rhythms. They drew inspiration from several directions including the campaign for political independence within the Caribbean, the liberation movements of Africa, and from the Civil Rights movement in the US. This early wave of Black Canadian writer-poets began to view the world through a different lens, keenly aware of the need to provoke fresh discourse about freedom, justice, and decolonization. Moved to give greater voice to the heart and soul of African Canadian sensibilities, they embarked on a new literary frontier. M. NourbeSe Philip, from Trinidad and Tobago, who emerged as an African Canadian poet, novelist, and playwright, recalls how difficult it was in the late seventies and eighties when she tried to establish herself in a hostile, sometimes indifferent, Eurocentric literary setting. "As a woman from the Caribbean writing in Toronto," says Philip, "there were no elders. There were no models that we could look to, to pattern ourselves on in terms of writing, so there is a sense in which ... we actually were almost creating the tradition as we were writing."

Two other sources of significant Black literary influences outside Canada were the Black Arts Movement (BAM) in Harlem, New York, and the Caribbean Artists Movement (CAM) based in London, England. The Black Arts Movement is said to have appeared circa 1965 after Malcom X was assassinated. Poet, dramatist, writer, and educator Amiri Baraka (Leroi Jones) is credited for envisioning the Black Arts Repertory Theatre/School (BARTS), an incubator designed for art activism. Out of this grew the Black Arts Movement, which Baraka co-initiated with Larry Neal, Hoyt Fuller, Don L. Lee, and others. BAM became the embodiment of Black pride. It created and promoted new independent forms of Black expression by cross-pollinating ideas from the Black power, civil rights, and Pan-African movements. During this period, Black American artists became increasingly politicized, lending their artistry to support conversations about race and racism. By synthesizing artistry with revolutionary ideals, they were using their creativity to compel American culture to reckon with the African American experience. Stridently critical of the political, cultural, and artistic norms of White America (the same norms that led to multiple assassinations), BAM began to promote a new Black aesthetic in which art and politics were fused. This has always been the case. BAM only made it more pronounced. Everything is political. Why not use art to expose the injustices of racism in White America? Why not employ art as a tool for political activism to support Black liberation struggles and self-determination? Through theatrical presentations, poetry readings, musical and dance performances, the Black Arts Movement brought a new appreciation for Black creativity in ways not seen or heard before. Their style, while open to varying interpretations, would eventually take root to become influential in the creative intellectual life of many who followed. Those associated with the movement included James Baldwin, Nikki Giovanni, Gwendolyn Brooks, Maya Angelou, Alice Walker, Toni Morrison, and August Wilson to mention a few, all of whom went on to make valuable contributions to American and world literature.

One group and artist emerging from the Black Arts Movement were Harlem based: the Last Poets and Gil Scott-Heron. The Last Poets came to public attention during the late 1960s with their Black nationalist rap—*"When the revolution comes some of us will probably catch it on TV with chicken hanging from our mouths."* Gil Scott-Heron, who in 1970 launched "Whitey On the Moon," followed up in 1971 with "The Revolution Will Not Be Televised." The Last Poets and Scott-Heron developed a performance genre that would become hip-hop's forerunner. Evidently, a new performance artist with a distinct Black aesthetic was coming to the fore. They were fearless, socially conscious, able to combine art with protest, and when called on, were prepared to render politically charged performances.

Founded during a similar timeline to that of BAM, the Caribbean Artist Movement (CAM) stirred to life in 1966 when Caribbean artists living or studying in England began to discover the power of collaboration. CAM was co-founded by Barbadian poet/philosopher Edward Kamau Brathwaite, Trinidadian publisher John La Rose, and Panamanian Jamaican writer Andrew Salkey, all of whom were residing in London, England. Their goal was to give prominence to the creative endeavours of Caribbean artists, writers, and poets who, despite their prodigious talent and prolific output, had failed to gain attention from mainstream publications or academic channels. This was nothing new. Black talent appears always to have been on the periphery, sometimes invisible, languishing in isolation. Seems like anything good or great was the preserve of White Eurocentric stock, with Black presence having occasional guest appearances. Realizing their exclusion, CAM members, which included dramatists, filmmakers, actors, visual artists, and musicians, banded together to celebrate and promote their own work at a time when no one else would. As outsiders, they became their own peer support network. They mutually enabled each other's creative output and aspirations and helped each other to develop their craft. CAM became a clearing house for sharing ideas on how to pique the consciousness of their community through the power of art. Live poetry readings were common. The movement lasted until the early '70s, and although it started in London, it would have ripple effects throughout the African diaspora. Among those involved in the movement were C. L. R. James, Orlando Patterson, Ivan Van Sertima, to name a few, and a younger generation of poets including Linton Kwasi Johnson. Professor Edward Kamau Brathwaite, who tenured at the Jamaica Mona Campus of the University of the West Indies, would go on to inspire many, including Oji, who would take up Brathwaite's challenge to forget Chaucer and instead create and promote a new vernacular—a *nation language*—one more suited to the unique Black African Caribbean experience.

In this regard, as far as performance poetry is concerned, it is difficult not to acknowledge the late Louise Bennett-Coverley (Miss Lou), who almost single-handedly led the way in making Jamaican folk language a valid form of oral, as well as literary, expression. Her influence is inestimable. From as early as 1962, she was courageous enough to write and perform poetry in the idiom (derisively described as a dialect or *patois* or broken English) of the common people, a way of speaking that was frowned upon by authorities who regarded this form of expression as uneducated and backward. Miss Lou, through the use of dramatic storytelling techniques rooted in the African Caribbean creole tradition, popularized the art form using satirical humour to get her message across—"*Wat a joyful news, Miss Mattie, I feel like me heart gwine burs / Jamaica people colonizin Englan in reverse.*" She undoubtedly influenced the evolution of dub poetry, an unflinching musical performance art form that sprouted in Jamaica, London, and Toronto during the 1970s.

Rooted in the African oral tradition, Dub poets employ a folk vernacular, reminiscent of Miss Lou, to deliver chantlike poetic speeches with pronounced, accentuated rhythms set to instrumental distilled reggae beats stripped down to the drum and bass lines. (The name dub comes from the fact that the vocal track of the original music is dubbed out, leaving only the instrumental tracks over which poets can rap.) The content, decidedly political in nature, served as an unapologetic social commentary on lived experiences relating to race and class oppression, covering such topics as poverty, violence, and the exploitation of the poor by the rich. Michael Smith ("*I and I alone ah trod tru creation / Babylon on I right / Babylon on I left*"), Oku Onuora ("*An de beat well red an de scene well drea*d"), and Mutabaruka ("*Free up de lan white man, free de Namibian*") were leading the genre in Jamaica, while Linton Kwasi Johnson and others was doing the same in England. In Toronto, Lillian Allen, Afua Cooper, Michael St. George, Clifton Joseph, and Ahdri Zhina Mandiela were some of the genre's earliest pioneers, their work influential enough to spark the first International Dub Poetry Festival in Toronto, May 8–15, 1993, featuring Mutabaruka, Oku Onoura, Benjamin Zephaniah, and others. Oji, who attended the festival, and many of the Young Poets, drew from this poetic wellspring. (As an aside, Calypso, a Southern Caribbean musical and satirical art form emanating from Trinidad and Tobago, can be said to serve a similar sociopolitical storytelling function as that of Dub poetry and reggae.)

By the 1990s, therefore, poetry in Canada, as elsewhere, had become more than a literary art form; for Black writers in particular, art had become a hybrid tool for sociopolitical activism intended to denounce oppression or to express dissent or to advocate for social justice and equality.

Maligned or ignored by the traditional Eurocentric literary world, Black writers and poets who often had their work or book proposals rejected by the mainstream publishing world found alternative means to get exposure. Many became disillusioned. However, rather than grumble, some saw it fit to create their own literary infrastructure, one best suited to their style and tradition; one more accurately reflecting their experience, interests, and needs. They wanted to have a bigger voice, one big enough to draw awareness to critical sociopolitical concerns that were hidden in plain sight. Denied a platform in the mainstream media, they created their own medium to share their observations. They operated within an anti-Black dominated environment that largely ignored them while at the same time giving them a disapproving eye. They pressed on regardless to create their own wall or soap box. In the words of Mutabaruka, *"A si down pan di wall a watch him a watch mi."*

Flyer promoting the Young Poets. The hate you give would return multiplied, and not in the form of guns, bombs, or knives. Rather, the answer back would be in the form of spoken words designed to chant down Babylon. (Poster produced on behalf of MACPRI/Oji Archives.)

When the Young Poets of the Revolution stood, the stage was therefore already set. At the time of their emergence, there was already a wellspring of inspirational influences from which they could pull. The Young Poets were literary poets as well as performance poets, not one or the other. They drew on both traditions. Performance poetry, as opposed to poetry readings, became their genre, a new revolutionary approach in writing, delivering, and experiencing poetry. In England, Linton Kwasi Johnson in 1974 had already set the tone with "Five Nights of Bleeding" in which he exploded about violence in South London, foreshadowing the 1981 Brixton riots: *"The song of hate was sounded / the pile of oppression was vomited / and two policemen wounded / Righteous war, righteous war."* In 1993, in "The Death of Joy Gardner," Benjamin Zephaniah, another British-based poet with Jamaican roots, made his contribution to the genre when he offered a moving eulogy—*"They put a leather belt around her / thirteen feet of tape and bound her / handcuffs to secure her"*—to mark the killing of a Jamaican student who died in 1993 after being detained during a police immigration raid at her home. In April 1990, when Zephaniah visited to perform in Toronto, Oji was there at the Bamboo Club to witness and write about the "Dub Poetry Messiah." He was not alone. He, along with a few students, artists, and activists, including Afua Cooper, met with Zephaniah personally at an event sponsored by the African Canadian Students Association to discuss revolution.

Cover artwork featuring Queen Nzinga produced by Minister Faust for *The Young Poets of the Revolution Special Edition 1992*. The poetry booklet featured the poems of all the performing artists to take the stage. All two hundred booklets produced were sold. (Poster produced on behalf of MACPRI/ Oji Archives.)

Performance-style spoken-word poetry laced with Black African resistance appealed to a younger demographic who latched on to the new idiom. If what preceded could be likened to jazz poetry, this new cohort was oriented to hip-hop styling. If the foregoing was rap, then this was dub. If the poets of the '70s were raw or vulnerable, this new batch in the '90s took their creativity a notch higher to reflect levels of extreme dread—crowd-pleasing emotionally charged performances without subtlety or apology, incisively critical of the establishment. For the Young Poets of the Revolution, there would be no holding back. They were grittier, much grittier. The leftover stultifying consequence of colonialism was screaming with maddening effect, and *times were crucial.* Betrayed by a country and a system that had failed them and their parents, the Young Poets refused to be silenced.

The images described by the Young Poets were necessarily grim, their messages unpleasant, rarely funny. But then, so too were their lived experiences. According to George L. Jackson,

> We must accept the eventuality of
> Bringing the power structure to its knees
> Accept the closing off of critical sections of our city with barbed wire
> Armoured pig carriers crisscrossing the city Soldiers everywhere
>
> Tommy guns pointing at stomach level
> Smoke curling black against the day light sky
> The smell of cordite
> House to house searches
> Doors kicked in
> The commonness of death

This was a community under siege, a community at war. With lyrically projected images of violence, the poets were deliberately intending to draw attention to their lived reality, realities often denied by the established order. Their poems were often a call to action designed to invoke greater vigilance in the face of violent acts inspired by White supremacist values.

In the words of Sister Amuna,

> When crackers talk about peace
> They mean peace in the grave
> And when they talk about love
> They mean how they love to get us there

Sister Amuna was referring to the killing by Montreal police of unarmed Marcellus François. François, a twenty-four-year-old Montreal citizen of Jamaican descent was shot fatally in the head by Montreal police on July 3, 1991. He was killed with an M-16 rifle by a member of the city's SWAT Team. For members of the Montreal Black community, this was a clear case of cold-blooded murder, an abuse of police power. For the police and the political establishment that came to their defence, it was a simple case of *"mistaken identity."* Sister Amuna's poem was a requiem, an ode to the dead and dying, a message to the living.

The Young Poets of the Revolution focused their artistry on unpacking the nuances of racism, highlighting its source, outlining its consequences. In their telling, racism was akin to genocide, an African holocaust. As far as they were concerned, the deliberate violence against African people was a global phenomenon. In this cold-bloodied landscape, every Black man "fits the description," were guilty until proven innocent, their only right being the right to remain silent. In their visualization, the Young Poets could see a straight line running from the ROM 11's clash with Toronto police on May 5 and June 2, 1990, to the LAPD beating of Rodney King on March 3, 1991. When on April 29, 1992, the White LA police officers Koon, Briseno, Wind, and Powell were acquitted, they could see the same connection. It was the same thread connected to Toronto police killing of Raymond Lawrence on May 2, 1992, a Black twenty-two-year old man allegedly dealing street crack-cocaine, a killing that sparked the Toronto Yonge Street uprising two days later. When Brother Oji was imprisoned in a Sarnia, Ontario, jail, sentenced to ninety-days for standing up for his rights, they would make the same association—all were conflated to become part of the same long, endless terror of racist police brutality.[35]

As each poet took to the microphone to perform, it became clear what their revolution was about. It was not one of guns, bloodshed, or retaliation, but rather one based on the power of words flowing from an ancient reawakened consciousness.

One evening, the opening poet stood to set the tone. Using poetic prose in a dub format, she unhesitatingly began uttering words in a distinctive rhythmic pulsating beat:

> In everything you read, books, newspapers, magazines you hear them talking about the founding people. In everything you hear, TV, radio, intelligent conversation, you hear them talking about the founding peoples. And even feminists sometimes talk about Canada's founding women. Well, tell me, who are these founding people and what did they find? Well, I was told in school they are the French and the British who came to this wild land and tamed it. Yes, I was told in school they are the British and the French who came to this wilderness and civilized it. Well, when they came here, did they not see something? Did they not see anyone? Did they not see nations, and civilizations and people who have been here since creation? Did they not see the Hurons, the Iroquois, Mi'kmaq, Mississaugas, Ojibwe and Cree? Did they not find people living on this land, living with it in harmony, founding nations, founding peoples? This land was not empty. It was filled with trees, sometimes prairies, bears, deer, fish, birds and people. Yes, people who had already known, who had already found this land. From the North to the South, this land contained people who had already known it.

This was the voice of Afua Cooper, an honorary member of the Young Poets. On that night in 1993, she and others performed before an audience of over seven hundred people. Afua, one of the young voices involved with the ROM protest, was an early generation Canadian dub poet. As her profile grew, she would become known as a "feminist, a Pan-Africanist, political activist, cultural worker, educator, rabble rouser, troublemaker." Born in Jamaica, she emigrated to Canada in 1980, quickly becoming a part of the nascent spoken word community in Toronto, later publishing essays and books of her own. Over the years, she would come to know more than a few things about race and racism and the ugly historical fault lines associated with oppressive social systems. For over thirty years, she would go on to use poetry and spoken word to get her social justice message across. In 2003, she co-founded the Toronto Dub Poets' Collective, eventually moving to Halifax in 2011 where, as Dr. Afua Cooper, she took on the role of associate professor at Dalhousie University's department of sociology and social anthropology. In 2018, Halifax proclaimed her its seventh poet laureate.

---

35 The case of the racially motivated murder of Stephen Lawrence, an eighteen-year-old Black teenager who was fatally stabbed by a mob of White men in Eltham, southeast London, on April 22, 1993, was also part of this global trend. The subsequent investigation by British police was found to be inadequate. After much travail, a public enquiry relentlessly pursued by the teen's mother subsequently concluded that there was institutional racism within the country's justice system.

Afua's powerful erudition would receive strong applause as would the other young poets. After greeting the audience, each poet would have an opening line typically using poetic irony to begin their set. With the audience clapping, whistling, and cheering, each poet worked the microphone, pulsating it with rage—rage and tenderness about history, self-empowerment or self-identity, peppered with heavy doses of social realism. The atmosphere was electrifying.

To end their sets, poets often concluded with an acknowledgment to MACPRI and the African Image Revolution and to the work of Brother Oji, who they referred to as *the Teacher*. Over the four-year span of performances between 1991 and 1995, a lively energetic crop of poets with colourful monikers emerged under the auspices of MACPRI: Sistah, Carolin Outten, Nosakhere, Miguna Miguna, Ndeje, and the Prophets of Rage. Other outstanding poets who led the way included N2; bi-lingual poet ONI, the Haitian sensation who performed in French and English; the Original One; Debra Ross; Annex; AKWM; Peculiar I; and others. The Original One went on to spawn his own poetry collective in Ottawa, while ONI and AKWM had stellar spoken-word achievements in their own right. At the core also were Jennifer Isaac, Muchoki Simba, and others to name a few. Present too was Mighty Hefty, a.k.a. Winston Anderson, the DJ of choice. Winston, Oji's younger brother, provided the necessary musical backdrop. Winston, who ran his own sound system, New Age Promotion, was a faithful ally of the Young Poets. He has been an enduring partner to his brother, providing the appropriate sound to accompany MACPRI related events.

As for Brother Oji, he already had his own recorded compilation of spoken-word, "To My Root," a politically charged, no-bars hold rendition of performance oratory which included, "ROM 11 Set An Example." With much audience appeal, he too would step to the microphone and perform his signature piece entitled "My Origin." Rooted in the oral tradition, rap poems are meant to be said, not read. Reading Oji's poem from a page is far different from hearing him live from a stage. The experience is mesmerizing. He would begin by signing, "*This is the land of my birth,*" to get his listeners relaxed attention, coaxing them into a festive mood before boldly hitting them, repetitively declaring, "Jamaica, the land of my birth but not my origin." With this introduction, he would launch into a gusty vocal recitation:

> I am Akan
> I am Ewe
> I am Yoruba
> And some Mandingo, Bambara, Wolof,
> Fula, Damongo, Bakongo, Baluba, Bakuba,
> Ibo ...
> My blood is filled to the overflow
> Making me a Pan-African
> That's why
> Gambia, Guinea, Guinea Bissa,
> Liberia, Serria Leone, Ivory Coast,
> Mali, Burkina Faso, Togo,
> Benin, Nigeria, Niger, Cameroon, Congo,
> Angola, Gabon ...
> Can claim me you see
> I am forever connected

I could have made dry bones
On the shores of Alkebulan
Near Lake Bosomtwi
My children could have sung songs to
Mawu
As they bade in the River Volta
My clan could have listened to
And followed the fire The fire
The firing thunder of Shango
I am forever connected
I am child of the burning sun—RA
That's why "I"
Long for those days Those days
Daaaaaaaaaaaaaaaaze …
When in my own Son I could gaze
And look at the place Where for thousands
and thousands And ten thousands of days
My ancestors walked in
Our own place
They call me a Kormantse
For I am stubborn to their will
Their ill-will
I am Sun the son of the great sun
Kofi and Kodjo
I am Son the sun of the great son of
Tachie
And Nanny of the Maroons
I am African from head to toe
Of me
Not concerned about the minor biological
invasions of me
I am African
Jamaica the land of my birth
But not my origin

It is difficult to measure what impact, if any, the Young Poets may have had in instigating broader social change. Their audiences were usually of like mind. It is yet to be determined if a galvanizing tidal wave of change was ever triggered by them. Yet it is never too late. Ripples from a detonation sometimes take time before hitting shore. Poems and spoken word can entertain, educate, uplift, and inspire. And words are said to be more powerful than the sword. The Young

Poet's body of work, no doubt, added to a very important public discourse, contributing a voice usually shutout from official debates. Whereas now it is generally accepted that youth should and can participate meaningfully in shaping public policy, back then it was less appreciated. Today, public consultations are said to be more broad-based and inclusive. In this regard, the Young Poets were pioneers, forerunners in youth public engagement. Their strident unapologetic attitude set the tone for what was to come. Their no-nonsense approach was sharply different from the more conservative differential mode of some of their predecessors and laid the foundation for future and more radical challenges to the status quo of systemic injustices.

At the very least, the poetry collective offered fellowship and kinship for individuals who otherwise would have been alienated from mainstream literary sororities primarily rooted in Eurocentric traditions. The Young Poets did achieve a minor milestone when through Oji's influence they got some of their work published in a special winter edition of the University of Toronto's literary publication *Acta Victoriana*, volume 116 number 1, to mark Black History Month. Uniting and organizing young Black poet-activists interprovincially to partner together in community was a significant achievement on its own. Young Poets of the Revolution showed what was possible. It served as an incubator, helping young poets and writers to sharpen their craft while providing them with the necessary motivation to advance their academic and other careers. The group would be an anchor in stormy weather, a place to vent, to articulate complex emotions and ideas; a place where performers and audiences alike felt empowered to become agents of change, if only for a brief moment. When the value of the Young Poets is fully assessed, it may be determined that they contributed to the transmission and preservation of a people's collective memory at a critical time in Canadian social history. And the record will show that they did so in the true spirit of African oral tradition.

MACPRI label on flyer promoting the Young Poets explaining the African Image Revolution. (Poster produced on behalf of MACPRI/Oji Archives.)

The 1995 flyer promoting the Young Poets' final stand. (Poster produced on behalf of MACPRI/Oji Archives.)

It is an indisputable fact that Ghanaians have deep respect and love for brothers like myself who devote their life and studies to the redemption of Africa. It is this commitment to my work that has sustained me in times of melancholy, and it is this commitment to Africa and African culture that has been my passport into many places I would not otherwise have been admitted.

—**Brother Adisa S. Oji**

Chapter 8

LOOK FOR ME IN THE WHIRLWIND

He went through his checklist. It seemed endless. Clothing, necessities; miscellaneous—toilet paper, toothpaste, soap, rags, towels, underwear, socks, T-shirts, pants, pairs of running shoes, tensor bands, handkerchiefs, track shorts, gifts, lotion, sunglasses, malaria pills, medication—the list went on; reading materials and books—*Race First, Afrocentricity, Bluest Eyes, Malcolm X, 100 Amazing Facts, Blacks Perfect Pictures, Africa on a Shoe String, Power to the People*; travel documents—passport, immigration papers, immunization card, student card, photocopy of initial name change document, MACPRI info stating purpose of trip, press passes, citizenship info, passport photos, phone numbers, addresses, contact list, etc.

After weeks of preparation, Oji was finally ready. He had everything except a visa.

Toronto International Airport. January 23, 1991, 11:30 p.m. As the plane taxied down the runway readying for take-off, Oji calmed himself. Not everything was settled. As he prepared mentally for what he was about to do, his mind turned to the missing visa. He was going to need one. He wasn't sure how he'd get it. He was embarking on a long trip with an extended stay-over scheduled to last fifteen hours in London with no definite plan as to how he was going to pass the time. His travelling companion and guide, Kwame, the friend of a friend who just happened to be travelling on the same flight heading to the same destination, had only introduced himself minutes before. They were virtual strangers. Kwame, who resided in Toronto, was originally from Kumase, a city in the Ashanti region of Ghana. He was making the same trip on the same day; for Oji, this was a small comfort. Travelling with someone who had made this sojourn many times before would be helpful.

This was Oji's first trip to Africa. Presently, his eyes were hurting. He could feel the weight of exhaustion. Yet his heart felt right. Deep down he could sense a change within himself as he relaxed into his seat to buckle up. He was going through a transformative journey of a special kind. No doubt, this trip heightened his awareness that much more. He felt a profound significance in its meaning. Yes, he was going home, but to put it more directly, he was coming home to himself, coming home to his mother land. At first, he didn't know if he'd ever make it to Africa. He never thought he would be able to afford it. Still, he believed. Things took a positive turn when a Rastaman in Kingston, Jamaica, told him to stop *believing* and *know* that he would go. From then on, what began only as a dream slowly morphed into reality. He was on his way to Ghana, gateway to his ancestral homeland, on his way to soul restoration.

He had been told to be careful, to hold on to his belongings, never to overstay his hospitality. Definitely no filming when dealing with officials. Most Ghanaians speak Gao and Ashanti, he was told. Kwame taught him a few useful phrases, phrases he soon forgot in the fog of fatigue. The awful-tasting meals he had to endure during the overnight flight didn't help either.

At eight-twenty the following morning, they finally arrived in London. He had not slept. Sleep had been erratic. It had been erratic over the past three years, made worse recently by the episode with the Royal Ontario Museum and the pending criminal charges hanging over his head. Preparing for this trip had been a whirlwind. Of nagging concern was the unresolved matter of the visa. Some people told him he did not need one; others told him that he did. Kwame advised him that a visa was essential, but not to worry, he could easily get one in Accra for about US$20. Still, not having a visa caused him anxiety. The whole trip could fall apart if he could not get one. It would be a disaster. As fate would have it, the long layover provided an opportunity to get a visa in London from the Ghanaian High Commission. It took effort, multiple phone calls, and money; forty pounds for taxi to 38 Queen's Gate and another forty for the visa itself. Initially, he was told he could not get the visa until the following Monday, time he did not have. To put in a rush order would cost him even more.

With Kwame's help, he was able to get the visa much earlier than expected. Thankfully, disaster was averted. After a taxi ride to Heathrow followed by the Speedlink airport bus to Gatwick, they returned to the airport to await their next departure.

Junk food and two beers later, the two travellers, tried as they may, still could not sleep. The noise and the airport's cold temperature made rest difficult. Tensions in the Gulf Region at the time meant they had to be on high alert. The world seemed to be sitting on a knife's edge, waiting for the worse. Security guards roamed everywhere, patrolling by every ten minutes as the public address system blared frequent announcements instructing passengers to hold on to their luggage or otherwise have them destroyed. In this surreal setting, the two men passed the time exchanging life lessons, mostly with Kwame offering language instructions on Ashanti conversational expressions such as "How are you?" and so on.

As time for departure approached, Oji made a phone call to Accra to arrange for his pickup. His contact was Aunty Gladys, the mother of Kofi Fefe, who lived in Toronto. Without hesitation, Kofi, on hearing of Oji's intention to visit Ghana, had offered his mother's place as a destination. Kwame again acted as his translator, helping to make the necessary arrangements during a lengthy phone call costing £1.50. Aunty Gladys had been expecting Oji for some time, excitedly preparing for his arrival, and she told him so. Nothing was going to be spared for his comfort. Having never met in person before, Oji had to offer up a description of himself—very tall, wearing black-rimmed glasses, and carrying a green army knapsack. He had identified himself to Aunty Gladys as Kofi's friend from Toronto; she in turn told him that she would be holding two signs with his name on it, a sign he should look out for when he arrived.

On January 25, 1991, at 6:40 a.m., Oji finally touched down at Accra airport. He was armed with his camera along with big yet-to-be tested ideas about Africa. He was in Africa at last and for the very first time. He wouldn't kiss the ground, at least not yet. He had no intention to. He was happy to be finally on the continent but was not sentimental about it. He kept his head, preferring to remain businesslike, practical. Even so, he could not escape his excitement. The first time he had ever set foot on a plane to go anywhere was when he was eight years old—seventeen years ago when he left Jamaica for Canada. Now, here he was setting foot in Africa, looking to meet a stranger named Aunty Gladys who was eagerly awaiting his arrival. He had heard about the sensationally profitable triangular trade between Europe, Africa, and the Americas in which the slave trade—the forced mass migration of millions of enslaved Africans—was the backbone. He had also learned of free Africans who travelled to the New World long before the arrival of Columbus. Now, here he was, a displaced African freely returning from the so-called New World to his traditional place of origin.

True to her word, Aunty Gladys stood waiting for him, her companion holding a sign emblazoned with the letters "OG." Oji had seen the sign but looked past it several times, never realizing it was meant for him.

After clearing immigration, the small delegation of Aunty Gladys and her assistant Bogardi, Kwame and Oji set off in a private passenger vehicle to the residence of Kofi Boako in LeBone. On arrival at the residence, Oji immediately experienced the greatest hospitality he had ever received up until that time; the feeling of being the recipient of unqualified deep generosity was consistent throughout his stay. It was an experience he had never before enjoyed to this extent. As refreshments were served, he settled into a spacious living room beautifully laid out with fine furnishings, the wall adorned with coloured as well as black-and-white framed family photos.

He had yet to see the entire house, but from where he stood, he could tell the place was expansive. The enormous room provided for his lodging was considerably larger than the largest room in his own home in Toronto. In it were three large armchairs, night tables, and cupboards in addition to two well-made beds adorned with stylish pillows. There were two entrances to the room, each having doors that could be secured. Conveniently located beyond another door was the bathroom. The entire property could best be described as an estate. Once he got to see it, he learned that there were several buildings on the property, including two beauty parlours, a tailor's shop, a kitchen, plus workers' accommodations. The property reminded him of a small self-contained community, the magnitude of it leading him to wonder at his good fortune. He was being hosted in the home of two African diplomats, one of whom had been a government minister in Ghana's first independent administration led by Kwame Nkrumah. The room in which he stayed was also the room in which Malcolm X was accommodated during one of the revolutionary leader's visits to Africa. For Oji, his first visit to *the* mother country was shaping up to be beyond his wildest imagination.

The thought of Malcolm X lingered as Oji wandered about the property. After he had broken ties with the Nation of Islam, Malcolm X's visit to Africa would influence his intellectual and spiritual evolution as he transformed himself into El Haj Malik Shabazz to become an independent Pan-African leader beyond the narrow polemic of US racism. As if in parallel, Oji contemplated on his own life and how it was about to change. Malcolm X's words—*Nobody can give you freedom. Nobody can give you equality or justice or anything. If you are a man, you take it*—had spurred him on. Quickened, Oji could feel a deep change impacting him, moving him in ways he himself could not immediately fully understand.

In the days that followed, he allowed himself to relax, immersing himself in the hospitality he was offered. He soaked up Ghanaian culture, its cuisine, and its vibe with ease, while spending time meeting and interacting with local children and grownups. They were grateful for his presence, even as he was grateful for their welcome. Whenever an opportunity presented itself, he would share what he knew, building bridges of understanding whenever he could. When Yaw, Kofi's cousin, for example, mentioned that he didn't know much about Malcolm X or Marcus Garvey, Oji took the time to share reading materials with him, enlightening Yaw through engaging conversations. This reciprocity—giving and receiving—would typify his entire stay.

"Look for me in the whirlwind," he said. He was a fierce fighter for freedom. He was a fraudulent imposter whose ineptitude led to the implosion of a mass movement. He led his people with pride and unbridled self-confidence. He was full of bombast, overly ambitious, and in the opinion of some, outlandish with no real sustainable program. He was the calm before the storm; he was the storm after the calm. He was a flash of lightning; he was the thunderbolt that followed. He was a game changer; he was changed by the game. He was a heartthrob; he was the heartbreak, a man whose heart was broken in the end. He made his people see themselves as kings and queens; he died a pauper in the shadow of obscurity. He was ferocious and defiant; he was led like a lamb to the slaughter. He spoke truth to power; he was overpowered by the truth. He bought his people's freedom with a heavy price; in the end, it is said he was betrayed then sold for rice.

In the whirlwind of public opinion, Marcus Garvey represents different things to different people. So long gone, his drums now seemingly silent, his message apparently subdued, he may be, for some, but a memory. Nonetheless, his unmistakable beats can still be heard by many, his voice enduring from generation to generation. He can be heard in the torrid whirlwind where contradictions swirl like a storm around his remembrance. You can see him in red, black, and green, and catch his essence at night-time on street corners far and wide where his light still glows. His rich spirit continues to permeate in and around the letters *U, N, I* and *A*, the organization he created—the Universal Negro Improvement Association. The depth of his passionate plea for unity in his slogan—"One God, one aim, one destiny"—still echoes like a clarion call throughout all the ages.

Better to light a candle than to curse the dark. Curse the dark, he did; but what a candle he was. While others hated them, he loved the dark-skinned people of the world. What he hated was the darkness that enveloped them. Reminiscent of a flamethrower, he punctured the dense darkness with his burning spear, scorching the unjust together with their vile injustices. The name and personage of Marcus Garvey remains a lasting symbol of insurgency, an iconic figure whose legacy is so deeply profound that many are apt to mythologize and canonize him along with his message. He has been called the Black Moses, often stylized as a liberator. For some he remains a prophet. By the end of his life, he seemed to have failed in achieving his dreams. In the latter days as he struggled to come to terms with his demise, a cloud of disappointment descended on him, a disenchanted man apparently brought low. His seeming fall from grace notwithstanding, Marcus Garvey, throughout his life and work, called on forces that were up until then dormant, forces that, when unleashed, could never be recalled. The man—his presence, his power, and his passionate love for Africa and people of African ancestry—would break the psychological stranglehold of the creed of White supremacy, unquestionably and forever. He came, he assessed, and he aroused, advocated, admonished, organized, and stomped. He stomped on the ideology of Black racial inferiority, crumpling it under his feet, crushing it in utter defeat. And then he was gone ... well, sort of.

When Oji decided to visit Africa, the philosophy and opinions of Marcus Garvey were already tucked away in his consciousness. Thoughts of Garvey meandered through his reflections as he went to bed late at night, mingling with more mundane memories of meals consumed during the passing days—meals of palm nut soup, fish and rice, and *kele wele* (a dish consisting of deep-fried plantains spiced with ginger and black pepper). As he settled down to rest, visions of traditional cultural dances he had seen at Coco Beach earlier in the day made their way into his reverie—the high-energy dancers, their brilliant colours. He could still hear the hypnotic pulsating drumbeats.

On cool mornings before mosquitoes went wild, Oji would awake to fresh fruits for breakfast. He often fraternized with the children, observing them as they played and spoke in their mother tongue. He would try to remember their names —Akos, Asibi, Naomi, Kofi, Kwame, Kobena, and so on. Regularly, he listened to Bob Marley songs, ever so popular among the children and people, and to reggaefied highlife music. Indeed, he lived and loved each day of his stay, feeling and knowing that he was the lost son and brother finally returning home, even as Marcus Garvey had urged so many to do.

Oji delighted in discussing history. Whenever the opportunity presented itself, he would talk culture and politics with his hosts or with folks he met and travelled with. Rarely did he ever have to pay for much. Most, if not all, of his needs were met through the generosity and kindness of those with whom he spent his time. For this he was truly grateful. He was aware that his hosts and their circle of relatives and friends, such as Esi, Chovies, Kofi, and others, were some of the wealthiest people in Ghana. They were members of a professional business class, independent, privileged, and certainly influential. The high standing of the women, all high achievers, particularly impressed him. Recognizing that Oji's budget was limited, everyone collectively went out of their way to ensure that he had all he needed. Aunty Gladys soon became his adopted African mother. She was very keen to see to it that his trip to Africa was fruitful. She refused to accept any monetary compensation from him despite his many attempts to discourage her. Ignoring his kind refusals, she went to great lengths to assure him that he was in good hands. She promised that he would gain weight before returning to Canada, meaning that she was going to feed him well. Indeed, upon his return to Canada, Oji would be pounds heavier than when he left.

Three days into his visit, Kofi called from Toronto to check on Oji. Oji was having a great time at Kofi's mother's home, and Kofi was pleased to hear. In return, Oji asked Kofi to reach out to his own mother, Geraldine. Oji wanted to assure her that he was okay. He promised he would write her soon. Oji also wanted to maintain contact with a number of associates in Toronto. To this end, he asked Kofi to keep them advised of his experiences, his hopes and expectations for when he returned. Aside from his mother, he especially had one woman who was close to his heart, lingering always in his thoughts. In all the fuss, he had found love, or its better to say love found him. Either way, he had a special greeting for this woman who held his affections. With each passing day in Ghana, it began to dawn on Oji that his visit to Africa was not only about him. His sojourn was also for many others who wanted to reconnect with their African roots and ancestry but who, for a variety of reasons, could not.

It is August 3, 1920, and New York's Madison Square Garden is ablaze with twenty-five thousand Black people. They had come from many directions—Bermuda, Jamaica, Nigeria, Panama, St. Lucia—but mostly from Harlem and urban America. This was not a protest. It was a celebration. They gathered to commemorate the inauguration of the first International Convention of the Negro Peoples of the World. Under a glorious sun, the twenty-five thousand strong marched in pomp and pageantry, a display of commercial power and civic pride as they gathered to showcase Pan-African strength. In the history of the modern world, no one had ever witnessed a gathering of this nature before. "Marching, marching, marching noon 'til night. Who knew that so many Negroes were on earth?" reflected Harlem poet, Langston Hughes.

The excitement began two days before on August 1 and would run through to the end of September. The convention began reverentially in the morning with prayer, followed by a solemn, silent, but powerfully moving march through Harlem streets. Then, only the rhythmic pitter-patter of marching feet could be heard. When the Universal Negro Improvement Association (UNIA) delegates convened at the association's headquarters at Liberty Hall in Harlem for the first time, the celebratory mood rose to a palpable pitch, the air charged with great expectation. Over the following days, delegates adopted and agreed on a formal charter and established a leadership structure for their organization. They would co-sign the Declaration of Rights of the Negro Peoples of the World, which, among other things, insisted that the miseducation of Black school children should cease, that Black school children be taught African history and a right knowledge of themselves. A president-general was elected, branches were recognized, and an anthem—the "Universal Ethiopian Anthem," composed especially for the occasion—was adopted. Red, black, and green were chosen as the official emblematic colours for the organization's flag.

With a new sense of organized empowerment, the parade snaked its way through New York City on August 3 as immaculately uniformed men and women quickstepped down Lennox Avenue, moving in unison to the masterful sound of majestic marching bands. With ceremonial swords in hand, the African Legion marched, so too, Black Cross nurses and children. It was epic, something to behold. Everyone smartly dressed, some in ceremonial suits adorned by badges, hands poised in white gloves, the scene was like a floating sea of crowns and headdresses of plumed hats. It was as if a levee had broken, setting free a river of liberated men, women, and children who now moved like an army, flowing forward as one people with one destiny.

The band played "Onward Christian Soldiers," radiating discipline, order, and decorum. There was a feeling that Black folks had finally arrived, ready to claim their inherent right to dignity, self-respect, and self-determination. Just a few days before, they had been invisible; like children, they were required to be seen, not heard. But today, it was different; today, they would be seen *and* heard. Just a few days before, they were lowly bellhops, cooks, maids, porters, stevedores, labourers, shopkeepers, and shoeshine *boys*. Yesterday, they were just common folk with no titles in front of their names, casually referred to as *boy* or *George* or, at other times, more derisively as *coons* or *niggers*. Today, they were royal citizens of a new kingdom. Yesterday, they were the wretched of the earth, victims of a historical wrong. Today, they were the salt of the universe rising in triumph, singing a new song. Yesterday, they were nobody. Today, they were somebody.

Heading the pageant, behind four mounted police officers, were the president of the Black Star Line and the secretary of the Negro Factories Corporation, both entities created by the UNIA. Both officials were also mounted on horseback. Bringing up the rear of the long spectacular procession were five hundred automobiles, trailed by two other mounted policemen. Somewhere further up front was a convertible seating the resplendent mayor of Monrovia. Beside him, regaled in full black attire, was a short heavyset man with the confident aura of royalty. He was dressed in his robe of office, wearing a feathered headdress, waving magnificently. This was Marcus Garvey the day before his thirty-third birthday. While some critics would colour this day in tones of a parody, painting the occasion as a ridiculously poor imitation of royalty, others more favourable knew "*thy kingdom had come,*" that a special spell had been cast. The pageantry orchestrated by the man with the feathered headdress would be a milestone in the annals of history. Seven years later, at age forty, Marcus Garvey would be serving time in a penitentiary. But on August 3, 1920, he was in ascendancy, leading New York and the Black world in a show of unity, igniting a movement that would have its visible beginning in this delirious and magnificent moment.

August 3, 1920, was the greatest demonstration of Black glory and power in the history of North America, then and since. The men, women and children who congregated were not begging for rights. They were claiming and affirming what was already theirs. When Marcus Garvey rose to speak later that evening, it would be momentous. For those who were present, it was breathtaking as it was empowering. For a while, the hellish existence faced by people of African ancestry momentarily ceased, held at bay, oppression briefly forgotten. The promise land seemed now only up ahead. Seven more UNIA conventions would follow this grand inauguration, four held in New York in 1921, 1922, 1924, and 1926. Two would be held in Kingston, Jamaica: 1929 and 1934. Toronto, Canada, would follow in 1938, punctuating the end of what was, in modern history, the first global mass movement of Black people in solidarity. Try as it may, the world could never return to what it used to be.

The 1920 Declaration of Rights of the Negro Peoples of the World insisted, among other things, that the miseducation of Black school children should cease (*Negro World*, July 31, 1936).

Marcus Garvey, in partnership with his wife Amy Ashwood, was editor and publisher of the *Negro World*. The broadsheet newspaper published weekly between 1918 and 1933 had primary distribution in New York. In an editorial written on February 6, 1926, Garvey wrote the following:

> It does not mean that all Negroes must leave America and the West Indies and go to Africa ... We say to all Negroes in America, West Indies and elsewhere, seize all opportunities that come to you, but remember our success educationally, industrially and politically is based upon the protection of a nation founded by ourselves. And that nation can be nowhere else but in Africa.

These words, written so long ago, appeared to have jumped off the pages of the *Negro World*, travelled across several generations before landing in the heart of a young man named Adisa Oji. For when promptings emanating from these words, written sixty-five years before, began to nudge him, he could do nothing else but respond affirmatively.

One day as he sat at Coco Beach observing the scene, Oji wondered if this was what Marcus Garvey had in mind. Situated along the Atlantic coast, known once as the Gold Coast, Coco Beach is now a place of leisure, an attraction for locals and tourists alike. It was a day of gaiety. Like any other day at the beach, people of all races rubbed shoulders, many dancing to live or recorded music. As far as the eye could see, there were local Ghanaians, adults, children, performers, and vendors far and wide. Among them were collections of tourists; some roving about, others seated beneath the shade of beach umbrellas to protect themselves from the searing heat. Altogether, it was a party scene, an incongruous wonder considering that close to five hundred years ago the European exportation of enslaved Africans from this beach was once a major enterprise.

More directly, Oji wondered how he would begin to put into practice Marcus Garvey's vision of self-determination and self-reliance. As was his habit, he engaged people in conversation looking for clues, trying to understand what Ghanaian life was like. Presently he was speaking to a soldier stationed on the beach whose assignment it was to guard against thieves and pickpockets. The soldier, seated at a table with a plate of food set before him, was armed with a gun and an ample supply of cigarettes. Beach patrons passing by showed great interest in his weapon. Some brave enough sought permission from the soldier to touch it. At one point, the soldier removed the cartridge to allow a man to inspect the unloaded weapon. Oji also reached over to touch it, but he was politely denied. In a moment of reflection, Oji was left to conclude: Whatever revolution Marcus Garvey may have had in mind, it would not be achieved with a gun, loaded or not.

In contrast to the crowded shores of Coco Beach was the placid compound of a wise, timeworn elderly woman who hosted Oji later that week. The profound encounter would leave a lasting impression. He already had set ideas about his African self-identity. He had no misgivings about his place of belonging when he entered her compound that day. He was therefore startled when the old woman addressed him as *Obroni*, a term roughly translated as "White man." The suggestion caught him off-guard. That he was out of place, that he was not quite African, that he was an outsider who did not belong had never crossed his mind. Despite this off-putting beginning, the elderly woman was kind. She offered to prepare plantains for him. Overcoming what appeared to have been an insult, Oji accepted her invitation. As time passed, he realized he had to leave earlier than planned; he would not be able to partake of the meal on account of how pressed he was for time. He anxiously hoped he would not disappoint or offend her by his sooner-than-later departure. After all, he already had a thorny start. As it turned out, the two had an invigorating conversation discussing an assortment of subject matters relating to Ghanaian history. The conversation was lively, made even more animated because of the elderly woman's growing curiosity. As she mellowed, Oji relaxed. As he relaxed, she offered him even more respect. As they talked, the elder grandmother probed the young man's understanding, querying why Africans who leave for America came back after a brief time more Americanized than Americans. She was curious to know how Oji was able to maintain his love and connection with his ancestral home. In the end, she expressed admiration for him. She was pleased that he was not a *sell-out* African who had forgotten his culture. Although his stay was too short to enjoy her plantains, he stayed long enough to impress her with his sincerity, thereby gaining her endorsement. By the time he was ready to leave, he had so earned her trust and respect she accorded him a tribute by referring to him as *Bibini*—Black man or African, a term of approval he would cherish for the remainder of his trip. With this anointment from an elderly grandmother, Oji's homecoming was now legitimate.

Through the old woman, he learned a lot about himself as she gently led him on an exploration beyond his own narrow self-perception. He could now see himself in a new and different light. Through this visit with the elder African grandmother, Oji came to better appreciate how others may see him and how he may see himself. Earlier on, he was not quite sure how he would be received in Africa. Now he could relax his fears and be himself.

Five days into the visit after much travelling, Oji began to experience flu-like symptoms. At day's end, he was exhausted, his energy failing him, preventing him from even showering after evening dinner. While he acknowledged his general fatigue, he attributed this instance to excess smoke to which he was exposed throughout his travels. To make matters worse, he had been caught in one of the downpours typical of the area. On this particular night, the electricity had gone out, leaving Aunt Gladys's home in darkness. While Aunty Gladys made sure he had candles, Esi offered him aspirins, which he refused. Oji, as a practice, did not take drugs. As an alternative, Esi offered him a special remedy. She gave him a bowl with water containing some kind of vapour. She told him to put it up to his face and to inhale while having a towel over his head. The reaction was swift. The strong vapour rapidly enveloped his face as it quickly entered his nostrils then into his lungs, causing him to cringe. As involuntary tears rolled down his face, he was tempted to violently throw the bowl aside but instead calmed himself. Once the excitement died down, he removed the towel from his head, his face stinging. Within five minutes his nose was cleared, his headache significantly less intense. Surprised and grateful for the quick recovery, he silently hoped he would be able to get some of the remedy to take back with him to Toronto. He slept peacefully that night, dreaming about how to bring Africa back to Canada.

Born and raised in Jamaica, Garvey spawned a Black nationalist movement that touched and influenced the lives of many individuals throughout North and Latin America, the Caribbean, Europe, and Africa. A far-reaching number of men and women either worked for or were members of his grassroots organization, which had branches worldwide. He was not the first or only proponent of Black pride and self-reliance; neither was he original in his ideas about Africa and its redemptive power. What Marcus Garvey gave to the theatre of race politics were his enigmatic qualities—his ability for mass mobilization coupled with his brash bravado and colourful self-confidence, which at the time were incomparable, certainly unimaginable for any Black person during his era. His innate gifts allowed him the distinction of becoming one of the most outstanding in his time. His vigour, his rapid-fire eloquence, his brilliant wit, his winning smile with flashing white teeth, his power of persuasiveness and ability to get people's attention were simply unparalleled. His belief in his mission, in himself, and the depth of his convictions seemed limitless.

Through Garvey's prolific work, multitudes came to espouse what has been termed the Back to Africa Movement. Before Garvey came to prominence, Africa had been caricatured as wild, primitive, and uncivilized. Africa was then popularly known as the Dark Continent, typified by images of backwardness. Christian refinements, strong injections of White sponsored cultural enlightenment, were considered to be remedies for Africa's woes. To many who were uninformed, Africa had no ancient history of which to boast, no culture, in the elitist sense, to celebrate or honour. Ties to Africa were frequently downplayed by Black people, if not denied. Indeed, prior to Garvey's arrival and during his era, to be associated with Africa as a Black person was seen not as something to be proud of but rather as a source of shame. *Disinformation* and *fake news* are not recent.

There is irony here. While popular propaganda degraded Africa as unworthy during this period, and while the African Black Diaspora was made to feel ashamed of being African, Europeans were making it their business to flock to Africa in large numbers in search of opportunities to enrich themselves. You will recall that Europe raided Africa in the late nineteenth century in what has been described as the Scramble for Africa, with the Partitioning of Africa soon to follow as Europeans powers, including Britain, Germany, Russia, France, Italy, Portugal, and Belgium, descended on the continent, dividing territories up between them like thieves sharing the spoils of a robbery. They did this through violence, warmongering, and gun-boat diplomacy, without any regard for the needs of local indigenous African communities. Realizing the staggering mutual benefits to be derived, a consensus was established in which European nations unleashed their imperialist agendas with one accord. By this means, they acted with great fervour and in relative peace, without worry about rivalling and fighting each other. Together, they jointly carved up the continent between them, using a range of questionable pacts and agreements with weak local leaders, imposing them by force if necessary, in a bid to expropriate a significant amount of Africa's natural wealth. During the preceding era of slavery, Europeans raided Africa for its human resources, exploiting its people for "free labour," Britain alone commanding the lion's share of over three million enslaved Africans. Now, during the era of imperialism, Africa was raided again, this time exploited for its natural resources—coal, cotton, diamond, gold, ivory, palm oil, rubber—and for its strategic and political value. It was also during this period that significant caches of African art and cultural assets were pillaged, carted off to Europe and to far-flung places throughout the colonial world where they were used in some cases as doorstoppers but above all acquired for profit and brandished as trophies.

Garvey and other radical thinkers were savvy enough to understand this duplicity. They understood that Africa's assets were being fraudulently devalued for good effect, that this was a prelude to stealthily taking away those same assets for the benefit of Europe. He, and others who were consciously aware, also understood that colonial domination was based on the idea of White supremacy and its corollary of Black inferiority. They also surmised that once the myth of Black inferiority was destroyed, then other myths would also collapse, and with it, the pervasive power of colonialism. It was upon this basis that the UNIA under Garvey's leadership sought to have representation at the Versailles Peace Conference following the conclusion of the First World War. It was Garvey's belief that Germany's former colonial possessions in Africa should be returned to Africans. He expected the Allied powers to consent to such an arrangement. He was absolutely convinced that Cameroon and Tanganyika (present-day Tanzania) should be transferred to UNIA's control. All these proposals were regarded as outlandish by the world powers of the day. As far as Garvey was concerned, this was all the more reason to put his proposals forward. Outlandish or not, standing aside or doing nothing and being a passive bystander, this for Garvey was preposterous. As far as he was concerned, imperialism had to be firmly challenged. Such was the breath and daring of Garvey's conceptualizations, always ambitious, invariably audacious.

This unprecedented demand may have been regarded as outrageous by others. However, for Garvey, the elevation of Africa was a matter of course, an outlook long overdue. For Garvey, it was justifiable time to invoke a strong belief in Africa's value, to highlight Africa's power to uplift and inspire displaced Africans everywhere. Garvey's fearlessness was also a reflection of his innate self-confidence and the faith he had in the cause he represented. As he was often quoted: "If you have no confidence in self, you are twice defeated in the race of life. With confidence, you have won even before you have started."

Garvey's self-confidence was uncommon. He came by it honestly as he struggled to find his own purpose. On his path, he encountered his share of setbacks and detours, frequently contending with strong opposition. He was up against strongly held negative belief systems and encrusted mindsets. Unwittingly, a number of unawakened Blacks living in North America and the Caribbean during the pre-Garvey years had internalized their timidity. They were afraid of their own shadow, a learned behaviour pattern. Largely existing in the shadows to which they were relegated, this segment of Black existence cared or knew little of their own or of Africa's power. While Europeans were confidently attaching themselves to Africa in ways that were enriching, numerous African descendants were divorcing themselves from the continent in ways that were self-defeating. According to Garvey, the "Negro slept a thousand years, while white men moved along, and so he sheds his bitter tears as white men sing their song." Before Garvey, Black consciousness seemed dormant; there appeared to be an anathema or an aversion to all things African, a dense prevailing apathy, a mentality that appeared difficult to break through.

In and around 1917, however, the transformative influence of Marcus Garvey began to erase this loathing or at least supplant it. As the charismatic and powerful populist activist advanced his radical African image revolution in the United States of America, a new generation, there and elsewhere, began to reawaken to their birthright. Tired and weary from the injury inflicted by oppression brought about by the philosophy and practice of White supremacy, Black folks began to embrace Garvey's ethos like an antidote. Sensing the arrival of a new day, many rose in exultation to claim or reclaim their African identity by reaching out to connect with a newly envisioned Africa, which they now regarded as a part of their inheritance. Instead of Blackness being a stigma, it now became a badge of pride. "The night is beautiful, so the faces of my people," wrote the poet Langston Hughes. The slogan "Black is beautiful" very likely had its roots here. Marcus Garvey is the shoulder upon which Black leaders, who followed, would stand. He is the first person in modern history to popularize Black consciousness on a global scale, empowering Black communities worldwide with an infused sense of dignity and destiny.

One day, Esi and Yaw took Oji to an art centre where he witnessed beautiful art pieces. He was so moved he began making personal connections with the artisans, many of whom expressed an interest in exporting their work to a wider global market. Their products were wide-ranging, including sculptures, carvings, and fertility fetishes from the Fanti and Ashanti cultures. Meticulously, Oji made notes of each piece he observed, making specific reference to their price in the local currency (cedi) together with a brief title or description. "Two heads are better than one," "Unity is strength," "Round fetishes are Ashanti," "Long fetishes are Cape Coast Fanti," and so on. He would document stall numbers. If the vendors were willing, he would, in addition, take down their phone contact.

The fetishes, he observed, were akin to personal identification. Wearing them identified where you were from and to which group you belonged. Voodoo doll fetishes were from Benin City, while other types were from the Ivory Coast. Some of the art forms told mini stories, while others told epic folk tales. One, a Fanti carving, illustrated a missionary transporting recently purchased "*slaves.*" Another, made of brass, depicted a woman selling goat milk, while another was illustrative of the water bearer. There were also games or board games such as a brass chessboard from Burkina Faso. Most outstanding was a brass piece depicting a king and queen playing a game called Oware.

Esi and Yaw later took Oji to visit the Ghana National Museum where a tour guide took him through the exhibits explaining their meaning and history. In order to take his camera along, Oji was required to pay a special fee, this in addition to an entrance fee. As a non-Ghanaian, he was furthermore expected to pay more than his hosts. Oji took this as an affront. He felt he was being overcharged. On a much deeper level, he saw himself as an African returning home. As such, he felt deserving of the same privileges as his African hosts and therefore questioned the differential treatment. He may also have felt that his legitimacy as a returning African was being questioned. "Who do you think you are? What are you doing here?" "Obroni!" Or maybe it was a lingering hangover having to do with a sore memory regarding museums and their often profit-driven fundraising practices conducted in the name of culture. Whatever the reason, he was less than enamoured with the museums' excessive demands.

Esi, however, persuaded him to remain calm, advising him not to be overly concerned. She reasoned that money was of little consequence, particularly when compared to the greater significance of his presence in Ghana. She reminded him that whereas the memory of his first visit to Africa and to Ghana would have lasting value, money on the other hand, which is only material in nature, is likely to come and go. Esi's compelling rationale made sense. As was typical, Esi, an independent businesswoman of means, covered Oji's cost. With less misgiving, Oji was able to continue his tour while enjoying the reassuring companionship of his hosts.

First founded in Jamaica in July 1914, the UNIA had as its tag line "Africa for Africans, at home and abroad." It was decidedly a Pan-African organization, which grew to worldwide prominence when the first North American branch was established in Harlem, New York, in 1917. The Harlem headquarters, aptly named Liberty Hall, spawned many other Liberty Halls around the globe. Garvey, through his fiery and compelling speeches and his indefatigable hard work, soon found wide support throughout the diaspora. From its inception, the UNIA was firmly grounded in a bottom-up as opposed to a top-down organizational culture. Garvey's used organic, people-centred approaches to harness the energy, natural skills of ordinary men and women to achieve extraordinary results. News of UNIA activities, for instance, travelled globally by word of mouth via migrant and domestic workers, sailors, and agents travelling far and wide. Also finding common cause with Garvey, if only for a time, were intellectuals and radical thinkers with revolutionary leanings toward the political left. By 1920, the association boasted a membership of two million, putting the organization in direct contention with other established power blocs. The American federal government, for one, was concerned about the considerable impact of Garvey's radical ideas. Consequently, Garvey and his organization were subject to surveillance, harassment, the Federal Bureau of Investigation (FBI) playing interference with their activities, covertly and overtly. Meanwhile, on the other hand was the Ku Klux Klan, another ominous threat, especially in the US south where UNIA membership surged. Between these two formidable antagonists, it is a wonder the UNIA thrived as it did.

An attempt was once made on Garvey's life. He became the target of gun fire, one shot reportedly hitting him in the leg. The alleged shooter, a Black man, was prepared to come forward to confess. Before he could do so however, he was discovered mysteriously dead. Garvey might not have been fearful, but he was pragmatic enough to understand the risk involved in pushing forward with his anti-racist, anti-imperialist agenda. He was known to have chameleon-like qualities capable of bending this way or that depending on the circumstances, while maintaining his integrity. Whereas before he vociferously challenged and condemned colonialism and Jim Crow, he later toned down his anticolonial/anti-White supremacy rhetoric, redirecting his focus instead on a race-first orientation, advocating for race consciousness along with promoting repatriation to Africa.

It was during this phase that Garvey was criticized for his seemingly ridiculous overtures to White supremacists, including the Klan. This made him vulnerable to harsh criticism from other Black leaders such as W. B. Du Bois, who was outraged by Garvey's pragmatism. Du Bois denounced Garvey for being a *lunatic or a traitor.* Garvey in turn shot back at Du Bois, calling him a *lazy dependent mulatto.* The acrimony between both men was disconcerting considering that they were both regarded as champions, each in their own right, in the fight for equality. This would be one of those divisive and low moments in the Black liberation movement. Instead of forging formidable alliances, internal feuding would fracture its support base. This would not be the first time, nor would it be the last.

As for Garvey's tango with the Klan, this was an example of the political tight rope he had to walk, the fire of coals over which he had to run in order to hold his organization together. Many among his growing membership lived in the American south where racism was rife. In the deep South—Mississippi, Alabama, Georgia—the Klan had legitimacy and acceptance. For this reason, Garvey refrained from declaring open war against the Klan for fear of jeopardizing the safety of his membership, their families and their homes. He had to be tactful while uncompromising. But even this too had its challenges. Despite these setbacks, and maybe even because of them, the Garvey's movement became a way of life for many who adopted his philosophy of Black pride, self-reliance, and Africentricity.

As with any ambitious Jamaican entering a foreign land with big dreams, Marcus Garvey was met with a mix of ridicule, suspicion, apathy, and a host of obstacles. These became even more pronounced when he ventured into the American political arena. Some individuals to whom he initially turned to for help began to regard him as a cocky upstart. In other instances, he was seen as an irritating nuisance from the *islands*. Because of his bold and unprecedented vision, it was not uncommon for others to ask "Who do you think you are? What are you doing here?" His legitimacy was frequently questioned.

Malcolm X's visit to Ghana in May 1964 was always a point of curiosity for Oji. He felt honoured to be dwelling in the same residence where this lightning rod of Pan-Africanism once stayed. At every possible opportunity, he would inquire about Malcolm's visit to Ghana from anyone who knew anything about it.

Oji considered himself a documentarian. For this reason, he carried his camera everywhere he went. He made regular checklists of items to photograph. The marketplaces where women carried loads of baskets on their heads intrigued him. So too the women with babies strapped to their backs, women vending at market stalls, basket weavers, and the crowded public scenes at bus terminals. Capturing vivid details of life in Ghana through photography—including animal life, farming activity, historical artifacts, people at work or at play, the essence of day-to-day existence—increasingly became his passion. He often took snapshots in public places such as restaurants or at the beach. Almost just as often, he was warned to keep a keen eye on his camera or not to carry it at all for fear it might be stolen. Esi called the camera his *lifeline*. Aunty Gladys described it as his *baby*. Oji agreed with both portrayals.

Of particular appeal were the images of children as they skipped or played or as they went to and from school dressed in uniforms or while they were in class learning. The children's natural joy, their beauty, their innocence appealed to him as he watched them go about their daily lives. He could see beyond the immediate, visualizing their real and future potential for greatness. They reminded him of his own childhood. It was as if his childhood gaiety was being reflected back to him. In turn, he wondered what it would be like if the children could one day see themselves being reflected back at them. One night, as he sat with a few of the children, he took the time to tell them a story of how and when Africans first came to North America and how they are now returning home to Africa. By so doing, he was describing how he and the children were inextricably linked. Together, they were like ends of a broken circle finally reuniting, each complementing the other.

During one of his tours, one important object above all caught Oji's eye. It would cost him 400 cedis. That was only to shoot it; that was how much he would be charged for each photo he took in the military museum. The object in question was the gun used by Queen Mother Nana Yaa Asantewaa in her fight against the British. Queen Mother Nana Yaa Asantewaa (1863–1923) is an important figure in the history of modern Ghana. When Ashanti men were fearful of fighting the British in the early twentieth century, she had the courage to rally her community, calling on them to join her in resisting British imperialist domination. Challenge, struggle, confrontation, and adversity were persistent themes weaving through the lives of the individuals who Oji admired and who inspired him even as he faced his own challenges and adversity. One such person was Martin Luther King Jr., who himself had made a bold statement declaring that the "ultimate measure of a man is not where he stands in moments of comfort and convenience, but where he stands at times of challenge and controversy." Another inspirational voice was Frederick Douglass, who was unequivocal when he said, "Power conceded nothing without a demand. It never will and it never did. Find out just what any people will quietly submit to and you have found out the exact measure of injustice and wrong which will be imposed upon them, and these will continue till they are resisted with either words or blows, or with both."

These words rang true for Oji and reminded him of the living legacy of Nana Yaa Asantewaa. That she was an exceptional woman in an exceptional time resonated strongly with him. Whenever he contemplated his own ordeal or thought about wavering in the face of injustice, he often took encouragement from her life and from all the other luminaries he admired.

At the end of each day, if he had the energy, Oji would go to bed reading or meditating on the lives of the heroes he admired. This became his daily ritual while in Ghana. He often thought about the Golden Stool and how the Ashanti king Osei Tutu (1671–1731), together with his friend, spiritual advisor and chief priest, Okomfo Anokye, envisioned the idea of invoking the power invested in the stool to unite the various people of the Ashanti kingdom. The stool is said to embody the spirit of the Ashanti nation, their power, wealth, health, bravery, and well-being. According to custom, the stool is required to remain permanently stationed in Kumasi to ensure the Ashanti nation's vitality and power. The founding of the Ashanti Confederation would inspire other confederations such as the Fanti and the Ga, both of which emerged at a later date in Ghana's long history. On many nights, with these and other thoughts drifting through his head, Oji would float off to sleep contemplating "Africa for Africans, at home and abroad" and the life of the man who inspired the idea.

Garveyism has had a long, colourful, dramatic history, a legacy that would not be complete without controversy. Garvey's fiery rage was unsettling for some. Some found his rigid determination distasteful. To his critics, his endeavours were grandiose, overly ambitious, out of reach, and unrealistic. He was regarded with skepticism by some of his contemporaries, many of whom were themselves leading public figures, some perhaps motivated by envy. But for others, Garvey's greatness was undeniable. By any measure, his audacity, the bold programs he initiated were tantamount to strokes of genius.

Garvey owned and ran several newspapers throughout his life including the previously mentioned *Negro World* (1918), *The Blackman* (1929), and *The New Jamaican* (1929). Through these outlets, he was able to advance his ideas, drawing attention to matters relating to the aspirations of the peasant working class. His ability to use print media to get his message across was unrivalled, his campaigns soon becoming the template for future media houses.

The widely disseminated *Negro World*, the UNIA's newspaper, had significant readership. Garvey's newspapers were considered so radical some governments banned their distribution.

Convinced that Black liberation could come only from Black success in business, Garvey, through the auspices of the UNIA, created the Negro Factories Corporation in 1920. The corporation's goal was to support the promotion and success of Black owned and controlled manufacturing enterprises, one of which was a factory specializing in the production of Black dolls. This one factory alone is said to have employed more than a thousand Black Americans.

The Black Star Line of 1919 was another ingenious scheme that helped to boost the Garvey movement, persuading many to believe in the power of collective endeavour. The enterprise owned three ships. One of them, the *SS Yarmouth*, an old ship purchased in Canada, was later renamed in memory of Frederick Douglass. Intended to serve as a commercial shipping line to foster Black trade, it also aimed to serve as a cruise line for Black passengers between America, Africa, and the Caribbean. However, after considerable negotiations the effort failed. The Black Star Line folded prematurely after only a few years of operation. Expensive ship maintenance, costly repairs, poor crew management, and organizational infighting undermined the effort. In 1922, when the American Federal Government indicted Garvey on mail fraud charges, the Black Star Line ultimately came to an end, demonstrating yet again how a great movement can be deterred, if not destroyed, by a lack of internal harmony. Undeterred, Garvey launched a second shipping line, Cross Navigation and Shipping Company, in 1924. This too failed.

True to form, Garvey was never fazed by failure. Despite the practical setback of the shipping enterprise, the mere act of acquiring ships to be part of a bigger ecosystem of enterprises was no minor matter. Moving from idea to bold attempt was a psychologically empowering act. The Black Star Line buoyed the hopes of many who were convinced in the rightness of the moment. The muscle of the UNIA may have been nascent, but it was definitely real.

It is thought-provoking to consider what the UNIA could have achieved had it not met with strenuous resistance from opposition. Garvey's opponents adopted sinister methods to stop or deter the rapidly mushrooming Black liberation movement, of which he was regarded as the presumptive head. It remains amazing what the UNIA was still able to achieve despite adversity. What might have appeared to be an unrealistic goal a few years before—Africa for Africans, at home and abroad, and the mass organization of people of African ancestry—now seemed very plausible.

One opposition faced by Garvey was the United Fruit Company (predecessor to the Chiquita Brand), a behemoth multinational company owning and controlling vast territories in Latin America and the Caribbean. Because a vast portion of their cheap labour force was Black, the company was understandably very concerned about the potential for Black labour unrest. There was fear of Black workers becoming radicalized by the Garvey movement. The entire British Empire also trembled. Already, the British were contending with a little brown man by the name of Gandhi from India in the East. At this stage, they were not inclined to deal with a little dark man from the West Indies by the name of Garvey, who was set to topple their fragile empire. As far away as South Africa, where UNIA branches were taking root, similar fears were expressed by the White ruling regime. Whether in Cape Town or Johannesburg, Paris or Lisbon, French or Spanish speaking, Canada or the US, wherever White colonial economic interests prevailed, there was great apprehension about Garvey's disruptive, destabilizing potential. Racism and exploitative business economics have had a long-standing relationship. Those benefiting from this arrangement were not prepared to have the two divorced from each other so quickly.

Convicted of mail fraud, Garvey was imprisoned in a federal penitentiary in Atlanta, Georgia. He would spend two years and nine months in incarceration between February 1925 and November 1927. Upon release, he was deported to Jamaica. Undeterred, he continued his efforts, writing, publishing, lecturing, and organizing conventions in Jamaica, Canada, and London. He ran a social centre in Kingston known as Edelweiss Park. The centre became an incubator for developing Black Jamaican talent in music, culture, and the arts at a time when Jamaica's cultural life was dominated by and constructed on White European norms. Garvey was indefatigable. Wherever he went, he was a man with purpose.

During the 1980s, a strenuous campaign, spearheaded by his two sons, petitioning the US government to issue a pardon for Marcus Garvey failed. Denied yet again, even so his legacy remains boundless.

As the days passed, Oji developed morning routines, rituals, and exercises designed to strengthen his well-being and invigorate his sense of purpose. Before breakfast, he would perform a thirty-minute physical workout, including pushups and other forms of calisthenics exercises. Eventually, he added a morning run. He was very determined. If and when he developed a cold with stuffy nose, this did not stop him. He continued to persevere in his routine. On finishing his exercises, he felt fresh, ready to face the day. Some days would be restorative. On such days, he fasted while resting, spending time reading or journaling. Despite having some tough physical days, Oji found himself sleeping much better than he ever did before. His health had deteriorated over the prior three years due to the stress of constant activity and poor sleeping and eating habits. But now, his well-being began to show remarkable signs of recovery. This was a relief to him, if for no other reason he could now reassure his mother that he was fine, that she need not worry. She frequently worried for him, her love giving her much needed faith that he would be okay.

Weeks into his trip, Oji developed diarrhea. It lasted some three days. This slowed him down, but not much. The body does not lie. Oji considered himself to be African, an African returning from the West. As such, he was aware of his overexposure to non-African ways of being. Now that he was returning to reconnect with his ancestral roots, he needed to divest himself of anything that was foreign to his system to rid his body of toxicity. If anything, the condition was a metaphor for ridding his mind, body, and soul of anything he no longer needed. His body needed to decolonize itself; in its wisdom, the body rarely lies.

In exploring West African religious thought, Oji sought out experts on the subject, experts such as Kofi Asare Opoku, a senior research fellow in religion and ethics at the Institute of African Studies at the University of Ghana. Africa, West Africa in particular, is known to be fertile ground for philosophy and spirituality given the many ancient Yoruba, Akan, Ibo, and many others cultural communities converging there. Ghana especially is known for its many peoples such as the Asante, Akuapem, Dagomba, Ewe, Fanti, Fon, Ga, Mende, and many more, each group making their own unique contribution to African religious thought. He learned that all Akan people speak variations of Twi, while many other Ghanaians speak Ga, Ewe, Fante, Ga, Hausa, or Nzima, depending on their origin. The rich unity in diversity impressed him. Oji made note of these distinctions and sought to better understand various aspects of West African worldview. He noted that *Onyame* was the Akan supreme being. He came to understand that the idea of *spirit* was an important concept in West African spiritual thought. West Africans believe that *spirit* can and do inhabit chosen objects, essentially making them their habitat. By this means it is possible for *spirit* to be embodied in material objects through which they exert their divine influence.

Oji was amazed at the degree to which his knowledge had increased and, along with it, his consciousness. In the short time that he had been in Ghana, he had learned more about African history and way of life than in all his years of Canadian schooling, including university. Excitedly, he wrote back to Toronto, eager to share his newfound knowledge, making sure to explain that there was so much more he needed and wanted to learn about Africa.

Oji's previous life as a Christian churchgoer offered a somewhat contrary understanding to the indigenous African worldview to which he was now being introduced. These conflicts he would have to resolve. He began to call into question the heavy European influences exerted on Western Christian dogma, beliefs that have led to deep prejudice against African concepts. Christianity and colonialism have conspired to label African philosophical frameworks as *primitive* and *uncivilized*. Those who subscribe to or practice tenets from an African worldview are usually regarded as *uneducated* and *superstitious* and are deemed to be ultimately in need of *salvation* through *conversion* or, at the very least, in need of some form of *Westernized education*. Oji was becoming more keenly aware not only of this bias, but also of the condescending nature of European patriarchy towards Africa. His increased awareness also spotlighted the contradiction between his past learning and the new understanding he was beginning to acquire—a contradiction he would resolve through his own continued self-education. He knew that the attempt to delegitimize and diminish African religious thought first began when the missionaries came. British anthropologist E. B. Taylor in the mid-nineteenth century is said to be one of the first to use the term *animism* to describe African spirituality. Other terms with negative connotations would soon follow, such as *pagan*, meaning any philosophy or practice that was not Jewish, Christian, or Muslim. The amulets and talismans used by Africans were regarded as *fetishes* and were never given the same level of reverence or respect accorded to other symbols or badges of faith such as the cross, fish, or rosary beads used in Western religious practice. As far as Oji was concerned, religion was another frontier for European colonization and control, another platform used by White supremacy to show contempt for Africa and Africans. With each passing day, his visit in Ghana enabled him to decolonize his own reality, allowing him to free his mind from the limitations imposed by the narrow-minded tendencies of Western philosophical thought.

Life, death, and dying are also experienced differently in West Africa. Oji was able to witness this first-hand at a wake held for a high-standing member of the Akwapim people in Ghana's Eastern Region. It was a traditional Akwapim service, elaborate as it was celebratory. As the community marked the transition to a higher calling of one of their own—a call to be with the ancestors—Oji looked on, observing with keen interest the Akwapim State drummers as they invoked the pulsating heartbeat of Mother Africa in their rhythmic percussions. Sitting with the Akwapim State drummers, he was able to hear and watch them play in their traditional style. Through drumming, the beating of rhythms, a community became united in a shared experience as they celebrated the journey of life from one plane of existence to the next. Each drum had its own significance, including the talking drums, which were either male or female. The female drum, placed on one side, had a higher pitch, while the male drum positioned on the other had a lower distinctive sound. Accompanying these were an assortment of other drums, some designed for lead roles, others assigned to follow and accentuate. The drums were played with sticks only. It was a violation of custom to touch them with bare hands. Oji, with official permission, was able to record and take photos of the drumming ceremony, thereby further deepening his knowledge of Ghanaian arts and culture. He learned that death does not mean absent or departed, that the separation between the living and those who have transitioned is not as final as in Western religious thought. Above all, he learned the highest honour one can receive is to be counted among the ancestors.

After returning to Jamaica via deportation at the end of 1927, Marcus Garvey tried unsuccessfully to enter Jamaican politics. He inaugurated Jamaica's first political party—the People's Political Party. The progressive platform he advocated—a brand of politics truly exemplifying "government of the people, by the people, for the people"—was unwelcome by the local elite and business community, descendants of the plantocracy, power brokers who benefited most from British colonial administration. Garvey's ideas were geared to the masses, working and unemployed peasants, many of whom were of African ancestry, the majority of whom were ineligible to vote because they did not own property or meet the required tax threshold. Garvey's ideas were too advanced, too radical to have currency in a country still overseen by British colonialism. Despite his apparent failure, his unconventional proposals—self-government, the protection of labour, land reform, minimum wage, the provision of legal aid, the promotion of local industry, etc.—have since gained traction to become cardinal features of modern sociopolitical life. Quietly and studiously, a local Black intelligentsia imbibed Garvey's philosophy. On entering public life, they would, in due course, go on to implement his forward-thinking blueprint in politics, culture, and education long after he was gone.

Garvey eventually moved to London in 1935 where he continued to work feverishly before fading into seclusion. In 1964, he was named Jamaica's first national hero. As is the case with most heroes, honour came after death. He had created something bigger than himself. He was a man for his time. He was a man beyond his time.

Garvey's life is one of seeming incongruities. The Garvey movement was the largest organized worldwide Black mass movement in history. In the 1920s, the UNIA was the single most powerful Black organization in the USA. Neither the NAACP or the National Urban League or the Nation of Islam, which later followed (all of which shared some goals in common), had the international reach of the UNIA. Each of these organization vied for the same membership. The membership of the UNIA was however unique. They were younger, angrier, poorer; and they generally tended to have darker skin.

That the majority of the UNIA members were overwhelmingly from the Caribbean was an asset not readily available to other groups. Between 1911 and 1924, so-called West Indians poured into the US in significant numbers, particularly into Harlem, New York, where the UNIA had its largest branch. Afro Caribbean people living in the US represented a peculiar demographic. It meant belonging to a double minority subject to discrimination from Whites on one hand, as well as resentment from native Blacks Americans on the other. Paradoxically, this would eventually become a liability in the Garvey movement as adversaries skillfully exploited the division between native-born Americans and Caribbean people. Some of Garvey's former colleagues would later openly criticize him after moving on to leadership roles in other organizations. Despite breaking off association, Garvey's detractors would continue to draw upon Garveyite philosophical principles for years to come.

One lasting irony of the UNIA may have been that it was too big, too successful, for its own good. Thousands of dollars were raised from grassroots contributors to invest in its various enterprises such as the shipping line, the factory corporation, and the Liberian Loan Fund. While Garvey was an extraordinary leader, the overall administration and management of the UNIA appeared to have sagged under the weight of heavy expectations. Adverse and unfavourable pressure applied from outside influences further added distress, aggravating already existing internal weaknesses. While some allies were drawn to Garvey's stubborn belligerence, others were not. As Garvey adroitly attempted to walk the political tightrope of race and power, antagonisms developed, leading to frayed partnerships, disheartening betrayals and deceit, which ultimately made him vulnerable. It was no secret that J. Edgar Hoover had Black spies disguised as UNIA sympathizers working as informants.

Garvey's widespread legacy is indisputable. His body of ideas, loosely known as Garveyism, has inspired innumerable individuals. Malcolm X's father was a Garveyite. So too was his mother. It is said both met at a UNIA meeting. A long list of noteworthy persons either allied themselves or crossed swords with Garvey: Civil and women's rights activist Ida B. Wells-Barnet; politician and pastor of the Abyssinian Baptist Church in Harlem Adam Clayton Powell Jr. and his father, Adam Clayton Powell Sr. before him; and A. Philip Randolph, a minister with the African Methodist Episcopal Church who influenced the life of Martin Luther King Jr., to name a few. Madame C. J. Walker, the exceptional and wealthy businesswoman who made her name manufacturing and selling hair and beauty products, was an ardent sponsor of the Garvey movement. Myriad more men and women, who played significant roles in the civil rights movement, also fed from the Garvey school of thought.

The same could be said of key figures in the African Liberation Movement whether in West, South, East, or Central Africa. Kwame Nkrumah of Ghana and Jomo Kenyatta of Kenya were both stirred by Garvey's message. Nkrumah was so moved by Garvey that, on the occasion of Ghanaian independence, he arranged for the purchase of one of the UNIA's Black Star Liners.

The Ghanaian flag's design is a derivative of the UNIA's banner. Many Caribbean leaders, writers, thinkers, and philosophers, including George Padmore, C. L. R. James, Claude McKay, and Norman Washington Manley, were also significantly inspired by Garvey's life and philosophy.

Many others today, far and wide, known and unknown, continue to carry forward Garvey-like ideas. The ideas and opinions of Marcus Mosiah Garvey continue to hold currency, moving many to return to their African roots either in body or in spirit. In dress, speech, music, or philosophy, many are reclaiming that which was once considered lost, borrowed, or stolen. Today, schools, parks, and urban streets carry his name. Reference to Garvey's work can be found in many major cities, towns, and countries across the world. Songs and poems have been written about him. Annual awards, such as the Marcus Garvey Prize for Human Rights, are given in his name. Resting in the Hall of Heroes in the Washington, DC, offices of the Organization of American States is the sculptured bust of this robust man. Today, his image regales empty spaces throughout the diaspora; today, the colours red, black, and green have become ubiquitous, unmistakable.

Interestingly, acceptance of Garvey's ideas did not come immediately or completely at first. The power of Garvey's insights eluded many during his lifetime. The value of his life and the importance of his work did not become palatable or fully understood until long after he was gone. His life and legacy ignited Black political and social consciousness, enabling Black African culture, for the first time in the modern era, to have significant worldwide impact on culture at large. In this and other ways, he continues to live. And yet, his value is given short-thrift in the canon of world philosophy. Marcus Garvey remains probably the world's most underappreciated philosopher, global thinker, and leader. He is truly the world's best kept secret.

By early February 1991, Oji's first trip to Africa was picking up momentum. He had been away from home for almost three weeks, during which time he continued to keep in touch with family and friends in Toronto through phone calls and letters. One particular person he missed very much was always on his mind. Rarely did he think about another woman more than his mother. In this case, he made an exception. Not only did this woman think highly of him, she was also loved by him. With love found and cherished, he was thankful to have her in his life. There was a connection between her and his trip to Africa. He felt this in a mystical way. It was as if one informed the other. Often, he would miss the warmth of his friendships in Toronto. However, missing this woman proved to be the most intense, causing him to feel lonelier than he normally would. The magnetism between them was strong, at least for now. She filled his inner spirit with joy, enduringly occupying his inner thoughts with her endearing face, her voice, and the memory of her touch. In the phone calls he received, everyone said how much he, too, was missed in Toronto, how he was being remembered by all with great honour and respect. However, it was about her, this one woman, that he remained most anxious.

Oji's tour in Ghana allowed him to visit many places of interest. He met many interesting people who embraced him. In addition to attending a wake or funeral in Kumasi of a prominent member of the community, he also visited institutions of learning, including Accra Polytechnic School and Ghana University in Legon. While at the university, he attended the African Studies Institute, the university's library, and the Commonwealth Hall, a men's residence. He also visited the Office of the Dean of Graduate Studies where he obtained information on graduate study programs for foreign students. Oji was particularly impressed by the colour, decor, the lush landscape of the campus, a scenery he described as vast and beautiful, one that dwarfed the Mona Campus of the University of the West Indies, making it seem like a "ghetto" in comparison. At the National Union of Ghanaian Students, he met the president of the student body, who invited him to address their members.

The highpoint of Oji's Ghanaian visit, if he were to choose, was to Cape Coast, Elmina, and Koromantse. Trips to these sites were spiritually transformative. To walk in the footsteps of his ancestors as they journeyed into enslavement, to see or to stand in the same place where they stood when they left African soil never to return—*The Last Stop*—was deeply moving, captivating beyond words. It was a soul-shifting experience proving to be one of many climactic moments of his pilgrimage. In Koromantse, he visited the Fort Amsterdam Castle. Through here, enslaved Africans were led away as they were forcibly taken to ships waiting at Cape Coast or Elmina. To mark the occasion, he engaged in a communal ritual with his host, the *Oykeame*, Kwabena Kotse, the official linguist of the Koromantse Chief. Libation was poured on the earth. Prayers were chanted to the heavens. Under the guidance of a local priest, a ceremony was held to honour the ancestors. Also acknowledged were Africans throughout the diaspora who were working to enable African liberation. In concluding, they offered Oji a blessing for his continued safe journey.

During this leg of his tour, Oji had other deeply moving moments, particularly at the shrine of Obosom Fo KwaataNana Gyewuru. Here as libation was poured, Oji finally dropped his guard. On the pathway where his ancestors once walked in shackles and chains on their way to a life of servitude, he kneeled to kiss the ground. Surrounded by newly made friends, along with a small delegation of community elders, Oji was visibly touched as he stood in the old Koromantse town where the Fanti once battled with the Ashanti. His experience was made even more moving when he was acknowledged as an honorary guest. He felt as if he had made a full and complete 360-degree revolution, finally returning to his beginning. It was here at this point he experienced one of his greatest fulfillments.

Significantly, it was also in Koromantse that he first witnessed poverty on a community-wide scale, villagers eking out an existence on a daily basis. Rather than dissuading him, this inspired Oji, further deepening his attachment to the town where he was welcomed with open arms. He made a personal resolve to return to Koromantse as an expression of his commitment to be a strong advocate for Pan-Africanism.

Despite Garvey's strong, if not often misunderstood, association with the idea of repatriation, there is no official record of him visiting Africa. He spoke often of Mother Africa, a place that must have preoccupied his thoughts.

Likely, he must have visited Africa frequently in his imagination. His Black Star Line shipping company after all was established to sail to and from the continent. One of his initiatives was a program to resettle Liberia. To this end, he sent numerous delegations to Monrovia. The beautiful irony of Marcus Garvey's life is that while there is no record of him having ever touched African soil or having set eyes on Africa's shores, he contributed greatly to the movement that ultimately led to the decolonization of Africa.

In 1938, Garvey visited Montreal, then Toronto, Canada, where he attended a convention. He lectured local UNIA leaders on African philosophy. (He made a previously recorded visit to Toronto in 1928.) Canadian authorities prohibited him from making public speeches. Otherwise, his international travel appears to have been curtailed. European colonial governors in Africa are said to have barred him from visiting their territories. The established authorities tended to limit his voice and platform fearful of his far-reaching influence and power. This limitation hampered his travels. Nonetheless, it is striking that a man who dreamt and spoke so passionately about returning to Africa did not actually do so himself.

Garvey was a strong advocate for African liberation, a staunch opponent of colonial domination. It could be argued that while he might not have been to Africa, Africa found its way to him. Today, in Africa, he is held in high esteem. Ghana's national shipping company is named after the Black Star Line, as is the country's national soccer team. The black star on the Ghanaian flag is a Garvey-inspired symbol; streets in Nigeria and Kenya, as well as in New York City, carry his name.

Ironically, Marcus Garvey died in relative obscurity in London, England, the heart of the British colonial empire. For over twenty years, he had been a candle glowing in the wind. Legal authorities hounded him frequently in an attempt to undermine his credibility even as his colonial enemies worked feverishly to contain him by restricting his movements and organizing capability. Efforts were made to strangle his organization by choking off funding sources and by stirring up membership discontent with the hope that his network would shrivel and die. Fissures and cracks within the solidarity of his organization were ruthlessly exploited to good measure with the intention of isolating him from his broad support base. In the end, the menace was overwhelming. Garvey was reduced to doing battle with nagging, petty organizational concerns. Still, he fought, dedicated to the end for the cause of justice and for the people he loved.

On June 10, 1940, his candle finally dimmed. He reportedly died from a brain haemorrhage. He was fifty-three years old. Still, he lives. The fire he stoked still burns. He predicted as much in his own words: "Look for me in the whirlwind or the storm," he said. "Look for me all around you, for, with God's grace, I shall come and bring with me countless millions of black slaves who have died in America and the West Indies and the millions in Africa to aid you in the fight for Liberty, Freedom, and Life."

A kente cloth is a magnificent colourful fabric of intricately woven threads crisscrossing over and under each other to create unique patterns. In 1964, twenty-four years after his death, Garvey's physical remains were exhumed in London for return to Jamaica. On November 15, 1964, the government of Jamaica proclaimed him Jamaica's first national hero. Arrangements were made for the reinternment of Garvey's remains to be enshrined in King George VI Memorial Park, formerly known as Kingston Race Course and later renamed in 1973 as the country's National Heroes Park. Two years after Garvey's body was returned to Jamaica, Oji was born. The Garvey legacy would continue its onward march, glorious and true.

Beyond sentimental romanticism, Oji has embraced Garvey's principles. The philosophy and precepts of Marcus Mosiah Garvey inform the model upon which he has built his life. These principles echo throughout his outlook, inspiring his life choices. Constructing a lifestyle based on the best of Garvey's ideas, Oji has transformed not only his own life but also the lives of others. He has walked the talk and talked the walk. Garveyism has become an integral part of his kente cloth. Garvey's Pan-Africanism is a central theme of his African Image Revolution. When Oji's feet touched down on African soil in January 1991, it would be a life-altering event. He may have been walking in Malcom X's footsteps, but he was walking in Garvey's shoes. When he first glimpsed African shores, he was seeing it through the eyes of the Most Honourable Marcus Mosiah Garvey. Upon leaving Africa after his first visit, he would confidently walk into his own whirlwind, each purposeful step thereafter planted with greater vision. Following this first trip to his ancestral homeland, Oji felt more empowered to confront Queen Elizabeth II and her representatives in an Ontario court; he was mentally and spiritually better equipped to face the prospect of incarceration or whatever the outcome would be. Garvey had spent most of his life contesting the legacy of colonialism. For this, he had been locked up a few times. Oji's aim was to carry on this effort and to *aid in the fight for liberty, freedom, and life*, even if it meant losing his own.[36]

---

36 See appendix "In His Own Words" for more on Brother Oji's reflections on the life, legacy, and current relevance of Marcus Garvey.

My soul, my spirit, is engaged in a cultural manifestation of marronage. I was never tamable. I am Koramantin with a stubborn will. Returning to Koramantin in Ghana is like making a complete revolution in seeing and feeling and knowing who I am as a descendant of the fighting Maroons of Jamaica.

—Brother Adisa S. Oji

Chapter 9
MARRONAGE

Individuals who are able to identify as part of a family tree spanning multiple generations are fortunate indeed. If you are able to recount the names and location of your ancestry going back in place and time, count that as a privilege. On the other hand, those without this memory—those unable to locate or define themselves in an extended intergenerational family tree—are like leaves blowing in the wind, drifting like a canoe without a paddle or ships without an anchor. Marcus Garvey famously said, "A people without knowledge of their past history, origin and culture is like a tree without roots." James Baldwin, in *Notes of a Native Son*, puts it this way: "We cannot escape our origin however hard we try. Those origins contain the key—could we but find it—to all that we later become." Baldwin, ever so eloquent, also said, "If you know from whence you came, there is really no limit to where you can go."

For people of African ancestry who have had their lineage snapped then erased by enslavement and colonialism, this is tantamount to a travesty. This is a profound and significant loss, a loss we are only now beginning to completely fathom and only now are beginning to fully assess and restore.

The colourfully magnificent kente cloth is a fabric of intricately woven threads crisscrossing over and under each other to create unique patterns. As part of his nomadic heroic journey, Brother Oji has gone to extraordinary lengths to reclaim his kente by restoring knowledge of his ancestral roots. This is the rock upon which he stands, the inspiration behind his African Image Revolution. As a result, he has created an impressive kente, one revealing a breathtaking journey. If laid out, you will see Malvern Hills in St. Elizabeth hovering above the district of Ridge Pen, a village nesting in greenery, inhabited by people some may consider poor but who are rich in fortitude, people who rise early each morning, standing tall, mirroring the nearby mountains as they utter "Thank God" from their full sun-kissed lips.

If you roll out his kente even more, you will notice the haze of the Great White North with its cold reluctant embrace, holding in headlock a shivering youth who wants to be free, who someday comes of age to run through traps and maze, even as he is cocooned by his close-knit family. If you spread his cloth out even more, you will bear witness to Brother Oji's reunion with Mother Africa, who welcomes him into her abundant heat without suffocating him, revealing to him her riotous splendour, and parts of himself previously unknown. You will see Ghana in all her glory, including Accra, Kumasi, Tamale, and Nkroful—home of the Nzima people and hometown of the late Kwame Nkrumah; you will see Larteh sitting in the Akuapem Mountains, site of the Akonedi Shrines, and Lawra, home to the Lobi people, otherwise known as the Dagari, kinfolk of Malidoma Patrice Some, the great shaman.

Looking deeper into the fine threads, you will notice Oji free-footed. He is reliving ancestral memories, walking reverently through pathways once taken by his predecessors who were dragged in shackles from Kumasi to Cape Coast—a distance of over 200 km—as they hobbled in trepidation, even as many others were moved involuntarily from the extremities of the far north via Yende, Salaga and Bolgatanga, moving through thick deep rainforest under the watchful eyes of slave traders. If you look even closer, you will bear witness to places of magnificent beauty, beautiful when seen through eyes that are free, but which can seem frightful in captivity. You will see the rainforest of Kakum, the canopy walk of the Central Region. You will see dreaded slave dungeons located in Cape Coast and in Elmina off the shores of the Gulf of Guinea where, at one time, each moment was drenched in bitter tears as men and women shivered from fear as they became unhinged with a sense of doom and utter finality. You will observe the humiliating "*Last Bath*" in Assin Manso, the gut wrenching "*Gate of no Return*" in Elmina, and perhaps the unbearable "*Last Stop*" at Goree Island in Senegal. With unimaginable dread, you will notice the wide Atlantic Ocean, billowing threateningly, waiting to take loved ones to the land of no-coming-back. If you unfurl this kente further, you will find an individual coming full circle. He is detoxing, decolonizing, rediscovering himself where he once began, a place where his ancestors were forced to disconnect and lose their way. Somewhere among the kente threads is the image of a man finding illumination in a place once considered *dark*, a man who embarks on a liberating journey of his own when the ending of his physical freedom loomed in a Toronto criminal court. Look and you will see a man who, like a broken branch reuniting with its vine, comes home to reclaim kinship with the Maroons.

Running from the Alfred Rowe's family farm is a zigzag line to Accompong Town. Nesting in the deep mountainous interior, Accompong Town is one of Jamaica's several self-governing Maroon communities. Located in upper St. Elizabeth, atop the rolling cockpit hills where the terrain runs steeply up and down like gigantic waves, Accompong stands amid lush greenery—untamed, unconquered, erect. Bathed in rarified air, the village's roots run deep, as deep as the Kindah or baobab tree, roots stretching back in time to January 6, 1738, when the Jamaican Maroons first signed a peace treaty with representatives of the British crown. After years of doing battle with the colonial military and keeping them at bay, the Maroons entered into an uneasy détente with the Englishmen who grudgingly agreed to leave them alone.

Before the British arrived in the seventeenth century, the Maroons had a fledgling presence in Jamaica. As far back as the Spanish occupation of the island, which ended in 1655 (the word *Maroon* is said to have originated from the Spanish word *cimarrón*, meaning "wild"), Africans had been escaping captivity and finding creative ways to survive. Some formed alliances with indigenous Arawak and Taino communities to produce Maroon characters such as Juan de Bolas and Juan de Serras. Accompong, like other Maroon village in the parishes of Trelawny and Portland, represents many journeys, some extending beyond and before European colonization, deep into antebellum and Africa's pre-colonial past. In Accompong's cultural fibre is a continuity of spirit, shared customs held in common with African civilizations dating back to ancient history.

Residing in Accompong is a family by the name of Rowe, one of whom lays claim to this unbroken past. An official in the Maroon community, Mann O. Rowe professes to have ancestral connections to two of Accompong's former leaders who also bore the name. Nanny, the fabled female Maroon warrior whose anglicized name was said to be Matilda Rowe, is also mysteriously connected to Mann O. Rowe. Oji's great-grandmother, Caroline Rowe (née Daniels), who is from Accompong, is part of this long chain.

Fabled in shrouds of mystique, secrecy, and intrigue, Maroon history is born out of a determined desire to be free from servitude. For Maroons, bondage was unacceptable. As far as they were concerned, they would rather be hounded than be impounded, rather be free than be in captivity. Their advanced thinking made them indisposed to waiting for others to liberate them; their elevated sense of dignity insisted on freedom, compelling them to emancipate themselves through whatever means available.

Eschewing the plantation life of slavery, African men and women fearlessly committed themselves to a lifestyle described as *marronage*. Born free in Africa, they were unaccustomed to the stultifying life of Caribbean chattel slavery imposed and overseen by Spain, Britain, and France. Due to the pervasive mythology of White superiority, it may be assumed that Maroons were unintelligent, uncivilized "bush" people lacking advanced thinking or culture. However, this assumption is false. Enslaved Africans brought across the Atlantic were trained talented individuals skilled in arts, science, and technology; some were griots, philosophers, warrior-kings or queens, while others were respected priests and priestesses who were held in high esteem by their home communities and who were dearly missed when they were violently removed or stolen from their villages. This massive drain of human resources via the Atlantic slave trade—tens of millions of Africa's ablest—has led scholars such as Dr. Walter Rodney to cite the European extortion of African human talent as the means by which Europe underdeveloped Africa. (Correspondingly, the exploitation of Africa's human resources and the subsequent pillaging of African natural resources have led to significant capital wealth accumulation for Europe and colonial North America.)[37] It is not surprising therefore that once captured, the immediate response of enslaved Africans was to use their skills to flee. Through organized strategic planning, they successfully sought and found freedom. Upon escaping, they established themselves in free self-governing communities.

In Jamaica, many of the Africans were Coromantees originating from Africa's Gold Coast. Known to be extremely fierce, endowed with the brave spirit of warriors, they did not, indeed could not, surrender liberty quietly. It was not in their nature to accept captivity kindly. Rebellious escape was, as it were, compulsory. Driven by a passionate stubborn need to resist oppression, they would unhesitatingly seize it whenever the opportunity for liberty arose using stealth, disguise, or cunning, abandoning slave plantations as soon as they could. Acting with determination and guile, they used varied creative skills to escape and to subsequently defend

---

37 Other scholars such as Dr. Eric Williams have provided evidence to demonstrate that the European slave trade was the catalyst for the growth of industrial capitalism in Europe. See Eric Williams's *Capitalism and Slavery*.

their freedom. Their uprising to unfetter themselves from their oppressors was no simple achievement. The slave plantation system in the Caribbean was known for its cruel oppressive brutality. It was a closed system insisting on total control by the slave owner of the mind, body, and soul of the enslaved. In escaping, the Maroons not only secured their physical freedom, they also broke free from psychological strangulation. Rather than passively resigning to plantation life, Maroons took to the luxurious hills of Jamaica where they appropriated land to bolster their self-emancipation.

With each flight, each rebellion, Maroon communities grew. Each arrival of newly liberated Africans made their community stronger, more vibrant. With bare feet and hands, they conquered the wilds of Jamaica's interior, establishing themselves as a fighting force. Occasionally, and prior to treaty agreements, they would return to plunder the plantations for supplies of ammunition and animals or to encourage the freedom of other African men and women. While the British crown may have regarded the Maroons as fugitive slaves, the Maroons regarded themselves as a free sovereign community with the inherent right to autonomous existence.

Life for the Maroons was no paradise. Conditions were harsh. They were viciously pursued by colonial military platoons whose sole purpose it was to serve and protect the plantation system. It was a cruel paradox living free in a mountainous haven while simultaneously having to face overwhelming conditions that could at any moment result in re-captivity, or death. To empower themselves, the Maroons relied on the power of ancestry to help them fight for and defend their community. A certain aura of mystique permeated their existence as they battled, allowing them to remain unmoved or unaffected by dire circumstances. They recruited natural land formations, using environmental conditions to aid in their guerilla tactics. To British soldiers, nature was a formidable foe. For the Maroons, rocks, caves, ravines, rivers, and foliage were faithful allies.

Not all Maroons shared the same African ethnic background. While a good number were Coromantees, others were Akan, Ebo, Fon, Yoruba, or from some other African ethnic group. However, they remain united in the face of a common enemy. Held together by powerful beliefs and dedicated to a common purpose, they were able to band together and blend into the surrounding hills, transforming themselves into a cohesive community. For almost forty years, between 1700 and 1738, Maroon communities held ground, glued together in solidarity long enough to become recognized as an independent autonomous entity complete with their own system of governance. Organized under a strong leadership culture, they evolved to become a formidable fighting force, attacking their foes and former captors with surprising speed, pulling back and disappearing as required. Their speed and cunning made them a constant threat to the colonial status quo, oftentimes bewildering colonial forces whose attacks were regularly repelled. It became almost a mystery how Maroons, under these hostile conditions, were able to defend themselves from such violent attacks while nurturing and protecting their villages from utter annihilation. For this reason, colonial administrations regarded the Maroons as more than a mere nuisance; Maroons were a challenge to their sense of superiority. To slave owners, escaped Maroons were considered lost assets to be recovered. To the colonial powers, they were regarded as a threatening liability to be contained or eliminated. Ever persistent in their quest for dominant control over valuable economic assets, colonial masters gave their armed forces open orders to attack, kill, or capture. In this, they would have partial, not complete success.

Jamaican maroon history invokes images of resistance, rebellion, and revolution and points to the power of self-determination in the pursuit of freedom, justice, and the right to exist. The slaveholders, however, had a more hostile appraisal and labelled Maroons as *runaways*, *fugitives*, *lawbreakers*, and *squatters*. By all accounts, the plantocracy, and by extension the British Empire, were overseers of a grossly inhumane labour intensive economic system. As far as slaveholders were concerned, the Maroons represented a threat to their plantation economy, a system that generated great wealth and power for them and for the British crown.

There is no historical evidence to suggest that the Maroons had any intention to topple this slave-based plantation system or to break the back of the British Empire. The race-based oppressive plantation economy would continue to thrive throughout the eighteenth and nineteenth century, and even beyond if we are to believe the late Professor George Beckford who, in 1972, published his pioneering masterpiece, *Persistent Poverty: Underdevelopment in Plantation Economies of the Third World*. As far-reaching as Maroon resistance was, theirs was by no means a revolutionary movement as we understand it today. When scrutinized critically, it does not appear that the full dismantling of the plantocracy was a Maroon objective. It also does not appear that the Maroons were motivated by any systematic organizational or ideological agenda or by race consciousness or Pan-Africanism or any other such esoteric worldview. The Jamaican Maroons did not have a vision of autonomous self-rule in an independent Black republic such as that envisioned by François-Dominique Toussaint L'Ouverture in Haiti. Rather, they contented themselves with peaceful coexistence with a British-sponsored slave society. In simple terms, they wanted to be free and to be left alone unmolested.

Interestingly, Jamaican Maroons mockingly displayed admiration for their Anglo-Saxon enemies through mimicry and emulation, adopting Anglo-Saxon monikers and titles, oftentimes copying British aristocratic bearing and manner. The adoption of English as a common language by the Maroons may have been deliberate, perhaps for the practical purpose of bridging the communication gap existing between diverse African linguistic groups. Mimicking the enemy in some ways conveyed admiration, underscoring who it is that had real power to dominate. In other ways, mimicking may also have been a means of deception. As actor Ossie Davis once remarked, "Some of the best pretending in the world is done in front of white folks." Mimicry notwithstanding, the Maroons as a group displayed a cunning ability to adapt and to evolve. They were pragmatists willing to do whatever was required to meet their needs and circumstances at any given time.

By 1738, the revolutionary potential of the Jamaican Maroons appears to have been spent. By this time, the Maroon-Plantation relationship had become one of convenient accommodation in which both agreed to peacefully coexist, relating to each other with a sort of live-and-let-live diplomacy. Once the treaty was signed in 1738, Accompong lost its radical dynamism, thereby becoming less threatening. Some have criticized this first peace treaty between the Maroons and the English as a disappointing *sellout* on the part of the Maroons. Those who are of this view cite the fact that the Maroons entered into this arrangement on condition that they would assist the English in preventing further revolts on the island. Once their own liberty was secured, the Maroons appeared to have abandoned the cause of freedom for other enslaved fellow Africans. By stopping short of overthrowing the plantation system altogether, they acquiesced to it, essentially aiding and abetting in its continuation; they had become, as it were, willingly or unwittingly, collaborators in the British perpetrated oppression of African people. The terms of the treaty required Maroons to search for, chase down, and recapture runaway Africans; and there are recorded incidents of Maroons capturing and returning escaped African rebels. By doing so, they were in effect conforming to, and condoning, the same system that once held them captive. Over the course of time, this counter-revolutionary behaviour led to an ironic but understandable state of affairs where enslaved Africans on the plantations became suspicious and distrustful of the free African Maroons, a sentiment bordering on mutual feelings of contempt.

There are considerable lessons to be learned from the challenges faced by the Jamaican Maroons in their quest to be free. Some argue that the revolutionary character of the Maroons lies within their pragmatism and strategic good sense. How do you escape from the *belly of the beast*—a dehumanizing system within which you are trapped? Once you have secured your freedom, what are your obligations toward those who are still in bondage? What are your obligations to those who are already freed? To understand who the Maroons were is to appreciate what they did and why they did it. Did the Maroons sell out, or were they pragmatic? Was it a revolutionary position to sign a treaty with their British enemy instead of continuing the fight? Or was the treaty a strategic concession made in the face of the realities of war? Could they have realistically destroyed the plantation system or transform it to suit their own needs and interest?

Maroons have their own answer to these questions, and one day their story may be told for all to appreciate. To their credit, theirs was a complicated time; their decision-making actions will have to be measured against a historical backdrop in which self-preservation was of preeminent importance. From all accounts, the Maroons did what they had to do in order to survive and to protect their independence. In their quest for freedom, it is apparent that the Maroons could no longer successfully hold off the British without sacrificing more Maroon lives. They were forced instead to consider other less combative methods of survival. It could be said that agreeing to peace was a victory in itself.

Maroons from the parish of Trelawny, as distinct from the Maroons in Accompong, St. Elizabeth, appeared to have been a little more stubborn in their resistance against British control. In 1795, the Trelawny faction acted in defiance of the treaty and declared open war against the British for a second time. Their timing was befitting. Although isolated in the mountainous interior of the cockpit country, it was as if they sensed a growing global resistance against tyranny. Their efforts were staged during an era of radical, social, and political ferment in at least two significant parts of the known world: the French Revolution in Europe, which was in full throttle, and the Haitian Revolution not far from Jamaica where an African revolt led by Toussaint L'Ouverture was underway—as it turned out, the only successful slave revolt in history. The potential for cataclysmic change was reverberating everywhere in the hemisphere with established political orders of the day on full alert.

Prompted by the outrage of ongoing injustice, the Trelawny Maroons took a bold step in challenging the British who they accused of repeatedly violating earlier treaty agreements. Interestingly and disappointingly, other Maroon communities, including Accompong, did not take part in this second round of hostility. They stayed out of it. As to why the Trelawny faction was forced to fight alone, speculations abound. The divide-and-rule strategy practiced by the British appeared to have had a profound effect in fracturing the growing Black African majority on the island. After a series of intense battles in which the Trelawny Maroons repeatedly and convincingly defeated the much larger British forces, the latter were again compelled to surrender and call for peace.

Unfortunately, the new and second Maroon treaty, agreed to in 1796 after a year of intense conflict, had dire consequences for the Trelawny Maroons. On this occasion, they were bamboozled by British negotiators. Trusting the British to honour their word, the Trelawny Maroons dropped their guard in readiness to sign a revised treaty. In characteristic fashion, the British took advantage of Maroon graciousness. Rather than complying with the agreement, the British instead used the opportunity to ambush and capture the Trelawny Maroons who were standing at ease. What the British could not win in warfare, they achieved through bluff and deceptive diplomacy; when the opportunity arose, they reneged on their commitment to peace, revealing a persistent pattern. Whereas British opportunism can be relied on, their word could not always be trusted. British soldiers captured a good number of the Trelawny Maroons, later deporting them to, among other places, Nova Scotia, Canada. The freedom of a people was again thwarted in the interest of British colonial domination. After a few years, as mentioned earlier, while some remained in Nova Scotia, many of the Maroons were later trans-shipped to a British settlement in Sierra Leone, West Africa.

Prevailing questions about the Maroons, together with their fabled struggle for freedom, captivated Oji's imagination as he explored his roots and his family connections. It was important for him to reclaim that which had been misappropriated, and to restore the honour of his lineage. Although there are no conclusive answers, he was gratified to know that he belonged to a community known for its long historical insistence on freedom. The Maroons were emancipated from slavery long before the growth of the abolition movement—before the 1807 Abolition of the Slave Trade Act and before the Slavery Abolition Act of 1833. They were independent long before national independence movements took hold in the Caribbean during the 1960s, and they were liberated long before the African liberation movements became prominent. They were the first freedom fighters to emerge in Latin America and the Caribbean. By their reputation, they were without doubt the first in the so-called New World to initiate the struggle for justice; and although they did not go as far as Haiti to set up a self-governing independent Black African nation in the Caribbean, they were the first to cast off, as best they could, the yolk of British domination and colonialism in an effort to re-establish their own sovereignty and self-determination. For this reason, the names of Nanny, Cudjoe, Tacky, Quao and Cuffee are the names of heroes in the annals of Jamaican history, heroes recognized for their uncompromising desire for freedom.

The history of the Jamaican Maroons is still being written, their mystery still being unraveled. The steep hills they roamed—Charles Town, Moore Town, Accompong—continue to hold many secrets. Many unanswered questions remain, some of which may never be resolved. Academics and intellectuals from the US and elsewhere have shown remarkable interest in gaining access to the culture and studying it. However, Maroons, given their history, are apprehensive about cultural expropriation for ulterior motives, and rightly so. Becoming entangled once again with foreign forces intent on exploiting their anthropological wealth is the last thing they need or want. The sacrificing of their soul is not the Maroon way.

The peace treaty signed by the Maroons with the British remained in force when Jamaica gained its independence in 1962. Although, the Maroons have continued to be an independent self–governing entity within the Jamaican political landscape, the viability of their community continues to be threatened by an array of forces, not the least of which is resistance to Maroon culture by some segments of the Jamaican community. On February 24, 2021, Richard Currie, at age forty, was sworn in as the new chief of the Accompong Maroons, the youngest to be so recognized. He is keen on upholding and developing Maroon sovereignty and is already facing challenges as he seeks to defend against modern-day encroachment on Maroon rights and privileges.

The zigzag line therefore continues, running back and forth through time from Africa to Accompong, Jamaica, and back again, with strands running here and there through varied places such as Canada, and through the Alfred Rowe family farm in the Ridge Pen District of St. Elizabeth where an obscure boy arrived in '66—a boy preparing himself for manhood, readying to make his own zigzag line through history. No one knew it then, but he, too, would have to face and answer critical questions regarding where, when, and how he would fashion and weave his own emancipation. He, too, would one day come face to face with the bitter anti-Black legacy of British colonialism; he, too, would be entrusted with figuring out how to help unfetter others who were still left behind in its bit and bridle.

Sunday, June 24, 2012. The scene was not Paris nor New York, LA, or Cannes. It wasn't Harlem or Toronto or London or Birmingham, Alabama, or any of the other cities where the documentary *Akwantu: the Journey* had been screened to packed riveted audiences. This was Ridge Pen, St. Elizabeth, a rural village known for the absence of amenities such as electricity; it was a farming community of villagers, many of whom could trace their origins back to the fearless Maroons.

On this hot Sunday afternoon in June, Ridge Pen buzzed with palpable excitement. The paparazzi were out, so to speak, in full force. It was a historical newsworthy event. Armed with high-powered cameras, Oji and his brother, Winston, expertly worked the party-like crowd as villagers gathered outdoor, converging on the yard in the late afternoon under a natural canopy of brilliant sunshine gleaming through clear skies, the sunlight flickering like silver-gold neon through the green-yellow webbing of tall coconut palm trees swaying majestically around the open compound. The stars were out too—village people glowing in their Africentric garb. They were milling about, walking among the other sixty or so women, men, and children parading and prancing, making their way up the prestigious makeshift green carpet of coconut fronds. They feted, they feasted, they laughed, and they joked. It was lovely.

Soon dusk came. Everyone took their seat anxiously waiting. A hush swept over the crowd as the documentary flickered to life powered by a mobile generator. What they were about to witness was a film made by one of their own—filmmaker Roy T. Anderson, Oji's older brother. The villagers would have already been instinctively familiar with the story of the Maroons. They would have heard it told to them through their oral tradition. However, they had never seen or heard it told in film until now. It was an amazing evening, amazing for Oji and his brothers, Roy and Winston, amazing for their families, amazing for the Ridge Pen community, and amazing for the memory of all Maroons.

The outdoor screening in Ridge Pen was revolutionary because this had never before been done in the village. No one prior deemed the remote pastoral village significant enough to be the site for a special film screening. Not until four children who at one time scampered about the yard multiple decades ago returned as adults with their families to offer this extraordinary treat. It had been billed as the Homecoming Screening, a significant part of the Rowe's family reunion. Hosted and organized by the Rowe household, many family members were present, including Oji's mother, his sister, and extended family members such as Oji's uncle, Packieman, who is featured in the documentary.

That the screening was held in Ridge Pen and, in this way, was as a result of the purposeful vision and determination of Roy and his production team, including Roy's wife, Alison, and his brothers, Winston and Oji. The effort it took to pull this together exemplified the same strength of will displayed by the eighteenth-century Maroons. With single-minded focus, fortitude, funded primarily through their own resources, Roy used their family heritage as a launching pad to document and pay tribute in film to the odyssey of the Maroons and their struggle for autonomy and freedom. "Groundbreaking, bold and timely" was how one Jamaican daily newspaper described the documentary. "It tells the history of this hemisphere's first successful Freedom Fighters."

The Homecoming Screening in Ridge Pen was one of three screenings held in Jamaica between June 20 and June 24, 2012. The Press and Industry Screening, held in association with the Institute of Jamaica, went off well on Wednesday, June 20, 2012, in Kingston at the Redbones Blues Café. Present were Vivian Crawford, executive director of the Institute of Jamaica, and UNESCO director Kwame Boafo. Present also were Anne-Marie Bonner, former Jamaica consul general for Toronto, and UWI Mona history professor Verene Shepherd.

On Friday, June 22, 2012, the World Premiere screening of *Akwantu* took place at Asafu Yard, a Maroon village in Charles Town, Portland. Organized in association with the Charles Town Maroon Council, the Institute of Jamaica, and the Jamaica Social Investment Fund, this too went off with resounding success. Billed as the Night of the Ancestors, the screening added value to the three-day Fourth International Maroon Conference that was being held concurrently on the island. The conference, which attracted an international audience, featured drumming ceremonies, dancing performances, and panel discussions on Maroon culture, history, and philosophy, as well as arts and crafts displays. Present among the guests were then United States ambassador to Jamaica, Pamela Bridgewater, and Shauntay Grant, the 2009–2010 Poet Laureate of Halifax and a descendant of the Leeward Maroons of Trelawny. Present also was Susan Robeson, the granddaughter of the late American bass-baritone singer, actor, and activist Paul Robeson, who accepted a special award on her grandfather's behalf.

While in Charles Town, Oji conferred with Colonel Frank Lumsden and other Maroon leaders in the community to discuss history and future business ventures. (Colonel Lumsden passed away in 2015.) Oji also took time to teach one of his favourite pastimes—Oware—coaching a stream of people, young and old, the game board situated between them as they sat on the ground or on loosely arranged chairs at Asafu Yard under a shady spot in the warm Portland sun.

But it was in Ridge Pen where emotions were most heightened and had the most personal significance. On this sultry afternoon going into evening, in an outdoor compound, Oji celebrated his family's heritage in company with many whose family histories were tied to his. Oji, his brothers, his sister, and their respective families were heartened as they stood watching the audience as they in turn viewed with pride and a sense of discovery the eighty-seven-minute documentary. It was a landmark for the villagers to see themselves reflected in a major documentary film of this quality; an uplifting experience to understand that they, too, were part of a heroic legacy—a recounting of the path to freedom and independence forged by predecessors.

Roy, the producer/director, writer, and narrator, had by now become a reputed Hollywood stuntman. He enlisted his younger brother, Oji, and MACPRI to be the documentary's chief stills photographer. Together they would go on to partner on future documentary productions including *Queen Nanny: Legendary Maroon Chieftainess*, produced in 2015. At the time of writing, Roy's third documentary film, featuring the Honourable Marcus Mosiah Garvey, was in production, slated for release in 2021.

When Jamaica celebrated its fiftieth independence anniversary in 2012, *Akwantu* was selected as a Jamaica 50 endorsed film. Since then, it has garnered critical acclaim within the African diaspora. That it has yet to attract commercial interest from others in the mainstream film industry says something for the low appetite for these stories among Hollywood power brokers. Hollywood or not, *Akwantu* remains a tribute to an important past. The documentary's three showings in Jamaica demonstrated its extraordinary power. It is a highly educational tool with the ability to inspire and motivate generations to come. As *Akwantu* continues its inexorable journey forward, expect a seismic shift on many levels.

June 24, 2012: At the Ridge Pen screening, Winston, Oji's brother, guides the children as they paraded and pranced up the prestigious makeshift green carpet of coconut fronds. (Oji/MACPRI Archives)

L–R: Documentary film maker Roy T. Anderson; Lewis Rowe, elder uncle of Oji; and Packieman, Oji's younger uncle. Elder Rowe went to join his ancestors in 2009 after his last interview for the *Akwantu* documentary. (Oji/MACPRI Archives)

When one lives in the belly of the beast and if you are still alive—to survive you are forced to eat some of what the beast eats ... the only time when you can exist without having to eat what the beast eats, is when you have the power and force to propel yourself to be vomited out to a new and completely self-determined environment. As complete self-dependence in this global world is no longer possible, we must make wise power-positioned alliances for ourselves and our people.

—Brother Adisa S. Oji

Chapter 10

THE NEW REVOLUTION

I will not beg or steal
I would rather die
Trying ...
Doing something for myself
For in independent achievement
I will feel the joy of true self pride
If I only have a single dollar
I will always be able to work wonders
With that dollar
I will not beg or steal
I will not feed the hands that bite me
Even though times are hard
My own dollar must work for me
I must invest my mind to develop
Ways to use that dollar
That hard to get
Well-earned dollar
To make something
I have many skills
I must use them
To create something new
And purposeful
For myself
My family
My clan
My nation
My children
I will not feed the hands that bite me
I will not buy crumbs
Eat crumbs
Be crumbs
To be eaten by
Vultures/scavengers
I will become self-reliant And we will live.[38]

Having knowledge of his past while being rooted in the present with an eye on the future, Brother Oji instigated his own revolution—a moving, living, organic revolution. Embracing a philosophy of life that embodies change, he is constantly innovating, always adding new

---

38 Entitled "Bacon" from an unpublished collection of poems. Used with permission.

elements to his profile and body of work, doing so with a distinction that makes him unique in his generation.

"I will not beg or steal," he declares, speaking his mind, going about his business as if uncaring of what others may think or say. "You may not like my politics," he once said, "but with me there are no tricks ... I say what I feel with love and let the chips fall as they may."

Anyone whose life history—not their individual chronological version, but their immemorial ancestral lifespan—has been disrupted by abuse, broken by acts of dehumanization knows how urgent it is to get beyond brokenness and to become whole again. Life becomes a quest to collect shattered pieces, an enduring effort to refashion them in some way that allows for self-worth and dignity to return. The task facing those of us living with the destructive legacy of colonialism and its derivatives is to restore self-value by liberating our potential—within and without. As was the case with the Maroons, freedom becomes an imperative; life becomes a quest in search of new and creative ways of being and becoming, a quest to forge a new self-definition out of the chaos. This is no simple task.

Brother Oji has pieced together his broken bits. First, he deconstructed and reconstructed his relationship with himself, then proceeded to redefine his relationship with neocolonial schemes designed to entrap and imprison him. How he accomplished this is instructive. Not that his life is a template to be rigidly followed or to be borrowed wholesale. Rather, he exemplifies what is possible. He challenges us to widen our vision, to be courageous, to bravely interrogate the self-limiting habitual norms that we have adopted as if they were true, norms which have been imposed on us against our will and better judgement.

As Brother Oji's multidimensional journey continued, and he with it, his life and work crystallized with stunning clarity. Once a mild boy-child, shy and reserved, he grew to become brash with a distinctive bravado, developing a swagger some found jarring, even outrageous. If nothing else, Oji preferred to be himself, to be his own walking, taking, active revolution. He led mostly not through words but primarily by example, uplifting not only himself but also those around him through his compelling manner. Overall, his life's work exemplifies an ever-increasing capacity for self-love and self-reliance. He knows the journey he is on is typified by struggle; that even if he should win the proverbial race, the act of self-determination will never be complete. There will always be resistance, streams of criticism from rivals and naysayers. He knows transformation is an ongoing process. This does not worry him.

While the ROM incident had won him acclaim as an activist, he did not wish to be defined by this singular episode. He was convinced there was yet a higher purpose. For this reason, he kept his eyes wide open with the end in view knowing that the benefits of his persistency would always outweigh the cost.

There are interesting features about Oji's revolution, not the least of which is that he is bringing others with him. Not only that, his sales gimmicks—such as his wearable store pictured above—are more than simple gratuitous self-promotion. Through his work, he is modelling self-emancipation. He is enriching the ground for the next generation, showing a way out beyond the *belly of the beast*. To follow his journey to self-autonomy is to understand the range of his contributions and the full meaning of his bloodless revolution.

I Will Not Beg or Steal

In June 2015, Oji held his first Business and Community Capacity Building Marketplace at Knowledge Bookstore in the city of Brampton, Ontario, west of Toronto. The event, which ran over the course of two days, was intended to support several Black enterprises in the Greater Toronto Area and beyond, including the Black Community Action Network (BCAN) of Peel, Ujamaa Nation, and the Ghanaian African Art Producers. The pilot initiative was part of Brother Oji's overall vision for his flagship enterprise, MACPRI. The event was held in partnership with Sean Liburd of Knowledge Bookstore, who acted as co-host and sponsor.

While family and friends gathered in the quiet Brampton suburb, community workers, members, and guests from the general public patronized the groundbreaking festive bazaar. It would largely go unnoticed by a wider audience. Many would not have heard of it on prime time news or have read about it in mainstream newspapers. Being outside of the dominant milieu was nothing new for a man accustomed to marching to the beat of his own drums. From the days of beating pots and pans as a boy while sitting under a tree in Ridge Pen, Oji always had a unique way of marking territory. His path has never been pebbled with ease or conformity. What suited many others have never quite suited him, and vice-versa. While the 2015 Marketplace did not attract mainstream attention, it was nonetheless indicative of an untapped potential and of what was possible.

Brother Oji came close but has never held a conventional full-time job. To ease himself through school, there were the occasional obligatory summer employment or short-term contracts. By this means, he took time to formulate ideas on how to become self-reliant or to travel as he pleased. He wanted to feel alive, not dead; he especially wanted to tap into his creative passion rather than emptying himself on the long treadmill of someone else's employment line. Following his own inner compass, he intuited that it was better to get caught in a quagmire of his own making rather than becoming entangled in the grind of an oppressive system—a set of orchestrated arrangements that had the tendency to devalue those deemed less than worthy, a system perforated with invisible cracks, sink-holes through which so-called minority groups and people of colour routinely fell at disproportionately alarming rates. Rather than becoming a casualty of *that shitstym*, he opted to create his own model of life and work, one in which there was no distinction between the two. He opted for autonomy over dependency, staying in his own lane, making his own way. Instead of each morning, Monday to Friday, answering the bell of an alarm clock to punch in to work at nine only to anxiously wait to leave at five, he instead answered the bell from within prompting him to stay alive, to stay true. Standing on the edge of a cliff with no other apparent choice but to fly or die, he chose to fly, learning how to do so while in mid-air. Rather than disconnecting from himself, he chose to stay connected to who he was, loyal to values rooted in the legacy of his chosen ancestry.

Going off the main path had its disappointments, certainly. Sticking with prescribed convention may have proven easier. But ease was never his goal. Everywhere he looked, he could feel the pressure to conform to a success-oriented culture heavily reliant on appearances. He did not succumb; he held ground. Going down a path along which many were funnelled would not satisfy him. Instinctively, he knew this would yield unacceptable results, an outcome inconsistent with his best and truest potential. And so, he chose a more challenging path, following it no matter how long it took or where it led. Positioning himself outside the prevailing paradigm of wage-salaried-employment, he took the steep, rocky road rarely travelled, one that went against the grain of the popular wisdom of his generation. He pushed through resistance despite setbacks, each step bringing him closer to that which made him feel more alive, more authentic.

Easier said than done, this decision would be costly. It called on everything he had—tremendous courage, patience, and an abundance of personal resources. Timely and loyal backing from his support systems would prove invaluable. There were times when life appeared as if it would come to a grinding halt, and many times it did. Yet, empowered, Oji pressed unremittingly onward. Through his endeavours, he discovered endless opportunities for growth, expansion, and community building. He pulled people in while avoiding others. He confronted dogma while creating his own, always moving forward. While some collaborators fell away, he would have the support of others who signed on to his vision and remained loyal.

The Business and Community Capacity Building Marketplace grew out of this need for autonomy. The event turned out to be a two-day success. The Marketplace demonstrated the power of community collaboration as a means of building self-sufficiency. By this approach, he was attempting to redefine the concept of private enterprise and to create alternatives to the so-called free market system of wage-slavery. Whereas in the framework of wage-slavery, businesses are established, owned and operated by private individuals for the sole purpose of selfishly reaping massive profits through the legal and extralegal exploitation of others, Brother Oji's business design offered a difference.

A quick survey of the compendium of business streams spawned by him reveals a progressive experimental attempt to use new methods of building self-reliance and community empowerment. His vision—a new revolution—was sustained by a higher purpose, one that would see him establish fresh family roots in Africa, while concurrently consolidating his reputation as pioneer, leader, and *Mwalimu* in Canada, Jamaica, and Ghana.

Road Less Travelled

On first entering the Canadian labour market, the few jobs held by Oji were low paying—what he considered menial dead-end work typical of an unskilled labourer. Some of the jobs he held were further up the employment food chain, but not far from the bottom. He wasn't above such work or scorned the people who performed them. Rather, he noticed that the labour market was riddled with traps, self-limiting and otherwise. Embedded in these work arrangements were plans designed to lock legions of individuals into prisons of powerlessness, subtly driving them helplessly and hopelessly into never-ending cycles of impoverishment. He discerned an inherent inequity whereby the many who sowed received little for their efforts while a few others reaped enormous benefits. He came to define this as a form of wage-slavery where individuals gave up their labour and talent—sometimes their souls—to others in exchange for an allowance calculated to allow them to get by or to only make ends meet.

As a youth in the late seventies, shortly after his arrival in Canada, Oji began delivering newspaper for the *Toronto Star*. As previously mentioned, he worked at a Candy Floss food stand at Exhibition Stadium during the annually held summer Canadian National Exhibition (CNE). He did counter duty at Dickie Dee Ice Cream in addition to working as a mobile vendor. He had a brief stint as a weed picker at an Orangeville onion farm. Far from being a slouch, he would do what he could even if it meant returning another summer to the CNE to work at the Time Out restaurant. He once worked in the "medical field" in material management, handling soiled laundry at Sunnybrook Medical Science Centre. He was once a peer career counsellor at Woodgreen, a local community agency, and also served as a leadership development programmer for an elementary school. He once worked for a start-up Canadian clothing company as well as for an electrical contractor. He was a labourer with a professional packing service and once worked for a moving business.

Most of all, however, he worked for himself. Motivated by the belief that ownership and control of his labour was foundational to the realization of his dream, he pressed on with a *Kujichagulia* (self-determination) mentality. With the support of family, friends, and a small circle of active well-wishers and people of like-mind, he leveraged his ingenuity to forge what he called his *black-print*, a roadmap to independence. By this means, he was able to, as he puts it, break free from the matrix. He developed an uncommon business acuity, ultimately leading to the formal establishment in 2000 of MACPRI enterprise, which initially began as a part-time endeavour but, in eight years grew to become his full-time preoccupation.

Some critics are apt to point out that Brother Oji is an underachiever, especially when compared to those who have chosen more conventional salaried day jobs covered over by a veneer of superficial success symbolized by mortgages, multiple garage homes with attendant nightmares of mounting debts. If Oji is to be understood, he must be seen as an outlier. While functioning outside the mainstream, he has built a business in Canada while assisting his wife in establishing her own in Ghana. He has assisted in the construction of a mortgage-free home for his mother in Jamaica and has built his own family home in Ghana. Brother Oji, while based in Canada, has established roots and branches in three different countries.

Formerly an acting president of the African Canadian Students Association (ACSA) at the University of Toronto, Brother Oji holds a Bachelor of Education and Teacher Qualification Certificate (1997) from the Ontario Institute for Studies in Education (OISE), together with an honorary bachelor of arts degree in history and sociology (1990) from the University of Toronto. He was part of the student body of the University of Ghana (1991) and once attended the University of the West Indies, Mona campus (1988–1989), where he respectively enrolled and studied courses in African Cultural Heritage and African Caribbean History and Development Studies. During the course of his studies, he met remarkable scholars, two of whom made a remarkable impression on him: Professors J. Edward Chamberlin and the late Edward Kamau Brathwaite. Not one to give acclaim lightly, Brother Oji holds both professors in high regard, not only as outstanding scholars of the highest order, but also as incomparable genuine individuals. Each in their own way have had a profound effect on him.

He refers to Professor Chamberlin (who some would cite as a *White man*) as Brother Ted; Brother Ted, in turn, addresses Brother Oji in like terms of endearment. In his usual candour, Oji is not shy to say that it is near impossible for him to accord this honour—of being called *Brother*—to any *White man*. Why he extends this exception to the now retired University Professor Emeritus at York University is telling. Professor Chamberlin has extensive research experience and interests in World Literature, English modernist and contemporary poetry, Caribbean literature, Aboriginal literature, oral and written traditions, and in stories and storytelling generally. But this is incidental. In some strange twist of fate, the professor became Oji's mentor and friend and was a character witness at Oji's trial. It was risky for a White university professor at a reputable Canadian tertiary institution to appear in court on behalf of a criminally charged young Black male. Yet the faculty member thought nothing of stepping forward in support of a young man he had come to admire. During the onset of their relationship at the University of Toronto, they had lengthy tumultuous arguments, conversations that ultimately led to mutual respect, friendship, and trust lasting many years. It is clear that they have a relationship that transcends race, one that allows for reciprocal enlightenment.

Professor Braithwaite (who, on the other hand, is a person of African Caribbean descent) had an uncanny historical understanding of the psychosocial anatomy of slavery and colonialism. As a philosopher-poet, he offered insightful restorative countermeasures on how to best approach this horrid history. He brought an immense spiritual-intellectual depth to his scholarship, teaching with a quiet passion that stirred many of his students while befuddling others. Oji, who is in the former group, came to admire the late professor's courage—courage to be himself while in the hornet's nest of academia. It was Professor Braithwaite who awakened within Oji a greater sense of connection with Africa and first introduced him to the concept of *marronage*.

Brother Oji internalized various aspects of the pedagogy of these two leading scholars. In his own practice, he has carried forward some of their revolutionary insights and teaching methodology.

Although qualified to teach from middle school through to the collegiate level, Oji rejected a teaching career in the formal school system. As part of his teacher qualification training, he taught one grade 4 class briefly at Kingsview Village Junior School, a school within the Toronto District School Board (TDSB). From this and other experiences within the formal system, he rapidly determined that there was an immediate conflict between his Afrocentric teaching philosophy and the Eurocentric outlook typical of local school boards. From this brief experience, he knew he would not be a suitable fit. Furthermore, his strict intellectual rigour and tough-love discipline led many to believe that he would be a mismatch for the liberal approach preferred by many Canadian grade school educators.

While he did not function in a structured setting, he held the reputation of being a community educator. He actively gave his time to help youth in underserved neighbourhoods. As a public speaker he was known for lecturing on a range of subjects, including West African history, philosophy, and culture; radical Black thought; and cooperative economics (otherwise known as *Ujamaa*). Despite having these noteworthy credentials, Oji has never seen it fit to build a professional career in the typical sense. He refused to *feed the biting hand*. Rather than embracing a full-time fixation with having a formal career or pursuing the comforts and security of a stable professional job, he opted instead to withdraw from the mainstream labour pool. His would be the road less travelled. Unhampered by the narrow confines of convention, he freed himself to pursue other and more enriching forms of endeavours. He was not interested in enrichment in the remunerative sense. He refused to see himself as a wage or salaried "*slave*" to monetary-based systems. Rather, his enrichment came in the form of redemption, of being able to live a bigger and broader existence in rhythm with the beat of his own self-awareness. His independence allowed him freedom of thought, freedom of action, positioning him outside the narrow streams customarily reserved for people of colour. Where Oji would make his most lasting mark is as a radical rebel, a provocateur business owner and entrepreneur, a creative activist who, over time, would build a remarkable portfolio based on his work as a photojournalist.

Awakening

Brother Oji's awakening did not come overnight or lightly. It took some time before he came to realize his ability to *work wonders*. Ms. Donna Whitmore, his sixth-grade teacher is credited with being one of the first to help him discover his voice. She made him feel valued. In so doing, she helped to facilitate his emergence.

Olivia Chow, then an Ontario School Board Trustee, was another catalyst. She opened the door that would initially lead Oji to discover his calling. Circa 1985, she introduced him to a peer career counselling program, later arranging for him to appear on a TVOntario interview series. Focusing on the theme "School Works," the interview spotlighted the Ontario school system's systemic discrimination against Black male students who were being routinely derailed into vocational courses, in effect redirecting them away from the more prestigious academic stream considered by many as the pathway to so-called higher learning. From this platform, Oji found his stride. He connected with other like-minded Black students who shared his passion. From here his fame grew. Soon he became known as a subject matter expert on matters relating to the Black student experience. This in turn led to an unpublished interview with *Maclean's* weekly news magazine during which he opined on the legacy of Dr. Martin Luther King Jr. From here, it was a natural segue into the growing Black student movement, an activity he entered with great relish to become an advocate for student rights. From then on, his opinions were much sought after, leading to various appearances on radio talk shows, including the campus community-based radio station CKLN, as well as an appearance on the Canadian Broadcasting Corporation's (CBC) premier morning show *Morningside*, with the late Peter Gzowski. Gzowski's program, which had a listenership of over a million Canadians, included Oji together with a panel of students from Halifax, Montreal, and Winnipeg. With national exposure, Oji reached an even broader audience enabling him to further extend his influence and reputation among a rapidly growing network of student activists.

Involvement with the Young Poets of the Revolution between 1991–1995 further sealed his growing profile as a leading young activist with a unique voice. Acting as what could best be described as a convenor-promoter, Oji, under his MACPRI brand, helped to organize and sponsor spoken-word events long before they would become popular in Toronto. The Young Poets had local and international reach. Together with his various collaborators (including businesses such as Caribbean Corner, Star Pak, Hefty Sounds New Age Promotion, and a variety of agencies such as ACCESS, TAMA Islamic-African Correspondence, African Canadian Youth Literacy Project, Ryerson African Caribbean Association, and community radio stations CIUT, CKLN, and CHRY), Oji brought together local Canadian poets as well as poets from New York, Jamaica, Ghana, Tanzania, and England. Their vision was multifaceted. As a collective, their goal was to improve mastery of their craft through peer support and shared expertise. In addition, they wanted to expand their exposure to a wider audience and were determined to have their work acknowledged as a legitimate art form.

Oji was aware of the growing tendency of event organizers to use spoken-word poets as an attraction without sufficiently compensating them. For this reason, he took a deliberate ethical business approach by speaking out against the exploitation of young poets and by introducing measures to ensure they were fairly treated. He encouraged artists to become self-reliant, to protect their work by assuming control of their intellectual property through the use of copyright, trademarks, or any other tools readily available. Not one to preach that which he did not practice, Oji was keen to see to it that poets received economic value from their creativity. By also performing his own poetry, he demonstrated his multifaceted range, making it known that he, too, had something to say. In these early days, while becoming a fledgling business leader, he was also mushrooming into an artist in his own right.

Student Activism

Between 1986–1992, while attending the University of Toronto, Oji rapidly gained leadership status as an authoritative voice for African student development and leadership. Following the departure of Akwatu Khenti, he assumed the role of acting president of the African Canadian Students Association (ACSA) from 1989 to 1990. Confidently, he entered the fray as an advocate, agitating on behalf of Black students' right to gather and organize. He emphatically argued for racial justice and equality. He was unapologetic in his stance.

In September 1989, he led the ACSA in a head-on dispute with the University of Toronto Students' Union (UTSU), then known as the Student's Administrative Council (SAC), itself ostensibly a student representative body. The contention involved the use of university space, specifically who had the right to use it and for what purpose. ACSA, which had their office located on the third floor at 44 St. George Street, was given an eviction notice by SAC on the grounds that the group did not "fit the criteria." ACSA, in response, decided to resist the order. SAC, in turn, escalated the controversy by changing the lock on the office's door in a bid to shut the group out. ACSA raised objections to these actions, claiming unfair treatment and proceeded to fight the eviction.

Former Black university students had struggled during the 1970s to transform campus race relations if only by carving out for themselves a dedicated space within the university grounds where they could meet, confer, and have caucus. This was seen at the time as a tremendous historical gain, a pathway to autonomy and empowerment for students of colour. Now, decades later, came an eviction notice to shut down the ACSA, a growing politically conscious student group insisting on racial equality and espousing Black revolutionary thought. With this as his backdrop, Oji led the charge, vowing, "We will not be evicted … we are not dead, we are just displaced."

SAC argued that ACSA served narrow ethnic concerns irrelevant to students at large. Consequently, the mood of the university administration toward ACSA's militancy became antagonistic. Undeterred, the group with Oji as acting president, pressed forward with their demands. When on September 25, 1989, sixty or so ASCA members stormed into SAC's budget meeting to challenge the eviction chanting "Hell no, we won't go"! Metro Toronto police were summoned to simmer things down. "Our hope is for SAC to realize that ACSA cannot continue to be pushed around. We're showing SAC we are not joking," said Oji in defiance.

ACSA forged alliances with other anti-racism advocates to create the United Coalition Against Racism. In October 1989, when the University of Toronto held its U of T Day celebrations, the coalition launched a public demonstration much to the embarrassment of U of T Day organizers. "We are going to show up the university for what it really is." said Oji. "We want to make them look bad. The administration doesn't care. The questions are not heard until we find a medium that forces people to listen."

By leading this anti-eviction campaign, he became part of the genealogy of Black campus activism. What he may not have known was that he was being prepared for an even bigger crusade laden with even more controversy.

By March 1990, Oji was impassioned enough to run for a seat on the University of Toronto's Governing Council (GC). In putting forward his candidacy, he served notice to the university community that the White elitist culture of the monolithic student administration must come to an end. With an anti-racism platform, he committed to bringing attention to institutional racism on the campus, highlighting particularly the university's heavily weighted Eurocentric course content and the glaring under-representation of people of colour in faculty and administration. In his bid for election, he declared, "I remember when I last went to the GC meeting. I looked at people at GC, and most are white, Anglo Saxon. The structure of GC and faculty represent only one group in society." While he did not win a seat, he made a lasting impression and found other ways to redirect his passion.

It was a heady time to be a Black student activist. The air was rife with protest. Black consciousness grew in response to revelations of anti-Black racism in the areas of law, education, employment, and society at large. As he confronted these issues in and outside of the classroom, on and off campus, Oji began to find his niche. At every turn, his involvements were thought-provoking, even entertaining, sometimes both.

The times he spent with kindred spirit, Lanchester, for example, were both funny and intellectually rewarding. He met Lanchester F. Anderson (no relations) while both were in their first semester. Each year hence, they had at least one class together. This cemented their friendship. Their partnership deepened further when Anderson joined MACPRI as a community outreach advisor, primarily serving as a liaison between MACPRI and other like-minded community organizations. Both also worked for *The Varsity* newspaper, Oji as a photographer, Anderson as a writer. As a team, they made it their business to inject African scholarship in campus print media news content, exploring for example anti-imperialist and anti-colonial themes, as well as posting articles on African liberations movements.

In an introduction to the Young Poets of the Revolution written for *Acta Victoriana*, the university's literary journal, Lanchester described the poets as "the dissenting voice," Africans who were "continually submerged in their induced nightmare of this supposedly peaceful Canadian society."

Oji in addition to his photo news assignment had articles of his own, a few of which were published under his old "slave" name. The focus of his subject matter was clear. A few titles illustrate his interest: "Freedom Ride," a 1988 article in *The Varsity* highlighting a road trip from Toronto to Montreal by anti-racism groups to protest the police killing of Anthony Griffin, and "Black Student Must Fight for Black Progress," a special report, again for *The Varsity*, in which he spotlighted an event held by the Anti-Apartheid Network. Noting that out of one hundred students present only six or seven were Black, Oji commented, "Silence has never worked for Blacks."

One memorable article Lanchester and Oji produced highlighted the work of Kenyan writer and academic Ngũgĩ wa Thiong'o, who himself often made reference to an African image revolution. Like two excited fledging radical intellectuals, the two met regularly in Kensington Market to work on joint projects. They debated and plotted strategy on how bring Africentric consciousness to the campus, comparing notes about their observations as they discussed how to detect White supremacist bias among faculty members and within the curricula. Of particular interest were discrepancies in the faculty's understanding of African history.

In one episode, they were provoked into action by Martin Klein, a professor in the History Department, who at least on one occasion made cynical remarks about "Mr. Adisa's revolution." Klein, who had seen *Into the Heart of Africa* twice, had concluded the exhibit was not "racist," and said so publicly. Much to Oji's and Anderson's dismay, and to make matters worse, the professor had a particular caustic attitude to what he labelled the "black identity movement." He regularly found fault with scholarly attempts to present a "glorified view of African history" and attacked the credentials of Cheikh Anta Diop and Walter Rodney, two intellectual giants who were preeminent pundits in the annals of Black African scholarship. Klein argued they were not true historians. Tantamount to academic blasphemy, this intellectual affront spurred Oji and Anderson into action. To assist in the professor's "re-education," the two young students regularly posted a variety of anonymous notices on his office door emblazoned with "Cheikh Anta Diop is a historian," and so on. If and when removed, another sign would soon go up. Such were the kind of creative acts of upheaval (or "good trouble," according to the late John Lewis, US congressman and civil rights leader) that Oji, Anderson, and others had to carry out in response to the barrage of intellectually abusive, biased, narrow-minded, Eurocentric scholarship prevalent at the time on the University of Toronto campus.

Besides pulling off these playful stunts, Oji distinguished himself as an influential, unflinching leading voice for African Canadian university students. He gained attention in a variety of student newspapers across Ontario universities including *The Varsity* and *The Gargoyle* (Toronto), *The Excalibur* (York), and *The Charlatan* (Carlton University) in Ottawa. As his reputation and visibility grew as a daring politically minded student-leader, so did the prominence of the ACSA. Leadership in the nascent student movement was a pivotal launching pad for Oji as he became the focal point through which other Black activists, on and off campus, began to channel their mobilization. As ACSA president, he established himself as a creditable voice for Black liberation, thereby widening his platform, popularity, and influence. Soon, he would become the nexus connecting various revolutionary threads running through Toronto's Black community.

When the ROM exhibit became a flashpoint for protest, it was only a matter of time before someone came looking for him. That person would be Afua Cooper, then a student of history at the University of Toronto. Afua, like many others who had seen the exhibit, came away disturbed. Sensing that action was needed, she decided to approach Oji, knowing he would be uniquely placed to provide the leadership required to rally community support. Although not initially interested, Oji in time would set in motion events leading to the creation of the Coalition for the Truth about Africa (CFTA), and the offices of the ACSA would become mission control for the demonstrations.

It was about December of 1989 when Afua first approached Oji on the St. George Street campus to discuss the well-promoted exhibit, which had opened months earlier. Ras Rico, who was meeting Oji for the first time, was also present. Ras Rico had become radicalized in 1978 after the Toronto police killing of twenty-four year old Andrew "Buddy" Evans at a nightclub on King Street West in Toronto. The coroner's inquest, which followed, exonerated the officer of any wrongdoing. The following year, Ras Rico noticed a similar pattern of complacency and official apathy when Albert Johnson was killed by Toronto police. Provoked into becoming a justice activist, Ras Rico jumped into action. He used his *Thursday Morning with Ras Rico I* show on CIUT FM as a platform to communicate his ideas. By 1989, when the ROM exhibit made its debut, he could not rest, which explains his presence alongside Afua in the office of the ACSA. Both were interested in launching a protest. However, they needed a leading energizer, one with the necessary organizational expertise to inspire and influence other young activists.

Afua, a fellow student at the St. George campus who majored in African history and who would go on to earn a PhD in African Canadian history, made a fervent appeal for a strong challenge and called on Oji to get involved. Both Afua and Ras Rico were aware of Oji's visibility and his effectiveness in organizing and leading campaigns to address Black-related student issues across Canada. Afua asked Oji to convene a meeting to organize students in concert with the Black community. At first, Oji held back. He did not have time; he was already too busy to be initially interested. Actively fighting ACSA's eviction notice, he was already preoccupied with campus politics. Additionally, he had a part-time job in Kensington Market, working to assist his mother as she single-handedly attempted to support her four children through school. He was also working hard to get through his studies while being a staff photographer for *The Varsity* newspaper, and he had ACSA's upcoming twentieth anniversary celebrations to plan for, an event scheduled for February 1990. As fate would have it, Oji relented. Afua's call did not fall on deaf ears. He urged her to return at a later date when he would have more time. To her credit, she did.

When significant discussions in the Black community began to spread regarding the ROM's exhibit, the debate eventually mushroomed, filtering throughout every facet of Black life, including the University of Toronto, Ryerson, and other college campuses. The St. George campus, which stood not far from the ROM, easily became a rallying point, particularly within the offices of the ACSA. Oji, in his capacity as acting president, along with other members, rapidly became a key leading influence in organizing and facilitating the ROM demonstrations that soon followed.

The ACSA must have been successful in their bid to remain at 44 St. George Street, because it was here on March 6, 1990, that the CFTA was born. Here, Oji met Brother Yaw for the first time. The two would go on to enjoy a long-lasting collaboration, one that would long outlive the ROM protest. Alliances were also formed with other student-led groups such as the Ryerson Anti-Apartheid Movement, whose president, Silbert Barrett, would become one of several leading organizers and spokespersons for the CFTA.

Likely, neither the CFTA or the ROM protest would have materialized had it not been for Afua's appeal to the ACSA and for Oji's responsive leadership efforts in mobilizing the coalition. The growth, development, and membership of the CFTA would also not have been possible had it not been for the hard work and input made by numerous individuals drawn primarily from this student-led united front. Afua, a founding member of CFTA, attended some of the demonstrations and remained an important enduring voice. Spearheading the charge were those who would eventually become the bulwark, those committed to the point where they were willing to be arrested—including Barrett and McKenzie—and who would later become known as the ROM 11.

Through these experiences, Oji began to further extend his leadership profile. Along with his formal education, he now gained even more street credibility. By collaborating with a range of organizations, like-minded individuals, and groups interested in advocating for anti-Black racism and advancing Pan-African approaches, he began to widen his scope and deepen his experience. Through his involvement with the ROM demonstration, he would also learn more about his strengths and weaknesses. He came to better understand his role in filling the perceived void in leadership and how he could best contribute to the broader movement for racial equality, social and economic justice. He was so utterly committed to achieving his vision that he was prepared to die trying.

MACPRI: The African Image Revolution

As he began to feel *the joy of true self-pride*, Oji expanded his range of interests, growing his enterprise to include other lines of business. In an effort to maintain self-employment, he developed a business entrepreneurial and self-reliance mindset. During its infancy between 1987–90, before officially launching, MACPRI—Mother Africa's Children Photographic Reproductions International—existed only as a single entity geared to showcasing photographic images. The initial goal was to use photography as a medium to promote greater understanding of African life and culture. Primary activities during this early genesis included visual photo displays, slide presentations, performances, lectures, and discussions. While he did not have command of extensive resources enjoyed by institutions such as the Royal Ontario Museum, it is evident that Oji was acting proactively early on to champion an alternative narrative in contrast to the imperialist storylines projected by Victorian-like museums and other postcolonial educational institutions.

Dedicated to developing the African Image Revolution, Oji positioned his company as an enterprise committed to global African partnerships in education, art, spiritual, intellectual and economic development. His intention from the outset was to create a business model reflective of African philosophical principles. To this end, he infused his business practice with African concepts such as *Ujamaa*, which became not only a guiding principle but also acted as a means of imparting African philosophy, history, and ways of living.[39]

In its early incubation period, MACPRI and Oji were initially supported by a group of young ardent African Canadians such as Lanchester Anderson, many of whom shared a mutual passion. They had similar ideas regarding self and community development, and emulated and inspired each other through their courage, curiosity, creativity, and through their relentless push for change and community empowerment. Most have since moved on to lead their own community development initiatives. Claudette Barrett was one of the first to be responsible for

---

[39] *Ujamaa*, regarded as one of the seven principles of *Kwanzaa*, refers to the collective creation and maintenance of infrastructure, businesses, and enterprises for the benefit of the entire community. *Ujima*, meaning collective work and responsibility, refers to the practice of having joint responsibility for making each other and our community better through collective effort.

MACPRI's public relations. Howard James helped with publishing. In recalling this period, Oji remembers many other friends who rallied to his vision: Grace-Ann Abena Osbourn-James and Kwabena Kwao, who both moved to Kenya; Kwaku Henne, who moved to the US; V. Anderson, who remained in Canada; Christine Decordova in Jamaica; and Kofi Owusu in Ghana. The sustained success of MACPRI might not have been realized had it not been for these early partnerships of young talent pooling their efforts to liberate themselves from institutional structures of dependency.

Based on the principle of *Ujamaa*, Oji also cultivated significant cross-border partnerships to further his objectives. These partnerships have led to collaborations in Jamaica, Ghana, and a variety of other Caribbean and African countries, including the twin republic of Trinidad and Tobago, Kenya, Nigeria, Tanzania, and Zimbabwe.

Two noteworthy associates related to the history of MACPRI were Brother Andrew and Brother Sankofa. Brother Andrew, who has invested significantly in MACPRI's success, served at one time as deputy chief (or vice president), a role he held for over a decade. His able contribution and presence helped to establish MACPRI's early success.

Brother Sankofa, meanwhile, has been a longstanding MACPRI collaborator on a variety of initiatives including the All-African Dance Party, a series of Toronto fundraisers for various causes. The dance parties, which were popular in the early 2000s, brought together vendors to showcase African fashion, food, art, and music, and featured a new wave of DJs—Apollo, Kokofele, and the Mighty Hefty—all of whom had a knack for Africentric Caribbean beats. In essence, the dance parties were a means of promoting the African Image Revolution. Brother Sankofa, an impresario in his own right, used his brand name Westside Cipher to host his own events and parties with MACPRI support. This cross-collaboration was not uncommon. It was one of many examples of *Ujamaa*—collective work and responsibility or cooperative economics—in practice.

Another illustration of reciprocity was exemplified when Brother Sankofa, a past president of the Prospect Primary School Alumni Association, requested assistance from Oji in support of a fundraising brunch to help with the primary school's building fund in Jamaica. In response, MACPRI donated African artifacts and photographs, which were auctioned at the event. MACPRI has also supported clothing drives and various fundraisers to support community endeavours such as the Marcus Garvey Day celebrations. By this and through other means, MACPRI has nurtured relationships to enable the advancement of the African Image Revolution through poetry, music, art, a newsletter, and a wide variety of community endeavours locally and abroad. Brother Sankofa and Brother Andrew each have their own stories, each in their own way adding to Oji's kente cloth, even as he has contributed to theirs.

Besides his family, other personnel who have played key roles in MACPRI's early growth and success include Michelle Munroe, who acted as publicist; Denise Maxwell, and Muchoki Simba, Oji's one-time financial advisor and right-hand man. Others such as Nene Kwesi Kafale, and the dear late Ekua Walcott have also made meaningful contributions.

Above*: Brother Oji standing with Brother Sankofa,
one of his main community collaborators.
Below*: Brother Oji with his sister, Suzette, at Artscape Wychwood Barns in Toronto.
(Oji/MACPRI Archives)

Sankofa Tours

Kwame Ben-Eden making his *sankofa* journey.
(Photo taken on behalf of MACPRI/Oji Archives.)

When Oji first travelled to Ghana in 1991, he knew he would return. He also knew he wanted to share his experience with others so they, too, could have their own *Sankofa journey*—their own opportunity to rediscover and restore connection with their African ancestry, a connection largely severed by European enslavement and colonialism.[40]

Oji's initial travel to Africa was inspired chiefly by the *call to return* made by the Honourable Marcus Garvey. This led to numerous subsequent visits culminating in 2002 when he launched MACPRI Sankofa Kingdom Adventure Tours as a means of bringing others to Africa. His inaugural tour included three of his friends—Kwabena, Kwaku, and Brother Yaw—all of whom had collaborated closely with Oji. To celebrate their return, a traditional welcome ceremony was held for the three *Sankofans* (referring to those who made the journey). The ceremony was held in the presence of local officials at the palace of the Akan chieftaincy in Techiman, Ghana. All three men were so moved by their experience that they later adopted Techiman as their honorary African Ghanaian home. Brother Yaw later relocated to Ghana after moving to the US. So too did Brother Kwabena, accompanied by his wife, Asantewaa; their connection to Africa restored, the couple would eventually move to Ethiopia before they finally settled in Kenya.

---

40 In the Akan language, *sankofa* means "Go back and get it" and is traditionally represented by the mythical Sankofa bird flying forward with a contorted neck looking backwards, a metaphor for remembering your roots and for knowing your history. Sankofa is also a commonly used name for males of African descent.

In 2003, Oji took a second group of five *Sankofans* to Africa. Collectively from Florida and Maryland, the group was escorted to Larteh, home to the Akuapem-Guan people, reputed to be the original settlers of Ghana. Here, they visited places of historical interest, including sacred shrines. As required by custom, a traditional welcome ceremony was held by members of the local chieftaincy. Visiting a village palace was diplomatically important. On entering a village, specific customs for both visitors and host had to be observed. Visitors, for example, first had to seek permission from the village leaders, clearly stating the purpose of their visit. These and other protocols were intended to be expressions of goodwill, a way of demonstrating courtesy. Oji had to correctly learn and adhere to these customs in order to gain reciprocal respect, build trust, and acquire credibility. To his credit, he was able to master these practices in the appropriate manner, thereby building sufficient rapport to earn recognition as a well-meaning emissary. Over time, he would be acknowledged as a trusted son of Africa, recognized as someone interested in completing his own *sankofa* journey while assisting others in completing theirs. Not only was Oji well received in Larteh, it is also said that the town became a famous destination among travellers as a result of his visits and as a result of his endearment to the area. In many subsequent trips to Larteh, Oji donated clothing, gifts, and school supplies to the families he adopted, and who adopted him. The African Image Revolution, indeed, had many sides.

Over the ensuing years, Oji continued to guide many more individuals on their first *sankofa* journey. Such journeys went beyond Ghana to include Togo and Benin, where he conducted tours of historical sites, including Allada, the hometown of the Haitian revolutionary leader Touissiant L'Ouverture. In many instances, he partnered with other guides such as Prince Judah, and in some cases collaborated with Nene Kwasi Kafele, himself an African Canadian *sankofa* organizer and conductor.[41]

One person who experienced his *sankofa* journey with Oji was civil engineer Kwame Ben-Eden. Moved by his deep love for Africa, Kwame has since acquired property in Ghana. More significantly, he and his wife, Marshalette Mactyson, have established the Love Africa Project, an initiative to build public washrooms in Ghana. The idea for Love Africa first came to him in 2014 when, on an early morning jog along the beach in the coastal community of Salt Pond, he discovered people congregating not to swim but to answer the call of nature. Kwame, after making his reconnection with his ancestral roots, was motivated to ensure that he and his wife played their part in contributing to Africa's growth.

The spin-off and ripple effects from Oji's trips are yet untold. Not only is he helping many to return, he is also opening the door to allow for the further development of West African communities. As he explains it: "If the triangular trade [the system of exploitative European commerce between European, African and American ports] led to the destruction of Africa—then engaging in the process of de-triangulation of Africa will aid in Africa's redemption."

Through working with a variety of groups and individuals to plan, organize, and execute cross-Atlantic African excursions to explore life, history, and culture, Oji was able to expand his repertoire of business competencies. He established connections in West Africa that have

---

41 My *sankofa* journey in 2015 with Nene is documented in Good Morning, Afrika: A Photo-Journey Home, self-published in 2016.

translated into mutually beneficial community business and educational opportunities. This aside, the greater learning he derived were lessons pertaining to himself. By embracing his multiple spiritual connections to the vast diverse expanse of West African traditions, he became more whole. By acknowledging the presence of a Pan-African body, he became less parochial and broadened his horizon. He could see with more clarity how bloodlines stretched from Gambia, Guinea Bissau, Guinea, Sierra Leone, and Liberia to the Ivory Coast; from Mali, Burkina Faso, Togo, Benin, Nigeria, Niger, Cameroon, Congo, Angola, and Gabon, all the way back to the Americas and the Caribbean. He learned to gaze at himself and see all of it. Now he could stare at a legacy bigger than himself; he could enjoy a birthright spreading beyond the land of his birth or place of citizenship to somewhere profoundly rooted in African soil.

On visiting Larteh in 2004, after conducting another *sankofa* tour, Oji took the time to meet with the families he had come to know. As usual, he brought gifts. They delighted in his company; he delighted in theirs. So profound was their bond of friendship, so remarkable their sense of kinship, that Oji was inspired to request, and was honourably offered, a ceremonial stool. This stool remains one of his prized possession.

Today, not surprisingly, Oji has a home and family in Ghana, West Africa, where he lives with his wife, Korkori, and their four children. In addition, for a number of years, Oji and his wife raised and cared for Akosua Kanji (Akos), an adopted daughter. As is the practice in Ghana, when a child's parents have both transitioned, the child is cared for by extended family. Such was the case with fourteen-year-old Akos, who remained in the Oji household for four years until she matured enough to care for herself. Akos, who enrolled in hairdressing school, has successfully completed her apprenticeship and has since established her own business. She is now on track to having a family of her own. The African Image Revolution, indeed, has many sides and sees to it that no one associated with it ever have to *eat or be crumbs*.

Photo-Journalism

Following his first visit to Africa, Oji needed a way to bring Africa back to those who were, for whatever reason, not able to make their own sojourn. It did not take him long to find a solution. Through the use of visual images, he has allowed many to have a deeper appreciation of the incredible richness of African culture, tradition, and way of life. His achievement as a photo-historian will likely be one of his most lasting legacy.

A self-proclaimed modern nomad due to his recurring trips between Ghana, Jamaica, and Canada, his body of work roams between all three locations depicting the daily life of people within the African diaspora as they exude joy, laughter, beauty, sadness, hope, and triumph.

His body of work collectively captures images that are as awe-inspiring as they are profound. Many have been exhibited in North America, Africa, and the Caribbean.

In 1979, after acquiring his first camera, Oji developed a passion for photography. During his stint as a staff photographer at the University of Toronto's *The Varsity* newspaper, his interest grew even more as he quickly increased his skill by expanding his use of equipment to produce captivating compelling images. While at the University of Toronto, he registered for a course in documentary photography at George Brown College to further hone his technique. This, together with influences from other student journalists including Isabel Vincent and Naomi Klein and photographers such as David Berman, Michael J. Cooper, and the late David B. Maltby, all of whom tended to view the world through a different lens, helped to shape Oji's unique aesthetic. Maltby in particular, who had an eye for social realism and an interest in the issue of homelessness, more often than not used a wide-angled lens to capture impactful street life images. This technique allowed Maltby to give his otherwise maligned subjects a sense of dignity. Oji admired Maltby's style and adopted a similar approach. "When I finally developed my own visual education concept," said Oji, "I had David to thank for the initial inspiration ... his memory will live on in my work."

By definition, the declared intent of the African Image Revolution, according to Oji, was to revolutionize how Africans at home and abroad saw themselves and how others perceived them. Through his eyes were revealed positive visual images. He reframed the African world from a perspective rarely seen in mainstream media, an antithesis to the negative demeaning images propagated by agents of neocolonialism and paternalistic relief development agencies operating in Africa. Consistent with his role as *Mwalimu*, Oji acquired a passion for presenting African history in ways he had not seen in the school books he read or heard in the classrooms and churches he attended. The result is a photographic portfolio that stands as a positive testament in tribute to people of African ancestry. His body of work offers fresh insights into the nuances of contemporary Black life and culture.

His first major photo exhibit took place in 1989 at 1621 Dupont Street, Toronto, former location of the Jamaican Canadian Association. This exhibit, sponsored by Professor Chamberlin, was entitled "Jamaica: A look at the Social and Cultural Reality" and signalled the scholarly significance of Oji's artistic focus. Another MACPRI exhibit entitled "Peoples of West Africa" was staged at A Different Booklist in 2001. This was followed up with an exhibit of the same name presented at the Celine Allard Gallery in Toronto in 2003 with the assistance of A Different Booklist Cultural Centre and other partners. This exhibit, featuring almost two hundred of Brother Oji's photographic concepts covering the vast diversity of West African culture and day-to-day life, was well received.

His next major exhibit, mounted at the Knowledge Bookstore Liberation Lounge Gallery in Brampton, took a while in coming; but when it opened in 2007, it was obvious why. "Mother God" was a landmark exhibit displaying over twenty years of Oji's work. In 2011, during the Scotia Bank Contact Photography Festival, he expanded his audience base by showcasing his work at Spence Gallery, then located in Mirvish Village, and known for featuring contemporary expressions of Caribbean, Latin, and African art.

As a photographer, Oji was never interested in Western art aesthetics for its own sake. "I am not a photography, per se," he was once quoted as saying. "Photography is merely the medium I have chosen to accomplish my ends—education that will lead to better understanding and uplift of the people of Africa." (Oji/MACPRI Archives)

"Mother God"
MACPRI © Adisa Oji signature photograph featuring Apana Ndaele (Bolgatanga, Ghana, 2006). Affectionately known as Mama Apana, she was at least 117 years old when she transitioned to be with her ancestors. As the oldest person in her village, many came from far and near to honour her.

"Ummu & Dudu"
MACPRI © Adisa Oji signature photograph featured as part of his "Mother God" collection. In the photograph taken at the Makah family home, Ummu, while preparing the evening meal, cradles Dudu on her back and takes a pause to look out at her garden. (Goree, Senegal, 2001)

Rowing Her Own Boat
MACPRI © Adisa Oji photograph featuring the world
famous "Village in the Lake" at Ganvie,
Benin, 2004. The village is known as the largest lake village in Africa.

Village in the Lake
MACPRI © Adisa Oji photograph featuring the "Village in the Lake" at Ganvie, Benin, 2004.

His subsequent exhibit, held in June 2012 at the Annual International Maroon Convention in Charles Town, Portland, Jamaica, also bore great significance. It was organized in conjunction with the Jamaican launch of his brother's debut documentary film *Akwantu: The Journey*. Oji, who was chief stills photographer for the documentary, also had his photography featured in Roy's follow-up documentary film, *Queen Nanny: Legendary Maroon Chieftainess*, which was premiered at the United Nations in New York late 2015.

Besides his photo exhibitions, Brother Oji served as a freelance photographer with *The Gargoyle* and other student publications, as well as with *Contrast,* a Greater Toronto Area weekly. He also wrote and published articles in *Voices of Harmony for Humanity* and *Power to the People*, community newspapers promoting revolutionary thought. He was an official photographer for *Power to the People*, which operated for a time out of the offices of the ACSA while he was president.

As a photographer, he had the honour of photographing Dr. Frances Cress-Welsing at the Fifth Conference for the Unity of African Students held in Toronto, October 26, 1990. Other notables who fell within the frame of his lens included Maulana Karenga, Professor Muhammed Ahmad, bell hooks, Ngũgĩ wa Thiong'o, and Nelson and Winnie Mandela when the couple visited Queen's Park in June 1990. In the realm of entertainment, Judy Mowatt of the I-Threes, Mutabaruka, and Public Enemy were among some of his more well-known photo subjects.

There is a hushed awakening that pervades Oji's photo exhibits as patrons peruse his collection with fresh eyes, a shaft of light steadily penetrating quiet darkness, stirring up consciousness, giving needed illumination intellectually, artistically, politically, and spiritually. As a photographer, Oji was never interested in Western art aesthetics for its own sake, an aesthetic sometimes held as the gold standard by which all others are judged. "I am not a photography, per se," he was once quoted as saying. "Photography is merely the medium I have chosen to accomplish my ends—education that will lead to better understanding and uplift of the people of Africa." His approach is to leverage art as a vehicle for social change and community development, to use art media as a form of contemporary resistance to oppression. By making the invisible visible and by giving voice to the voiceless, his photography has served to rebalance the scales of power.

Oji often quotes Chinua Achebe, who has been credited with saying, "Art for art's sake is just another piece of deodorized dog shit." The renowned author is also known to have said, "Art is man's constant effort to create for himself a different order of reality from that which is given to him." This could also be said of Oji's photographic archive, a collection dedicated to stirring our imagination, opening our eyes to witness images previously overlooked, caricatured or misrepresented. Oji's body of work may not qualify as *high art* or be regarded as an artistic *tour de force*. It is a powerful collection, nonetheless. By paying tribute to people of African ancestry, he is making a strong philosophical and artistic statement. This *is* the African Image Revolution: to instigate new, yet not so new, discoveries; to manifest African culture and Black life in ways not possible through colonial xenophobic lenses. Now, new observations can come to light; at last, our eyes can behold the beauty of what was previously despised, and *we will live*. "We cannot return to the past," says Oji, "but we can use our knowledge gained from history to develop a new vision for the future with a greater sense of cultural integrity."

Top: Children playing Oware in Ghana.
Below: Children playing Oware in Toronto. (MACPRI)

Oware

Brother Oji is the chief executive officer and founder of Oware Canada, another cultural business pillar. Through Oware Canada, he has become known as the primary Canadian supplier and promoter of Oware, an African-inspired board game comparable to chess. The game has become increasingly popular among local communities and schools following his launch of Canada's First Toronto International Oware Tournament in 2011.

Here is how he describes the game in a promotional video:

> There is a legend in Twi, the language of the Asante people of Ghana, that the game got the name Oware when a couple began to play endlessly. So as to allow them to complete the game, they got married. This way they could always be together. Hence the name: Oware or Wari meaning he/she marries. In another context it translates: A lifelong affair bearing on marriage. Oware is one of the world's famous games, having its roots in antiquity from Kuma temples of Egypt to ancient Zimbabwe and Uganda. It has many names. In Ghana there are five different versions of play. But no matter the version, the game is intensely exciting and alluring. It is hard to stop once you begin. Oware is a game of numbers. To play you better know how to count. It is an excellent way to teach mental math skills. Children, who would scoop out holes in the earth, using pebbles or seeds as counters, played Oware, in the old days. Oware is a numbers game. 12 represent the number of cups. 4 represent the number of seeds in each cup at the start of every game. 1 and 2 represent the amount of seeds an opponent can capture when the last seed is placed on the opponent's side. Oware is a mental game, a strategic game where seeds are moved in a counterclockwise direction with a view to get or capture as many seeds as possible. The Oware board is a beautiful ornament. The two-row version is used almost universally north of the Equator. Kings played it on beautifully carved ivory boards embellished with gold. Today Kings and Queens still play Oware.

When he came across the game during his first visit to Ghana, he knew immediately he needed to introduce Oware to Canada. He knew the game would make an extraordinary impact on the lives of Canadians, young and old alike. As a teacher, he was able to visualize the game's merit as a teaching aid, a tool to help students master basic math skills such as counting. In addition, the game called for clear thinking, strategizing, and problem-solving—mental skills adults could benefit from. While doing teacher qualification training at Kingsview Village Junior School, he experimented with integrating the game into his lesson plan. By using the game in this way, he noticed how better engaged his students became as he applied it in a range of learning activities including art, social studies, math and even a field trip. Immediately, he realized the game's educational value and its potential to captivate students. Furthermore, he envisioned Oware as an excellent way to uniquely introduce Canadians, students and non-students, to African history and culture.

As he began to learn more about the game, he came to appreciate Oware's long history as a "pit and pebble" game originating in Africa in places such as the Nile Valley dating back thousands of years. He discovered that there were approximately three hundred versions of the pastime, which had migrated beyond Africa to various parts of the world. He began to appreciate the impact of cultural appropriation. More importantly, he began to better understand the impact of cultural migration on the interconnectedness of African people worldwide. While the Egyptians or Arabs called it Mancala, the game would become known as *Ware* or *Warri* in the Eastern Caribbean. *Ware* is the national game of Antigua. The Philippines, Indonesia, India, and Germany also have their own versions of the game. When Oji learned that there was an entity called the Oware Society of England, he conceived the idea of launching Oware Canada under the MACPRI banner. The outcome was Canada's First International Oware Tournament in the fall of 2011. Since then, Oware Canada has continued to fulfill its mission of promoting knowledge of the game, locally and nationally.

Through this annual tournament, an abundance of young people, particularly those of African descent, have become attracted to the game, causing many of them to become more constructively engaged and aware of their own heritage and achievements. After staging these tournaments for a number of years, it is evident that the game of Oware has served to bring people of varied backgrounds together, both young and old. As Oji anticipated, the young are becoming increasingly attracted to playing the game. As they play, they are building self-esteem even as they interact with the game and with each other. Everyone who plays the game, regardless of background or age, develops a greater appreciation for the world and people around them.

The annual Oware tournaments have expanded to become a community family day, an all-ages celebratory affair spiced with Africentric music, food, and cultural vendors. A warm uplifting festive spirit pervades the atmosphere. The people gathered are happy to see one another. It is as if they are of one heart, one purpose, joyful even. The Oware competition remains the centrepiece spectacle, a round-robin playoff in which many players enter but one champion emerges. Gathered in pairs with an Oware game board between them seated along several lengthy tables laid out in an auditorium, players of all ages and gender ready themselves to compete as surrounding families and friends cheer them on. From the opening round to the final playoff, the accented sound of beads hitting the boards have become the tournament's soundtrack. Visible at each table is the palpable intense concentration on each competitor's face as they contemplate their next jump, bead by bead, moving steadily until only two players remain.

On that historic day, October 29, 2011, when MACPRI held its first tournament, there were forty-eight players who squared off under the watchful eye of two hundred spellbound spectators. As the series whittled down to the last two contestants, an old man and a young boy emerged as the tournament's best players. The old man would prevail as the crowned king. However, the young boy was no less a crowned prince. His was a brilliant challenge up against an octogenarian, a man who had been playing Oware for most of his life and who knew every trick, every twist and turn on the game board. It was an apt ending, a beautiful final game culminating with much uproar, a validation of MACPRI's African Image Revolution. On that day, two hundred people watched as a community began to see itself differently while at the same time transforming the way they were seen by others.

By way of outreach, Oji has expanded the field of play by introducing Oware to various school boards and districts. Consistent with MACPRI's business model, Oware game boards are produced in Ghana by Ghanaian artisans. Sankofa Kingdom Enterprise is responsible for acquiring the games in Ghana, while Oware Canada is responsible for promoting the game in Canada, which are in turn marketed by MACPRI.

Through Oware, Oji had created *something new for his children.*

Crowned king and prince of the 2011 Oware Tournament. In front, second from the right, is Suzette, Brother Oji's sister. His mother is fourth from the right in the rear. Brother Andrew is second from the left. (MACPRI)

Made in Africa Awards

The culturally conscious business entities created by Brother Oji afforded him independence and the ability to support numerous community projects. As a photojournalist, entrepreneur, teacher, and activist, he continues to evolve his vision, regularly looking for opportunities to serve and contribute to the African diasporic community. His most recent endeavour is the Made in Africa Awards Movement, a showcasing of iconic awards and original recognition pieces created by African artisans using raw materials indigenous to Africa. The craftsmanship of these awards is exceptional. The signature pieces are stunning. Through this means, Brother Oji has drawn public attention to the need to celebrate and recognize new names with new and different monuments while memorializing a new era of historical achievements.

In keeping with the objective of his African Image Revolution—changing the way in which people of African ancestry see themselves and how they are seen by others—Oji advanced the idea that individuals and groups within the African diaspora should be recognized with Africentric African-made awards. Although individuals and groups within the African Canadian community were being presented with accolades, they were being honoured with trophies and plaques that were neither made by Africans nor sourced from Africa. According to Oji, "When you have an opportunity to support what is produced by your own people, why not give that a try? We have African Canadian Awards, African Achievement Awards, African Entertainment Awards, African Community Development Awards. Why not choose a trophy award made in Africa?"

In alignment with his business model, he saw this as a way of supporting self-sufficiency in Africa, a way of "supporting our own ... supporting economic development, job creation, entrepreneurship, and self-esteem." He argued that award recipients within the African diaspora would "feel a closer connection to their awards if they were made by the hands of their own people."

Emelia and Wilson Aboagye from Aburi, a town in the Akuapim South Municipal District of the Eastern Region of south Ghana, are members of MACPRI's Made in Africa team. Said Wilson, "We want it to be great! We want to get more orders. You will benefit. The carvers will benefit. My wife will benefit, my children will benefit. Even all our workers will benefit. Even here in Aburi the community will benefit, because we are going to use the monies we get to buy something from Aburi ... we are supporting the economy of Aburi. In five-years everybody in Aburi is going to enjoy if our business is going good."

On December 28, 2016, the Made in Africa Awards Movement reached a significant milestone. On that day at the WEB Du Bois Memorial Centre for Pan-African Culture, thirty-four African Caribbean diasporans were granted their Ghanaian citizenship. Presiding over the ceremony was Ghana's immediate past president, John Dramani Mahama. As part of the ceremony, the president was presented with a Made in Africa award produced by master carver Albert Buamah. In this defining moment, it became clear that Oji had accomplished his goal of *creating something new for his nation.*

(MACPRI)

Workshops, Seminars, and Public Speaking

Building a self-reliant business model rooted in community partnerships has not been without challenges. There have been some hard lessons. Working with high-spirited, passionate individuals to build trust while having to resolve conflicts between strong egos possessing diverse styles, needs, and interests is hard at the best of times. Additionally difficult is the task of establishing partnerships within disenfranchised communities where sharp rivalries exist due to disunity flowing from a long history of divide and conquer. Nevertheless, this is the aim of the African Image Revolution—to counter negative effects with an equal or greater positive force. It is never possible to know how difficult this is until it is attempted.

In September 2010, Oji disappointingly had to notify his deputy director, Brother Andrew, that their annual African Business and Community Development Conference would have to be cancelled. Although a date had been booked and a location secured, subscription leading up to the conference was lethargic. Only three people had officially signed up. Two others expressed regrets. It would have been MACPRI's fifth African Business and Community Development Conference, a forum in which Oji discusses his life's work with community partners while brainstorming on strategies for future community development. This particular year, the gathering, which also included feasting and fellowship, had remarkably low uptake. Disheartened, Oji recognized this as an indication of the multiple challenges he and others were facing at the time (there was a climate of uncertainty due to an ongoing recession) and pressed on.

Finding the right time, the right place, and the right people to embrace his bold, broad vision would be one of many obstacles he would face. In particular, finding investors willing to take a risk on his ventures was never easy. It is a wonder he was able to accomplish as much as he did without sacrificing his independence. His abrupt, straightforward manner sometimes did not help; his assertive, no-nonsense attitude was off-putting for those unprepared for it or for those unable to get past it. It took someone special to look beyond Oji's abruptness to see his genuine character and trustworthiness. Undeterred, he continued to secure opportunities wherever he could with partners who understood and agreed with his ideas. When funding was not forthcoming, he worked tirelessly to raise money on his own. For two of his exhibitions, expenses ran upward of CAD$15,000 for which he had to pay out-of-pocket. In order to meet these expenses, he had to be creative with his gifts.

Consistently self-reliant, he made do through lectures, workshops, seminars, or through other public appearances locally in Toronto or beyond, sometimes as far away as Ottawa. While Oji welcomed invitations to speak, he loathed not being compensated for his efforts. This may seem selfish, but to him, a request to speak without renumeration was but another example of the exploitation of Black expertise, an example of the replacement of slave labour with volunteer labour. A subject matter expert on a range of justice and African history related subjects, his presentations were often lofty but down to earth, covering such topics as *Institutionalized Racism* (presented to the African Canadian Student Association, September 1990), *The White Lie* (presented to the Ryerson African Caribbean Student Association, October 1990), *Pan-African Unity* (presented in March 1991 to the Institute of Professional Studies in Ghana), and *Race First and Self-Reliance* (presented in June 1991 to the African Canadian Community Education Service in Ottawa).

Never shy of controversy, on November 28, 1990, he spoke at the Ryerson Polytechnical Institute (now a university) on the topic *Religion, the Bible and Mind Control: Exploding the Myth*. By this time, he had been through the ROM protest, was arrested, and charged. He therefore had first-hand lived experience of what it was like to run afoul of the status quo. His presentation that night was worth the price of admission.[42] Enlivened by his transformation into an African liberation activist, Oji shifted into high gear, speaking out against racism at engagements such as the Malcom X Speaker Series in Ottawa in November 1991 and other like forums

As his standing grew as a penetrating public speaker who can sometimes be scathing but honest, so too did the demand for his voice particularly on Pan-African related matters. On August 18, 2001, he had the honour of making the keynote address at Garvey Day celebrations held at Toronto's Coronation Park, choosing as his theme "Taking Responsibility for Our Children's Education." This and other such engagements cemented his reputation as an Afrocentric educator, the *Mwalimu*.

Oji often requested and received, where possible, a stipend for his lectures. Should he wish to, and he sometimes did, he would levy an enrollment fee for his conferences and workshops. To supplement his earnings, he made and sold audio tapes of his speeches. By this and other means, he reinforced his self-reliance, funding his ventures when other sources failed to materialize.

"I am not trying to be a capitalist," he said. "Ninety percent of the money I make is cycled back into my community in a process of de-triangulation." By this, he is referring to his numerous other pioneering projects in Canada, Jamaica, and Ghana, which collectively are designed to combat ignorance and dependency while developing self-esteem and self-love within the African diaspora. The Mwalimu African Teaching Institute (ATI) Family Renewal Centre, together with the Mwalimu ATI Annual Community Gathering in St. Elizabeth, Jamaica, are but two examples. His initiative "Blacks Dolls Please," whereby Black dolls are donated to MACPRI for distribution to pre-schools in Ghana, is another.

---

42 Ryerson was named in honour of Egerton Ryerson, considered to be one of the leading architects of Canada's Indian residential schools. It is unlikely that Oji knew this at the time—this news only came to popular attention as recently as June 2021. However, his presentation must have been no less apt.

Ujaama

Herein lies his revolution.

Ujamaa, one of the seven principles of Kwanzaa practiced by individuals and communities for mutual benefit, refers to the principle and act of cooperative economics. While the goal may be economic sustainability, the impact spreads beyond material gain and contributes to community wellbeing, solidarity, and improved quality of life for all concerned.

In Toronto and in the Greater Toronto Area (GTA), in West Africa as well as in the Caribbean, Oji has been a strong proponent of *Ujamaa*. Community building is a part of his expanding body of achievements, a part of his DNA. And he is not alone. Within the GTA specifically, he has worked with many African and Caribbean Canadian community groups and individuals to build mutual capacity for major contribution to Canadian life. His list of partners are impressive, including collaborators such as the African Canadian Heritage Association, A Different Booklist Cultural Centre, Black Community Advisory Council in Peel Region, the Harriet Tubman Community Organization, the International African Inventors Museum, Sean Liburd and Knowledge Bookstore, Success Beyond Limits, Taibu Community Health Centre, the Love Africa Project, and the Zero Gun Violence Movement to name but a few.

Collectively, Oji and partners are creating fresh opportunities for wealth creation and community achievement, locally and globally. Jointly, they are creatively building sustainability and community self-reliance through mutually beneficial and cooperative business ventures. This is the new liberation. Chances are this revolution will never be televised or make the front-page news. Or will it? We will wait to find out. In any case, it does not matter. This revolution is already underway.

Roots and Fruits

Contrary to assumptions, Brother Oji is neither a cop-out nor a dropout, for this would suggest that so-called mainstream expectation is the one and only standard by which we should all be measured. On the contrary, Oji's decision to pursue his life path was premised on the willful exercise of his right to self-determine his own course and to do so on his own terms. In the long run, his example of taking the road less travelled may become the standard by which we are all judged.

The road less travelled is Oji's strength and emancipation. Unfettered, he has overcome great hurdles to pursue and fund his education and to meet his own needs and that of his family. As we have seen, he has, over time, financed the building of a modest home in Jamaica for his mother with whom he shares a close loving relationship. He makes regular financial contributions to support his close-knit family home in Toronto, and he is known to support and contribute to various development initiatives in Jamaica and in Africa. He is the spearhead of a new revolution. Yet he knows he cannot do it alone. According to him, "It takes more than one person to lay the foundation on which any family structure or society will be built."

There is a commonly manufactured narrative based on the stereotyping of people of African ancestry, one made popular by the Western purveyors of cultural thought—the mass media. It is a narrative focused principally on depicting backwardness, persistent impoverishment, violence, mayhem, and destitution. This viewpoint is displayed for example in late-night infomercials and projected in the glossy brochures of well-meaning aid agencies preying on public sympathy with images of abandoned, emaciated faces of dark desperately looking but otherwise beautiful African children in need of charitable support. One can be forgiven for believing this is the whole truth (and nothing but the truth) about people of African ancestry. While these conditions cannot be denied, we must be mindful that this is a subtext, not the full text. For amid injustice, brutality, marginalization, exploitation, and war, there is an even greater story of profound humanity, stories of startling achievements by African people who continue to move with great dignity in the face of extreme odds and adversity.

Where would we be had it not been for the massive contributions made by Africans in the fields of art, architecture, astronomy, economics, literature, philosophy, political science, mathematics, medicine, and more? How easily we are made to forget these great accomplishments, overshadowed as they are by the vulgar and distorted representation of the African diaspora in Western media. How quickly we forget the foundation built by African ancestry and their descendants; how casually we dismiss and overlook the growing self-empowerment of those who choose self-liberation and *Ujamaa* over victimhood and selfish individualism.

The accomplishments of people of African ancestry lie not only in antiquity or recent modern history. They are also emerging today in real time. In Toronto and throughout Canada, Africa, Latin America, the Caribbean, and across the world, there is a groundswell of a new exciting crop of scholars, poets, writers, thought-leaders, entrepreneurs, and innovators who are following in the footsteps of those who went before, pioneering new paths while contributing to the greater good. As a creative community builder, Brother Oji is doing his part. Through the practice of *Ujamaa*, he is nurturing and internationally showcasing African artistry, excellence, and economic viability. In one of his poems, "Offspring," he concludes, "I have sown the seeds / And nurtured the seedlings … The fruits have matured / And now I am ready for the harvest." In the end, we will all benefit.

The Real Revolution

A revolution is not necessarily always about bombs, guns, and violent overthrow of oppressive regimes. It is often about people rediscovering themselves; masses of ordinary folk bonding in communion to elevate each other beyond the disaster created by injustice, exploitation, and hatred.

Ernesto "Che" Guevara, in giving a speech in August 1960 to Cuban medical students and workers, said this:

> I was telling you that to be a revolutionary requires having a revolution. We already have it. *And a revolutionary must also know the people with whom he or she is to work.* I think we still don't know one another well. I think we still have to travel a while along that road. (Italics mine)

Brother Oji is still travelling along his road. He is continuing to discover more about himself and others. He has had to make some tough selective choices about who he aligns himself and the African Image Revolution with. Some decisions have been hard, while some have been easy. Decisions, such as that relating to Michael Evans, owner and president of Evans Electrical Services, for example, is of the easy kind.

Evans, who has been a friend and supporter of the revolution as far back as the early 1980s, is not a blood relative of Oji, but he may well have been. (The Andersons and Evans have been neighbours and close family friends for many years. Oji babysat Evans' first-born child, cementing a lasting bond between them.) Then and now, Evans, who is an entrepreneur, strongly believes in Oji's life and work. He has made significant contributions to many of MACPRI's projects, including the Oware Tournaments, doing so with grace, generosity, and trust.

As if this was not enough, in an unbelievable act of selfless kindness, Evans assisted Oji's wife and children in their planned 2013 visit to Canada. Unfortunately, the Canadian Embassy in Ghana denied Oji's wife the opportunity to travel on a visitor's visa on the basis that she was a "flight risk." However, their two children, Nana and RA, came at the time and had a wonderful visit with their extended Jamaican Canadian family.

Evans went even further. He insisted that the two children, after visiting Canada, should also visit Jamaica, "The Land of [their father's] Birth." "You can't let them come this far and not visit Jamaica," Evans mused. Thanks to Evans, with three plane tickets and pocket money in hand, Oji was able to take his two children home to his birthplace in Ridge Pen. Here, the children had a memorable time walking down dusty roads where their dad once roamed and played bare-footed. Evans also acted as chauffeur, travelling to Jamaica himself on an earlier flight so that he could pick them up at the Montego Bay airport before dropping them home in Ridge Pen.

And that wasn't all. When Korkori, Oji's wife, a beauty consultant, completed her training in cosmetology at a beauty college in Ghana and wanted to branch out to establish a consulting business and a teaching practice of her own, it was Evans who once again stepped in to provide the start-up loan. The agreement required Korkori to pay back in two years. Korkori worked hard. Her business showed great promise as she established her shop in three short months, travelling from Ghana to Nigeria by road to acquire supplies. In a very surprising and amazing twist of events, characteristic of Evans, he pardoned the loan and wrote it off. The news brought Korkori to tears and the ever so stoic Oji ... well almost.

And Mr. Evans has never even been to Ghana.

To share this piece of private personal anecdotal detail is unusual for Brother Oji. He is customarily discreet with personal private details such as this. It is likely his way of expressing gratitude for the love and generosity he has received from Evans and from many others over the years. But there may be another reason—to demonstrate that the African Image Revolution, indeed, has many sides.

In closing his aforementioned speech, Ernesto "Che" Guevara ended with a short quote from one of his own heroes—Cuban poet, philosopher, essayist, journalist, and professor José Martí—"The best form of saying is doing."

One day, Michael Evans will visit Ghana. And when he does, he will see firsthand what he has contributed to. One day, everyone will see what the African Image Revolution is doing.

RA and Nana (*left and centre*) visiting the land of their father's birth seen here with extended family as they are escorted by Packieman in the background. (Family album/Oji Archives)

Above: "The Bearded Ones" - The author with Winston "Hefty" Anderson to the left and Lee Miller, close friend of Brother Oji and long-time supporter of MACPRI, to the right. (MACPRI/Oji Archives)
Below: Brother Oji and Brother Andrew schooling the Honourable Jean Augustine on the finer points of Oware at one of the annual tournaments while a guest looks on. (MACPRI/Oji Archives)

Where Heaven Rests

Behold Woman
Beautiful Being
Anointed
Holiness in flesh
I will come when you call me
To be "Born again"
In your abode of happiness
Your place of peace is like no other

(Excerpt from a poem by Brother Adisa S. Oji)

Chapter 11
FAMILY

In the fall of October 1992, Oji was on bail pending appeal of his sentence. He continued to study while feverishly building his business, making the best of youth. As if he did not already have enough to worry about, he and his family now faced another significant loss.

With summer gone, nature began preparing for regeneration, autumn leaves gently floating to damp ground. A chill slowly crept in, foreshadowing the dreary days of winter. It was here between summer and winter that Theophilus Anderson, as if knowing, elected to take his last breath. He had seen enough of Canadian winters, had enough of suffering. He would shed his police uniform, his tool belt, and his aches, pains, and disappointments for the very last time and lay his burdens down to rest. Finally, he would be free—free from fear, doubt, guilt, and the nagging anxieties that haunted his once steely footsteps.

When Theophilus Anderson died, Oji did not shed a tear. He had intended to declare *war* on the day of his father's funeral. For this reason, he attended dressed in olive-green army fatigues complete with a beret and Dr. Martens boots. As it turned out, there was no war after all. Instead, Oji landed in limbo, suspended emotionally somewhere between anger and despair, a place approximating ambivalence. He was not indifferent. From a safe distance, he had watched his father suffer. For months prior, his father had been slowly deteriorating, physically and emotionally, as leukaemia mercilessly attacked his body, a severe nightmare, an unkind escort into the afterlife, rudely striping the once proud man of his vitality and everything he held dear. Life before death had not been pretty for the *old man*. Nor had life been pretty for Oji's family when his father was alive and well. And now life was uglier still as the one-time head of the family stood ready to make his final exit with no chance of recovery. Everyone knew his end was near. When the end finally came, Oji felt numb.

On the morning when he heard of his father's passing—he heard just hours after the time of death—Oji could not cry. No tears came. His father was dead; dead before his fiftieth birthday. *He called this upon himself ... he abandoned the family ... turned everyone against him ... brutal man ... stubborn ... unrepentant ... There are no tears for this. None can be found ... Forgiveness? Maybe.* This crossed Oji's mind. Maybe there was something he could do for his father in death that was not possible while he was alive. *Forgive ... release ... perhaps.*

Suzette, his sister, had encouraged him to *let it go*. In the absence of tears, thoughts of forgiveness slowly began to protrude like grass returning after winter, a recognition that Theophilus Anderson was, is, and always will be father of four ... *My father.*

On the day of the funeral, it rained unremittingly, the sky laden with dark clouds. As family and friends gathered to say their last farewell, the heavens shed the tears Oji could not. Thunder roared. Lightning clapped. Was this a good or bad omen? Was the sky laden with grief or relief? As the legacy left by the *old man* hung in judgement, his son weighed him in the balance and found him wanting.

Mud stuck to mourners' shoes as they slowly marched towards the gravesite, slugging through deep slush, leaving behind soggy footprints to complement dark heavy clouds suspended above. As everyone stood somber watching the coffin descend gradually, Oji looked on. Anger tugged at him, tearing him away from more tender emotions. Relentlessly, memories of fatherless years flashed across his mind. There are moments in a man's life when having a father to turn to, someone to confide in, is more precious than gold. Oji had encountered such moments—he was facing one now, times of personal challenge when a bond with his father would have been priceless. Instead, in the bitter glare of estrangement, love between them had turned to dust, leaving Oji to rely on his own manliness without a father to say, "Well done, son" or "Son, take good care" or "What's up, son, what's going on?"

While standing askance in the rain-soaked graveyard looking intense, Oji, despite his anger, softened as he slowly crossed an invisible line, surrendering to the pain beneath his rage. The empty loneliness that comes with father-hunger finally broke loose. As he acknowledged his hunger—a hunger no one else could satisfy—he turned to watch the man who gave him life, the man who nurtured that hunger, a brutish and abusive man, disappear into the earth. He had missed his father. And now he felt it like a sharp knife. He had missed his father for a long time. He just couldn't bring himself to feel it. He had missed his father more than he was willing to admit. Like the rain, he broke and cried, tears coming from his soul more than his eyes.

There, at that time and on that October day at his father's burial, Oji buried his anger, setting aside his sword and shield—a ceasefire between father and son. He took a cache of sand he had brought back from his first trip to Africa and, with it, he showered his father's coffin. Dust to dust, ashes to ashes. *To Africa he shall return.* Finally, he forgave the man who once tormented the family before abandoning them, the man he called father. From here on, Oji would choose to remember only the good. He picked up a shovel then heaped dirt onto the vanishing coffin as it sank eternally into the ground. The war between father and son was over. The rain was a good omen after all. Where once there was angst, there was now peace. He wished his father Godspeed. Surrounded by his mother, two brothers, and sister, and as friends circled in mourning, Oji found rest along with Theo.

It was done.

One of our greatest fear is that we may inherit the sins of our fathers. Theophilus Anderson was a stubborn man. So was Oji. When one of his grade-school teachers suggested that he was likely to become abusive because he grew up in an abusive home—a case of like father, like son—he thought the idea was "absolutely crazy."

"I don't want to tell you what happened to that teacher when she told me that crap," he recalls. Oji was suspended for a week. It is unclear exactly what he did say or do that day. But he was adamant. "She's wrong. I'm not like my father ... and none of us are."

One of our greatest desire is to outrun our father's faults. Mr. Anderson senior was "a brutal man," but he was also diligent. By all accounts, Theophilus Anderson was a disciplined hard worker who provided for his family, a man who made sure there was a roof over their heads, clothes on their backs, and food on their table. He assisted in sponsoring other extended family members to Canada and led his family to church services. One of our greatest privilege is to honour our parents. To honour his father, Oji built a house in his father's name, a house situated on land his father initially purchased from Alfred Rowe in 1966. In this way, Theo Anderson's legacy continues to live on.

The home built in Jamaica was co-dedicated to Oji's mother. Oji may be self-determined, but he is not self-made. He credits his family for his successes and gives credit above all to his mother. She gave life to him and three others. She would have raised five but lost one. When asked about heroes who inspired him, Oji is likely to single out Monifa Owusu; Donna Whitmore, his grade six teacher; Chinua Achebe (Things Fall Apart); Marcus Mosiah Garvey; Malcolm X; Professor Yosef A. A. Ben-Jochannan; Sidney Poitier; Samora Machel; Professor Edward Kamau Brathwaite; Professor Ted Chamberlin; and a number of other notable icons, some of whom have already been mentioned. Top of that list would be family members Lewis Rowe, grandparents Alfred and Geraldine Rowe, and his brother Roy T. Anderson. Queen of them all would be his mother, Geraldine Scarlett.

Even though Oji steered clear of wage labour, he admires his mother for her love and for the commitment and dedication she displayed throughout her forty years of hard work and sacrifice as a factory worker. Once a mother, always a mother, Geraldine is Brother Oji's biggest supporter. Without her, there would be no coming or going forth, no becoming. She allowed him to live rent-free in her Canadian homes for most of his life. While at times she feared for him, she always gave him her blessing, granting him the freedom to pursue his passions. She gave him latitude to travel and allowed him the emotional space required to develop his ideas. "Oji is Oji," she would often say with a placid smile, looking away and shaking her head in her usual understated way. After all, she is his best friend. Whether sitting down together chit-chatting over a cup of tea or having easy informal conversations as she reclines in bed, Oji seated on a sofa nearby, there is a deep unspoken connection between them, one that Oji rarely shares with anyone else. Held in high esteem by his mother, Oji has been entrusted with the role of the family's presumptive spiritual head, the one who guides them toward a deeper understanding of ancestral roots, traditions, and culture.

Finding love then letting go ... finding it again at last. Oji met Genevieve, affectionately known as Korkori, the woman who would become his wife, in November 2004. Less than a year later in March 2005, they would complete their first rite of marriage with a second to follow in June of the same year. The final and third rite of marriage to Genevieve Aryee Oji occurred on January 21, 2007, in the presence of Korkori's family. Present also were Roy and his wife Alison, and several of Oji's friends and advisors, including Andrew Martin, Michelle Munroe, and Yaw Owusu Akyeaw. When Roy visited Africa to attend the ceremony, it would be his first trip to Africa, the first time another member of Oji's blood family would be visiting the continent. It was a moving ceremony for all who participated.

Korkori, an "offspring of the Ga," gave birth to their first child—a girl—on January 21, 2006. The timing had special meaning for the couple. Korkori gave birth at the same age as Oji's mother when she gave birth to him. Nana's birth was as peaceful and quiet as his own. Oji would say, Nana Akpaabe Adessa Oji came as a "guide back to love." He knew his life would never be the same. The joy of having his first child with Korkori, a child born in Mama Africa, was beyond words. It was a sobering reality to know that the cycle of life would continue.

This was further validated *many moons* later with the arrival of RA Ndemelle. With RA's arrival, Oji had a dilemma. He wanted to name his first son Roy, after his older brother. However, the thought of an Anglicized name did not appeal to him. While wanting to honour his brother, he also wanted to remain true to his African ancestral roots and continue to embed this into his family bloodline. As if in a dream, the name came to him one morning as he awoke with images of the first two letters *R* and *A* imprinted on his consciousness—*R* for Roy and *A* for Anderson. As it turns out, RA also denotes the sun in ancient Egypt. If Nana was the "guide back to love," RA was sunshine—the giver of life. As life and love continued to flow through the Oji's family home, they were joined by Akos, who was adopted at about this time.

Nine years, later, Naa Shika Isaga Oji arrived. And in the summer of 2020 came the last born, Naa Joomo Oji, the seal.

Queen Mother—Brother Oji's mother and best friend, Geraldine Anderson. (Oji Archives)

Four generations of African women (*L–R*): Korkori's mother, Korkori, Nana, and Korkori's grandmother. (Oji Archives)

A strong cast of family members have supported Brother Oji's life and work, even as he has supported theirs. His grandparents and great-grandparents and their ancestors loom large as part of his extended entourage.

Christine Decordova (a.k.a. Cuz Nene), granddaughter of Ivan Rowe (younger brother of Alfred Rowe), remains one of his closest collaborators in several community initiatives in Ridge Pen. Similarly, Clifton Rowe (a.k.a. Packieman), last in a line of children for Geraldine and Alfred Rowe, and a favourite uncle, has also been a supporter, lending his efforts to the Mwalimu African Teaching Institute in Ridge Pen.

Roy T. Anderson, referred to as senior brother, grew to become a seasoned stuntman and stunt coordinator with blockbuster movies such a *Spiderman 2*, *Shaft*, and *Bourne Ultimatum* to his credit. As previously mentioned, he is also a filmmaker, his latest project being a documentary film on Jamaica's first national hero Marcus Garvey. Although they are a study in contrast—one on the ground, the other airborne—Oji and Roy share an enduring friendship and partnership. When Oji was mired in community activism in 1990 on Toronto streets, Roy was busy setting a stunt record by leaping twenty-eight feet between two Toronto high-rise buildings. While Roy is more inclined to practice tactful diplomacy, Oji can be relied on to be more forward, preferring to call it as he sees it. Yet they are closely tied, their brotherly affection readily apparent. Roy admits he does not fully understand the depths of Oji's beliefs, yet he respects his younger brother for his controversial positions. He admires Oji's studious and determined attitude and applauds him for sticking to his convictions—no matter the cost. Oji in turn is proud of his brother's accomplishments and is very supportive of Roy's cinematic endeavours, particularly when it comes to the telling of African-related narratives—or what Roy calls "Our stories." Their partnership can be seen in their joint work on Roy's three films. Oji's love for Africa, African culture, and history has influenced Roy not only on a personal level but has also helped to professionally inform Roy's work as a filmmaker. Acting as an advisor, liaison, and guide, Oji has accompanied his brother on various film projects across Canada, Ghana, Jamaica, and the USA. Their relationship continues to grow, their mutual love and respect not likely to be extinguished, for even though they may employ different means, they are both fearless and in all likelihood share a common purpose.

Sister, Suzette Anderson, aside from being the only female, is an anomaly within Oji's sibling line. She is the only one who is not self-employed. Similar to her mother, she has remained employed with the same organization all of her adult life. This steadfastness has given her the ability to offer her brother significant on-the-ground logistic support. By virtue of her stability, she has been able to make travel arrangements and provide administrative support to enable various missions between Canada, Africa, and Jamaica. Given her acquired business experience and management acumen, she has been quietly instrumental in the execution of her brother's vision and has been a valuable business advisor to Oji and to MACPRI generally. Suzette, who can be seen in and around Toronto at Oji's events along with their mother actively working or volunteering, is very loved and appreciated for her loyalty and keen enthusiastic contribution. The family's legacy and well-being is in no small way due to her efforts. In turn, Suzette admires Oji's love for his immediate and extended family and the undying commitment he has shown to his values and mission. Next to his mother, she is one of his strongest cheerleaders.

Winston "Hefty" Anderson, the youngster of the family, like his brothers before him, has followed an independent path. An all-rounder, Winston appears to have taken the best from his father and made the best of it. A construction contractor with multi-disciplinary skills ranging from plumbing, electrical, tiling, painting, drywall, plastering, etc., he is also a DJ with his own creative pursuits. As previously mentioned, he has provided music, equipment, and audio for a variety of MACPRI-related events, including the All African Dances Parties and the Young Poets of the Revolution. When Oji was going through his legal ordeal, Hefty held fundraising dance parties in support of his brother and the ROM 11. To understand their relationship is to appreciate that Oji and Winston are each other's right-hand man. Oji has, in the past, when possible, accompanied Winston on various jobs as a helper, performing demolition and cleanup services, sometimes helping with finishing touches on stained wood surfaces. Their loyalty to each other cannot help but be noticed. Rarely do you see one without the other at MACPRI events held in Toronto.

When Oji stands, he does not stand alone. His family—functional, knitted and well-integrated—stands solidly with him. These include his extended family of in-laws, who have in common a shared ancestral tradition, and a strong sense of self, respect for elders, and love for their young.

Brother Oji and family standing with the Honourable Marcus Mosiah Garvey as their backbone. (Family album/Oji Archives)

Top: Primary school principal and Packieman exhibiting gifts of Oware board games in Jamaica in 2012. (MACPRI Archives)
Bottom: Brother Oji with extended family at 2012 family reunion in Ridge Pen. His mother is seated centre in red, sister Suzette is seated rear centre, and Packieman on Djembe in foreground. (Family album/Oji Archives)

What will it benefit me to participate in the ROM/CFTA reconciliation commemorative event? The last time I linked up with my CFTA people they unceremoniously asked me to leave. You know my volatility. You really think it is a good idea for me to be at such an event? Especially, because the community and the institution STILL have not done well by me regarding my sacrifice and the huge amount of money I had raised on my own to defend my case. We celebrate 25 years plus later, and I am still holding the bag.

—Brother Adisa S. Oji

Chapter 12

REPAIRING OLD WOUNDS / SMALL AXE BIG TREE

In the 1960s, Black power rose to prominence. So did the Afro. One was a philosophy, the other a style. Together they comprised a way of life. When combined, the resulting persona was distinctively impressive, undeniably cool, and iconic. Walter Rodney had one, Kwame Ture had one, so too Angela Davis. Huge body of natural Black hair signalling beauty, poise, presence, calibre. More than simply style, the look symbolized substance and power.

Take Walter Rodney for instance. From Georgetown, Guyana, Walter Rodney—young, vibrant, comfortable with who he was—represented a new kind of Caribbean man, a unique combination of political activism and scholarship, a grassroots everyman with intellectual gravitas. A sandal-wearing soul brother, he cross-pollinated Black power, Pan-Africanism, and Socialism into one high-octane cocktail. Rodney created an empowering revolutionary concoction that would have wide appeal stretching from the ghetto to ivory towers of learning, from the Caribbean to Africa. Pro-colonial governments with oppressive tendencies feared him. He was evicted from Jamaica during the '60s. In 1980, at age thirty-eight, he was assassinated, killed in Guyana by a car bomb during one of his political campaigns. In his short but remarkable life, he achieved much. His explosive thinking and the detonation he discharged by his thought-provoking ideas continue to reverberate with lasting potency even after his voice has long been violently silenced.

Kwame Ture, formerly Stokely Carmichael, is another soul brother. He popularized the term Black power. He is said to be the first to publicly use the expression and to politically apply it, not as a counter to White power, but as a form of radical democracy. Rather than waiting for it to be given or shared, Black power called on African Americans to proactively seize for themselves the levers of political power and economic privilege denied them by entrenched institutionalized racism. With an unmatched eloquence, he urged Black communities to empower themselves through united coordinated action. By exhorting his listeners to lead themselves and to determine their own destiny, he earned the right to be among the upper echelons of transformative leaders. More than that, he walked the talk. He was arrested for his activism more times than he could remember. Through his on-the-ground activism, he earned the right to be part of the pantheon of inspiring leaders. He was a rare embodiment of Martin Luther King Jr. and Malcolm X combined. Yet he occupies his own unmistakable place in the historical imagination, having lived longer than his two role models to influence a new global generation of Pan-African thinkers. Ture moved to Conakry, Guinea, where he died in November 1998 at the age of fifty-seven.

Also walking the earth during the late sixties was the contemporary reincarnation of Harriet Tubman and Sojourner Truth rolled into one feminine body. Caught in a man's world, Angela Davis was neither intimidated nor limited by gender or race. With her sharp-toothed grace and soul-powered 'fro, she stood tall, fighting alongside others while risking her life and freedom for a cause best described as justice and anti-oppression. Known for her fearless aplomb, her never-back-down attitude, she was removed, as a result of her activism, from her professorial teaching position at UCLA. In 1970, the establishment paid her a compliment by placing her on the FBI's Ten Most Wanted List. Based on a slew of charges, an intense police search followed, forcing her underground and into hiding. When apprehended, she would be incarcerated for over a year, culminating in her trial and acquittal in 1972. Davis was a soul philosopher revolutionary. "In the act of resistance, the rudiments of freedom are already present," she declared unapologetically. "The independence of the master is based on the dependency of the slave," she intoned. To this day, the expression "Free Angela" carries a special resonance in which she personifies not one woman, but collectively all persons arrested by institutionalized racism and anyone unjustly trapped within the oppressive law enforcement-judicial-prison industrial complex.

Rodney, Ture, Davis, and many others, were transformative figures who, in one way or another, raged against oppressive strongholds. Through their examples of Black consciousness, we came to better understand the cost, sacrifice, and dedication required when in pursuit of justice. Collectively they represent the sixties, an era beguiling and turbulent. It was, as someone described it, the last romantic gasp of the twentieth century, a period of intense political, military, and social conflicts, some of which were inextricably linked to conditions within the African diaspora. It was the era of counterculture, a time ripe with opportunities for resistance and protest, and a period in history marked by the creative and dynamic proliferation of opinions about identity, roots, and culture. Ideas pertinent to political independence, freedom, and justice ran rampant then. And with these ideas came a rich explosion of artistic expressions, the sewing and blossoming of seeds in various forms. Women, men, and communities awakened, stood up, sensing it was time for insurgency, riot, and rebellion, time to push back. It was also a time of reactionary oppression and slaughtering, a time of White backlashes and whitewashing. It was a time of destruction, a time of creation. It was the best and worst of times, majestic, messy. And all at once, full of joy and pain, losses and gains.

From this generation emerged characters of social and political action who threw themselves headlong and wholeheartedly into the pursuit of justice and liberation. They acted with the belief that a new world was/is possible. Emerging as warriors, they sacrificed their bodies even as they spiritually battled against inequality and discrimination. Their hope ultimately was the creation of a brighter future in which injustice, racism, and poverty no longer held sway. They were prophets with uncommon messages. They appeared to the world as dreamers who grew long hair, often criticized for their so-called identity politics as if the practice originated with them. They were seen as rabble-rouser or troublemakers. Alive with righteous indignation, they paid a price for their protest, paid heavily for fighting vigorously with defiant eyes, dying if they had to, calling incessantly for freedom and a new day. They not only talked about revolution, they went about triggering social change through activism. Eventually, Brother Oji would become one of them.

Today, instead of an Afro, Oji wears an unkempt beard, forcing others to wonder about his deportment. In the late eighties, early nineties, however, he sported one of his own. It accentuated his tall thin frame, accessorized by beads and African ornaments. His Afro gave him an aura of stoic resistance, adding to his height, allowing him to have an appearance of cool command. His updo, like a throwback, offered a statement suggesting he was living outside of his milieu, projecting backward in time, carrying himself as if Black power still had relevance. But even beyond this superficial likeness in appearance, deeper down he shared a fearless passionate drive for justice. Realizing this was his purpose, he, too, stood stubbornly against oppression in addition to being a radical teacher and educator and soul rebel. Like his hair protruding skyward, he would put himself out there, emitting a particular image that said, "Don't even listen to my voice. Just look at me and hear me and know that I love my people." This love would cost him.

The price was paid on April 29, 1992, when he was found guilty as charged and sentenced to ninety days in jail. Actually, he had been paying long before. After being charged on June 2, 1990, a dark cloud hung threateningly over Oji's head for two years while he was on bail.

Following their arrest, Oji and others formed the ROM 11 Legal Defence Committee to raise funds and public awareness. Solidarity among the group was still high. A trip with Ras Rico and Jennifer Issac to Ottawa-Carlton would be one of many speaking tours in which Oji participated. When all the other accused had their charges withdrawn in November 1991 after they signed a peace bond to keep the peace for six months, the case stretched on into March 1992 for Oji and Yaw, who continued to fight the charges levelled against them. Throughout the life of their case in court, various judges adjudicated the matter, with the judge denying most of their critical defence motions. The crown called their defence motions a fishing expedition, and the judge usually agreed.

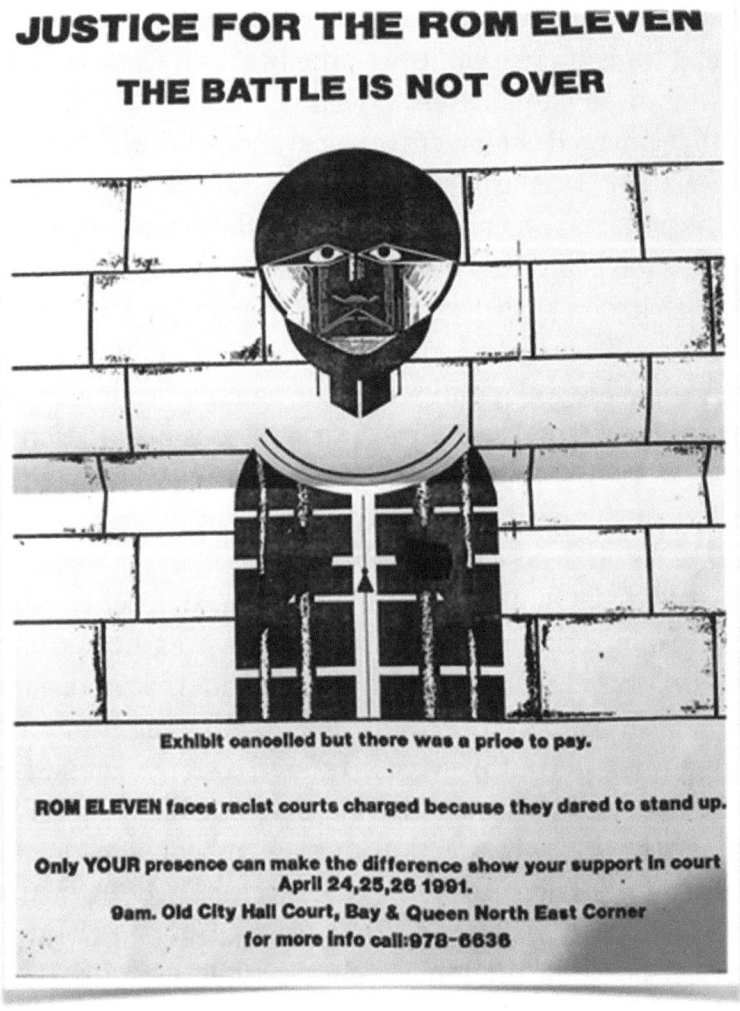

In the beginning there were eleven, then there were two. Now, only one stood: Brother Oji. (Oji Archives)

For the most part, Oji kept himself busy throughout; he kept on moving, travelling, teaching, presenting workshops, and giving lectures. He had been one of eleven individuals charged in the ROM ordeal. Eventually, Yaw would be acquitted on a technicality. Now, as the walls caved in, Oji stood alone.

Time and space become warped when in confinement; the two dimensions blend, stretch, then break into irreconcilable pieces as the mind tries to make sense of the confusion. Handcuffs, police vans, Europeans, Africans, shackles, jail cell, the smell, the yelling, endless procedural madness, the pesky questioning, booking, fingerprinting; the stripping down—a never-ending spiral of indignities, humiliations ... sights, sounds, bad odours, and a soul-numbing loneliness. Bondage behind bars.

As he entered the infamous Don Jail, the authorities seized Oji's red, black, and green bracelet then confiscated his Rodney King button. Stripped of his shoes, hat, and "African" attire, he was provided in exchange with jail footwear and "some dirty stinking Aryan blue clothes to put on." Jail authorities also provided him with a "care package" consisting of toothpaste and toothbrush along with a bed sheet, which he took with him as he was escorted through a series of heavily grilled security doors eventually leading to a prison cell. He was ultimately placed in maximum-security—a level within the institution where on arrival he could not help but notice the disproportionally high number of "brothers." After overcoming his initial shock of seeing so many, on second thought, he wasn't surprised.

To keep himself grounded, Oji decided to fast and meditate, a practice that had served him well in the middle of the madness. Before long, a *Rasta brethren* approached him. Recognizing Oji was new to the horror house known locally as the Don, the Rastaman, like a veteran coaching a novice, took the time to orient the newcomer by imparting basic survival wisdom. Don't whistle, never address anyone as buddy unless you want to end up dead, said the *Dread*. For entertainment, Oji attempted to pass time by playing cards. The game was distracting, but unsatisfying. He attempted to make some phone calls but had no success.

Sensing his own restlessness, he tried to settle down, to take the edge off. He needed time to take stock. *Day one in jail. Felt so much longer.* Time is warped. *Eighty-nine to go.* He had to remember to breathe, to take deep breaths. He noticed his breathing had become shallow, short, as if he was slowly suffocating, fading out. He felt far away from everything he knew and loved, far away from the things that mattered most. Never before in his life had he ever felt this far removed, cut off.

The three days spent in the Don Jail felt like eternity. During his stay, correctional authorities assessed his level of risk, an intake method used to determine who goes where. The classification officer concluded that the public good would best be served if Oji were to serve his sentence at the Maplehurst Correctional Centre in Milton, Ontario, located fifty-seven kilometres west of Toronto. And so, early May 1992, before sunup, with hands and feet shackled, he was escorted at 5:00 a.m. by guards to a waiting paddy wagon—a maximum-security transport van where he witnessed the sight of chains on Black bodies aside from his own, mist still hanging in the chilled air. *Welcome to modern slavery*, he thought as he shuffled along, caught in another backward time warp. Suddenly, he was reliving ancestral memories. Except this time, he was not taking a ritual walking tour of routes taken by his ancestors who were dragged involuntarily through thick rainforest under the watchful eyes of enslavers. This time it was *he* who was shackled. With the exception of not having constraints around his neck, it felt *just like slavery*. This was not the Gold Coast in the sixteenth century. Rather this was Toronto 1992, in a prison built in 1864 that was once a medieval dungeon—another monument to British colonialism located east of the Don River. Still, it felt eerily similar. *Just like slavery*. In times past, it had been soldiers, slave raiders, and missionaries. Nowadays, police, judges, crown lawyers, and jail guards were imperialism's neocolonial custodians. *Just like slavery*. Like the shackles around his feet, he couldn't shake the thought from his head. Black incarceration had become the new slave trade.

Time dragged on. Memory of the terror of slave trading ships cruising threateningly along Africa's Gold Coast crept to his mind as the van did round-ups at other local custodial facilities to onboard more imprisoned bodies. Seated in the dark confines of the jail-bus, Oji sensed the arrival of other inmates as they were herded in from the East and West Detention centres. Together, they travelled on what's familiarly known as the *goose*, sitting upright with their hands and feet steadfastly shackled. On what seemed like an endless joyless ride, the *goose* took its passengers for further pickups in London and Chatham located over two hundred kilometres away. It was as if they were being taken on an involuntary field trip through southwestern Ontario, known ironically as Canada's proud gateway to freedom—the Underground Railroad. In the windowless confined space, Oji became disoriented. Unable to tell where he was or where he was going, he closed his eyes and imagined *the middle passage*.

That night, instead of Milton, the goose landed in Sarnia, 290 km from home. Housed in a jail colloquially known as a *bucket*, Oji's despair deepened. Toronto, he knew well. He had a mental vision of the city, his home, his family, his friends. He could situate himself there with images of himself moving around through city streets. In Sarnia, he had no such reference. Nothing to visualize. Pushed further into darkness, he felt even more removed from everything he knew and loved. The only thing that gave him reassurance was the knowledge that he was his mother's son and always would be, that he was the beneficiary of ancestors who walked this way before him. On their shoulders he stood. That he was *Mwalimu*—the teacher on a journey not yet complete. Much had been taken away from him. But he still had his mind, his body, his soul. He'd cling to that and remain free. Between the hard metallic banging of prison bars, the rattling of keys, and the din of jail chatter, there was enough noise to drive a normal person insane. Self-contempt and self-pity pressed in on him like an inexorable force. *Resist it,* he reminded himself. Somewhere in the quietude of his mind he said a prayer for his mother as she gently entered his thoughts. She came frequently. He prayed that she be given strength, peace of mind. He prayed too for his entire family, prayed for their safe keeping even as they were surely praying for his.

Despite the conditions he faced, Oji had no sense of guilt or remorse about what he had done. He knew the CFTA and the ROM 11 were justified in condemning the *Into the Heart of Africa* exhibit. The group had done everything in its legal power to expose the racist nature of the event, to shut it down. Protest was one thing. To sway public opinion and to counterattack the ROM's propaganda was another. In order to do this, they had to initiate a public information campaign of their own. They had tried diplomacy. This, too, had failed. They tried lobbying decision-makers and politicians such as premier David Peterson. This yielded little, only empty platitudes. *White supremacist indoctrination could not go unchecked. The flagrant insult and oppression of African people could not continue. No way! We had to act. And we did. The mis-education must end; the stereotyping of Africans as barbarians must stop; the racist Babylon system must fall; someone else should be in jail, not me.* The thought of putting British colonialism on trial brought a fleeting smirk. It was an amusing thought.

The ROM 11 spent two years fighting their arrest through the criminal court. When the case first began in late 1991, Oji was seized by a spirit of righteous indignation. He quickly burned through several lawyers, none of whom were advocating for racial justice in a manner satisfactory to their rebel client. As the case dragged on, pressures came from all sides, including intimidation and surveillance. A range of destabilizing influences came from a variety of quarters. Schemes were applied to force the group to cave in, to give up. The ROM even launched a lawsuit for lost revenue so as to intimidate the group into backing off. Uncompromising in his stance, Oji had no concessions to offer. He was defiant. He sincerely felt they tried to kill or harm him. He told the court, "For a long time in this city, the pol-lice and the in-justice system have been getting away with a lot of things against our people ... We engaged in peaceful protest and still we get our asses kicked. The museum brought out the pol-lice to beat our asses ... Two women were subjected to humiliating strip searches ... pol-lice stuck their hands up their..."

No way was he intending to compromise with this clear case of injustice.

Oji knew the police did not attack him and his peers because they were violent or posed a physical risk of harm to the public or themselves. They attacked because he and others dared to stare White supremacy in the face, dared to challenge it publicly and dramatically. For this, the group had to pay. They had to be baited into a violent confrontation so as to create an excuse for an arrest. Now that the matter had moved into the legal arena, it was important to continue the attack on White supremacy inside the court as they did outside. After all, the museum and the court were part of the same system, weren't they?

The thought of bringing the system to justice brought a momentary smile to his face, small, cold comfort while on cold ground. The idea of authorities attacking him and his peers with tear gas and high-powered weaponry was a strange irony. For in contrast, the only weapons they, the demonstrators, had were made of words, pencil, pen, and paper. *Yes, we Africans are armed and dangerous.* The pen can be mightier than the sword. In a weak attempt to quell his growing despair, he allowed himself another smile. Initially, the ROM had not taken them seriously. The ROM had been dismissive, ignoring them at first, treating them as if they were inconsequential, nobodies, or like they were hooligans.

"Who are these nonentities? Who do you think you are? You are not curators. Leave us alone and let us do our jobs. We are the experts." They thought they could go on with business as usual. Thought the protest would wane and go away. *But we didn't! In the absence of wider public support, we just got stronger and more intentional. They didn't know what hit them! I bet they didn't see us coming!*

Realizing he was having a useless tête-à-tête with himself, thoughts relentlessly rushing back and forth through his head like a broken record, Oji tried to settle down in an attempt to come to terms with his situation. It was difficult not to rehash, hard to put the whole thing aside, as hard as the bed he attempted with difficulty to rest on.

The hope of turning the case into a tour de force to draw attention to racism in Canada emerged as a possibility, taking the matter through to the ultimate—the Ontario Human Rights Tribunal, the Supreme Court—wherever. Organizing the demonstration was a political act. The decision to enter the ROM building legally as citizens was a political act. The decision by the ROM to bar individual demonstrators from legally entering a publicly owned institution was no less political. The decision to bar only Black people was even more politically charged. It could be argued that all incidents flowing from this state of affair were political in nature, including arrest, trial, and incarceration. If so, then Oji was no ordinary inmate; he was a political prisoner. He had appealed his conviction *and* his sentence knowing the crown's case was flawed. Yet only a few within the coalition believed much would come of it. Fear was deep—fear of losing a career, of missing the chance for higher education, fear of damaging a well-crafted reputation. Money was scarce. Some argued it was a waste of time. Many had seen and had enough. Furthermore, the exhibit came down. Wasn't that enough? For Oji, it certainly was not. He remained adamant. Not everyone within the movement had agreed with his antics in the courtroom as he vigorously continued to argue their case.

Although he tried to ward them off, thoughts continued to press in on him just the same. *Plea deals were made ... couldn't believe it ... peace bonds were signed ... just can't believe it ... Where once there were ten of us young people and one elder facing criminal charges—in the end only two of us were left; and when the court proceedings were over, there was only me left standing, my co-accused, Yaw getting off on a "technicality," leaving me to hold the bag.* (Apparently, the crown was not able to positively identify Johnson at the scene of the crime.)

Years later, in vernacular, Oji would poetically describe his predicament this way: "Me and Brother X To carry on the battle / Without fear I an' I soldier brother step in there / In a dem throat without fear / The X get off on a technicality / And for I boldness dem send I go a prison."

Grassroots organizations fighting against injustice sometimes have difficulty sustaining solidarity even at the best of times. Intensive internal/external pressures can cause them to buckle or fold before their mission is achieved. Justice seeking groups slowly fray at the edges or splinter apart if they can't find a way to sustain their activism. Rivalries, polarizing opinions, clashing egos, the unrelenting pressure from the outside to divide and conquer can become distracting, eventually debilitating the group's effort or blurring its focus. In the crucible of the struggle with the ROM, segments of the Black community pitted against each other, separated by age, class differences, strategic objective, and tactical considerations. Organizations such as the Black Business and Professional Association preached accommodation, compromise, conciliation, and amelioration, while the CFTA espoused a radical militant approach, demanding nothing short of a nose-to-nose confrontation with institutional racism. Tensions ran so high, the strain reached deep into CFTA's sense of solidarity, shredding apart the consensus they had previously worked so hard to build.

The matter of the peace bond, or *bond-age* as Oji calls it, is a sensitive one. On one hand, the agreement entered into by some of the ROM 11 pointed to the collective strength of the CFTA's efforts to galvanize public opinion on their side. Public pressure pushed the crown to negotiate. Crown representatives are likely to argue that public opinion had nothing to do with their decision to settle, that the decision was based purely on legal grounds. Be that as it may, public officials could not entirely ignore public outrage. On the other hand, there are those who believe that the bonds were a buyout-sellout agreement in which the state sought to divide the group by siphoning off the soft parts while isolating more hardcore targets—the main protagonists. Whatever the reason, Oji loathed this arrangement; he was decidedly against it, calling it a *peace bond with Babylon*, something akin to signing away one's right to dignity. He believed their cause was righteous and just. Firmly rooted in his strong African pride, which he embodied, he could not bring himself to buckle under, especially to an unjust system that espoused White supremacist values. For this reason, he ignored the advice of lawyers and stood his ground, risking abandonment by old friends and allies who, for one reason or another, could not stomach his unapologetic, uncompromising challenge to White supremacy. He alone would pay the full price of being charged, arrested, convicted, and jailed—in effect tagged with a criminal record and the burdensome limitations that came with it. Because he refused the peace bond, they would make an example of him to deter others from ever wanting to follow his footsteps.

A nagging apprehension nibbled at the edge of his awareness as he reflected on having a criminal record. It was a slippery slope. One record could lead to an even longer rap sheet. Could his criminal record open the door to more convictions? *No way ... no way this was going to happen ... no way.* Banking on a favourable outcome to his appeal, Oji laid down to rest with little success.

For Oji, there was no mistaking who he was or the role he had to play. He was a child of the sixties, not the father. He was not the groundbreaker; but like others of his generation, he felt as if he, and people of African Ancestry, should be much further ahead, standing on higher ground. He was, after all, born into a highly politicized generation, one that had witnessed the epic battle for civil and human rights, an invigorating era captivated by characters such as Medgar Evers, Malcolm X, Martin Luther King Jr., Angela Davis, Stokely Carmichael, and the Black Panthers, all of whom worked to build mass movements and lead united struggles. He knew about Nanny, Cudjoe, Tacky, Quao, and Cuffee, freedom fighters in pre-emancipation Jamaica, and studied the revolutionary life of Marcus Garvey, the liberator. He knew of Kwame Nkrumah, Ghana's Pan-African visionary.

Closer home in Toronto, he was in varying degrees familiar with the activism of the Black Action Defence Committee with Dudley Laws, Charles Roach, Lennox Farrell, Sherona Hall, and Akua Benjamin, and knew of the groundbreaking anti-racism work of Bromley Armstrong and others. Trailblazers, past and present, frequently entered his thoughts as he went in and out of his cell, their presence on the gallery wall of his mind urging him to remain steadfast and to keep faith. While he was disappointed that most of the elders in Toronto who were in the struggle failed to openly support the CFTA, Lennox Farrell being a notable exception, Oji felt a responsibility to build on their legacy. He knew that the justice they and many others had fought so hard for remained long overdue. It was time to reap the benefits of past struggles, time for freedom and justice to be fully realized. Imbued with this sense of urgency, he came to regard himself as a custodian of the aspirations of those who came before him and who paid for his liberation. On this he would stand or fall.

In this time warp, he recalled other voices beckoning to him, voices he responded positively to. Voices such as Samora Machel, the Mozambican revolutionary leader who led an armed struggle against Portuguese colonial domination and who could be heard shouting *"A luta continua"* after a resounding victory in 1975; of Chinua Achebe, the Nigerian author of *Things Fall Apart*, a 1958 novel and masterpiece that told the story of colonization from an African point of view; and of Yosef A. A. Ben-Jochannan, the American historian and author who wrote such books as *The African Origins of Major "Western Religions"*, *Africa: Mother of Western Civilization*, and others, all of which contributed to a new and growing understanding of African-centred thought and philosophy. As he laid on his bunk staring up at the ceiling during his stay at the Sarnia bucket, he was surprised by the things he remembered, surprised by how valuable these memories now became and how much they meant to him.

He smiled when Sydney Poitier entered his consciousness. There was *To Sir, With Love* and *Guess Who Is Coming to Dinner*. But it was Poitier's role as African American homicide detective Virgil Tibbs that made him brighten up. During the 1967 film *In the Heat of the Night*, Poitier modelled a new way of responding to racism. His character was wise, forbearing, decent, and proud, a precursor to the Black power ideal. He was strong and dignified, albeit idealized in a way now appearing outdated. "They call me Mister Tibbs" was his famous signature line as he stood up against bigotry, refusing to be dehumanized and belittled. Oji remembered watching Poitier, admiring the man's carriage and deportment, a code of conduct he would emulate. Besides, at a time when it was unheard of, Poitier later in his career assumed more control of his work to become a behind-the-scene power broker and civil rights activist, a forerunner to other Black film director-producers who would follow his footsteps.[43] Oji wondered what Mr. Tibbs would do if he were in jail. The thought broadened his smile, if only reluctantly. It was an amusing thought.

Mr. Tibbs aside, Oji's paradigm was set, his course charted. There was no way he could hide or fade from his ultimate calling. He was who he was. That was it. He simply had to accept it and live with the outcome, do or die, come what may.

---

43 Sydney Poitier, February 20, 1927 – January 6, 2022. R.I.P.

To pass the time, he reflected on his first visit to Africa a year earlier in 1991. He had always loved Africa. He loved it even more now. For as long as he could remember, he had always wanted to travel there. He was glad he had the chance to stay at the house of the late Kofi Baako—a sportsman, teacher, and politician and the first minister of defence in the Nkrumah government during the First Republic of Ghana; to have slept in the same house and room where El-Hajj Malik El-Shabazz (Malcolm X) was hosted while in Africa. The experience left a remarkable cumulative impression on him. As he languished in a Sarnia jail, so far removed from Africa, the memory lifted his spirit, warmed his heart, giving him courage. *The ROM exhibit was all wrong. He knew it. They knew it.*

In the freedom of his mind, he revisited the history, traditions and life in Ghana he had come to know. He traversed the country's many landscapes, watching it change along an extended trip from Techiman through to Kintampo then up further north to Tamale into Bolgatanga just south of the border with Burkina Faso. He watched with fixated fascination as the scenery of West African flora transformed itself with a variety of tree lines—trees standing tall and still in wide-open expanses that seem to go on forever before giving way to grassland, then desert, then more stretches of grassland with one or two solitary trees here and there; trees like the baobab dotting the landscape interspersed with one or two round huts at the side of the road … to be a guest of the chief … to see the compounds where communities were organized … to be a part of it … *The ROM exhibit was all wrong. He knew it. They knew it.*

In this dreamlike way, time passed with restless sleep during which he was struck by a staggering irony. While he could feel a deep connection with Ghana, Africa, so many miles away, he could feel none with Sarnia, Ontario, Canada, where he was now locked up. His vivid imagination ran amok, his mind wandering, venturing to places not so pleasant, warping space and time, looking at the past through a cell door in the present. His controversial stand was costing him friendships. Not everyone was as uncompromising as he was. United action was hard to sustain when things became precarious. The ROM exhibit opened in the fall of '89, but it was not until February/March the following year when he became involved that the protest really took off. No one else had the influence, leadership, and gumption to push the agenda or forcefully galvanize the effort; everyone had ideas, but no one was prepared to execute, put shoulder to the wheel. No one else was ready to take the hit if and when things got rough. And when Oji stepped up, it did get rough. And when it became rough, everything and everyone became hypersensitive.

If he were to choose a nemesis, Oji would identify the late Christie Blatchford, a staff writer with the *Toronto Sun* during the time of the ROM protest. She delighted in referring to Oji and Yaw as the ROM 2. Though he often disagreed with her, Oji admired Blatchford's courage to speak her mind. She publicly bashed him every chance she got. "It was like watching the country go down the toilet," she reported in November 1991 in describing Oji's bold attempt to defend himself in court. Oji is said to have hopped "over the gate" in court to demand both Judge John Kerr and crown attorney Jim Ramsay recuse themselves from the case.

Not everyone could tolerate this kind of public embarrassment. When things got going, once CFTA was up and running and the heat came, many ran away. For some, protecting their careers and reputations was more important. When it came down to it, only a few stood fast until the end. Even those loyal to him felt compelled to part ways when the going got testy.

Cracks in personal relationships suddenly appeared in places where they weren't so obvious before, friends for personal or political reasons finding it necessary to disassociate and go their separate ways. The loss of one particular friendship carried an acute pain. Even love can cave in when stakes are high, and this one had to fall away. Fear sometimes can be stronger than love.

Rolling over on this depressing thought, Oji tried to find a comfortable spot to sleep on the cold hard truth. But as with some of his friends, sleep was lost, hard to find. Fitfully tossing and turning, he remembered an old saying perhaps first told to him by his grandmother: You make your bed, you sleep in it.

Today, Oji holds no grudge against the other nine who also stood gallantly, faithfully sacrificing their time, their future for a cause they believed in. Together they stood up against a major institution. Their collective dedication contributed to the eventual success of the protest. Many from all walks of life came and went, each adding fuel to the movement, many anonymous faces White and Brown, some prominent, others in the background, all significant in some way. Participation in the ROM protest took tremendous courage. All the members of the CFTA coalition who participated and especially those who were charged and arrested—including the late Jennifer Isaac, Silbert Barrett, Sandra McKenzie, Brother Yaw, Ras Rico, and Andre Bratu, the only member of the eleven who was notably not of colour—gave a part of their lives to something that was bigger than themselves. Some for career purposes chose to remain unidentified. Yet they too marched, staying up on many late nights to plan and strategize, enduring personal hardships as activists, advocates, and organizers engaged in a revolt against an exhibit they considered repulsive, racist, and denigrating, an exhibit staged by a public institution that should have known better. If reparations for the harm done by the ROM were to be considered, the indemnity when tabulated would be substantive.

After spending six days in a Sarnia jail, Oji was released on bail pending his appeal. He remained on this second stretch of bail until the matter was resolved the following year. On his behalf, lawyer Jack Gemmel called on the Ontario court to squash the conviction and to order an acquittal. This was denied. As secondary options, the lawyer requested a new trial and, if not, for the sentence to be reduced to time served. At the appeal hearing in the spring of 1993, the court upheld Oji's conviction. His sentence was reduced to time served. He was finally free, though still encumbered with a criminal record.

The person who helped with his bail was an elderly businesswoman, Ms. Yvonne Grant, known affectionately by her many customers as Ms. Yvonne. She had no political axe to grind, but upon hearing of Oji's plight, she offered up her house and business as collateral to help get him out of jail. No other member of the community with whom Oji worked and served and who were in good financial standing seemed willing or openly prepared to support him with his legal fight.

When Ms. Yvonne drove westbound down highway 401 from Toronto to Sarnia—a 290 km desolate stretch of road running through farm country variously known as the Kings Highway or the Macdonald-Cartier Freeway—to post Oji's bail, it would be the first time she ever considered doing such a thing. She had been operating a small, humble family-owned tropical food store aptly named Caribbean Corner in Kensington Market since 1977, which had become a hub for people of Jamaican and Caribbean background. She first met the Anderson family—mother, daughter, and sons—when they lived near Spadina and Queen Street West. The Andersons frequently patronized her store, allowing Ms. Yvonne to get to know Oji who was then a university student. She was moved to act when Muchoki Simba asked her to consider helping out. Muchoki, Oji's close friend—always a present help in times of trouble—was a long-time customer of the store. He along with Lanchester Anderson and executive members of the African Canadian Heritage Association were frantically hustling to rustle up the needed funds for Oji's bail, and not without difficulty. When Muchoki explained the urgency of the situation, Ms. Yvonne knew what she needed to do. She was aware of the ROM controversy and considered Oji to be a decent, respectful young man. As far as she knew, he was from a good family and was simply trying to tell the truth. Sensing an injustice, she volunteered for the humble role of playing a small part in his release.

As she went through the rigmarole, she was struck by the heavy bureaucratic barriers involved. The level of security applied to the young man seemed to her to be extremely high, so high it was as if he were in for *murder*. It was as if he was on Canada's most wanted list, or so she thought. She came to learn that the reason he was placed so far from home in Sarnia and not closer in Maplehurst or Toronto was because the authorities wanted to place him in a remote location so as to keep his whereabouts a secret. They were afraid of the public attention his presence might attract. With many hoops to jump through, Ms. Yvonne did what she had to do. To this day, she has no regrets about going to all that trouble.

Three women—Oji's mother, Ms. Yvonne, and Ruby Johnson, Brother Yaw's mother—plus Brother Yaw himself came to meet Oji when he walked out of the Sarnia bucket. For some reason, he was expecting to see others there to greet him; he was disappointed to see there weren't that many others waiting, those with whom he had struggled in comradeship over the past number of years. While pleased to be released at long last, he was crestfallen, caught in the crosswinds of mixed emotions. He would later recall this as one of the most painful and revealing days of his life. What grieved him as he sauntered out was not the old miseries that tend to haunt released inmates. He wasn't embittered or feeling revengeful, nor was he contemplating a life ruined. It wasn't the need for housing, employment, or income support that weighed on him. No, these were no bother. What pressed down on him was the loneliness of it all, the sense of desertion after working so diligently to energize a mass united front and then having to watch the whole thing collapse around him. He felt acutely abandoned. In a state of anguished relief, he embraced his mother and the other women who came to greet him. He thanked Ms. Yvonne. "Thank you! Thank you!" he said repeatedly. He knew words were not enough, but that's all he could say. He embraced Yaw.

Like a funeral procession, the small contingent streamed quietly toward the parking lot where Brother Yaw's old grey Volvo sat waiting. On the long, almost three-hour eastbound journey back to Toronto, Oji cried, the full realization of what he had been through suddenly bearing down on him. Rarely since has he spoke openly about his brief taste of prison life and the leftover scar. He had no intentions whatsoever of looking back except to remember fondly the three mothers and a brother who came to welcome him home that day.

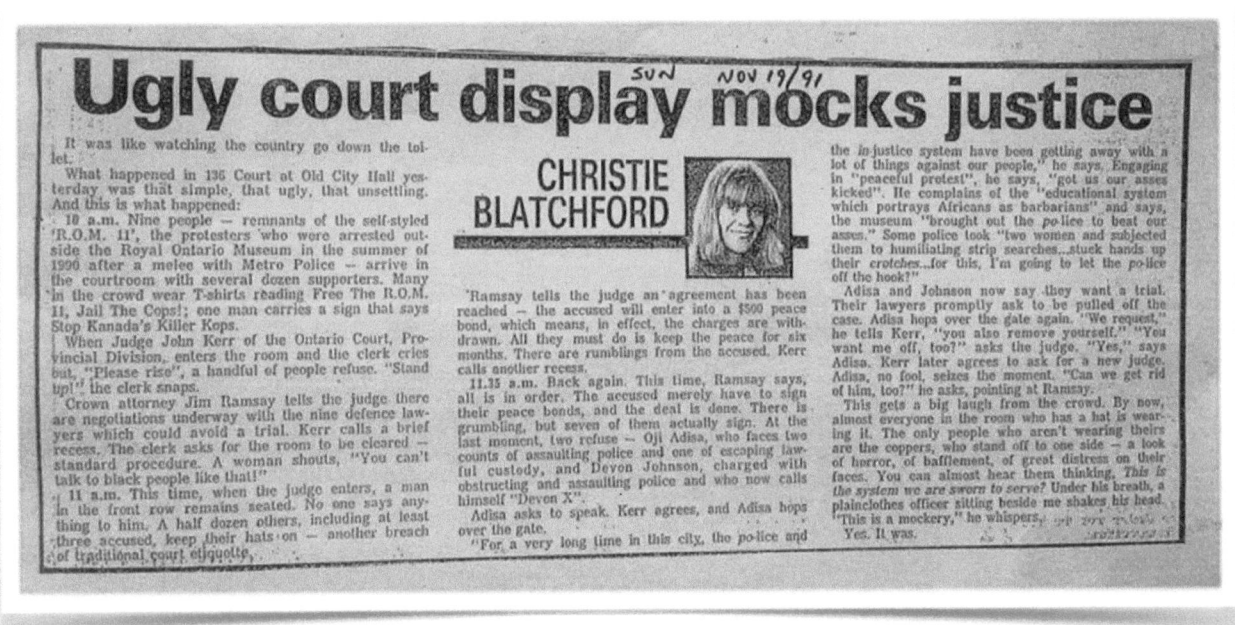

"It was like watching the country go down the toilet," reported Christie Blatchford in November 1991 in reference to Oji boldly defending himself and his community in court. Oji is said to have hopped over the gate in court to demand Judge John Kerr remove himself from the case as well as crown attorney Jim Ramsay. (*Toronto Sun*)

Twenty-four years after Oji's arrest on June 2, 1990, the Royal Ontario Museum offered a public apology to the Coalition for the Truth about Africa (CFTA). By extension, the ROM apologized to all African Canadians. Apparently, the public institution founded in 1914 was slow to assume public responsibility for its transgressions.

Since the shutdown of their 1989 flagship exhibit, the museum chose to remain silent on the matter. The notion of an apology actually first surfaced in 1991, months after the exhibit prematurely closed. ROM management in consultation with a hastily convened community group of eminent African Canadians had come up with a pacifier—an exhibit celebrating festive art related to Caribbean costumes and masks. The *Caribana*-like exhibit scheduled to run during the summer of '92 would include presentations, films, and lectures. However, there was one condition. The consultative group insisted the ROM first apologize, signaling that they would not endorse the exhibit if this condition was not met. Grudgingly, the ROM agreed, and its public rigidity began to melt. They issued a statement admitting to their "racial indiscretion" and conceded that a greater degree of consultation on exhibits was needed together with "employing more minorities at all level of the ROM's hierarchy." Said acting director John McNeill, "To this day, the ROM remains disturbed that offence was felt by some over the exhibition." As it turned out, in the opinion of the Black advisory group, this apology was not good enough. The apology lacked any admission of responsibility; there was no recognition of the direct harm caused. As such, the apology appeared tepid, half-hearted. Talks subsequently went sideways, and in the following decades, the issue seemed to have disappeared from the ROM's public agenda altogether.

Their exhibition *Into the Heart of Africa* appears not to have been the ROM's favourite subject or finest moment. Indeed, their national and international reputation suffered as a result, and possibly their revenue when other museums opted out. The price tag for mounting the display was $25,000.

"I am shocked by some of the visual material," said Davis Hemphill, director of the Vancouver Museum, one of the four museums to subsequently cancel their run of the exhibit. "Our regular supporters would not be pleased to support something so controversial," he concluded.

A quick survey of the ROM's online platform between the hasty departure of director Cuyler Young in 1990 and the turning point arrival of Janet Carding in 2010 reveals a conspicuous absence of any obvious mention of the event. The intervening directors/CEOs—John McNeill, Lindsay Sharp, William Thorsell—in their brief, heavily edited, online video introduction of themselves, omitted to publicly mention the failed exhibit or its likely impact on their mandate.

In a guest article in the *Globe and Mail*, December 4, 2000, entitled "Stay tuned: The ROM has a story to tell," Thorsell, then ROM president, disappoints anyone interested in hearing about the doomed exhibit. "Over the next six months," he declared, "the ROM's masterplan will be refined and, most critically, a financial reality check will be done to assess what supports exists for this vision. In the neighbourhood of $200-million over seven years, the project falls well within comparable museum initiatives elsewhere, but $200 million isn't chopped liver either." His evasion of the subject was striking.

Similarly striking was the absence of any reference by Janet Carding in her November 28, 2014, interview with the *Globe and Mail* captioned "Exit interview: The ROM's departing CEO and the museum's challenges." During her interview, Carding gave a retrospective on her tenure in which she spoke about all else except the 1989/'90 fiasco. While she was not present at the ROM during the debacle, she was the first CEO to publicly offer an acknowledgement of responsibility. Despite her involvement as a fixer, she, too, in her interview with the *Globe and Mail* was silent on the matter, stunning if for no other reason that *Into the Heart of Africa* was probably the ROM's most troublesome significant exhibit to date. Like the exhibit, the subject appears to have gone into storage.

For the intervening years prior to the apology, the shadow cast by the ill-fated "racist" exhibit haunted the museum. Trapped in dogma of the past, the ROM fell victim to its own confirmation bias (focused on information consistent with their mind-set only while rejecting anything contrary) and other forms of thinking errors when it ignored concerns expressed by the African Canadian community. This they did at their own peril. Old and archaic in its policies and practice, the museum's administrators had a cavernous unacknowledged blind spot, one that prevented them from clearly seeing the legitimate concerns expressed by a significant segment of their public audience. Stemming from this myopic view, they proceeded to make erroneous assumptions regarding communities they had very little empathy for or knew very little about.

They appeared not to have cared, at times coming across as insensitive. The mistake was, in hindsight, comparable to lunacy, a disastrous lesson learned the hard way. When the scandal caught up with them and the wreckage began to unravel, the museum's local and international credibility would be on the verge of ruin, leaving them scrambling to find a way back to public legitimacy. The exhibition, which was initially intended to go on tour in several other cities, soon lost favour. With cancellations came a financial fallout. "Shell-shocked" was how one-time staffer, Dan Rahimi, former director of collections and vice president of programming at the ROM (currently executive director of Galleries at the University of Pennsylvania Museum of Archaeology and Anthropology), described it. Rahimi, an anthropologist who had been with the ROM since 1987, said the protest was a "wakeup call" that fundamentally changed the way museums did business.

Cannizzo, the curator, was fired. Her initial declared intention was to expose colonialism by putting it on full display, to offer a presentation of the ill-begotten acquisitions of the ROM's collection. However, her effort backfired, blowing up in her face. Facing harsh criticism and a nasty backlash from students at the University of Toronto where she lectured, Cannizzo took a quick medical leave. She left the country, never to return. Museum director Cuyler Young also took flight after the exhibit came down, exiting his contract two years ahead of schedule. For years afterwards, the ROM remained mum. And for a while, as if nursing a grudge, the institution continued to cling to outmoded museum models based on eighteenth-century ideas. Pompously, piously, the ROM shuffled along, snobbish and stuffy, attempting to save face by maintaining innocence. Under the leadership of predominantly British-trained administrators, funding and infrastructural concerns appear to have been the ROM's paramount preoccupation in addition to dwindling attendance. According to Rahimi, "There was no leadership. The museum didn't have a voice the community would listen to, and they weren't, I'm guessing, in much of a mood to talk to the ROM. It was highly polarized, and I don't think there was much effort to de-polarize it."

Modest signals that a shift was taking place surfaced when between October 2, 2010, and March 5, 2011, a new exhibit, Position as Desired, was launched at the museum. Curated by Kenneth Montague, consisting of photographs from his Wedge Collection, the exhibit was described as an exploration of African Canadian identity; this was coupled with musical performances, film screenings, and a conversation with Montague. Supported by the TD Bank Group, Citizenship and Immigration Canada, the Canada Council for the Arts, the Ontario Arts Council, and the Toronto Art Council, the ROM appeared to be back in the business of showcasing art from the African diasporic community in Canada, this time with acute sensitivity.

It was not until 2013, the year of the ROM's centennial when it launched its Of Africa project, that the ROM publicly demonstrated a wish return to the "scene of the crime" and reopen dialogue with selected members of the CFTA. Of Africa was the big comeback, billed as a "multiplatform and multiyear project aimed at rethinking historical and contemporary representations of Africa." Co-organized by a crew of in vogue, cosmopolitan, and more diverse curators including African Canadians Dr. Julie Crooks and Dominique Fontaine, along with Dr. Silvia Forni, the grand affair was ostensibly an attempt to review the damage caused by *Into the Heart of Africa*. Intended to run for three to five years, maybe more (2013–2016/18), the project proposed to explore African experiences through exhibitions, lectures, performances, and events. To open the series, Dan Rahimi hosted and facilitated a conversation: "Learning from 'Into the Heart of Africa.'" He conversed with two of the people prominent in the 1990 protest: scholar, historian, and poet Dr. Afua Cooper and Ras Rico. Yaw Akyeaw also participated in other conversations held throughout the series, as did Geraldine Moriba, an organizing member of the CFTA.

"It really stems from the desire to show the public that we have transformed and want to do things differently," said Italian-trained Dr. Silvia Forni, ROM's curator of Global African Art and Culture since 2008, a new position created by the museum as an expression of their renewed commitment to mounting African art and exhibitions sensibly. "We want to start a different conversation about Africa that is mindful of the past. We cannot forget what has happened here, and that, yes, we are that museum, but we also want to look at the present and the future while we recognize that there were serious mistakes made here," added Forni, who has been responsible for leading the ROM's major Black African exhibits in the latter years.

By 2014, after laying their public relations groundwork, the ROM was ready to come clean. It was as if they could not properly celebrate a centennial without first acknowledging a major turning point in their history. Above the signature of Janet Carding, then new director and CEO of the Royal Ontario Museum—the first woman in the history of the ROM to occupy the role—an invitation was issued for October 22, 2014, to a private event entitled Acknowledging the Past, Forging the Future. With this, the ROM initiated a program to rehabilitate their public image. By hosting a weekend-long symposium, which included invitations to CFTA members and other activists who were involved in the demonstrations, the ROM was hoping to, in the words of Silvia Forni, offer "a direct public acknowledgement." "We are owning our past, not hiding it," said Forni.

Said Carding, "The exhibition and protests that followed represent a painful chapter in the ROM's one-hundred-year history. Into the Heart of Africa brought to light the problematic colonial premises on which museums were established and the consequent difficulty in engaging effectively with Canada's diverse communities. On reflection, the ROM during this time did not address the important issues of inclusiveness and representation brought to the fore by the protesters." (An important aside: By the end of 2015, Janet Carding would be gone from her post.)

"The ROM expresses its deep regret for having contributed to anti-African racism. The ROM also officially apologies for the suffering incurred by the members of the African-Canadian community." With words to this effect, the in-private apology was given.

Notably present, among others, were Dr. Afua Cooper, Yaw Akyeaw, Ras Rico, and other members of the CTFA. Collectively they accepted the ROM's apology and commended the museum's effort in righting a wrong. Said Ras Rico, "I would like to formally accept, on behalf of the African community in Canada here, the apology of the ROM." His words triggered applause and cheers. "We want our community to know: the ROM did not slip or slide, nor hide. They came forward and showed themselves and worked with us," he added.

The by-invitation-only event was billed as an "acknowledgement" and was intended to be the initiation of an extended reconciliation process eventually leading to a full "apology" to the wider public. Through the efforts of Cheryl Blackman, the museum's assistant vice president of audience relations, together with CFTA members, the ROM proceeded to organize a series of public engagement programs to continue the "apology" conversation. The conversation continued after Carding's departure. The task of offering the wider public apology was assigned to Josh

Basseches, her replacement appointed in 2016. This apology was presented and accepted on November 6, 2016, two years after the initial acknowledgement.[44]

Under an angular glass ceiling, members of the CFTA gathered that evening with ROM officials and staff to celebrate the occasion. Pictured standing together in a straight line posing in a wing of the ROM not present in 1991, the dignified group stood poised with an air of achievement, a self-congratulatory image of pride and joy in finally realizing this milestone. Present from left to right were Ajamu Nangwaya, CEO Josh Basseches, Ras Rico, Dr. Mark Engstrom, Dr. Afua Cooper, Cheryl Blackman, president of the Board of Trustees Martha Durdin, Geraldine Moriba, Dr. Silvia Forni, and Yaw Akyeaw.

Noticeably absent was Brother Adisa Oji, his long shadow eerily haunting the gathering. Ras Rico in his remarks had mentioned Oji in passing—regretting that Oji could not be present. But otherwise, there was no mention of his name; and rightly so. Oji would rather have distanced himself from the entire affair. He would be conspicuously absent from this or any other event, private or public, having to do with the ROM's reconciliation efforts. Had he been there that day in November 2016, there might have been poetic symmetry to this impressive group of celebrants. For there would have been eleven individuals standing up to rejoice instead of ten—a newly revised version and, hopefully for the ROM's sake, a less intractable edition of the ROM 11.

Although disheartened upon his release from jail, Oji was far from broken. The ROM incident brought him some public acclaim; however, as time went on, he eschewed public notoriety. Preferring to move in a direction more important than fame related to the museum, he responded to other expectations. He did not want to be defined by this one incident; he wished it was left out of his storyline entirely. Racism makes stereotypical caricatures of its victims. This he knew to be true. He did not wish to become a one-dimensional cardboard cutout pegged and remembered only as a *Racist Ontario Museum* demonstrator. As always, he continued to choose his own path, moving forward, lunging beyond the ROM, busying himself with building his African Image Revolution with only occasional backward glances.

One such glance took place in a radio interview held August 27, 2003, with then host Andy Barrie of CBC's *Metro Morning*. In the interview, Oji can be heard reviving the debate about the ROM protest. Since his release eleven years prior, he had been "keeping a low profile." When asked why he was now speaking out, Oji insisted he was implored by others to do so, namely by documentary filmmaker Lana Lovell and journalist Adrian Harewood. "It was time that the most significant issue against museums in North America be brought back to the fore; it had been dead and should not be kept dead," he added simply.

---

44 See appendix for full text.

Dan Rahimi was also a co-guest on Barrie's show. Amazingly, as Barrie noted, it was the first time since the protest that a ROM official and Oji—or any member of the CFTA or the ROM 11 for that matter—had been at the same table. According to Rahimi, the ROM, after the fatal exhibit, had made efforts to consult with individuals and groups they "could work with" from the Black community. Incredibly, however, for thirteen years the Royal Ontario Museum either bypassed or sidestepped the CFTA and the ROM 11.

Oji's meeting with Rahimi would prove instrumental. Both had an engagement later that evening at A Different Booklist (a Toronto bookstore doubling as a Black community meeting place) where both were each scheduled to speak. Captioned "Into the Heart of Africa Revisited," the program included a screening of Lavell's related documentary film.

For Rahimi's part, on entering the room to sit with Barrie for the interview, he "sensed distrust, tension, and hostility" coming from Oji. However, this misperception would soon subside, giving way to mutual understanding between the two. Oji and Rahimi would have several in-person conversations thereafter, during which time they developed a mutual respect. Whereas Rahimi was not directly involved with the ROM's '89 exhibit, he was aware of its controversy. He was also aware of the antiquated character of museum scholarship and of its resistance to change. He had no problem acknowledging that senior North American and European anthropologists tended to be dismissive when it came to matters relating to Afrocentricity. In fact, they were illiterate when it came to this branch of investigation. According to Rahimi, despite the influential controversial work by Martin Bernal, *Black Athena: The Afroasiatic Roots of Classical Civilization*, first published in 1987, museums and Eurocentric scholars remained largely unimpressed, stuck as they were in outmoded traditional thinking.

With his progressive outlook, it did not take long for Rahimi, who grew up in New York City during the sixties, to find common ground with Oji. Sensing an opportunity for reconciliation, they initiated a process by which CFTA members and the ROM 11 could formally begin to participate in ROM consultations. On Rahimi's invitation, Oji made several personal private visits to the ROM where the two continued to build rapport. It was a tremendous personal victory when Oji crossed the threshold of the ROM entrance. It was a small reconciliation of sorts. He never thought it was possible, nor did Rahimi. Oji would make a subsequent visit, more openly, when during one March break he held an Oware workshop for a diverse group of grade school students. When Oji mentioned the game to Rahimi, Rahimi jumped at the opportunity to recommend Oware as part of the ROM's March break programming featuring games from around the world. The delightful engagement of the students as they learned numeracy through play was obvious. More obvious was Oji's joy as he went about doing what he loved—teaching African culture and facilitating learning through play. It was a beauty to behold as he graciously stood surrounded by students in the basement of a building from which he was once previously unpleasantly ejected.

In his interview with Barrie, Oji noted that within the overall voice of any community, there are going to be different factions advocating for different methodologies in approach. He cited, for example, the gap between the older generation within the Black community and the young of which he was a part. Interestingly, internal gaps also emerged within the younger cohort of activists. As the ROM-CFTA consultations got underway, before long, divergencies began to appear. The differences in approaches were so sharp, group cohesion became untenable. Over time, Oji would withdraw his involvement.

Sentiments about what happened during the ROM affair and since are not universal. It is exceedingly difficult to establish with any degree of certainty some of the minutiae of what occurred—who did what and why, before, during, and after the protest. Over time, memories fade, perspective change as lives move on, and characters evolve. A more thorough and authoritative review will be required. Notwithstanding, Oji has never wavered in his perspective. When the ROM began to warm up to an apology, he opted out, preferring not to be a part of the ROM/CFTA reconciliation efforts.

The reconciliation effort was a botched exercise from the outset, at least in Oji's opinion. He came to this conclusion when the ROM attempted to negotiate his participation. Initially, following their CBC appearance, most if not all of his interactions with the museum had primarily been with Dan Rahimi. Together they unofficially explored what a CTFA/ROM reconciliation could look like. As the conversations became more formalized, others were brought in to mediate the relationship between Oji and the ROM. Rahimi, meanwhile, would soon step aside, opting out to secure a new assignment at his alma mater, the Penn Museum at the University of Pennsylvania.

In discussions with Oji, ROM negotiators flatly refused to compensate him for the legal costs he incurred arising from his participation in the demonstrations. Thinking as a business strategist, Oji intentionally approached these discussions as if undertaking a business-to-business transaction. While he was not asking the ROM to unconditionally pay for or to reimburse all his legal fees, he was determined to establish his value and to hold the ROM accountable for the damage done. The ROM's efforts at reconciliation needed to be substantive, not merely symbolic. With this in mind, he posed what he considered to be reasonable questions: *What will I get out of participating? Who will compensate me for my legal fees? Will I receive an honorarium?* The ROM's response to this line of inquiry—cleverly mediated through a person of African ancestry—turned out to be unsatisfactory. In his assessment of the institution's sincerity in making substantive reconciliation, Oji found them wanting. In his estimation, the response they offered was insulting, tantamount to further abuse, leaving him with distaste and a harsh conclusion. "Colonialism revisited" is how he would describe it. Lucidly, he could see the long arc of history recycling itself. By insisting on Black volunteerism—free labour—the ROM appeared to be invoking a new brand of slavery; it was as if the ROM had taken a line out of the colonialism playbook by replicating How Europe Underdeveloped Africa, except now there was a more specific application: How to Underdevelop Oji and Keep the Black Community Impoverished.

As he weighed the situation, Oji came to the conclusion that he was being used; he was being asked, in the name of community reconciliation, to freely do the ROM's bidding while they reaped the major benefits. He was being asked to lend his name and reputation to the ROM in order to help them repair theirs; he was being called on to assist ROM officials build their own careers, while he got nothing substantive in return. Given the violence he and others had to endure on the steps of the ROM, and the subsequent torture of prison and a legal bill, he did not consider this to be a fair reciprocal exchange. At the very least, he was hoping for a demonstration of real sincerity in the form of a more substantial proposal. If the ROM seriously intended to repair the damage done and to reconcile, then they would need to put money where their mouth was. When he realized this was not going to be the case, Oji concluded it was time to step away. For him, the protest did not end when the exhibit came down; the revolutionary struggle needed to continue through to the next level. And the next level was here and now in this moment when the ROM needed to own up to its fiduciary responsibility relative to its history of abuses. On arriving at this fork in the road, Oji disengaged, choosing instead to remain true to his convictions and the cause to which he was committed: justice. On this he would stand—or fall, as some certainly hoped he would.

While he applauds those of his colleagues who participated in the ROM's reconciliation, and acknowledges their accomplishments, he questions if anything meaningful was achieved by the exercise. As far as Oji was concerned, the so-called reconciliation by the ROM was no more than a "high level political promotional publicity stunt." He likened the ROM's reconciliation exercise to that of the abolition of the European enslavement of Africans, which, according to him, did not end because of so-called abolitionists. In his interpretation of history, slavery ended because of the slave masters' recognition that the slave system no longer served their purpose—it was no longer viable or profitable. The termination of slavery as an economic system was in the best interest of those who had the power to end it. Therefore, they agreed to abolish. To save face, they then set about creating and promoting the illusion that abolition was an act of humanitarian triumph. In Oji's view, the abolition of slavery was a business necessity, or else it might have continued even longer. Similarly, the ROM's reconciliation efforts, according to Oji, was strictly business as usual. The ROM apologized because it was no longer viable or profitable to remain obsolete.

This perspective is not as far-fetched as it may seem. Indeed, slavery as an institution had become too expensive and had outlived its economic value. With the onset of the Industrial Revolution, machines, not intensive human labour, were becoming the new norm. Astonishingly, once the governing bodies decided to abolish the practice in 1833, and after profiting from slavery for some two hundred years, the British offered compensation to slave owners to the tune of £20 million. £20 million was the incentive given to slave owners to enable the release of their African "property." But what of the enslaved? After years of exploitative forced labour upon which a massive empire was built, generating lasting residual intergenerational wealth, there was not much by way of compensation for the emancipated, no reparations for all the harm—the torture, abuse, loss of freedom, etc.,—endured by people of African ancestry who, as a direct result of colonialism and slavery, suffered and died in telling numbers. The most ex-enslaved Africans received was "free paper," a proclamation declaring they were free at last.

This was the heart of Oji's objection. Why is it that the people most exploited by systems of oppression are the ones required to bear the burden of paying for its overhaul, while the beneficiaries of those systems are allowed to prosper even more?

As outrageous as it may seem, Oji's super-conflated analysis had some validity. The ROM, a crown public institution, had been functioning on a tight operating budget, half of which came from the Ontario government. The other portion came from endowments and donations from wealthy benefactors, the most recent, visible, and dramatic example being the Michael Lee-Chin Crystal, opened in 2007—an angular space-age-looking geometric structure of glass and aluminum jutting out from the original old building—an impressive if not ghastly sight for street-side gawking. (The same wing under which the public apology was staged.) Nevertheless, despite this opulent show of magnificence, most of the ROM's galleries remained empty. Lacking in variety and quality programming, the massive building served more like a sophisticated warehouse for relics rather than what it purported to be—one of North America's leading institutions of learning. Public attendance was sluggish; there was brick-and-mortar, but no heart and soul. By the time Janet Carding arrived as director and CEO in September 2010, the Toronto museum was in dire need of new life—and significant funds. Who knows what other strife may have been playing out behind closed doors from the staff up to the board level? Evidently, the ROM needed to transform itself. In order to stay relevant and or to remain viable, it needed new direction and an injection of new life. And fast. If they were looking to Brother Oji to provide this momentum, they must have been sorely disappointed. Perhaps a little hellraising by Brother Oji may have been what the ROM needed; however, there seems to have been no appetite for his brand of drama.

Andy Barrie, on closing his interview with Oji and Rahimi, implored the two men to promise they would continue to meet. Well known for his erudition, Barrie ended by saying, "I hope that the word 'truth,' forever as it must be, is ever elusive and no one will claim absolute ownership."

As it turned out, Oji's truth was unequivocal and incisive. In his assessment of the ROM, he offers what appears to be a harsh indictment: As it was during the end of slavery, so it was during the ROM's reconciliation efforts—nothing more than self-serving propaganda aimed at restoring the ROM's reputation for the purpose of maintaining or increasing revenue stream. And so, partly business, partly in principle, Oji stayed away, preferring to disaffiliate himself from the ROM's reconciliation plans. He was not alone. There were other members of the CFTA—too burnt, hurt, disenchanted, or otherwise engaged—who opted out for reasons of their own. Out of respect for his colleagues who wanted to go ahead, Oji held his tongue. He was in effect a conscientious objector. The reconciliation would have to go ahead without him or his truth. No truth, no reconciliation.

Immersed in its colonial bourgeois disposition, the ROM could not see eye to eye with Oji. Opened in 1914 under the auspices of Prince Arthur, Duke of Connaught, Governor General of Canada, third son of the late Queen Victoria, the ROM and Oji came from diametrically opposed worldviews; they couldn't have been further apart. Smack in the middle of the ROM's perpetual blind spot stood Oji. They could not see or hear what he was saying, even if they wanted to. He was not highbrow. He was not Michael Lee-Chin (Jamaican Canadian billionaire, businessman, and philanthropist) offering a Crystal. Nor was he Helga Schmidt (president and CEO of Toronto-based ABC Group of Companies and Hatch Ltd., an international engineering project and construction firm) carrying a $3-million gift donation. The ROM consequently muted him out, failing to appreciate how their well-meaning efforts at reconciliation could possibly fail. How could anyone possibly interpret their well-intentioned effort as opportunistic race-based exploitation?

While the ROM was willing to entertain the values of multiculturalism and to admit responsibility for offending the Black community and to repair old wounds, ROM administrators were not prepared to acknowledge the deeper and more decisive questions related to racial injustice and oppression. Leery as they were of the possible complex negative risks and ramifications (they were already ultrasensitive about their troubled public image), they could not have been happier when Oji—a risk manager's nightmare—removed himself from the picture. With Oji's withdrawal, the ROM may have felt greater freedom in moving comfortably forward with less intractable parties, softer targets who were more amicable or more inclined to compromises.

Years following Oji's meeting with Rahimi, the museum began staging a number of follow-up exhibits and events, such as Of Africa, featuring contemporary African art, as well as Black artists, writers, and scholars. Evidently, the ROM felt it was ready to make peace, ready to reflect a more balanced positive view of Black African life and culture. It had learned from its past. Likely, there were backroom conversations held with "experts" in the Black community—known and unknown—who assisted in its rebranding.

In June 2017, the ROM held a presentation with the auspicious title the Coloniality of Existence: Africa in Scholarships and Museums. The featured speaker was Professor George Dei, the beloved esteemed Canadian scholar and teacher known for his leading-edge anti-racism work in the field of education. The presentation was described thus: "Explore the limitations, challenges and possibilities of studying Africa and the African Diaspora in Western academia. From the responsibilities and roles of national cultural institutions in the West, such as museums and universities, to the critical academic scholarship and educational lessons, this lecture suggests an alternative way forward to how we teach, learn and research Africa."

With this description, it appeared the ROM was embarking on a new era in which it was prepared to interrogate alternative and more modern curatorial methodologies consistent with best practice. Clearly, the museum also needed to lure African Canadian audiences back into its space by rebuilding trust and by offering an enticing array of African focused exhibitions and events. One such exhibit was Art, Honour and Ridicule: Asafo Flags from Southern Ghana, which ran for a year between September 3, 2016, and September 4, 2017. The show, which featured handcrafted flags, costumes, artifacts, and videos, had wide appeal among African Canadian audiences and continental born Africans who viewed the exhibit with dignified delight. Curated by Dr. Forni, the staging allowed viewers to celebrate and learn about an aspect of African culture seen through the eyes of indigenous Africans—not through the eyes of colonizers, but from "the people who conceive and wave them."

In February 2018, during Black History Month, Dr. Afua Cooper was featured in an interactive solo poetry performance in support of another ROM's exhibit entitled Here We Are Here. Afua, whose voice had been ignored by the ROM in 1990, was billed as a poet "inspired by the African Canadian experience" and whose poetry "delivers rich nourishment for the imagination." It was as if the stone that the builders had initially refused had now become the new cornerstone. Here We Are Here: Black Canadian Contemporary Art, staged between January 27 to April 22, 2018, featured artists Sandra Brewster, Chantal Gibson, Sylvia D. Hamilton, Bushra Junaid, Charmaine Lurch, Esmaa Mohamoud, Michèle Pearson Clarke, and Gordon Shadrach. The show was co-curated by Dr. Forni together with Dr. Julie Crooks and Dominique Fontaine, both independent Black curators who were instrumental in helping to spearhead rehabilitation of the ROM's image. With refreshing forthrightness, the exhibition was framed from a non-colonizer's point of view with the goal of challenging preconceived notions of Blackness in Canada by using current and historical objects, images, and ideas "to blur the longstanding perception that Black bodies belong on the edge of Canadian history." According to the curators, "In presenting multiple voices and sensitivities, this exhibition disrupts simplistic and comforting narratives, while affirming the longstanding relevance of Blackness to the fabric of Canada."

Included in the line-up for the Black Contemporary Art series was artist Jessica Karuhanga. Described as an artist of colour, her captivating performance of "When blue falls in to the ocean" was showcased as part of the ROM's original exhibition Here We Are Here. Even NourbeSe Philip joined the retinue of writers and performers to give a rendition from her collection of poetry featuring *Gregson v. Gilbert*, a legal decision focused on a rarely known case at the end of the eighteenth century in which Africans were murdered by slave traders on board a slave ship in order to claim freight insurance. What previously had been outside its walls in the 1990s as a protest message had now legitimately entered on to the ROM's main space as part of its adaptation to a new era of diversity and inclusion.

Credit for this shift can be traced back to the agitation of the CFTA and the resistance of the ROM 11. Many who earlier distanced themselves from the young rebels would later benefit from their rebellion. As government agencies and institutions began to navel gaze and look for "people they could work with" to air brush their public image, opportunities that were hitherto scarce began opening up. One tragedy of the ROM protest is that the young people who led it did not earn any immediate gain from their efforts. Disenchanted by the negativity they faced, they may not have realized the positive lasting power of their impact. At the time, they were regarded as pariahs and cast aside, lived mostly in fear of repercussions, anxious about an uncertain future. While they paid a heavy price for their actions, those who shunned them gained significantly from the aftermath of their struggle.

Many of the demands made by CFTA in the early nineties have now purportedly been met. Rahimi, before he left, developed guidelines on how to mount exhibits with community consultation. African Canadian communities now have greater input and a voice in shaping future exhibits. Black Canadian independent curators such as Dr. Julie Crooks and Dominique Fontaine were contracted to work with Forni, a curator and anthropologist with a specialization in African art and culture. With these and other changes, patrons could sense that African Canadian communities now had a positive place of belonging in the ROM's programming.

In common with other civic-minded institutions that have recently rediscovered a new and heightened sense of social responsibility, the ROM on its website (August 2020) have seen fit to declare its stand on race and racism. According to their posted statement, "In these times of extraordinary change, a global movement is underway to dismantle systemic, institutionalized racism. In order to serve our communities, to transform lives, and to help people navigate their world, we must recognize our own position in it and commit to our own transformation through anti-racist work including institutional self-reflection, inclusive practice, dismantling racism, pursuing reconciliation."

ROM director and CEO at the time of writing, Josh Basseches, in a letter to the ROM community posted on the museum's website (August 2020), admits that "as a museum, our work over the last 106 years has at times reinforced colonial perspectives and ideas that further entrench systemic oppression ..." Further he says, "We must continue to work toward ensuring the ROM becomes an even more inclusive, equitable and anti-racist institution, so that people not only feel welcome but see the Museum as a place of belonging."

This is a step in the right direction. To acknowledge the problem and to accept ownership of the responsibility to act proactively and retroactively to implement remedies are part of right practice; exercising the will to dismantle structures of institutionalized racism is praiseworthy, especially when accompanied by timelines and executive accountability. Members of the African Canadian community hold diverse opinions about the significance of the ROM's turnaround. There is cautious optimism among the various perspectives. Some are more cynical. Reserved in their congratulations, they are apt to regard this as *fake* and to say: "We have heard this all before."

Racism has blown up to become a complex ill phenomenon with many messy sides—disproportionately high dropout rates and school suspensions among racialized students, their mass derailment into lower grade or vocational streams, the disproportionately high rate of incarceration among racialized and Indigenous people, the high rate of poverty and negative health outcomes in racialized communities, ghettoization of Black life and culture, the absence of racialized people in corporate boardrooms and in the annals of political and economic power, and so on. These realties have historical roots traceable back to colonialism and slavery. How can the Royal Ontario Museum, an institution with global standing, a public body dedicated to research, learning, and public education, respond to these prevailing concerns? Can it? Should it?

Within this broader context, some are guarded in their appraisal of the ROM's about-face. They are suspicious of institutional piecemeal measures buttered up with lip service. As a public agency owned by citizens, the ROM will need to find its way to new relevancy. By becoming more responsive to these and other grappling human needs, the ROM may one day overcome its past; for the ROM to meet these challenges, more embedded expertise will be required in order to drive the envisioned changes. Critics point to greater need for racial diversity in the senior administration, trusteeship, and governance of the ROM.[45] Meanwhile, similar to Holocaust

---

45 Member of the Order of Canada, Rita Shelton Deverell is a media and theatre professional, a writer, and scholar renowned for being one of the first Black women to be a national television host and network executive. She is a member of the ROM's Board of Trustees, the governing authority responsible for the museum's policies, operational continuity, collections, and other assets. Ms. Deverell has a track record of social activism and brings to the board an equity and social justice lens together with a range of other creative and communication expertise.

museums for example, others claim there will be no real progress until targeted inclusive programs focusing on the experience of racialized communities become more mainstream.

Still, others are calling for more far-reaching changes. They suggest that consultative participation is not reparations, that justice will not be complete until Canada institutes or supports a museum dedicated specifically to the African diasporic experience, or a section thereof. According to some, if the ROM wishes to demonstrate the sincerity of their apology, they can contribute to these efforts either through direct donations or through targeted fundraising.

Moreover, Eurocentric museums are called upon to make cultural restitution by relinquishing ownership and control of items of African cultural significance that are currently in their collections—items that have been misappropriated, looted, or plundered through imperial conquest, not unlike how Nazi stolen art pieces are currently being returned to their rightful owners or how Indigenous sacred objects are being repatriated. Other museums throughout the world are currently engage in this targeted form of deaccession. According to this perspective, Eurocentric museums born out of colonialism such as the ROM lack the culturally appropriate expertise necessary to be competent stewards of items reflecting African cultural heritage, nor do they have the capacity to showcase them with integrity or the moral authority to own them. At the very least, these items should be repatriated or entrusted to the care of organizations best able to honour and house these artifacts respectfully.

The disciplines of anthropology and archaeology were integral to the establishment of empires and the spread of colonialism. Museums established during this era derived their collections through imperialist arrangements. Such museums were founded on racist ideologies seeking to justify and institutionalize White supremacy. Decolonization therefore will mean more than simply dismounting an exhibit or changing labels. Museum decolonization involves rigorous and critical reframing of imperialist ideologies and practices. Beyond making pronouncements, decolonization requires conscious methodical creation of pathways to knowledge, skills, and values that will promote and encourage anti-oppression. All aspects of museum business will have to be reappraised, including human experiences, policies, programs, and activities. Colonialism and slavery cultivated inequity, injustice, and human degradation. Museums interested in transformational change will need to help their constituencies unlearn associated attitudes and behaviours.

To respond to a singular event with a knee-jerk reaction and fleetingly move on with "business as usual" once the issue withers away is to fall short of the goal of meaningful change. Colonization took four hundred years. Decolonization will need to be a long-term project.

Recently in March 2021, the University of Aberdeen decided to repatriate a Benin Bronze sculpture to Nigeria, admitting that the sculpture of an Oba, or ruler, of the Kingdom of Benin, had been looted from Nigeria in an "extremely immoral" fashion. This was one of thousands of objects taken from the Kingdom of Benin by the British during their occupation—art, and monuments routinely plundered then auctioned off to Western museums and private collectors.[46] Pressure is mounting as public institutions are being compelled to return to their places of origin treasured items stolen by colonial powers. Will the ROM follow the University

---

46 For more on the "not-so-polite" history of British colonialism and museums, listen to podcast hosted by Marc Fennell entitled "Stuff the British Stole" at https://www.cbc.ca/listen/cbc-podcasts/1030-stuff-the-british-stole.

of Aberdeen's example? At question is whether or not the ROM can decolonize itself and seize the opportunity to rid itself of the systemic traps of the past. It is doubtful that it can or ever will. It may need to begin by first changing its name.[47] (Be wary of any institution with the word "Royal" in its name. The Royal African Company, for example, was one of the most successful slave-trading enterprise in the history of British commerce. The company interfaced with banking, insurance, and shipbuilding to create an engine of economic growth that continues to reverberate even today. The trail of victims, past and present, in the wake of this quest for dominance is so extensive, it is beyond comprehension.)

An obscure reference to the *Into the Heart of Africa* exhibit appears on the ROM's 1980s ReCollects website. It reads succinctly, "The exhibition opens in November with good attendance at the public programs. Early in the next year, protests begin and escalate. *ROM changes the process by which exhibitions are proposed and approved*" (Italics mine).

Previously highbrow, the stuffy exclusive preserve of an elite group, a place where even well-meaning amateurs were not welcome, museums now regard community consultations as a critical step in their curatorial process. Whereas before, public input was never considered a priority, now it has become essential for museums to invite diverse bodies of academics and non-academics alike to the table and to engaged them before and during development—not after exhibits have been fully conceptualized. It is now standard practice to consult with community advisory groups. For curators and students of museum history and practice, the ROM's *Into the Heart of Africa* exhibit has become a landmark case study on how *not* to mount an exhibit.

When all is said and done, Oji—an Afro-wearing lightweight imprisoned for his pugnacity, a descendant of African Maroons, a *lickkle bwoy* from Jamaica born on a day dedicated to the elimination of racism who crossed *hill and gully* to come to Canada with his family in '74—is satisfied that he was able to open the door in some small way to allow for other voices to be heard. He is gratified that even in the absence of social media, he was one of the early leading voices in the movement to politicize modern museums, laying the groundwork for tackling institutionalized racist historical propaganda.

In recent years, statues and monuments have been falling. Some have been vandalized, others desecrated—the monuments of John A. Macdonald, Canada's first prime minister; Christopher Columbus, the so-called discoverer; Cecil Rhodes, the South African empire builder; and Edward Colston, a seventeenth-century slave trader in Bristol, come to mind.

---

47 A number of museum organizations have already embarked on the task of decolonizing their institutions, including the Museums Association, Group for Education in Museums (GEM), the Association of Independent Museums (AIM), and others. They have jointly made declarations to reappraise their respective history and the colonial mind-set upon which they were built. They have committed to proactively support anti-racism in their heritage collections and in all areas of museum work.

Recently, the legitimacy of Henry Dundas has been posthumously called into question. Dundas, a wealthy, well-connected, powerful Scottish member of the British House of Commons and the House of Lords in the eighteenth/nineteenth century, regularly blocked anti-slavery efforts and argued for the British empire's continued involvement in the transatlantic slave trade. Previously held in high regard, his legacy has been memorialized on Ontario street names and various important civic places of interest, including one town named in his honour. Who knows who else in the White elite have tarnished historical reputations? Many are the roads leading back to colonialism and slavery. Other representative symbolic icons of colonialism and slavery better watch out, for the multitude is coming—a new worldwide wave of activist-protest movements. Never mind them; the general population is more widely aware and are becoming increasingly impatient with the covering up of historical crimes by historical lies masquerading as fact. Insisting on having honest and transformative discourses, this new era of rebellion is dedicated to nothing less than questioning and attacking institutional racism. They are interested in setting the record straight. Images invoking memories of oppression that are rooted in racist colonial value systems are now being exposed for critical re-evaluation.

As a result, museums, galleries, and art institutions globally are on notice; their CEOs are now impelled to take stock of injustices embedded in their respective collections and archives. More than ever, they are being asked to be self-critical of the objects, artifacts, and symbols within their care; to relook particularly at how they archive, label, juxtapose, or present historical memory related to people of African ancestry. No longer can they ignore or fail to re-examine the role played by dominant cultures in perpetuating human abuse and exploitation.

Before the British-born and trained Janet Carding knew she would be coming from Australia to Toronto to lead the ROM in 2010, *Into the Heart of Africa* was already a case study in her professional curriculum; how fortuitous. This would likely not have been so had it not been for Brother Oji and the CFTA. The gaping flaws within the '89 exhibit would likely have flown under the radar had it not been for their uproar. The exhibit did not, as Cannizzo presumably intended, expose the nasty underbelly of colonialism. It took the demonstrators to do that. What the ROM exhibit did was to resurrect the glorification of colonialism and aggravate festering wounds. It took the outrage of demonstrators to draw attention to the disreputable record of British imperialism and to call for the ROM to cease and desist in perpetuating racist mythology. And cease and desist they did, albeit stubbornly. Through their work, Brother Oji, the ROM 11, and the CFTA triggered the tsunami that eventually led to the closure of the exhibition and to the introduction of anti-Black racism principles in the management practices of museums worldwide. Collectively, they smashed the prevailing colonial misrepresentation of Africa and the Black experience.

Because of this, other historically excluded communities have likewise benefitted. The anti-racism movements we see today—and liberation movements generally—are a continuation of the struggles initiated and sustained by freedom fighters since the inception of Black African enslavement. In this genealogy, it is befitting that we offer Brother Oji a place of belonging.

What's more, it must be remembered that he did not take "the deal" as others did. Some may be resentful or critical of Oji for his stubborn foolhardiness, but he cannot be faulted for exercising his single-minded autonomous self-respect. In doing so, he established a bar of moral leadership unknown among his peers. Through this remarkable defiance, he led others to discover the meaning of commitment without compromise; through his epic struggle against oppression, in word and in deed, he inspired many young onlookers who though hungry for heroes could find none close at hand who looked like them. In Oji, they found a relatable revolutionary at last, a hometown role model they could emulate and call their own.

As someone who has been a militant crusader for Pan-African freedom and who has contributed to the stream of anti-racism political protest, Brother Oji is grateful that, in a brief moment in history, he was called on to be the small axe up against a big tree.[48]

While others stood proudly inside the ROM November 2016 to accept an apology, Brother Oji stands proud outside in 2018, unapologetic—a small axe up against a tall tree. (Photo by Eryck B.)

---

48 A review of the history of the Canadian Museum Association (CMA), an association founded in 1947, as outlined on its website, would suggest that despite the global significance of the fiasco associated with Into the Heart of Africa, the exhibit hardly made a blip on the association's radar, this despite having as its declared values "Collaboration and community, boldness and courage, accountability and professionalism, diversity, inclusiveness and social responsibility, excellence and creativity." During the 1990s, the CMA appeared to be more focused on the survival and viability of Canadian museums rather than whether or not they were conduits for racism. In response to the 2015 Truth and Reconciliation Commission of Canada's final report containing ninety-four calls to action, the CMA has established a body of experts in Indigenous culture and museum practices to respond to call to action #67, which "calls upon the federal government to provide funding to the CMA to undertake, in collaboration with Aboriginal peoples, a national review of museum policies and best practices to determine the level of compliance with the United Nations Declaration on the Rights of Indigenous Peoples and to make recommendations." Unlike other museum organizations, the CMA has no obvious stated equivalent declaration of commitment to address anti-Black racism or to push for decolonization practices among its members or affiliates, at least not any this author could easily identify. Notwithstanding the efforts of Brother Oji, the ROM 11, and the CFTA, the big tree may still be standing, though not as tall.

"One of the CFTA demands was for the ROM to return art stolen from Africa. This was very strategically omitted from any reports on the reconciliation. Return all art stolen from Africa, now!" (Brother Oji) (Oji/MACPRI Archives)

My Origin

My children could have sung songs to Mawu
As they bade in the River Volta
My clan could have listened to
And followed the fire
The fire
The firing thunder of Shango
I am forever connected
I am child of the burning sun—RA

(Excerpt from a poem by Brother Adisa S. Oji)

EPILOGUE

Speaking of revolutions, in the words of Black Panther leader Fred Hampton, "You can jail a revolutionary, but you can't jail a revolution."

Speaking of revolutionaries, following a botched uprising against Cuban dictator Fulgencio Batista in 1953, Fidel Castro and other insurgents were arrested and charged. In his own legal defence, Castro spoke for four hours, concluding fearlessly, "Condemn me. It does not matter. History will absolve me."

These words became the template, the motto that would later inspire the lives of young truth-seekers with a revolutionary consciousness, young men like Oji, who found kinship with the lead characters of the Cuban revolution. Not that he wanted to be like Fidel Castro. Instead, what they shared was an uncommon passion for attempting the impossible, both blessed with a daring moxie defying good sense, each with an acute ability to see the long arc of history. At various junctures in their lives, each in their own way became a lightning rod of controversy, both at times being so far out others often wondered about their sanity. While they both matured in a different time, faced vastly different circumstances and are different in fundamental ways, both faced sharp criticisms and disagreements, and both shared an unwavering tenacity in the face of opposition. Shared in common also is the ability to transform the situations in which they respectively find themselves, disrupting patterns of subordination and servitude, even if it means using unconventional attention-getting maneuvers.

For his part, Fidel Castro, against all odds, remained true to his cause, this despite the mayhem of numerous assassination plots motivated by US interference. Standing tall, unshaven, dressed in his customary olive-green military garb, Castro personified the ultimate nonconformist. When Oji's father passed way, rather than showing up respectfully dressed as ordinary folks would when attending funerals, Oji appeared at the ceremony wearing army-like boots, outfitted in military fatigues, à la Fidelista. He was seemingly unapologetic and uninhibited; some would say disrespectful, even misguided. It was one of those "Who do you think you are? What are you doing here?" moments. On the surface, he seemed as if he was a man at war. And to some degree, he was. He was not immune from the typical tug-of-war tension common between fathers and sons. Deep down, however, his bravado belied a young man's search for peace, for meaning, and for a better way, a way beyond that which was blazed by his father. He was searching for ways to transcend the past. His search would not be in vain.

Ernesto "Che" Guevara in 1952, before he became a world-famous icon, had himself embarked on a journey of self-discovery. Argentinian by birth and a physician by training, he made his trek through Latin America's Bolivia, Peru, Ecuador, Panama, Costa Rica, and Guatemala. His sojourn, now a matter of legend, is said to have been the source of his emotional and political maturation. Through his escapades navigating the waterways, mountains, and plains of Latin America and relating to everyday people, young Guevara eventually found and embraced his life's work.

Eight years later, in 1960 after becoming a Cuban citizen, Guevara delivered a speech to a group of Cuban medical students. In his speech, entitled *"Un Niño de mi Ambiente"* (A Child of My Environment), he gave an account of his personal odyssey in which he described his transformation from a student of medicine into becoming an active revolutionary. He said,

"The revolution today demands that they learn, demands that they understand well that the pride of serving our fellowman is much more important than a good income; that the people's gratitude is much more permanent, much more lasting than all the gold one can accumulate."

Oji has had his own odyssey of discovery. His sojourn took him through various outposts of what was once the British Empire, beginning in Jamaica through to Canada then West Africa. He also faithfully kept a diary very much the same way Guevara did. And similarly, Oji's convictions were deepened and strengthened by his experiences. Throughout his journey, he found himself embracing with increasing relish his life's purpose even as he found solidarity with the land and the people he visited. Informed by a strong sense of history and a strong connection with ancestry, Oji, in spirit and in deed, echoed the sentiments delivered by Guevara. He did so by taking pride in serving a greater cause, even if it meant sacrificing "all the gold one can accumulate." His life became his work, and his work became his life. He embodied tangible aspects of revolution, bringing such ideals forward into the present. It may be obscure, but a new direction is emerging through Brother Oji's life and work, a new era of right activism; new ways of righting historical wrongs are beginning to take shape. Through his drive, his persistency, Brother Oji has remapped the neocolonial landscape, giving us clues on how we may move forward.

This biography is a modest attempt to chart the evolution of the life and work of an exemplary young man who endured significant challenges along his hero's journey. He is best understood when seen not in isolation or in abstraction. Brother Oji's light shines brightest when seen within the context of the prevailing conditions that impacted his life and times. Beautifully, passionately, his life unfolds like a canvas, a gift of grace, telling of turbulence, defiance, and hope. His life, and the circumstances running in, out, and throughout, can be likened to that iconographic motif—the kente cloth—his own historical quilt, which when unfurled reveals the birth of a new, yet ancient, radicalism. He did not conform to what others thought he should be or become. Nor did he succumb to societal pressures to pursue a "good income," nor did he bow to dehumanizing systems when they required him to be subservient or be helplessly dependent. Instead, he raged against it, defying it at great odds. Daringly, he stood up fearlessly, seizing his humanity with both hands to challenge and disrupt lopsided power relations, if only a touch, at times appearing to be an anomaly as he used his genius in the cause of liberation.

Anomalies play a special role in nature. That which does not fit conventional patterns have something to tell us. If we pay attention, and if we are willing to listen, they can meaningfully inform us, give us insights we would otherwise miss. Brother Oji's philosophy and practice—whether it be his Pan-African revolutionary vision or his insistence on self-determination (*Kujichagulia*), the idea that we have the right to determine our own destiny; his passion for *Ujima* (collective work and responsibility) and *Ujamaa* (co-operative economics); the way he confronted questions of identity and belonging through what he described as *Maroonage* and *Sankofa* (the return); or his activism for economic freedom, justice, and human rights through a process he calls *de-triangulation*—all these practice philosophies are great examples from which we may learn. Some may find Oji's views and attitude objectionable. This notwithstanding, his body of work to date is, and will remain, a historical treasure, one that qualifies him—while he is alive and well—for iconic status.

In 2017, Canada celebrated its 150th birthday, boasting its reputation as a diverse nation speaking over two hundred different tongues. (French and English remain the two official languages.) According to census data, 22 percent of the Canadian population at the time were said to be born elsewhere; over 7 million "visible minorities" within the multicultural mosaic accounted for this distinction, jumping from 1 percent during the sixties. At the time of Canada's 150th anniversary celebrations, 1.4 million (4.3 percent) identified as "Aboriginal." As it turned out, many Indigenous communities distanced themselves from the fanfare, some openly condemning it as another illustration of imperialist Eurocentric arrogance. Moreover, indigenous people had little to cheer about, having been in mourning for the past four hundred years over the loss of many of their own due to hostile White European encroachment. Entrenched in their ways, Canadian authorities pressed ahead with their festivities nonetheless, making a big splash in a self-congratulatory mood, applauding the settler-nation as the first country to ever pass a national multiculturalism law in 1988.

About the same time, I was staring at the cover of a major glossy Canadian magazine, a *Canada 150 Special Edition* marking the 150th anniversary of Canadian Confederation. Emblazoned on the red-and-white cover was "**Happy Birthday to US!** *From Celine to poutine. The people, places and things that make our country so damn cool.*" I cracked the covers to see if I could find myself. Flipping through to the last page, all 130 of them, I was unable to find any images that looked like me. Missing also were images of Indigenous people and many other communities of colour who have made this country *so damn cool*. Disappointed, and in disbelief, I looked again to double check. This time I found two images of individuals not considered White: The Weeknd and Oscar Peterson, two entertainment celebrities. They were part of a photo collage on page 3. If multiculturalism was a fundamental value in Canadian society, it certainly was not reflected here in this slick commemorative publication.

The erasure or *invisibilizing* of Black presence and contribution is nothing new. Disconcerting and disturbing, this happens with numbing regularity. In scanning through *Canada: A People's History, Volume One* by Don Gillmor and Pierre Turgeon—"a richly illustrated book (telling) the epic story of Canada from its earliest days to the arrival of the industrial age in the 1870s"—I was hoping to find mention of Mathieu Da Costa or Josiah Henson or Richard Pierpoint, the Black Loyalist, or the story of Marie-Joseph Angélique of Montreal, an enslaved woman who was tortured for wanting to be free. Described as a "story of the people who created this vast nation," I was expecting to discover more about the enslavement of Africans, their emancipation, and the growth of African Canadian communities. Regrettably, none of the above Black historical characters appeared in the text or index, nor were any of the topics I was looking for referenced in this beautiful, glossy volume that ran over 292 pages long. However, the Shadd family—Abraham, Mary Ann, and Isaac—were mentioned.[49] They were mentioned on the same page as the Underground Railroad.

Granted, there are limits to what can be included in any academic work. The authors understandably may be forgiven for working within frameworks that are restrictive in scope. Regardless, in a book intended "for every Canadian home" and which purports to be about "the people who found themselves in extraordinary circumstances in a vast and promising land," it is disappointing to see blank spaces where the presence of Black lives and their stories ought to be. It is as if Black lives in Canada don't count and have little citizenship or place of belonging. If Black presence is mentioned at all, it is usually on the down-low or down below in positions of subservience or in need. Maybe a more comprehensive history is accounted for in volume 2. I don't know. I was too frustrated to go looking for it.

Today, we are faced with a sore dispute, a not-so-pleasant debacle. No one knows when it will end, or how, except that it will likely be sorry if not soon. At the core of this debate is the lived experience of extreme inequity and inequality endured by disadvantaged groups within the North American mosaic. The fraying loose threads in the fabric of Western democracies are becoming increasingly visible as we come face to face with the long-term consequences of intergenerational inhumanity. No one seems to be immune from this harm. *Everyone* suffers from the adverse moral and other deleterious effects of unjust inhumane systems. Yet some are likely to suffer more egregiously than others.

Many who are debased or injured by racial discrimination continue to suffer in silence. They are afraid of complaining lest they become victims of further reprisals. Many more are slowly becoming cynical, even tired, due to their lack of confidence in the system's ability to positively correct itself. Others are embittered and are convinced: "They don't really care about us!" There is a growing alienation among those who increasingly believe that they, their children, and their grandchildren are more likely to face significantly higher rates of discrimination and harassment, not less. For parents rearing children in this environment, conversations about *Babylon and the Beast* are equivalent to, if not more significant than, the bird and the bees, especially if they are raising teenage boys. Beset by racism, more than a few individuals assume they have no meaningful available recourse or remedy, prompting some into acts of hopeless desperation or reckless abandon, thinking they have nothing more to lose. Racialized communities have become familiar with seeing themselves missing in powerful influential places of sociopolitical and economic rank. They see themselves packaged more often in negative media representations; they are disproportionally over-represented in humiliating degrading social conditions and live daily with an intimate over-familiarity with structural barriers, keenly

---

49 Anti-slavery activist, journalist, publisher, and lawyer, May Ann Shadd is regarded as the first woman publisher in Canada and the first Black woman to have that distinction in North America. For more, see Rosemary Sadlier's 1995 book *Mary Ann Shadd: Publisher, Editor, Teacher, Lawyer, Suffragette* by Umbrella Press.

aware of their own apathy and lack of power. There is growing dissatisfaction with the failure of social and political leaders to make a difference. As the world churns from one global crisis to another, the equity gap accelerates even more, while faith in our social systems continue to erode. Should this be allowed to continue as it is, a social collapse as we have never seen will overtake whatever meaningful gains Western democracies have been able to make over the past one hundred years.

As we advance our understanding of the intersection between race, sex, gender expression, religion, place of origin, and ethnicity, each dimension with its own claim to legitimacy, we are faced with an even more complex controversy rife with heated debate. In this larger prism, Black redemption becomes subsumed, lost in a troubling arrangement in which sub-sets compete for attention, a rivalry that oftentimes distract from the insidious legacy of anti-Black racism instead of highlighting it.

The deepening of anti-Black and other forms of racism, have not stopped or diminished since Oji and his family first arrived in Canada in 1974. On the contrary, as Canada comes of age, there have been increased reports of various forms of racism. Evidence reveals that racism has mutated into new and virulent strains, evolving to the point where it has infiltrated every aspect of social, economic and political life.

The ROM incident is but one example of modern expressions of structural and institutionalized racism. Debates about what transpired before, during, and after the demonstrations, inside and outside of the ROM's walls, will likely continue. Oji's role will always be controversial and provocative. Criticized by some, he will be much acclaimed by others for his stubborn tenacity in standing up defiantly against the status quo of racism. He insisted on having a unique voice, on creating platforms for the voiceless. With each act of defiance, he contributed to the tapestry of resistance, each occasion finding ways to remain invigorated or inspired, drawing upon a web of interconnecting influences far and wide. The ongoing debate about his role is a measure of his lasting impact, the ultimate outcome of which is yet to be fully realized.

Although some of us have been able to live in relative comfort, wealth, power, and significance remain unequally distributed. Poverty and degradation remain overly concentrated among people of African ancestry. Despite immense progress in education, employment, technology, sports, and entertainment, and despite having unimaginable access to a variety of tools, people of colour remain the primary target of neglect, abuse, exploitation, and dehumanization. We still have not "solved" racism. James Baldwin refers to this fixation as an addiction; others refer to it as an industry. We may refer to it as a twenty-first-century failure of historical magnitude. In an era of modern human civilization in which men have landed on the moon, billionaires have been launched into space, the world is on the verge of becoming petrified as we stand transfixed by a viral pandemic even as many helplessly gaze at the Medusa-like face of unbridled greed and wealth accumulation. The prioritization of race-based material gain and disproportionate wealth generation over basic human dignity continues to be a striking trend, as is the racialization of poverty, crime, and policing.

It is in this context that *I AM Brother Oji* calls on us to contemplate the meaning of our lives, the nature of existence, our place and purpose in it. Its narrative calls us to consider how, if at all, we may make a difference for good, even as we pursue inner fulfilment. Begging for our attention is the appalling presence of polarizing conflict. This protracted struggle, characterized by an everlasting push and pull between contending forces, is beginning to dominate our lives;

it always has, but now it has become painfully inescapable. It is a struggle between *us* and *them*; between Black and White, oppressor and oppressed, victims and victimizers, outsiders and insiders—a never ending cycle of suffering as one side squares off against the other in an ongoing contest filled with angst and despair. It is a sometime deadly controversy in which people of African ancestry rage against anti-Black injustice. They are calling for equal rights, equity and full citizenship, and in many instances are demanding reparations—some refer to this groundswell as an uprising, or a reckoning. On the other hand, members of the White establishment continue to hold ground, act in bad faith or push back, inflicting punitive measures on people of colour, overtly or covertly, routinely eliminating threats to their monopolized dominance and power. At the same time, many from both sides are trapped in the middle. Although they too are infected by the toxicity of oppression, they watch as if they are spectators, head rotating side to side as they stand on edge. Unsure in their bewilderment of what to do, they wait anxiously for a break in the tension uncertain of what may happen next. Others weary just the same stay out of the fray completely, consumed as they are by their own particular escape or preoccupation. Insulated from the pushing and fighting, they are less fixated on the struggle but are no less concerned. Will this bitterness ever end? If so, when and how? Is there a pathway to peace beyond death, destruction, rage, and despair?

To be clear, purveyors of racism do not act alone. In 1990, for instance, the ROM's refusal to heed calls to drop its White supremacist representation was not an isolated event. This was part of a pattern, a bigger picture of systemic racial oppression. Racism's persistent pervasiveness was and is made possible by a prevailing worldview held and promoted by leading minds in positions of influence who with their supporters have normalized and embed this mentality into institutions, systems, policies and programs. The silence of many further enables racist practices. (Howard Zinn was probably right: You can't be neutral on a moving train.)[50]

When Brother Oji and others stepped forward in 1990, they intended to raise their voices. Brother Oji in particular was moved to take an uncompromising stand in opposition to the ingrained philosophy of White supremacy. No one challenges this leviathan without paying a price. When Oji emerged from the protest demonstrations, he may have been chastened, but he was certainly not dispirited. Emboldened, he continued with his African Image Revolution, refashioning as best as he could the sociocultural, political, and economic landscape in which he found himself.

This history should not be forgotten. It is a significant milepost in a significant era. Although his life and work has yet to be preserved in national memory or commemorated in film, monuments, paper bills, or postage stamps, Brother Oji is already worthy of recognition as a staunch fighter for racial and social justice. He did so at great personal cost, not the least of which is the handicap of a criminal record. A campaign for his full exoneration should begin forthwith.

---

50 *You Can't Be Neutral on a Moving Train* is the title of Zinn's memoir published 2002, and also the title of a 2004 documentary featuring his life and work as an intellectual and justice advocate.

When it comes to race and racism, there is a tendency to regard Canada's standing as distinctly better than that of the USA. Depending on whom you ask, Canada is a "raceless" society where no one sees colour, a colour-blind culture where there is a polite innocent benevolent understanding of human diversity. Wendell Adjetey, during his post-doctoral fellowship and tenure in the Department of History at Harvard University, described Canada as "arguably one of the greatest liberal democracies on earth, our shortcoming notwithstanding." This is usually positioned in contrast to the more virulent racism practiced and experienced in the United States. On the other hand, Saje Mathieu, a professor of history at the University of Minnesota, had this to say: "Canadians have contributed handsomely to a myth that makes us feel morally, politically, legally superior to the US at least on the question of race."[51] Indeed, dotted throughout Canadian history are examples of racism directed at Indigenous, African, Chinese, Japanese, South Asian, and Jewish people—severe acts of racism that were far from benign, some of which could be classified as "crimes against humanity."

In the broader Canadian society, there appears to be a lack of true understanding of racism and its many sides. To begin with, generally, there is a low appetite for race-based discussions. Conversations about race and racism are akin to walking on eggshell or through minefields. Best advice when entering such conversations, if at all, is to do so cautiously. In mixed interracial company, relationships suddenly may become fragile and fraught with fear if and when the subject is raised. Most tend to shy away from the conversation altogether given its general discomfort. Strong emotional reactions are often triggered, judgement becomes cloudy, and communication becomes distorted. In particular, any critique of Canadian culture and history pointing to racism can lead to closed doors or a deep sense of guilt or strenuous denial.[52]

This notwithstanding, there is currently an opportunity for increased awareness of the history of racism in Canada and to assess its lasting effect on the body politic generally, and specifically on those who have been negatively affected. Currently, we are faced with an opportunity to strengthen our capacity for greater understanding and to begin or continue the work of dismantling discriminatory barriers at all levels across a wide range of institutions. Brother Oji's story serves as an early warning sign. His life story suggests that racism is a form

---

51 Both Wendell Adjetey and Saje Mathieu comments were made on CBC's radio program *Ideas*, on a 2018 edition entitled "The resistance of Black Canada: State surveillance and suppression." Adjetey, Ghanaian by birth, made the above statement in the wider context of Canada's racist practices. He used declassified materials to reveal how, during the 1960s and 1970s, US and Canadian security services cooperated to undermine and arguably sabotage Black community activism on both sides of the border.

52 "White fragility" is a term made popular by Robin DiAngelo. In a 2011 edition of the *International Journal of Critical Pedagogy*, Vol 3 (3), he states, "White people in North America live in a social environment that protects and insulates them from race-based stress. This insulated environment of racial protection builds white expectations for racial comfort while at the same time lowering the ability to tolerate racial stress, leading to what I refer to as White Fragility. White Fragility is a state in which even a minimum amount of racial stress becomes intolerable, triggering a range of defensive moves. These moves include the outward display of emotions such as anger, fear, and guilt, and behaviors such as argumentation, silence, and leaving the stress-inducing situation. These behaviors, in turn, function to reinstate white racial equilibrium."

of pathology; that window-dressing or petty tinkering is overrated, even counterproductive; and that we should consider overthrowing systems of oppression altogether once and for all, now, sooner rather than later, for the benefit of all.

The life and times of Brother Oji is a reminder of the importance of bringing these conversations to the forefront. Rather than silently pretending, "sweeping the dirt under the rug," it is high time to take down the "exhibition." His story, given its undeniable breadth, helps to underscore the universal adversity and suffering flowing from the divisive social phenomenon of racial injustice. His story helps to uncover the historical origin of race and racism, explaining to some degree how these concepts have woven their way into the social fabric of life and political culture in Jamaica, Canada, and Africa. Nestled in his narrative are clues on how to navigate this territory and how to pluck this blight from its safe and snug habitat.

Brother Oji's story illustrates that a healthier form of liberal democracy is long overdue, one based on fairness and equity and one whereby we are in right relationship with ourselves and each other; one in which we are willing to hold courageously honest, authentic, respectful, uncomfortable conversations about racial hierarchy.

Before the nation (or institutions) can arrive at a mature place of shared understanding, there will be need for a higher level of dialogue regarding Canada's unequal heterogeneity. This must be coupled with a willingness to examine nationhood beyond narrow economic parameters based on GDP, income levels, market shares, profit margins, and consumerism. In addition to economic power, justice as a valued principle needs to be enshrined as an important benchmark for true nationhood.

In 1992, when Brother Oji was going through his legal ordeal, there was a riot on Toronto's Yonge Street. The riot (some called it an uprising) came on the heels of Peel Regional Police killing of Raymond Lawrence. Anger was further inflamed by the acquittal of the four Los Angeles Police Department officers involved in Rodney King's beating, a saga unfolding during the same time period. The so-called riot led the government of the day to commission Stephen Lewis, a respected politician and diplomat, with instructions to examine race relations and policing in Ontario. Following Lewis's examination, he recommended among other things that the Task Force on Race Relations and Policing be reconstituted. He also recommended the creation of a commission on systemic racism in the Ontario Criminal Justice System.[53] An excerpt from the Stephen Lewis report compiled some thirty years ago (1992) is worthwhile quoting if only because it describes an ongoing reality:

> First, what we are dealing with, at root, and fundamentally, is anti-Black racism. While it is obviously true that every visible minority community experience the indignities and the wounds of systemic discrimination throughout Southern Ontario, it is the Black community which is the focus. It is Blacks who are being

---

53 Studies of these matters appear to be never ending. Lewis, in his report, called for a redo of a previous 1989 task force report on the basis that it contained shortcomings. As for his proposed commission, its mandate was to study and make recommendations on all facets of Ontario's criminal justice system. In 1995, when the commission finally released its 450-page finding, one of its recommendations was to develop guidelines for police discretion to stop and question people, with the goal of eliminating differential treatment of Black and other racialized people. Today, racial profiling continues. We can expect further reports, examinations, and inquiries.

shot, it is Black youth that is unemployed in excessive numbers, it is Black students who are being inappropriately streamed in schools, it is Black kids who are disproportionately dropping out, it is housing communities with large concentrations of Black residents where the sense of vulnerability and disadvantage is most acute, it is Black employees, professional and non-professional, on whom the doors of upward equity slam shut. Just as the soothing balm of multiculturalism cannot mask racism, so racism cannot mask its primary target.

It is important, I believe to acknowledge not only that racism is pervasive, but that at different times in different places, it violates certain minority communities more than others. (Stephen Lewis Report on Race Relations in Ontario, June 1992, Pg.2)

I AM Brother Oji calls attention to the fact that anti-Black racism has a remarkable ability to adapt and survive. This form of oppression has had an unbroken line from inception in the sixteenth century to the present. Lamentably, racial oppression is far from over; racial disparity is far from decreasing. Progress in the fight against racism is oftentimes short-circuited by the very same institutions charged with the responsibility for addressing it. Stranger still is the fact that the people from whom ameliorative help is sought are sometimes the same people who are the prime beneficiaries of the system. In a strange way, the *Into the Heart of Africa* exhibit is still up. While not mounted in the halls of a museum located at 100 Queens Park, the exhibit remains in full display in our schools where Black youth are stigmatized, their future jettisoned or derailed by negative labelling and classification. It is on full display in the mass media where stereotyping continues to abound and on the streets where the erasure of Black lives persists without mercy. The *Into the Heart of Africa* exhibit remains on display in our legal, correctional and justice system, in corporate and political boardrooms where power is wielded for the exclusive benefit of a privileged few at the expense of many who are not part of the in-group. If the story of Brother Oji teaches us nothing more, it teaches this: without popular united social agitation from below, there will be no active positive change from above. For there to be revolutionary momentum, individualistic aspirations, and the personal quest for wealth accumulation will have to be outpaced by collective united action for justice.

Today we are witnessing a major push for real transformational change focused on the realization of justice, equality, and peace, not just for some, but for all. However, those who have observed the face of anti-Black racism throughout the long course of history can't help but conclude "the more things changed, the more they have remained the same." *Forms* may have changed, but the *substance* or the *impact* prevails. Words and vocabularies may have been updated, but the inequitable outcomes resulting from decision-making still persist like a grim perennial groundhog day. The racial landscape may have changed, but systemic conditions remain unchanged. Fact is, Western liberal democracies have failed to live up to its own ideals. We have failed to arrest the forces of racism.

In this regard, Cannizzo was correct—the colonial racist past continues to bleed into the present despite the initiatives, policies, and programs invented to intervene, stop, or mitigate it. The collected lived experience of people of African ancestry who reside in these jurisdictions is glaringly out of sync with the glowing promise of justice, equality, peace, and prosperity. The progress promised has not been realized. Between the gap of promise and fulfillment is a chasm through which many have fallen. People of colour in general, but more particularly people of African ancestry, are still held in check at the bottom of the hierarchy; they are still not seen as equal partners but as the subservient "help." (Think Meryl Streep and Robert Redford in the 1985 film *Out of Africa*.) Any attempt to assert Black self-empowerment creates anxiety or triggers a backlash from the power base. Why? At what point do we have the right to become impatient, disgusted, enraged? Racism is more than an aberration practiced by a "few bad eggs." This "ism" has been part of the foundation of Western democracies for the past four centuries.

Reactionary confrontation opposed to real transformational change is also clearly visible. Denial abounds. We have seen how racism mutates, how it possesses an afterlife in a so-called post-racial world. Racism has a peculiar dynamic that has been largely ignored, its nuances misunderstood or otherwise romanticized. We think it is gone when it is not. Each person's experience with racism may be different, but because you can't see it doesn't mean it's not there.

An early advice I once received, no doubt well-intended, was this: If you look for racism, you will find it. If you don't, well ... you won't. And I get it. Whatever you focus on expands. However, even those with this positive thinking have been confronted with prejudice and discrimination when they least expect it, if not openly, then in subtler terms. The fact that you are not holding racism in your consciousness does not mean someone else more powerful than you isn't.

Racism does not disappear simply because we say "Stop!" The end of slavery did not mean the end of White supremacy. Similarly, the closing of the *Into the Heart of Africa* exhibit and the offer of an apology does not create structural change. These are incomplete projects with necessary steps yet to be taken. *Whiteness*, White power and privilege remain pervasive, proliferating everywhere throughout public organizations and institutions, a concept and practice that have held sway for a long time, beginning with European colonial rule. In this macrocosm of White supremacy, *Whiteness* is so entrenched it makes room only for itself. And has very little tolerance or appetite for anything other than itself.

Not surprisingly, the historical forces that drove slavery and colonialism are similar to the contemporary influences fueling environmental degradation. Increased atmospheric radiation; excessive toxicity in our lakes, oceans, and rivers; the warming of our planet due to greenhouse gas emissions; the depletion of our forests; the growing extinction of our wildlife; and the disabling of our habitat and ecosystems are primarily sponsored by a small wealthy corporate network—an oligarchy with hegemonic interest—even as vast majority of people, mostly Black, Indigenous, and people of colour, suffer the brunt of catastrophic consequences. This crisis is undeniably urgent and real. The parallel injustice is no less disturbing. As with racism and oppression, so too with environmental destruction: The people least responsible for the problem are the ones most likely to suffer the horrible results and are the ones most often called upon to bear the burden of fixing the disaster.

In reference to the abolition of slavery, someone said, "We went from animal to people because someone said something." In reference to inaugurating a new era in which there is true diversity, inclusion, and equity, we say this: "We will move from White supremacy to true equality when people stand up and say enough is enough." To restore human goodness will mean all good people standing up, rising to become more than simply observers. No longer can we remain passive bystanders. A colossal breakthrough in human history is currently unfolding, one that will finally change our and our children's existential condition. On which side of this history would you rather be? To follow Brother Oji's singular example is to accept personal responsibility and to enter the fray, contributing whatever possible toward the revolution.

Clearly not everyone may have experienced this type of oppression, abuse, and exploitation. You may have had a completely gloriously rewarding life free from struggle. But the questions remain: What are you doing? How are you using your blessings to assist others not so fortunate? Have you been silent or vocal? Are you aware that your benefits may be derived from an unfair unjust system? Are you okay with that?

I AM Brother Oji invites us to consider how we can collectively change the old worn-out paradigms and the orthodoxies that have led to the current state of affairs. It is time to shift gears as we enter the next decade. Can we move from resisting change to embracing it? Can we move from a model of oppression to one of empowerment? Can we change our stance from reactive to proactive? Can we move from being passive to becoming active intentional leaders of change? Can we move from being merely followers of orthodoxy to becoming mindful transformative leaders of a modern inclusive community? When can we finally move from selfish ego driven leadership to leaders who possess a high level of self-less compassion? Who among us can begin to lead this transformation?

But that is not all. *I AM Brother Oji* also calls attention to our individual explicit and implicit biases, inviting us to decolonize our minds by re-examining the walls we have personally erected through conditioning to keep others down and out. To the extent that we can break down our personal walls and cultivate openness, spaciousness, and compassion for others who are unlike ourselves; to this extent, we may begin to contribute to a different kind of revolution. If we are able to properly check our individual assumptions, restrain our ethnocentric rationalized judgements and any narrow-minded thinking that may shrink our abilities to see people for who they are; if we can stretch our imagination beyond its previous and current limits to invite a new range of human possibilities and permutations; if we can fruitfully begin to dissolve our rigidity so as to widen our circle of compassion; if we can disable hate and greed and take care of one another, then collectively maybe we can begin to globalize empathy, allowing each nation-state to authentically say in their own language, *bienvenue*!

Perhaps the best place to start is to simply see individuals as they are, not who *we want them to be* or who we *think* they are. How we translate this on a systemic scale or global level, I will leave for other scholars and philosophers more insightful than I to opine.

Over the next months, years, decades, we will need to figure out a way to cultivate more community building, to practice mutual support, and to encourage the cross-pollination of transformational ideas. It is time for each of us to become transformational leaders and to create a new day, not only for individuals of African ancestry, but for all those who face abuse, exploitation, and oppression and are treated unjustly because of their identity. Let this be the beginning of a journey, not the end. May all of us find our place in this revolution in some way, shape, or form.[54]

---

[54] See appendix for a few select ideas on how you may actively contribute.

So what can we do? We know the system is merciless, differentially cruel to some while protecting others, and is rigged to self-perpetuate itself. Knowing this, what then?

The character of racism is such that it allows perpetrators to dominate the lives of targeted victims. This control can extend to life or death decisions, not to mention access to health, prosperity, and peace of mind. Racism, if properly understood, in basic terms, is a form of violence, a type of psychological terror that, by its very nature, rob victims of their autonomy, disempowering and demoralizing them in the most demeaning ways. Anti-racism means reversing or countering this dynamic through determined retaking of personal jurisdiction, a decisive rejection of the idea that others control, overrule, or govern your autonomy. This is where the real revolution begins—the taking back of personal power, taking command of our sovereignty, driving our own circumstances in a self-determined manner in ways that are uplifting and fruitful for ourselves and others. Herein lies our liberation, our nobility, and our strength.

This is the example Brother Oji offers us. He refused to allow the deception of racial inferiority to infect his self-image. Divesting himself of the ideology of White superiority, he consistently rejected any and all false body of knowledge that implied his inferiority. This is the real overthrow. Once this tyrant is toppled, there is no limit to what one can achieve or where one can go. We become the author of our condition. This is true emancipation, the core message of the Honourable Marcus Mosiah Garvey.

Individuals possess the ability to shape their lives for better or for worse, not through denial, but through self-determination. We are all capable of creating the required personal tools with which to do so. Although prevailing circumstances may seek to alter this truth, through determined, purposeful, creative, intelligent application of effort, it is possible to take or retake authority of our life condition. Circumstances do not have the last word. Complaining and resigning to the forces of oppression is never an option for revolutionaries. Instead, they resist, then rise in the knowledge that *Goliath* can be slain, that the age old oppressor is already at death's door desperately trying to stay alive. By using the hidden powers and inner gifts at their command and by partnering in solidarity with others, the revolutionary's handiwork lives on long after they are gone. Brother Oji's life, as it stands, is illustrative of this reality. He broke the bond of slave-like dependence to set himself free. Meanwhile, he continues to evolve, constantly redefining his limitless potential as he collaborate with others.

For *new jacks*—the *nowadays*—Oji's story may seem anachronistic, outdated, an old-fashioned story in a post-racial virtual world where skin colour supposedly no longer holds significance. This is understandable. Unfortunately, there has been a breakdown in communication between one Black generation and the next—a kind of broken telephone that has led to an intra-cultural chasm of knowledge separating one age cohorts from the next. Sadly, too many—both young and older—are unable to appreciate, or are unaware of, the path paved, and price paid by Oji and others to secure gains we now take for granted. Hopefully, this biography will help to bridge this gap.

The reasons for this divide are many. Chief of these is our failure to encourage the transfer of right knowledge from one generation to the other, a failure reinforced by poor schooling and miseducation perpetuated by an ever-expanding hyperactive commercialized mass media dominated by an overbearing narrow-minded focus on the ghetto-centric escapist primal aspects of Black African life and culture dazzlingly packaged for gullible mass consumption. Sustained by today's highly materialistic culture of immediate-gratification, this intense propaganda has been partially responsible for our sleepwalking, the consequence of which is a malaise, a general disinterest in deep history, and a generation of estranged youth—significant sliver of them—using whatever ill-begotten means at their disposal to find refuge, to patch up their brokenness—like laughing to keep from crying, except not as benign. On arrival, revolutionaries call us out of this soul-paralyzing slumber. They awaken and invite us to break this cycle of numbing ignorance. *I AM Brother Oji* opens the door to this awakening.

My hope is that Brother Oji's story will help to reignite a passion for justice and reverberate enough to create a rippling wave of collective urgency across many different communities and ages. May this conversation meaningfully continue; may the change longed for come at last, on an individual as well as on the collective level.

Finally, citizenship and home.

In his groundbreaking book *Capitalism and Slavery*, first published in 1944, Eric Williams in discussing the end of one historical era and the onset of another concluded his analysis by saying:

> An outworn interest, whose bankruptcy smells to heaven in historical perspective, can exercise an obstructionist and disruptive effect, which can only be explained by the powerful service it has previously rendered and the entrenchment previously gained.

It is an uncomfortable truth that not everyone enjoys the benefits of Canadian and US citizenship equally. The historical debilitating trace effects of enslavement, colonization, and racism—outworn interest whose bankruptcy smells to high heaven—continue to be felt and heard everywhere in the mind, soul, and body politic. To reinforce his point, Williams went on to say,

> The ideas built on these interests continue long after the interests have been destroyed and work their old mischief, which is all the more mischievous because the interests to which they correspond no longer exist.

Enslavement and imperial colonialism may be over. This notwithstanding, the ideology and practice of racism continue to "work their old mischief."

There are several philosophical questions raised by Brother Oji's story. Should Canadian citizenship be based on ideas built on interests that have long been destroyed? Do some people deserve belonging more than others? Do some have more rights than others? Is there a multi-tiered level of citizenship where some communities deserve to be regarded as more Canadians than others, and if so, on what grounds? Who has a legitimate right to be part of the frame? As Canada, North America, and the West struggle to resolve *their old mischief*, many individuals will continue to suffer from the adverse impact of waiting, waiting for change that has been promised but which is long overdue.

I AM Brother Oji, if nothing else, is a biographical meditation on belonging, home, and citizenship. The story illustrates that while Canada may be considered unique and can be proud by virtue of its diversity, there are lingering prevailing systemic conditions within the body politic that continue to create homelessness—second and third-class citizens who have no true sense of belonging. Outwardly and officially, there is professed mutual respect and tolerance, yet beneath this veneer remains a habituated tendency within the nation to marginalize many of its inhabitants who are denigrated because of race. This biography serves as an open love letter to Canada, a place where many have flocked to, arriving with open hearts ready to offer their love only to discover they are not genuinely loved in return. They have fallen casualty to an unrequited affection. *I AM Brother Oji* is an impassioned challenge to Canada, a nation where a great human experiment in social justice is underway but in which many still wait in vain to enjoy freedom and justice equitably and to meaningfully participate with substantive dignity in democratic life.[55] *I AM Brother Oji* reveals that there can be no real democratic ideal until there is racial equity, no national integrity until there is racial justice. How can a nation boasting freedom, justice, and equality continue to keep people of African ancestry underfoot by allowing unbridled racism to continue unchecked?

Rather than waiting for an answer to this question or waiting to be integrated or included, Brother Oji has chosen to act. He has found a way to extricate himself from the enduring traps of colonialism. While the world stands, waiting to see what happens next, he has already made his stand: Africa. Africa is no safe haven either, but he has found his home there. Many people of African descent are discovering or rediscovering their roots in similar fashion, returning to where their roots first began, hoping to recover parts of themselves that had been lost or

---

55 Deviating from the norm, Prime Minister Justin Trudeau, in June 2021, appointed Inuk leader and former ambassador Mary Simon to be Canada's thirtieth governor general—the first indigenous person to be appointed to this role. Approved by Her Majesty Queen Elizabeth, Mary Simon, in accepting her new post, said, "I can confidently say that my appointment is a historic and inspirational moment for Canada and an important step forward on the long path towards reconciliation. This is a moment that I hope all Canadians feel a part of because my appointment reflects our collective progress towards building a more inclusive, just, and equitable society." Later in 2021, the federal government enacted a new federal statutory holiday—the first National Day for Truth and Reconciliation to be observed on September 30 in honour of Indigenous children who died while attending residential schools, survivors, families, and communities affected by the legacy of Canada's residential school system. Meanwhile, for years prior, despite issuing an apology, the federal government continued to defend itself against a class action lawsuit brought by students who attended residential schools. Government lawyers argued that Canada had no residential school policy and never intended to eradicate Indigenous languages and culture. This matter has since been settled after much resistance by the government. However, other Indigenous-related lawsuits for compensation and reparations against the Canadian government remain outstanding. The bipolar tendency of Canadian politics—to give with one hand while taking with the other—continues, particularly when it comes to justice for Black and Indigenous people of colour.

stolen. As for Brother Oji, he is aspiring to a home beyond Africa. He is convinced that his life, so far, has not been wasted; that he is on a path to becoming an honoured member of the retinue of ancestors by virtue of the way he has lived and continues to live his life. But for now, he is grounded in African soil.

Marcus Garvey, who exhorted his listeners to emancipate themselves from mental slavery, also said, "I know no national boundary where the Negro is concerned. The whole world is my province until Africa is free." In stating one of his core beliefs, Garvey declared, "Our success educationally, industrially and politically is based upon the protection of a nation founded by ourselves. And the nation can be nowhere else but in Africa."

Echoes of Garvey's exhortation can be heard in Brother Oji's own declaration: "Here I am with banana in one hand and cassava in the other. Still planted in Mama Africa, in Ghana, on the land where I make my stand. I AM Brother Oji, the first and surely not the last." More than a quixotic gesture of reconnecting with ancestral roots, this proclamation has tangible meaning and will have profound practical application for generations yet unborn.

Given Jamaica's rich talent running the complex gamut of race, colour, class, and gender, Adisa Oji is certainly not the only "poor boy" from Jamaica to make good. He definitely will not be the last. He is but one model amoung many, representative of individuals from the Third World who have forged a path forward to make a mark for themselves. Oji, however, represents a peculiar kind of legacy. He has no interest in climbing corporate ladders or in becoming a billionaire through capitalist orthodoxy and no interest in endeavours embedded with Eurocentric worldviews. Not that he is interested in being poor; far from it. Oji lives in a different place. He is a teacher-educator, an entrepreneur with an uncommon mission. He is decidedly Pan-African, keen on fundamentally changing the status quo, not playing up to it. He is, for better or for worse, set on instigating a revolution, serious about the restoration and preservation of African pride, history, culture, and self-efficacy. His definition of success is not measured by individual self-seeking achievements but by the degree to which he honours the legacy of his ancestry by contributing to the wider community within which he finds himself. We look forward with anticipation to his next iteration.

In closing, we esteem the dreamer and his dream and all those who dream with him. According to Brother Oji, the dreamer "will never die … There will always be one whose Soul-purpose is to dream the impossible, and in the infiniteness of the universe, we call this collective soul The Dreamer … A wanderer of the earth in search of tomorrow … Anything he touches with his bare hands grows and flourishes."

And if I may add, anything the dreamer touches becomes the roots, the rock, and the revolution to buoy many wanderers for generations to come. You can jail a revolutionary, but you can't jail a revolution…

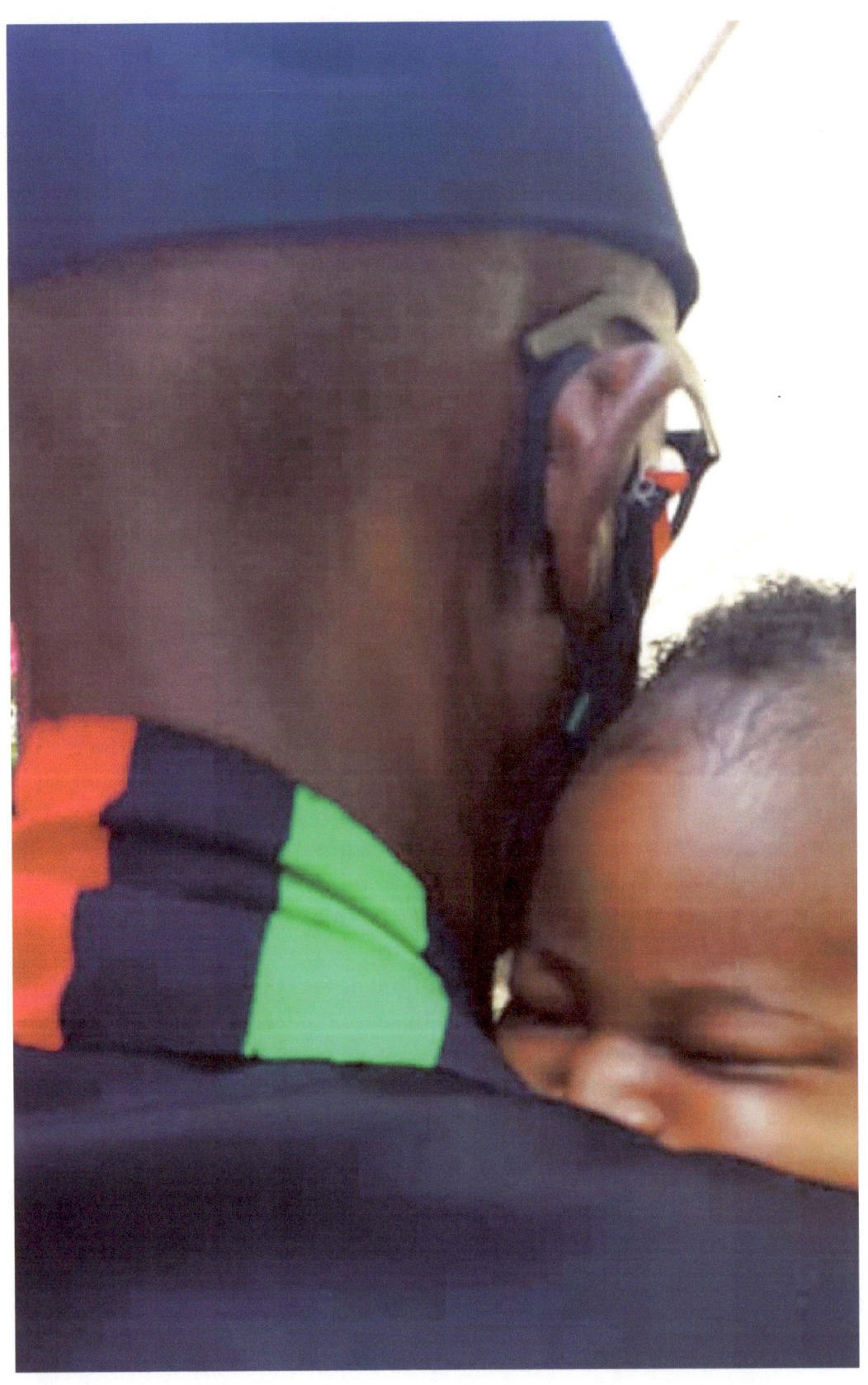

APPENDIX

In His Own Words
Speech by Adisa S. Oji

Speech prepared in Accra, Ghana, by Adisa S. Oji, August 13, 2020, on the occasion of RBG (Red, Black, and Green) Day commemorating the centenary of the first UNIA convention held in New York City when the Declaration of Rights of the Negro Peoples of the World was first unveiled. In his presentation, Brother Oji pays homage to the Honourable Marcus Mosiah Garvey, founder and visionary of the mass movement, and applauds his friend and former ROM 11 collaborator Yaw Akyeaw. The RBG100 celebration was envisioned by MACPRI and executed in partnership with MADA Ghana and ASTAR International led by Yaw Akyeaw. With pandemic protocols in effect, approximately sixty Garveyites, their children, grandchildren, and supporters—Africans from the diaspora who have elected to return to their ancestral homeland—were in attendance. Ras Kofi Munko, Ghana coordinator of the Love Africa Project, was in attendance as was Sylvia Morrison, founder of Links Across Borders, a charitable organization responsible for building eight libraries in Ghana's Volta Region.

In preparing for this presentation, I came across a website marketing the Canadian identity. And I choose Canada as an example because Canada is where I grew up, where my business is based and where I live part of the year. I am very familiar with Canadian branded items because—THEY ARE EVERYWHERE—in our homes, in our classrooms, in our garages when we go to fix our cars, in our offices, in the factory where my mother worked as a machine operator for over 40 years. And in the fast-food joints we go to buy our hamburgers and hotdogs ... I don't mean to offend vegetarians. I am just breaking down the Canadian scene in general.

So, what are some Canadian branded souvenirs? Among them are: Chiefly, the Canadian flags and flag pins; anything with the Maple Leaf or the Canadian flag on it from T-shirts, cups, caps and so on. Maple Syrup (for pancakes), Molson Canadian and Crown Royal Hockey Jersey (TML) and Mini Sticks, stuffed Moose and Beavers, Tim Hortons, Loonies and Toonies

Now, a listing like this is not unique to Canada. Because all countries, Ghana included, have their own branded products—not just souvenirs—to self-promote and give visitors something to take home. But more importantly, is that if these items are marketed very well, strategically, and at opportune times, they can generate significant income for the country and its merchants. And the marketing campaigns are usually deliberate, planned, well executed in national self-promotional interest.

So, it is clear that, on a national and international sovereign nation level, self-promotion of cultural identity is deliberate. It is not a bad thing where economic development and wealth creation is concerned.

Now, please take note in the context of our RBG100 Commemoration. The Canadian branded items mentioned above, their production and marketing have over time developed a life of their own, especially in the hands of quick, opportunity seeking merchants who get them made and stock them in their shops and warehouse. Even if sales trickle in, they can maximize at key moments like Canada's Centenary Celebration and Canada at 150. I myself have marketed Canadian souvenirs during Canada Day as a youngster ... That was before I became a Garveyite of course. And now that I have become a man, I have put away another man's things ... And then, just the other day it dawned on me, as a Garveyite that ... I cannot expect others, and especially those who do not necessary share my ideals, to market me.

I hope you understand where I am going with this. While the President of Ghana gave a wonderful tribute to Marcus Garvey that has gone viral, nothing else has been done for the people of Ghana to let them know that August 13 is a great day. No newspaper made mention of RBG 100. No RBG flags were sold. No pins, no mugs, no hats. Who can be blamed for this? No one but ourselves ...

As Pan-Africanist, as Garveyites, as Black people, who have left Babylon to come home to perch on our own piece of freedom rock we have got to develop a deliberate individual and collective self-promotion marketing plan where each individual in the collective can benefit. There is hope for us and I say this because this event has been a test; and a successful one at that ... as a business entity that can make possible what we desire, MADA GHANA stands strong in my vision.

MADA GHANA has great potential and great leadership willing and capable of bringing Garveyites in Ghana together to strategize around realizing some of the objectives of the UNIA and Marcus Garvey.

I have mentioned the example of production and marketing of souvenir items. Ghanaian artisans who produce for my MACPRI Canada business, have provided a few tangible samples here today. As you know many of our people, including myself learn by seeing. We need to be the example and show our people more of what we need to learn ... And specifically, as it relates to what I am sharing today in the context of UJIMA—collective work and responsibility; and UJAMAA—Cooperative economics ... And again, MACPRI a Canadian based Garveyite company, working with MADA Ghana and Astar International, Ghanaian based Garveyite companies—we have made ourselves the examples ... and in doing so we have accepted Marcus Garvey's challenge: "... If we cannot do what other races have done, what other nations have done, then we have got to die."

Marcus Garvey was a master orator and a great manipulator of words and sentiments capable of firing up the human spirit. He had a clear formula in his speeches: tell the truth, break them down, rile up emotions ... then build them back up by igniting the flame of hope and possibility.

And in answer to the question, can we do it? The Honourable Marcus Garvey answered for himself and for us all ... Can you all say it with me ... (Please stand up!). The question is: "Can we do it?" And the answer is: "Yes, we can!" Everybody! Can we do it? Yes, we can! (Thank you very much. Please be seated.)

And since, he is the ultimate example here and since Marcus Garvey also answered his own question ... Yes, we can ... What did he accomplish?

Thanks to the Velvet Lounge website, I was able to get a very powerful and succinct list of Marcus Garvey's "Yes we can" accomplishments:

1. Marcus Garvey built factories, and his factories made clothes and they also made Black dolls for Black kids to play with.
2. He built a hotel.

3. He built a chain of grocery stores.
4. His organization had their own trucking company.
5. He built schools.
6. He built restaurants.
7. His organization had their own printing press.
8. He started 3 newspapers.
9. His main newspaper was called *the Negro World*, and that newspaper was published in English, Spanish and French.
10. His organization bought 3 ships and they started practicing international trade and commerce.
11. Marcus Garvey's organization owned office buildings.
12. His organization also bought an auditorium in New York, and that's where Garvey did most of his speaking and that place was called Liberty Hall.
13. By 1922, Marcus Garvey organization had 6 million members.
14. His organization had over 900 branches in 40 different countries.
15. Marcus Garvey also started his own political party, and he named it The Peoples Political Party.
16. Marcus Garvey was the first Black leader that changed the (mindset) of Black people. He taught Blacks to love themselves, and he taught us to be proud of the way that God made us.
17. Kwame Nkrumah became the first president of Ghana, and he said that Marcus Garvey was his hero and his biggest influence. Nkrumah named Ghana's shipping line the Black Star Shipping line in honor of Marcus Garvey. He also named Ghana's soccer team the Black Stars.
18. Jomo Kenyatta became the first president of Kenya, and he also said that Marcus Garvey was a major influence on him.
19. Nnamdi Azikiwe became the first president of Nigeria and said that Marcus Garvey was a major influence on him. He said that reading Garvey's *Negro World* shaped his view.
20. Julius Nyerere became the first president of Tanzania and he also said that Garvey's teachings were a major influence on him.
21. Malcolm X parents were members of Marcus Garvey's organization.
22. The honourable Elijah Muhammad the leader of the Nation of Islam praised Marcus Garvey. He said that Garvey was the forerunner and laid the foundation for what the Nation of Islam is doing. He said that they are carrying on the work of Garvey.
23. Marcus Garvey said that his organization employed 1000s of people through the businesses that they created.

Marcus Garvey did all of this without any help from white people or the government ... and he did it with an 8th grade education. He did this during a time when there were no televisions or computers.

MACPRI is currently affiliated with 3 of the UNIA branches ... and all three—Toronto, Buffalo and Queens—are responsible for the UNIA-ACL 1920–2020 MADE IN AFRICA/GHANA Commemorative Kente Sashes. By agreement with UNIA-ACL Toronto, we have been granted permission to make a limited quantity of 100 for the 100 Commemorative Kente Sashes available to UNIA supporters and Garveyites in Ghana for a special price of 100 ghc. Once 100 have been sold they will not be reproduced. For everyone who purchases one, I will ask you to put it on and join in our group photo. We will send the picture along with Centenary greetings to the UNIA-ACL President General Michael Duncan who is currently in Liberia. We will also send one to the President of Liberia. In the package will be two sashes, one for each president courtesy of Astar International.

Brother Yaw, please step forward. In honour of your work with MADA and what you have done to make this event possible for all of us, on behalf of my family, MACPRI and our partners in the UNIA-ACL, I wish to bestow on you this gift, one of the 100 only, officially Made in Ghana UNIA-ACL #RBG100 Commemorative Kente Sashes. May our Ancestors always be pleased with what you do.

In closing, I would like to share a few of my favourite quotes and lesson learned. From the Black Velvet Lounge: Nothing is impossible, the word itself says I'm possible. From Marcus Garvey: "If the Negro is not careful, he will drink in all the poison of modern civilization and die from the effect of it."

From myself: I am the piper, I pay myself. I call the tune! And finally, one of the greatest lessons I have learned from the Honourable Marcus Mosiah Garvey is that if you are going to make yourself special in this world, you are going to have to be an anomaly. Thank you very much.

Reprinted with permission.

Reprise: Our Home on Native Land

Early European colonial ventures were sponsored by organized syndicates, private promoters, and investors who launched travel expeditions under license from their respective monarchs. By this means, groups of speculators flocked to the "new world" accompanied by gangs of thuglike mercenaries. First a trickle, then a wave, European influx consisted of a mixed assortment of expendable undesirables including drifters, panhandlers, prisoners, and dissenters—marginalized miscreants hoping to discover a new life and a way out in an ancient sacred world they heard of but knew little about. Although some did return to their homeland, they did not come simply to visit. They came to settle with the intention of claiming a stake. As the European presence increased, so too did their desire to subdue, control, or convert, rapidly moving into Indigenous territory as if it was their natural right, bringing with them imported germs and diseases against which Indigenous communities had little or no protection. For the most part, European settlers encountered local people who welcomed them with generous helpings of native hospitality. Often Europeans were assisted in their explorations. At other times, European aggression provoked resistance from, and wars with, Indigenous warriors—notably the Iroquois—who took umbrage with their impolite imperialist intrusion.

Engrossed in a hegemonic power struggle in North America, the primary contenders, Britain and France, jostled for colonial dominance. In this mortal combat, they competed for Indigenous support, respectively allying with one community or another, essentially bribing and pitting one Native group of warriors against the next. Greedy for silver and gold, they set forth to colonize and Christianize. They hoisted flags, erected crosses, claiming possession for king, queen, and church. Imprinting their brand everywhere they went, they rechristened locations in the likeness of their motherland—New France, New Scotland, Nova Scotia—and gave their names to landmarks such as Hudson Bay and James Bay to immortalize themselves and pay tribute to their nationalistic ambitions. If humanitarianism and goodwill were motives for colonialism, it must not have been high on the agenda. The lure of wealth, the possibility of reaping immense profit through mercantile trade in fish, fur, forestry, or through fiduciary monopolies, the tantalizing sight of seemingly limitless uninhabited tracts of land appealed to the settlers' greed. Propelled by an insatiable desire for more, Europeans advanced their plunder, ignorant or uncaring of the people whose land space they had violently invaded. As far as European settlers were concerned, the people who greeted them in this *newfound land* were *savages*, an ironic characterization considering the source of most of the unprovoked unleashed savagery. Trouble is, Native communities stood in the way of French and British imperial designs. What to do with *these native savages* would become an enduring question for colonizers.

In the spirit of congenial cooperation, Indigenous communities allowed Europeans to settle permanently. However, in the twisted ways of colonialism, tides turned as the Europeans proceeded to become more acquisitive, forcibly capturing and systematically privatizing wide sections of Indigenous assets while enforcing their own rights, entitlements, and systems of governance. By 1763, when the Treaty of Paris was signed between Britain and France (and the United States) to mark the end of seven years of hostilities, the British crown had full ownership and control of what was then understood to be Canada. Indigenous people who fought as allies with the British were not invited to the peace talks or negotiations. Instead, they were dealt with subsequently as if part of a subplot in which the British crown used its leverage as a super landowner to "negotiate" all manner of self-serving treaties with the Native people under the guise of "mutual benefit."

The benefits were neither equal nor mutual. Treaties in a colonial context are not what we ordinarily consider them to be—binding agreements, an accord or pact entered into by equal partners. Rather, these were disingenuous manipulative instruments used by representatives of the British crown to gain footholds in Native territory. Over time, law, and politics were (dis)ingeniously used by British agents to push sovereign Indigenous nations into a state of dependency. Gradually, Indigenous people themselves would become colonized to the extent that their communities were no longer genuinely self-governing but rather came under the control and regulation of agents of the British crown. The authority of previously autonomous Indigenous communities steadily eroded as numerous "agreements" came into effect. These agreements inevitably undermined Indigenous independence, negatively impacting their capacity for self-sufficiency, which soon diminished to the point where only a fraction was left. Through this means, Indigenous cultures began to lose stability, internal strength, and vibrancy. Increasingly, Indigenous groups were reallocated to reserves thereby putting pressure on their ability to maintain social, economic, and political viability, their freedom and cultural identity. The host nation had become, at best, guests in their own home; at worse, aliens in their own country, and in extreme cases, hostages.

It is claimed that nation-to-nation treaty arrangements governed the relationship between White European settlers and Indigenous people. However, evidence suggest that such treaties were either dubiously administered, broken or dishonoured, that the so-called treaties served as a cover under which Indigenous people were exploited and or pushed closer to extinction. Indigenous communities entered these agreements with integrity, expecting the same from their co-signatories. However, with each treaty, Indigenous people lost rather than gained. The British had become masters of using cunning and deceit to advance their colonial agenda. They had fine-tuned this approach into an ugly art form. They practiced similar double-dealing in India, and repeated similar deceits in Jamaica during their negotiations with the African Maroons. They used the same playbook in their relationship with other native populations throughout the world, and as more records are revealed and as reparations movements surge, we are only now beginning to better understand the full degree of bad faith and duplicity that enabled and characterized the British Empire. As far as sleight of hand goes, it is curious that Indigenous land claims are being adjudicated in courts established by the same colonial powers who confiscated or expropriated the land in the first place. In this curious arrangement, the crown is responsible for administering the same system in which it stands as a litigant. In this British-based Canadian legal system, where justice is supposedly blind, all sorts of double-dealing craftiness are possible.

During the Riel Métis uprising in 1885, a number of other Indigenous groups took up arms to defend themselves against Canadian rule. After squashing the rebellion, the Canadian government in an effort to discourage future uprisings proceeded to severely punish all Indians who questioned White Canadian domination. They also used the occasion as a pretext to renege on previous treaty agreements. Colonial controls tightened even more, leading to further dehumanization of Indigenous people.

As the Canadian government increasingly claimed supreme control over the daily lives of Indigenous peoples and their communities, the malicious stereotyping of Indigenous people began to take root. Fiction became fact as new fabricated narratives began to flourish. Consistent with the tendency of colonial imperial administrations to infantilize the populations they dominate, the Canadian government pressed on with its efforts to treat Indigenous people as children. This paternalistic attitude served to justify their ongoing supervision and control of every aspect of Indigenous life. It also served as a psychological instrument to subjugate and to secure further submission. This stereotype was promoted frequently enough by thought leaders and with such absolute conviction that the belief soon took on a life of its own. Leading minds within the White-only Canadian government knew that if this stereotypical parent-child relationship is accepted by the Indian population under domination, the chances of them rising up to claim equality would be significantly reduced. Or so they thought.

Following 1876, when the Indian Act was introduced, First Nations people became official wards of the state. Every aspect of their lives were regulated by crown representatives —their land, their livelihood, their resources. Meanwhile, status Indians—as defined by the Act—were disenfranchised. They were not permitted to vote, an undemocratic exclusionary limitation that existed until 1961. Even the definition of who was an Indian was determined by the Act. Native people could not dance or have religious ceremonies without approval; they literally needed permission to be themselves. A pass was needed in order to move freely. They could not engage in commercial pursuits such as the buying of goods and services. To conduct commercial transactions, approval from a crown agent was required. If Indigenous persons dared to pursue higher learning, they stood the risk of "losing status." It was as if in Canada being Indian *and* being educated were incompatible. It was as if Europeans knew what it meant to be Indian more so than the Indians themselves. Traces of this arrogant paternalism can still be found in so-called Indian policy today.

One major outcome of the Indian Act was the reservation system, what someone described as a holding pen. Indigenous people who reside on reserves apparently do not own their land. It is crown land held and managed in trust by a governance system authorized by the crown. The Indian Act stands in opposition to traditional hereditary clan leadership; it is essentially a subversion of Indigenous sovereign rights. Which explains why, in some instances, Indigenous communities have rival and competing leadership models—hereditary chiefs versus band chiefs for example—and why some Indigenous persons are attempting to break free from this oppressive legal framework by giving up their Indian status, while others are striving to keep or gain it. It is a cruel conundrum.

Ward status imposed by the Canadian government in the late nineteenth century was a perfect pre-condition for what came next. As Canada began to establish itself as an independent nation based on sugar-coated White supremacist ideology wrapped in liberal fluff, Canadian leaders and policy makers began to make a concerted effort to assimilate Indigenous people who were variously stereotyped as "wild," "instinctual," or "primitive." The stated official solution was to "civilize" or "Christianize" the Indians. In effect, this meant Anglicization, a process implemented largely through the use of Residential Schools and other orientation programs.

First established in the 1870s, the Indian Residential Schools of Canada were a coast-to-coast network of so-called boarding schools for Indigenous children—First Nations, Metis, and Inuit—which led to the forcible separation of children from their families and communities. Poorly funded by the Canadian government, the estimated 128 schools were administered by prominent Christian churches, notably the Catholic and Anglican, and to a lesser extent Mennonite, Presbyterian, United, Baptist, and other non-denominational bodies.

By this means, 150,000 or more Aboriginal children were forcibly removed from their families and housed in crowded, underfunded, and unhealthy facilities with the specific intent of erasing all traces of their ancestral culture. It was a brainwashing exercise purposely designed to "killing the Indian in the child." According to John A. Macdonald, Canada's first prime minister, celebrated father of Confederation, in reference to the Indian Act, "The great aim of our legislation has been to do away with the tribal system and to assimilate the Indian people in all respects with the other inhabitants of the Dominion as speedily as they are fit to change."[56] Residential schools were an extension of this "re-socialization" policy, which ultimately led to the further stultification of Indigenous communities. Evidence suggest "re-socialization" was but one part of a more insidious impulse. Better described as an act of cultural genocide, residential schools resulted, intentionally or otherwise, in the mass physical and sexual abuse of several generations of Indigenous children. Those who survived the residential school experience continued to suffer post-traumatic stress, many induced to stumble, stagger, and die through excessive use of intoxicants and high rates of suicide. Intergenerational trauma can also be traced to this history. The inhumane mistreatment of Indigenous people, in which churches of various denominations played a role, flowed from the presumed notion that White European ways were superior to all others. At the heart of this ideology, Indians were likely regarded as less than human, not far removed from Black African slaves, worthy not of dignity but more suited for exploitative abuse, disposable once spent. The last Residential School remained opened as recently as 1990. While many lived through this trauma, many untold others have died unaccounted for. As recently as May 27, 2021, the remains of 215 Indigenous children were uncovered on the site of a former Indian Residential School in Kamloops, British Columbia. One month later, another 751 unmarked graves would be discovered, this time at a cemetery near a former Indian Residential School located approximately 140 kilometres east of Regina, Saskatchewan. These numbers are preliminary. Of the many other 127 schools scattered across Canada, who knows how many are surrounded by unmarked graves containing the remains of children who never returned home to their families and were never seen or heard of again.

---

56 It has become popular to (dis)credit John A. Macdonald as the "architect" of Indian Residential Schools. However, he was not the sole proponent. There were a cadre of public officials, leaders, and influencers who advocated for and supported this project. In 1879, Nicholas Flood Davin, Toronto lawyer and journalist, prepared a report recommending residential schools in partnership with churches. In 1920, then deputy minister of Indian Affairs Duncan Campbell Scott said he was looking forward to the day when "there was not a single Indian in Canada who has not been absorbed in the body politic." The mass decimation of native Indigenous culture could not have occurred or lasted as long as it did without the widespread complicity and approval of the dominant non-Indigenous White culture. John A. Macdonald did not act solitarily on his own accord.

We may never know how they died. Many discreditable institutions practiced a scorched earth policy by destroying culpable documentary evidence to conceal institutionalized violence and abuse. For this reason, we may never know exactly how many innocent children died too soon. The half is yet to be told.

Adding to the atrocity is the Sixties Scoop, in which tens of thousands of Indigenous children (those not sent to residential schools) were forcibly removed from their homes by the Canadian government and adopted out to mostly non-Indigenous families. Currently, the issue of missing or murdered Indigenous women and girls continues unresolved. So too the over incarceration of Indigenous men and women and the daily sometimes deadly encounter with racism experienced by First Nations people across Canada.[57]

Reconciling with this unsavory history has not always been high on Canada's list of pre-occupations. In fairness, reconciliation attempts are of relatively recent concern and are ongoing at federal and provincial levels. Since the 1990s, there has been a resurgence in the call for Indigenous self-government and self-reliance and for reconciliation. In 2007 the Indian Residential Schools Settlement Agreement was reached in which 134 residential schools were identified and former students made eligible for compensation. Submissions have been made to add other such schools to the list. Some of those requests have been denied. In 2008, the Canadian federal government issued a limited apology to former residents of Indian residential schools, an apology repeated in 2017. On September 28, 2016, the Supreme Court of Newfoundland and Labrador allowed for compensation to be provided to those who attended residential schools in that province and to those who may have suffered abuse. The settlement also includes provisions for therapy and for any related commemorative events. Other provisions relate to a call to action outlined in the *Final Report of the Truth and Reconciliation Commission* published in 2015. Also significant is the 2013 report following an independent review by Honourable Frank Iacobucci on First Nations representation on Ontario juries, a report that revealed that "the justice system, as it relates to First Nations peoples, and particularly in Northern Ontario, is in crisis. Overrepresented in the prison population, First Nations peoples are significantly underrepresented, not just on juries, but among all those who work in the administration of justice in this province, whether as court officials, prosecutors, defence counsel, or judges."

Spurred by the recent groundswell in public consciousness regarding institutional violence against Indigenous people, the Canadian Parliament in June 2021 enacted a new federal statutory holiday to be effective September 30, 2021, to mark the first National Day for Truth and Reconciliation. And on September 4, 2021, the Canadian Conference of Catholic Bishops (CCCB) apologized, acknowledging the role of the Catholic church in the horror experienced by Indigenous people in federally funded residential schools. In addition, the bishops followed up

---

57 In November 2014, based on a public poll, CBC News reported that "Racism is still an uncomfortable truth in Canada," particularly in the city of Winnipeg, where "a deep racial gulf between aboriginal and non-aboriginal citizens" is said to exist. Thunder Bay does not appear to be any different. As recently as early 2017, after a visit to Thunder Bay, Renu Mandhane, chief commissioner of the Ontario Human Rights Commission, was led to remark that "community members told me about their concerns related to policing and child welfare, trafficking of Indigenous women and girls, and everyday racism in almost every facet of their lives including employment, housing, healthcare and retail. Most strikingly, people talked about being 'garbaged'—literally having garbage thrown at them while walking down the street, all because of their Indigenous ancestry" (Quoted from "*Leadership Needed to Fight Racism-Viewpoint* by Renu Mandhane," special to the *Chronicle Journal*, July 25, 2017).

with a $30 million pledge to support Indigenous reconciliation projects for residential school survivors, their families, and their communities across the country. (It is not the first time the Catholic church has pledged money to support residential school survivors. They did so before as part of the settlement agreement in 2005, agreeing to raise $25 million for survivors but, in the end, paid out very little, using the money raised instead for church infrastructural projects.) It is noted that the Vatican has yet to apologize.

In spite of these efforts, healing of the wounds inflicted on Indigenous people is far from complete, their treaty rights are yet to be fully honoured; their inalienable right to the land that is indubitably theirs is yet to be completely adjudged.

Indigenous and Native communities have not been passive. For generations, they have been fighting back to regain that which they have lost or to maintain what little they have remaining. In the spring of 1990, just when the ROM protest was about to get underway, a crisis called Oka also made the news. It was one of many Native land disputes, this one involving the Mohawk in Quebec who faced off with provincial police, the RCMP, and the Canadian military forces. The Mohawks were protesting the town of Oka's decision to build a golf course plus condos on sacred Indigenous territory, an area the Mohawks called the Pines. For hundreds of years, Mohawks had been unsuccessfully attempting to have Oka legally returned, an area known to them as *Kanesatake*. In response to official indifference, after years of waiting, they decided to occupy the land. The armed stand-off, which began in the summer of 1990, lasted for seventy-eight days until September, resulting in one or two fatalities.

Confiscation of Indigenous land, broken promises, and the use of lethal force were repeated in the 1995 killing of Dudley George in Ipperwash Provincial Park on Canada's Labour Day weekend. George was unarmed when he was killed by the Ontario Provincial Police (OPP). He and the Stoney Creek First Nations had taken occupation of the land in Southwest Ontario near Sarnia to protest the government's failure to return ancestral Indigenous territory. History records that the Canadian federal government initially expropriated the land as part of their 1942 war effort, using it as a military training base. They had promised to return it but did not. Long after World War II ended, the land continued to be in the military's possession. The land claim dispute continues, with the property yet to be completely transferred to its rightful owners. The incident at Ipperwash illustrates how protests can go fatally wrong, especially when law enforcement is involved.

There is considerable insight to be gained from Indigenous ancestral knowledge and customs. Yet in their narrow-minded ethnocentricity, the Canadian colonial government refused to appreciate Indigenous wisdom. They refused to allow this outlook to thrive. Although Indigenous communities have their own valuable unique way of relating to each other, to other people, and to the environment, this was never acknowledged or given credit. Rather than respecting Indigenous worldviews or seeking to better understand, the governing English and French settlers in their presumed superiority dishonoured Indigenous traditions. With a colonial mind-set, they demonstrated disdain for Indigenous people, treating them as inferior, devaluing an entire nation-community. By this means, a series of deadly consequences followed lasting for multiple generations. Interestingly, while English and French colonial settlers were pushing Indigenous communities to the brink of elimination, they were meanwhile appropriating from First Nations people whatever profit-generating opportunities they could exploit.

The belief that First Nations people are equal partners in the founding of Canada instead of inferior subordinates still remains a radical idea. Colonial sentiments continue to prevail. Some propose that the abolition of the Indian Act—a source of iniquities and inequities—is a good place to begin true reconciliation. If and when the history of the Indigenous people of Canada becomes fully and finally understood, the Seven Grandfather Teachings of Native American culture—love, respect, courage, humility, wisdom, truth, and honesty—will resonate with even greater meaning.[58]

---

58 In 2016, the government of Canada endorsed the United Nations Declaration on the Rights of Indigenous People and committed to its implementation. In December 2020, Canada introduced legislation to implement the declaration. If passed by Parliament, the legislation will provide a roadmap for the government and Indigenous peoples to work together to implement the declaration. The declaration, a non-legally binding resolution, was adopted by the UN in September 2007.

The ROM Apology and Other Initiatives

On November 9, 2016, the Royal Ontario Museum (ROM) issued the following statement at a reconciliation event held at the museum in collaboration with the Coalition for the Truth about Africa (CFTA). The reconciliation included ongoing steps for the ROM and CFTA to work collaboratively.

> "The Royal Ontario Museum produced the exhibition Into the Heart of Africa, which opened at the Museum in November 1989. This exhibition was intended to critically examine the colonial relationships and premises through which collections from African societies had entered museums. The exhibition displayed images and words that showed the fundamentally racist ideas and attitudes of early collectors and, in doing so, unintentionally reproduced the colonial, racist and Eurocentric premises through which these collections had been acquired. Thus, Into the Heart of Africa perpetuated an atmosphere of racism and the effect of the exhibition itself was racist. The ROM expresses its deep regret for having contributed to anti-African racism. The ROM also officially apologizes for the suffering endured by members of the African Canadian community as a result of Into the Heart of Africa."

The ROM statement was delivered by Dr. Mark Engstrom, the Museum's Deputy Director, Collections and Research, who has guided the reconciliation process for the ROM, Josh Basseches, Director and CEO of the ROM, and Martha Durdin, Chair, ROM Board of Trustees. This statement was accepted by Rostant Ras Rico John, on behalf of the CFTA.

In addition, the ROM announced a number of steps it will take in the coming years to continue to strengthen collaboration with African-Canadian communities and help shape the museum of the future. These include enhanced partnerships with Black educational networks, opportunities for training Black youth interested in museums, and continued support of events and lectures that address the history and cultures of Africa and the Diaspora. Working with the CFTA and other community partners, the ROM is committed to sustained and meaningful programming, and acknowledges the importance of dialogue and collaboration toward enhancing its collection and public events.

Rostant Rico John, CFTA Spokesperson said, "Greetings, it is good and pleasant that, on behalf of the CFTA and the African community in Canada, we would like to express our pride in having reached this point of reconciliation after twenty-seven years. It took many gallant efforts by people inside and outside of the ROM to reconcile and both the ROM and CFTA worked diligently, persistently, and consistently to arrive at this agreement. We would like to congratulate all the participants in this effort: The ROM's Dr. Mark Engstrom, Cheryl Blackman, and Dr. Silvia Forni; and the CFTA Rico John, Yao Akyeaw, Dr. Afua Cooper, Geraldine Moriba and Ajamu Khalfani for working together to achieve this historic milestone. And also, I thank CFTA members for their significant efforts, analyses, and intents which stood the test of time."

Mr. John continued, "The CFTA's community gracefully accepts the apology advanced by the ROM. We jointly look forward and will work fervently to see other initiatives as agreed upon come to fruition. We would like to say on behalf of the African community again, a heartfelt thanks to those people in our community who have worked hard to bring this to fruition. Jah live!"

(Text reprinted with permission from the Royal Ontario Museum. https://www.rom.on.ca/en/about-us/newsroom/pressrelease/royal-ontario-museum-and-the-coalition-for-thetruth-about-africa)

Department of Art and Culture Internship

In 2019, in conjunction with its Of Africa program and as part of its diversity and inclusion initiative, the ROM launched a dedicated internship program for Black students. Five young people have already benefitted from this opportunity. Overseen by the Department of Art and Culture, the internship offers one paid position for undergraduate and graduate students with interest in the arts and cultures of Africa and the Diaspora. Offered to senior undergraduate-level and graduate-level students with preference given to applicants who self-identify as African or of African descendant, the program gives interns an opportunity to explore museum careers and to gain professional experience and training. The internship began in October 2019 and is ongoing with funding secured until 2024. Fund raising for this and other related initiatives are in progress.

For more information on the Of Africa internship Program visit:
https://www.rom.on.ca/en/blog/department-of-art-cultureofafrica-internship-for-undergraduate-and-graduate-studentsfall#:~:text=The%20OfAfrica%20Internship%20Program%20awards%20a%20parttime%20internship,to%20the%20ROM%E2%80%99s%20Afric an%20Arts%20%26%20Cultures%20collections.

Staffing and Representation

As senior curator of Global Africa and deputy head of the Department of Art and Culture, Dr. Silvia Forni has been with the Royal Ontario Museum since 2008. She has curated and co-curated several partial gallery reinstallations and exhibitions including Of Africa, a multiplatform project aimed at promoting the cultural and creative diversity of Africa and its Diaspora. Dr. Forni has been instrumental in helping to rebrand the museum through transformative programs of contemporary relevance consistent with diversity and inclusion values.

Swarupa Anila, senior vice president for exhibition and gallery development, joined the ROM in April 2020. A former director of interpretive engagement at the Detroit Institute of Arts, she brings experience related to "visitor-centered interpretation for exhibitions." With nearly two decades of museum experience, she has led the development of award-winning interpretation and exhibitions and has produced numerous publications on innovative and critically progressive practices for visitor-centeredness and community engagement. A widely recognized leader in her field, Swarupa regularly participates in and shapes national dialogues about best practices in issues of representation and inclusion in the museum field. She is a founding board member and current president of the Association for Art Museum Interpretation.

Other Programming

The ROM intends to continue building on gains achieved since "the apology" by bringing new and interesting perspectives into the museum's exhibition space that reflect a diverse range of public interests, particularly the interest of communities who have been historically underserved or under-represented. Community consultations are held prior to the staging of exhibits.

In its effort to favourably spotlight African artists, the ROM opened Tightrope in July 2021. Tightrope featured the work of contemporary Ethiopian artist Elias Sime. His mixed media compositions combine discarded electronics such as keyboards and circuit boards, and prompt questions about the precarious balance between technologies that permit human connectedness while impacting on the natural environment. A community advisor panel was convened to offer feedback and suggestions and to help inform the exhibition's curatorial team. Although the pandemic limited exposure, Tightrope received rave reviews.

How to Join the Revolution

The process of revolution is essentially the process of people finding themselves.

—C. L. R. James

1. Be the best version of yourself; be the best you can be. Be the change you want to see. Seek positive self-change and become a model or source of transformative living.
2. Eschew hate and revenge. Invoke hope, optimism, love, forgiveness, and compassion. These are some of the first casualties of racism.
3. Beyond structural/systemic barriers, the revolution begins with self-liberation from self-entrapment, a reclamation of your self-worth, respect, and dignity. Consider how best to overthrow self-imposed limitations then incite a revolution to reclaim your personal power.
4. Write a book, a blog, a song, a poem. Read, study, and educate yourself; become part of a change agent community and learn how to form alliances with others.
5. Launch a self-owned business or social enterprise aimed at achieving a higher purpose in service of our shared humanity, one that disrupts the status quo of oppressive power relations.
6. Define what moral courage means to you then outline a step-by-step plan to act on it.
7. Go beyond your comfort zone by connecting with someone or a community seemingly different from you. Be aware of and learn about your own misgivings or apprehensions while paying keen attention to how you may become more compassionate to or understanding of others.
8. If you found this book useful, share it with family and friends. Become an ambassador for justice, truth and human rights.
9. "Don't wait for leaders; do it alone, person to person" (Mother Teresa)
10. Respect yourself. Be an active participant in your own liberation.

You cannot use someone else's fire. You can only use your own. To do that, you must believe you have it.

—Audre Lorde

End Notes

Adisa S. Oji v Regina

1. "We want African experts and scholars to be consulted as to the mounting of any exhibit on Africa. This is the first exhibit on Africa in the 77-year history of the ROM and look at the mess they have made. We want a formal apology specifically to the African community and to all the people and citizens of this province." - Metro Morning, August 27, 2003, CBC audio tape.
2. One picketer, his face earnest with conviction, carried a sign declaring The ROM Endorsement: Over One Million Africans Murdered by Europeans. – Getty Images, Andrew Stawicki, May 21, 1990, Toronto Star.
3. The late Charles Roach, lawyer, justice activist and elder in the Black community, was among the distinguished group of twelve invited to the screening. – Share Newspaper, July 19, 1990, Art confrontation by Ahmed Elamin, & The Varsity, March 12, 1990, Protestors call ROM "Racist Ontario Museum" by T. Clive Thompson.
4. According to Marshall, "the cumulative tone of the exhibit was paternalistic, and paternalism is the form of racism we encounter most often in Canadian society." – Globe and Mail, April 21, 1990, Letter to the editor, Paternalism promotes racism at ROM.
5. In a public statement, Roach said: "We were chilled from the very beginning. What we saw was a glorification of imperialism. What we saw in it was the roots of apartheid and the genocide that has gone on in Africa. We would have no objections if they labelled it as such, but they do not." – The Varsity, March 12, 1990, Protestors call ROM "Racist Ontario Museum" by T. Clive Thompson.
6. A professor of History at Wilfrid Laurier, Terry Copp, who visited the exhibition, saw nothing wrong. - Globe and Mail, April 21, 1990, Letter to the editor, Paternalism promotes racism at ROM.
7. While critics argued that the exhibit presented Africans as barbaric and primitive, Cuyler Young, then director of the ROM vigorously defended it. "It is a historical examination of Canada's involvement in Africa. It has to tell a story that is historically true," said Cuyler. – Share Newspaper, July 19, 1990, Art confrontation by Ahmed Elamin.
8. A ROM spokesperson, Linda Thomas, reiterated his view by saying the exhibit was presented from the perspective of missionaries and soldiers and as such was "historically accurate and historically based." – Toronto Sun, May 10, 1990, ROM protestors standing firm by John Schmied.
9. But then, came the retort from Molefi Kete Asante, an African American professor and philosopher specializing in African studies: "This is the defence of the indefensible. The defence of the Museum is the same arrogance the missionaries had." – Share Newspaper, July 19, 1990, Art confrontation by Ahmed Elamin.

10. Stubbornly, the ROM refused to heed their advice, leading Afua Cooper, one of the lead voices among the protestors, to remark, "This was a classic example of White people not listening to what Black people were saying, of knowing what's best for Black people." - NOW Magazine, Toronto, December 8-14, 2016, ROM recovers cred: Apology for 1989 racist exhibit is a start – now diversify the board by Susan Crean.
11. Finding common ground with the ROM demonstrators were protests related to cruise missile testing, Inuit or Indigenous rights, the abusive use of police powers against Africa Canadian citizens—all found voice at the Queens Park demonstration. – Sunday Star, May 20, 1990, photo headlines.
12. Meanwhile, across town in the East-end community of Scarborough, the Black Action Defence Committee would hold its own demonstration during the month of May with close to 300 protestors marching in opposition to police brutality chanting repeatedly, "Who are we? Africans! Africans! African people must harmonize. African people must organize." – Toronto Star, May 27, 1990, Metro officers listen to abuse from protestors by Michael Tenzen & Toronto Sun, May 27, 1990, The march made good TV but ... by Christie Blatchford.
13. According to the much-disputed pseudo-scientific research of Professor Philippe Rushton of the University of Western Ontario, Blacks were at the lower end of the ladder of human intelligence. – The Varsity, September 10, 1990, Western forces Rushton to lecture via video tape by Karen Hill (Canadian University Press); The Varsity, October 1, 1990, UWO anti-racism policy useless: Critics by Karen Hill (CUP).
14. The content and presentation was so troubling, the Toronto Board of Education declared the exhibit unsuitable for elementary age students. – Share Newspaper, May 24, 1990, School Board confirms Black's concerns - Exhibition unsuitable.
15. Silbert Barrett, a CFTA spokesperson and then president of the Ryerson Anti-apartheid Movement, was also arrested that day. – The Buffalo News, June 10, 1990, Toronto exhibit on Africa is called racist by Barry Brown and David Cooper.
16. Other media reports suggest demonstrators had "blocked" the entrance before being removed by police. – Share Newspaper, July 19, 1990, Art confrontation by Ahmed Elamin.
17. Metro police detective claimed, "They charged at the museum. The security staff called for help." – Toronto star, May 6, 1990, Police hurt, pair arrested in protest at museum. See also Toronto Sun May 6, 1990, Cops hurt; 2 Held after ROM battle by Tom Godfrey.
18. What happened next depends on who is telling the story. Police and mainstream media reveal there was a "scuffle" or "clash" with two officers receiving minor injuries. Demonstrators would have a more dramatic version. – Toronto Sun, May 10, 1990, ROM protestors standing firm by John Schmied
19. Said Ras Rico, "Since our demonstration started, a lot of Black people from out of town, and others who are in no way connected to us, have been turned away from the museum because the guards are afraid they might be members of the Coalition who want to destroy the exhibit." Share Newspaper, May 10, 1990, Protestors arrested.
20. "We weren't fighting them. We were trying to get away," said Ras Rico – Ibid.
21. Demonstrators claim that for every protestor there were five police officers. Outnumbered in the chaos, they scrambled for safety shouting, "Don't shoot! Don't shoot!" – Charlatan,

Carlton University, Ottawa, November 14, 1991, Black fight police brutality over ROM by Mo Gannon.

22. Before the day was done, the demonstrators marched to the police station where Barrett and McKenzie were being held to chant and to push for their release. – Toronto Sun, May 6, 1990, Cops hurt; 2 Held after ROM battle by Tom Godfrey.
23. This was the fourth shooting of a Black citizen by Metro-area police over the previous six months setting off another protest of about 500 demonstrators who on May 19, marched from Queen's Park to police headquarters on College Street, women carrying hand-written banners listing 11 recent victims of police violence with the caption: WE WON'T FORGET. – The Toronto Star, May 20, 1990, The time for talking is over, black protestors tell police by Jack Lakey and Jane Armstrong.
24. "Two big white men in business suits jumped out of a car and grabbed me," he said. "They never identified themselves as police officers and they never answered my question about why they were grabbing me. I thought I was being abducted." – The Varsity, July 1990, Former ACSA head Oji Adisa (sic) arrested by George Sewell.
25. Said Joma Nyakorema Nkombe, chair and founder of the Pan African Law Society of York University, "The 11 politically accused were out there risking their lives in order to restore the dignity of the African heritage, plundered by over 400 years of racism, which in conjunction with colonialism contributed to freezing our heritage in a particular time and space." – Share Newspaper, July 19, 1990, Art confrontation by Ahmed Elamin, pg. 3.

What a Bam Bam!

1. Twenty-four years later, as Fitzroy began to claim his own ties to Africa, he too would come to acknowledge Rastafarianism intellectually as a form of resistance, a stirring attempt to reclaim an African persona decimated by colonialism. – The Gargoyle, Black History Month Supplement, Rastafarian movement proves hard to define by Oji Adisa, February 1, 1990.
2. According to Dennis Forsythe, quoted in a 1980 edition of *Caribbean Quarterly*, "Rastafarianism is the first mass movement among West Indians preoccupied with the tasks of looking into themselves and asking the fundamental question, Who am I? or What am I? As such it reflects the spirit of Garveyism ... it is an alternative call for a counter-culture more suited to the needs of black people ..." - *Jamaica Journal*, Quarterly of the Institute of Jamaica, Vol. 17, No.1, February 1984. See article by Velma Pollard: Word Sound - The Language of Rastafari in Barbados and St. Lucia.

Our Home on Native Land

1. Remarkably, years later when Canadian crime rates ballooned, particularly in urban centres such as metropolitan Toronto, Black crime would be blamed as the culprit. More specifically, the driving force would be identified as a "Jamaican crime problem."

This prompted Canada in the late 1990s to launch a series of mass "criminal removals" in which significant number of criminally convicted persons without citizenship were routinely deported to Jamaica. - *Toronto Sun*, June 2, 1990, How alone our police must feel by Christie Blatchford; *Maclean's*, February 17, 1997, A trade in criminals by Maureen Sheridan and Naomi Morris.

2. While this history is rich in content, this inhospitable aspect of Canadian life is rarely communicated. The practice of slave auction blocks, the benefits derived from the international commerce of Black bodies have been whitewashed or erased. - *CBC Ideas. Slavery's long shadow: The impact of 200 years of enslavement in Canada.* https://www.cbc.ca/radio/ideas/slavery-s-long-shadow-the-impact-of-200-years-of-enslavement-in-canada-1.4733595

Young Poets of the Revolution

1. Now the children of the oppressed would speak up and speak out, uttering words as if they were *"bullets from a gun."* - Power to the People Newspaper, Volume 2, number 8, We Are At War.
2. According to the Minister: "What we are doing as poets as young people is to kick reality on what is being done to us, and it is that point when people wake up from their dream." – Ibid.
3. M. NourbeSe Philip, from Trinidad and Tobago, who emerged as an African Canadian poet, novelist and playwright, recalls how difficult it was in the late seventies and eighties. "As a woman from the Caribbean writing in Toronto," says Philip, "there were no elders. There were no models that we could look to, to pattern ourselves on in terms of writing, so there is a sense in which ... we actually were almost creating the tradition as we were writing." – UWI Today, University of the West Indies, St. Augustine Campus, March 2010, article 10.
4. The Young Poets did achieve a minor milestone when through Oji's influence they got some of their work published in a special winter edition of the University of Toronto's literary publication *Acta Victoriana*, volume 116 number 1, to mark Black History Month. – Jamaica Gleaner, January 1, 1992, Young Poets, Afrocentric Vision for campuses by William Doyle-Marshall; see also *Acta Victoriana*, volume 116 number 1.

Marronage

1. Roy, Producer/Director, writer and narrator, had by now become a reputed Hollywood stuntman. – Gleaner Extra NA, July 1-7, 2010, J'Can-Born Hollywood stuntman traces his roots by Paul H. Williams.

Look for Me in the Whirlwind

1. Oji was amazed at the degree to which his knowledge had increased, and along with it, his consciousness. In the short time that he had been in Ghana, he had learned more about African history and way of life than in all his years of Canadian schooling including university. – The Varsity, February 28, 1991, Roving Varsity reporter in Ghana Researching African history leads to a return home by Oji Adisa.

The New Revolution

1. Following the departure of Akwatu Khenti, he assumed the role of acting president of the African Canadian Student Association (ACSA) from 1989 to 1990, confidently entering the fray as an advocate, agitating on behalf of Black students' right to gather and organize, and emphatically arguing for racial justice and equality. – The Varsity, October 10, 1989, ACSA loses vote to save its space by Hilary Bain.
2. In September 1989, he led the ACSA in a head-on dispute with the University of Toronto Students' Union (UTSU), then known as the Student's Administrative Council (SAC), itself ostensibly a student representative body. – The Varsity, September 18, 1989, Opinion and Editorial, SAC space allocation controversy: What is fair? By B. Khamisa Baya and Adisa Oji. For more on eviction controversy see also in The Varsity ACSA continuing its protest of SAC policy by Wanda Stride, September 18, 1989; The Gargoyle, Vol 34, number 8, February 1, 1990, The ACSA eviction brings racism to surface by Raghu Krishnan.
3. With this as his backdrop, Oji led the charge vowing, "We will not be evicted...we are not dead, we are just displaced." The Varsity, September 11, 1989, ACSA locked out by Karen Hill; see also ACSA protest at SAC, September 21, 1989.
4. When on September 25, 1989, sixty or so ASCA members stormed into SAC's budget meeting to challenge the eviction chanting "Hell no, we won't go"! Metro Toronto police were summoned to simmer things down. "Our hope is for SAC to realize that ACSA cannot continue to be pushed around. We're showing SAC we are not joking," said Oji in defiance. – The Varsity, September 28, 1989, Student group demands speaking rights: ACSA protest axes SAC's meeting by Sandy Williamson.
5. ACSA forged alliances with other anti-racism advocates to create the United Coalition Against Racism, and when in October 1989, University of Toronto's Day celebrations were being held, the coalition launched a public demonstration much to the embarrassment of U of T Day organizers. "We are going to show up the university for what it really is." said Oji. "We want to make them look bad. The administration doesn't care. The questions are not heard until we find a medium that forces people to listen." – The Varsity, October 19, 1989, Anti-racism coalition protest U of T Day by Shelagh Young.
6. In March 1990 he was impassioned enough to run for a seat on the University of Toronto's Governing Council (GC). Putting forward an anti-racism platform, he committed to bringing attention to institutional racism on the campus, highlighting particularly the university's heavily Eurocentric course content and the glaring under-representation of people of colour in faculty and administration. – The Varsity, March 5, 1990, Five

students run for two GC spots by Berton Ung; see also The Varsity, Opinions/Letters, Vote Joffe, Adisa, March 12, 1990.

7. In an introduction to the Young Poets of the Revolution written for *Acta Victoriana*, the university's literary journal, Lanchester described the poets as "the dissenting voice," Africans who were "continually submerged in their induced nightmare of this supposedly peaceful Canadian society." - *Acta Victoriana*, volume 116 number 1, Young Poets of the Revolution, Introduction by Lanchester F. Anderson.

8. On one occasion, they were provoked into action by Martin Klein, a professor in the History Department who at least once made cynical remarks about "Mr. Adisa's revolution." – Globe and Mail, July 14, 1990, Protest at the ROM

9. During its infancy between 1987-90 before it was officially launched, MACPRI—Mother Africa's Children Photographic Reproductions International—existed only as a single entity geared to showcasing photographic images. – African Business & Culture, Vol. 2 No.16 2001, The need for the African Image Revolution by Sister Ekua Azami-Walcott.

10. Ras Rico who became radicalized in 1978 after the Toronto police killing of Andrew "Buddy" Evans (24) at a nightclub on King Street West, and in which a coroner's inquest exonerated the officer of any wrongdoing, was also present. – Power to the People, (Date and issue unknown) Struggle in Toronto as seen through the eyes of Ras Rico I.

11. His next major exhibit, mounted at the Knowledge Bookstore Liberation Lounge Gallery in Brampton, took a while in coming but when it opened in 2007 it was obvious why. "*Mother God*" was a landmark exhibit displaying over 20 years of Oji's work. – Gleaner Canada Extra, September 13-19, 2007, Photo exhibit opens in Brampton.

12. "When I finally developed my own visual education concept," said Oji, "I had David to thank for the initial inspiration ... his memory will live on in my work." – The Diversity News, Vol. 3 Issue 11, November 2003, In the eyes of a "CAMERA" – A Photo Historian's personal journey by Usheak Koroma.

13. Now, new observations can come to light; at last, our eyes can behold the beauty of what was previously despised, and *we will live*. "We cannot return to the past," says Oji, "but we can use our knowledge gained from history to develop a new vision for the future with a greater sense of cultural integrity." – Ibid.

14. On August 18, 2001, he had the honour of making the keynote address at Garvey Day celebrations held at Toronto's Coronation Park, choosing as his theme, "Taking Responsibility for Our Children's Education." This and other such engagements cemented his reputation as an Afrocentric educator, the *Mwalimu*. – Jamaica Weekly Star, August 16-22, 2001, Afrocentric educator keynote speaker at Garvey Day Celebration

Repairing Old wounds

1. Following their arrest, Oji and others formed the ROM 11 Legal Defence Committee to raise funds and public awareness. Solidarity among the group was still high. A trip with Ras Rico and Jennifer Issac to Ottawa-Carlton would be one of many speaking tours in which Oji participated. – The Charlatan, Carlton University, Ottawa, November 11, 1991, Blacks fight police brutality over ROM by Mo Gannon.

2. Throughout the life of their case in court, various judges adjudicated the matter, with the judge denying most of their critical defence motions. The crown called their defence motions a "fishing expedition," and the judge usually agreed. – Toronto Star, March 26, 1992, Judge views tapes of museum brawl by Jim Wilkes.

3. He told the court: For a long time in this city, the pol-lice and the in-justice system have been getting away with a lot of things against our people ...We engaged in peaceful protest and still we get our asses kicked. The museum brought out the pol-lice to beat our asses. – Varsity Newspaper, November 31, 1991, ROM 11 have day in court by Naomi Klein.

4. On one hand, the agreement entered into by some of the ROM 11 pointed to the collective strength of the CFTA's efforts to galvanize public opinion on their side. Public pressure pushed the crown to negotiate. – Ibid.

5. The matter of the peace bond, or "*bond-age*" as Oji calls it, is a sensitive one. On one hand, the agreement entered into by some of the ROM 11 pointed to the collective strength of the CFTA's efforts to galvanize public opinion on their side. Public pressure pushed the crown to negotiate. Crown representatives are likely to argue that public opinion had nothing to do with their decision to settle; that the decision was based purely on legal grounds. – Ibid.

6. The notion of an "apology" actually first surfaced in 1991, months after the exhibit prematurely closed. ROM management in consultation with a hastily convened community group of eminent African Canadians had come up with a pacifier—an exhibit to celebrate art related to *Caribana* focusing on festive Caribbean costumes and masks. – The Toronto Sun, April 5, 1991, ROM apology uproar & The Globe and Mail, March 7, 1991, "ROM hoping to mend fences" by Kate Taylor.

7. She publicly bashed him every chance she got. "It was like watching the country go down the toilet," she reported in November 1991 when describing Oji's bold attempt to defend himself in court. – Toronto Sun, November 19, 1991, Ugly court display mocks justice by Christie Blatchford.

8. Their exhibition, *Into The Heart of Africa*, appears not to have been the ROM's favourite subject or finest moment. Indeed, their national and international reputation suffered as a result, and possibly their revenue after other museums opted out. The price tag for mounting the display was $25, 000. ("I am shocked by some of the visual material," said Davis Hemphill, director of the Vancouver Museum, one of the four museums to subsequently cancel their run of the exhibit. "Our regular supporters would not be pleased to support something so controversial," he concluded.) - The Varsity, September 27, 1990, ROM exhibit is rejected by Stephanie Campbell.

9. In a guest article in the *Globe and Mail*, December 4, 2000, entitled "Stay tuned: The ROM has a story to tell," Thorsell, then ROM president, disappoints anyone interested in hearing the story about the doomed exhibit. "Over the next six months," he declared, "the ROM's masterplan will be refined and, most critically, a financial reality check will be done to assess what supports exists for this vision. In the neighbourhood of $200-million over seven years, the project falls well within comparable museum initiatives elsewhere, but $200 million isn't chopped liver either." His evasion of the subject was

striking. – Globe and Mail, Review, December 4, 2000, Stay tuned: The ROM has a story to tell by William Thorsell.

Epilogue

1. An excerpt from the Stephen Lewis report compiled some thirty years ago (1992) is worthwhile quoting if only because it describes an ongoing reality. – Stephen Lewis Report on Race Relations in Ontario, June 1992, Pg. 2 may be found here https://archive.org/details/stephenlewisrep00olewi. See also NOW Magazine, Toronto, May 4-10, 2017, Yonge "Riot" and Rebellion: New documentary marking 25th anniversary of uprising that exposed Toronto's divide asks, "What does it take for Black people to get justice in this society?" by Simon Black.

Sources and References

Archives and Collections
Brother Oji Archives and dairies including photo collection and digital files.

Brother Oji's court transcripts: Regina v. Devon Johnson and Adisa Oji; Her Majesty The Queen and Adisa Oji Appeal.

Books highlighted but not mentioned in the bibliography
DiAngelo, Robin. *White Fragility: Why Is It's So Hard For White People to Talk About Racism.* Beacon Press, 2018.

Grizzle, Stanley. *My Name is Not George: The story of the Brotherhood of Sleeping Car Porters: personal reminiscences of Stanley G. Grizzle.* Umbrella Press, 1st Edition January 1998.

Hill, Lawrence. *The Book of Negroes: A Novel.* Harper Collins, 2011.

Ruck, Calvin Woodrow. *The Black Battalion 1916-1920: Canada's Best Kept Military Secret. First edition 1987.* Republished with foreword by Lindsay Ruck. Nimbus Publishing, 2017.

Tattrie, Jon. *The Hermit of Africville.* Pottersfield Press, 2020.

Journals and Magazines
Jamaica Journal, Quarterly of the Institute of Jamaica, Vol. 17, No.1, February 1984.

Zoomer, Special Collector's Edition, Canada 150, Vol. 33, No. 5, 2017

Oral Histories and Interviews
Anderson, Geraldine. In-person interview. Toronto, Ontario, October 2010.

Chamberlin, Professor Ted. Telephone interview. September 2013.

Oji, Adisa. In-person interviews. Toronto, Ontario, September 2008 – September 2010.

Rahimi, Dan. In-person interview. Toronto, Ontario, August 2013.

Public Media

Buffalo News. Toronto exhibit on Africa called racist by Barry Brown and David Cooper. June 10, 1990.
https://buffalonews.com/news/toronto-exhibit-on-africa-is-called-racist/article_04e093ac-987c-54f6-b188-a43282787520.html

CBC. Racism is still an uncomfortable truth in Canada. CBC News posted October 7th, 2014.

CBC. CBC Ideas, 2018 Edition. *The resistance of Black Canada: State surveillance and suppression.*

CBC. CBC Ideas, July 5, 2019. Slavery's long shadow: The impact of 200 years of enslavement in Canada
https://www.cbc.ca/radio/ideas/slavery-s-long-shadow-the-impact-of-200-years-of-enslavement-in-canada-1.4733595

CBC. Stuff the British Stole. Podcast hosted by Marc Fennell.
https://www.cbc.ca/listen/cbc-podcasts/1030-stuff-the-british-stole

Canadian Museum Association. About the CMA.
https://www.museums.ca/site/aboutthecma

Challenges Faced by Racialized Licensees Working Group: Interim Report on Convocation, April 2015. A copy of the report may be found at
http://welpartners.com/resources/WEL_Pages_from_convocation_april_2015_equity.pdf.

Maclean's Magazine. Canada's Race Problem.
http://www.macleans.ca/news/canada/cover-preview-canadas-race-problem/

Museums Association. On Decolonizing Museums.
https://www.museumsassociation.org/campaigns/decolonising-museums/#

Ontario Human Rights Commission (OHRC). *Leadership Needed to Fight Racism - Viewpoint* by Renu Mandhane, Chief Commissioner of the Ontario Human Rights Commission, Special to the Chronicle Journal, July 25, 2017.

Ontario Human Rights Commission (OHRC) *"Timeline of racial discrimination and racial profiling of Black persons by the Toronto Police Service, and Ontario Human Rights Commission (OHRC) initiatives related to the Toronto Police."* (ohrc.on.ca).

ROM. *Message from the Director on Equity and Racial Justice,* Josh Basseches.
https://www.rom.on.ca/en/about-us/message-from-the-director-on-equity-and-racial-justice

ROM. Toward Greater Inclusion and Equity at the ROM
https://www.rom.on.ca/en/about-us/toward-greater-inclusion-and-equity-at-the-rom

The Star. *Race Matters: Blacks documented by police at high rate* By Jim Rankin, Staff Reporter, Saturday, February 06, 2010.

Toronto Public Health. *Racialization and Health inequities in Toronto* by Jennifer Levy, Donna Ansara, and Andi Stover, October 2013.

Toronto Star. Commentary: Police stops damage lives of black Torontonians by Professor Scot Wortley, September 28, 2013.

Truth and Reconciliation Commission of Canada. *Truth and Reconciliation Commission of Canada: Call to Action,* 2015.
https://fncaringsociety.com/sites/default/files/truth_and_reconciliation_commission_of_canada_calls_to_action.pdf

NOW Magazine Toronto. Why is our city council so white? by Jonathan Goldsbie, November – December 2014 edition.
https://nowtoronto.com/news/city-councils-race-problem/

Recordings
Metro Morning Audio Recording, August 27, 2003.
Young Poets of the Revolution Audio CD, 1992.

Illustration and Photo Credits
Every attempt has been made to attribute appropriate credit and source. Some images, particularly those from Brother Oji's archive, have had a long life. Due to their vintage, it is not always possible to determine who took the photograph and when. Apologies beforehand for any errors or omissions.

Front Cover
Designed by Mello Ayo in partnership with Xlibris design team. Flyer originally prepared by Minister Faust for Young Poets of the Revolution, 1991. Quote attributed to Fred Hampton.

Title Page
Photo of Brother Oji by Mesfin Aman (?) Or Winston Anderson. Oji Archive.

Enter the Mwalimu
Lead photo: Brother Oji at the United Nations, New York HQ for world premiere of Queen Nanny, October 19, 2015 Photo from Oji Archives courtesy of Action For Reel Film Works.

Adisa S. Oji v Regina
Lead photo: Self-portrait, 1990. Oji Archives.

Photo of Canadian monuments photographed 2018 (St. Thomas, Ontario) and 2021 (Kingston, Ontario) by Mello Ayo.

Photo of demonstrators Gerry Cromwell and Tia James by Neville White, 1990. Used with permission.

Oji screaming by Gerry Cromwell June 2, 1990. Oji Archive.

List of organizations in CFTA coalition, CFTA Brochure created by CFTA, 1990, from Oji Archives.

Catalogue cover of *"Into the Heart of Africa"* exhibition, mounted November 1989. Photo by Reverend A.W. Banfield. Used with permission.

Cover of *Illustrated London News Vol. LXXX, No. 2099*, Saturday, September 6, 1879, as displayed by the ROM.

Police clash with protestors outside 100 Queens Park at the Royal Ontario Museum. *Toronto Star* ©, June 3, 1990. Used with permission.

"What's wrong with this picture?" - CFTA flyer, created by CFTA, 1990. Oji Archives.

ROM 11 supporters outside Old City after ROM 11 first court appearance. Photo by Adisa Oji for MACPRI, 1990. MACPRI/Oji Archive.

ROM's east entrance, the Hilary and Galen Weston Wing. Photo by Mello Ayo, 2021. Mello Ayo Archive.

Who Am I
Lead photo of Brother Oji by Winston Anderson, 2006. Oji Archive.
Children playing in the rain at Ridge Pen. Circa 1970. Photographer unknown. Oji Archive.
Geraldine Rowe. Photo by Adisa Oji, 1988. Oji Archive.
Alfred Rowe and Brother Oji. Photographer unknown. Oji Archive.

What a Bam Bam!
Lead photo of Brother Oji and mother, Geraldine Rowe. Photo by Winston Anderson, 2012. Oji Archive.
The boy named Fitzroy, 1974. Photographer unknown. Oji Archive.

Oh Canada!
Lead photo contact sheet image of Brother Oji by David Maltby, 1988, property of MACPRI.
Theophilus Anderson at Roy Anderson's historic high-rise leap, March 26, 1990. Photo by Adisa Oji. Oji Archive.
Young Brother Oji as a budding draftsman, 1986. Photo by Winston Anderson. Family album/Oji Archive.

Our Home on Native Land
Lead photo of Brother Oji by Mesfin Aman (?) or Winston Anderson working on the details
Brother Oji with Eddie Carvery, during Marcus Garvey film shoot, 2017, courtesy of Black Star Line Films. Oji Archive.
Brother Oji teaching the game of Oware in North Preston, Dartmouth, Nova Scotia, in 2011. MACPRI/Oji Archive.
MACPRI posters courtesy of MACPRI. Oji Archives.
Adisa S. Oji Documentary Photographer at age twenty. Photo by David Maltby, 1986. Oji Archives.

Young Poets of the Revolution
Lead photo of Brother Oji, private photo shoot at Studio 44, Toronto, 1988. Property of MACPRI.

All posters/flyers from Young Poets of the Revolution, courtesy of MACPRI. Cover artwork featuring Queen Nzinga produced by Minister Faust for The Young Poets of The Revolution Special Edition 1992. Photo of N2 by Adisa Oji with art work by Winston Anderson, 1991. MACPRI/Oji Archives.

Young Poets of the Revolution in Kensington Market. Photographed by Adisa Oji, 1991. MACPRI/Oji Archive.

Look for Me in the Whirlwind

Lead photo of Brother exiting Na's palace to feed the royal horse. Photo by Kwaku Henne, 2003. MACPRI/Oji Archive.

1920 *Declaration of Rights of the Negro Peoples of the World. Negro World,* July 31, 1936.

Marronage

Lead photo of Brother Oji photographed by RA Oji, 2021. Oji Archive.

Roy T. Anderson, Lewis Rowe, elder uncle of Oji, along with Packieman courtesy of Action For Reel Filmworks, 2009. Oji/MACPRI Archives.

Rowe children on green carpet photographed by Adisa Oji, 2012. Oji Archive.

The New Revolution

Lead photo of Brother Oji by Winston Anderson, 2017. Oji /MACPRI Archive.

Brother Oji standing with Brother Sankofa in Portland, Jamaica, during the Annual Charles Town Maroon Conference, 2012. Oji/MACPRI Archive.

Brother Oji with sister, Suzette, at Artscape Wychwood Barns in Toronto at Black Unity Market photographed by Sepo Acheampong for MACPRI Archives.

Kwame Ben-Eden making his *sankofa* journey photographed by Adisa Oji. MACPRI/Oji Archives.

Oji as a photographer captured by Louis March or Mesfin Aman. MACPRI/Oji Archive.

Mother God, Ummu and Dudu, Rowing Her Own Boat, and *Village in the Lake* photographed by Adisa Oji. MACPRI.

Children playing Oware in Toronto and Ghana photographed by Adisa Oji. MACPRI/Oji Archive.

Crowned King and Prince of the 2011 Oware Tournament photographed by Adisa Oji, 2011. MACPRI/Oji Archive.

Honourable John Dramani Mahama photographed by Adisa Oji, December 2016. MACPRI/Oji Archive.

RA, Nana with cousin, Shauna, and Packieman in Jamaica photographed by Adisa Oji, 2013. MACPRI/Oji Archive.

Winston "Hefty" Anderson, Mello Ayo, and Lee Miller photographed by Adisa Oji, 2016. MACPRI/Oji Archive.

Dr. Jean Augustine photographed by Winston Anderson, 2016. MACPRI/Oji Archive.

Family

Lead photograph of Oji & Ko at wedding. Contracted property of the Oji family.

Queen Mother, Geraldine Anderson photographed by Adisa Oji. MACPRI/Oji Archive.

Four generations of African women photographed by Adisa Oji. Oji Archives.

Brother Oji and family standing with image of the Honourable Marcus Mosiah Garvey, May 26, 2018, courtesy of Black Star Line Films. (Oji Archive)

Chantelly Primary School principal and Packieman exhibiting gifts of Oware board games in Manchester, Jamaica, photographed by Adisa Oji, 2012. MACPRI Archives.

Brother Oji at family gathering in Ridge Pen photographed by Winston Anderson, 2012. MACPRI/Oji Archives.

Repairing Old wounds

Lead photo of Brother Oji on film set courtesy of Black Star Line Films, 2018.
Justice for the ROM 11 poster created by CFTA, 1991. Oji Archive.
Ugly Court Display Mocks Justice, Christie Blatchford, *Toronto Sun*, 1991. Used with permission.
Brother Oji standing outside the ROM photographed by Eryck b., 2018. Used with permission.
Brother Oji with raised fist and sankofa staff photographed by RA Oji, 2020. Oji Archive.

Epilogue

Lead photo of Brother Oji with sankofa staff photographed by RA Oji, 2020. Oji Archive.
End photo of Brother Oji with son, Joomo, photographed by Christine Selassie, 2020. Oji Archive.
Back Cover designed by Mello Ayo in partnership with Xlibris design team. Photo of Brother Oji at African Entertainment Awards, Toronto, photographed by Winston Anderson, 2017. MACPRI/Oji Archive.
Good Beautiful Morning art piece by Mello Ayo is a Mello Ayo logo associated with Good Beautiful Morning, a Mello Ayo registered company.

Bibliography

The information used throughout has been acquired over many years of reading and research, as well as through conversations with a variety of experts from a variety of fields. As you read and become more curious, you, too, may be motivated to do your own reading and research to draw your own conclusions.

To assist, here is a brief bibliography sourced from my personal library. All were useful or inspiring in one way or another, in part or in whole, and are all worth digging into. I thank the authors, researchers, and academics on whose work I relied and who have provided me with many hours of pleasurable insightful reading. I trust that I, in turn, have done the same for you and many others.

Asante, Molefi Kete. *Maulana Karenga: An Intellectual Portrait*. Polity Press, 2009.

Backhouse, Constance. *Colour-Coded: A Legal History of Racism in Canada, 1900–1950*. The Osgood Society, 1999.

Beckford, George L. *Persistent Poverty: Underdevelopment in Plantation Economies of the Third World*. Oxford University Press, 1972.

Bernal, Martin. *Black Athena: The Afroasiatic Roots of Classical Civilization, Volume 1, The Fabrication of Ancient Greece 1785–1985*. Rutgers University Press, 1987.

Bogle, Donald. *Toms, Coons, Mulattoes, Mammies and Bucks: An Interpretive History of Blacks in American Films*, New Third Edition. Continuum Publishing Company, 1989.

Bumsted, J. M. *The People of Canada, A Pre-Confederation History, 3rd Edition*. Oxford University Press, 2010.

Burnett, Paula, editor. *The Penguin Book of Caribbean Verse in English*. Penguin Books, 1986.

Commission on Systemic Racism in Ontario Criminal Justice System. *Racism Behind Bars: The Treatment of Black and Other Racial Minorities in Ontario's Prisons*. Publications Ontario, 1994.

Cooper, Afua. *Copper Woman and Other Poems*. Natural Heritage Books, 2006.

Davis, Angela Y., and other political prisoners. *If They Come in The Morning*. Signet Book, New American Library by arrangement with the Third Press, Joseph Okpaku Publishing Company, 1971.

Fanon, Frantz. *Black Skin, White Masks*. Grove Press, 1952.

Foster, Lorne. *Writing Justice: Voicing Issues in the Third Media*. Multicultural History Society, 2011.

Gillmour, Don, and Pierre Turgeon. *Canada—A People's History, Volume 1*. CBC, McClelland and Stewart Ltd., 2000.

Grant, Colin. *Negro with A Hat: The Rise and Fall of Marcus Garvey*. Oxford University Press, 2008.

Guevara, Ernesto "Che." *The Motorcycle Diaries: Notes of a Latin American Journey*. Ocean Press, 2004.

Hass, Jeffrey. *The Assassination of Fred Hampton: How the FBI and the Chicago Police Murdered a Black Panther*. Lawrence Hill Books, 2010.

Harris, Matthew, and Ron Harris. *The Black and Blue*. Hachette Books, 2018.

Head, Harold, editor. *Canada in Us Now*. New Canada Publications, 1976.

Iacobucci, Frank. *First Nations Representation on Ontario Juries, Report on the Independent Review*. Ministry of Attorney General, 2013.

Joseph, Peniel E. *Stokely: A Life*. Basic Civitas, 2014.

King, Thomas. *The Inconvenient Indian—A Curious Account of Native People in North America*. Anchor Canada, 2012.

Manley, Rachel. *Slipstream: A Daughter Remembers*. Key Porter Book, 2008.

Marable, Manning. *Malcolm X: A Life of Reinvention*. Viking 2011.

Marqusee, Mike. *Redemption Song: Muhammad Ali and the Spirit of the Sixties*. Verso, 1999.

Maynard, Robin. *Policing Black Lives: State Violence in Canada from Slavery to the Present*. Fernwood Publishing, 2017.

Mensah, Joseph. *Black Canadians: History, Experiences, Social Conditions*. Fernwood, 2002.

McCormack, Bill. *Without Fear or Favour: The Life and Politics of an Urban Cop* (as told to Bob Cooper). Stoddart Publishing, 1999.

Multicultural History Society of Ontario (MHSO). *Ontario's African Canadians 1865–1915*, researched and written by MHSO and included in program *From Drummondville to Africville, Songs of Freedom, Images of Hope*, a performance by the Nathaniel Dett Chorale. February 2000.

Paris, Erna. *Long Shadows: Truth, Lies and History*. Vintage Canada, 2001 edition.

Poe, Richard. *Black Spark, White Fire: Did African Explorers Civilize Ancient Europe?* Prima Publishing, 1997.

Rhoden, William C. *Forty Million Dollar Slaves: The Rise, Fall and Redemption of the Black Athlete*. Crown Publishers, 2006.

Roberts, Randy, and John Smith. *Blood Brothers: The Fatal Friendship Between Muhammad Ali and Malcolm X*. Basic Books, 2016.

Sadlier, Rosemary. *Mary Ann Shadd: Publisher, Editor, Teacher, Lawyer, Suffragette*. Umbrella Press, 1995

Sinclair, Justice Murray, Chief Wilton Littlechild, and Marie Wilson. *Truth and Reconciliation Commission of Canada, Truth and Reconciliation Commission of Canada: Interim Report*. TRC Canada, 2012.

———. *Truth and Reconciliation Commission of Canada, Canada, Aboriginal Peoples, and Residential Schools—They Came for the Children*. TRC Canada, 2012.

Tharoor, Shashi. *Inglorious Empire: What the British Did to India*. Scribe, 2016.

Van Sertima, Ivan. *They Came Before Columbus—The African Presence in Ancient America*. Random House, 1976.

Walters, Ewart. *To Follow Right, A Journalist's Journey*. Boyd McRubie Communications, 2011.

Williams, Eric. *Capitalism and Slavery*. Chapel Hill, 1944.

Williams, Chancellor. *The Destruction of Black Civilization*. Third World Press, 1987.

Wright, Robert. *Three Nights in Havana: Pierre Trudeau, Fidel Castro and the Cold War World*. Harper, 2008.

INDEX

A

Aboagye, Emelia, 228
Aboagye, Wilson, 228
Abolition of the Slave Trade Act, 111, 192
Accompong Town, 187–88, 190–93
Achebe, Chinua, 223, 240, 256
Adjetey, Wendell, 285, 285n46
African Business and Community Development Conference, 229
African Canadian Cultural and Educational Services (ACCES), 143
African Caribbean Students Association (ACSA), 41, 204, 207, 209–10, 229
African Image Revolution, 145, 153, 155, 211–12, 215–17, 223, 226–27, 229, 233–34, 264
African Liberation Month, 30
African National Congress (ANC), 77
African spirit, 83
Africville, 114–15, 119–23, 137
Akos (adopted daughter), 9, 163, 216, 241
Akwantu: The Journey, 31n4, 223
Akyeaw, Yaw, 50, 52, 57–58, 263–64, 295
Alchemists of Kush, The (Faust), 143
Alexseyev, Vasiliy, 125
American Revolution, 112
A. Murray MacKay Bridge, 120, 122–23
Anancy, 83
Anderson, Fitzroy (*see also* Brother Oji), 21, 64–72, 76–78, 83, 87, 89–90, 93–103, 108–9, 112–14, 117, 120, 128–29
Anderson, Geraldine, 65, 242
Anderson, Lanchester F., 208, 211, 259
Anderson, Roy T., 69, 194, 196, 240, 243
Anderson, Suzette, 66, 98, 213, 227, 238, 243, 245
Anderson, Theophilus, 65, 99, 238–39
Anderson, Winston "Hefty," 66, 96, 98, 153, 194, 196, 235, 244
Anglicization, 302
Anila, Swarupa, 16, 308
apartheid system, 45–46
Asante, Molefi Kete, 44
Asantewaa, Nana Yaa, 173–74
Ashwood, Amy, 166
Augustine, Jean, 30, 96, 106, 235
Aunty Gladys (Kofi Fefe's mom), 160–61, 163, 168, 173

B

Back to Africa Movement, 89, 168
Baldwin, James, 147, 186, 283
Ballantyne, Terrence, 96
Baraka, Amiri, 147
Barrett, Claudette, 211
Barrett, Silbert, 15, 50, 52, 210, 258
Barrie, Andy, 264, 268
Basseches, Josh, 16, 263–64, 271, 306
Beckford, George, 190

Persistent Poverty: Underdevelopment in Plantation Economies of the Third World, 190
Bedward, Alexander, 83
Ben-Eden, Kwame, 214–15
BenJochannan, Yosef A. A., 256
Bennett-Coverley, Louise, 148
Berlin Conference, 38, 38n6
Birth of a Nation, The, 48n10
Black Action Defence Committee (BADC), 41, 45, 56–57, 61n12, 255
Black Arts Movement (BAM), 147
Black Arts Repertory Theatre/School (BARTS), 147
Black Battalion 1916–1920: Canada's Best Kept Military Secret, The (Ruck), 117
Black Canadians, 113, 117, 128
Black consciousness, 89, 170, 208, 249
Black history, 29, 30n3, 30, 144, 155, 270
Black History Month, 29, 30n3, 30, 155, 270
Black liberation, 19, 147, 172, 175, 209
Black Lives Matter, 141
Black Loyalists, 112–13, 119
Blackman, Cheryl, 263–64, 306
Black Star Line, 165, 175, 182
Blatchford, Christie, 257, 260
Bloody Sunday, 78
Bogle, Paul, 61, 80
Book of Negroes, The (Hill), 112
Brathwaite, Edward Kamau, 88, 129, 147, 204, 240
Bratu, Andre, 50, 258
Bridging the Gap Peer Career Counselling Program, 101
Brooks, Wilson, 30, 147
Brother Andrew (friend), 212, 227, 229, 235
Brotherhood of Sleeping Car Porters, 137
Brother Oji, 5, 16, 18–25, 31–34, 121–22, 124, 143–44, 152–53, 183, 186, 199–205, 213, 217, 223–24, 227, 231–35, 240, 242–45, 249–50, 268, 274–76, 280, 283–87, 289–93, 295
 "Mi Bibini," 17, 21
 "Offspring," 232
Brother Sankofa (friend), 212–13
Brother Ted. *See* Chamberlin, J. Edward
Brother Yaw (friend), 210, 214, 258–59, 298
Brown, Allan, 96
Brown, Andrew, Jr., 142n32
Bryant, Ma'Khiah, 142n32
Buamah, Albert, 228
Bushman's Brew (Head), 146
Business and Community Capacity Building Marketplace, 201–2

C

Canadian Bill of Rights, 125
Canadian Black History Month, 30
Canadian Charter of Rights and Freedom, 125
Canadian Conference of Catholic Bishops (CCCB), 303
Canadian Human Rights Act, 125
Canadian Museum Association (CMA), 275, 275n44, 275
Canadian National Exhibition (CNE), 100, 203
Cannizzo, Jeanne, 42, 47, 262, 274, 287
Capitalism and Slavery (Williams), 291
Carby, Jermaine, 142
Carding, Janet, 261, 263, 268, 274
Caribana, 107

Caribbean Artists Movement (CAM), 147–48
Caribbean Corner, 108, 206, 259
Caribbean Islands, 87, 95
Caribbean people, 95–96, 106–9, 125, 179
Carnegie, Herb, 113, 138
Carvery, Eddie, 122
Castro, Fidel, 279
Catholic church, 303–4
Chamberlin, J. Edward, 204, 217
Chauvin, Derek Michael, 142n32
Chow, Olivia, 101, 205
Coalition for the Truth about Africa (CAFTA), 40, 260, 306
colonialism, 22–24, 36, 38–39, 41, 47, 58, 71, 80, 84–85, 89, 114, 122, 127, 130, 151, 169, 172, 177–78, 183, 186, 193, 200, 204, 214, 252–53, 262, 266–67, 271–72, 274, 288, 291–92, 299
Coloniality of Existence: Africa in Scholarships and Museums, 269
Columbus, Christopher, 84, 273
Comaneci, Nadia, 125
Committee for the Truth about Africa (CFTA), 40–45, 48–50, 59–60, 144, 209–10, 246, 252, 254–55, 257–58, 260, 262–65, 268, 270, 274–76, 306–7
Constitution Act, 125
Cook, Sophia, 56, 57n11, 142
Cools, Ann, 96
Cooper, Afua, 15, 44, 124n29, 148, 150, 152–53, 209–10, 263–64, 270, 307
Copp, Terry, 43
Crawford, Haseley, 126
Crazy Eddie (Africville hermit), 121
Crooks, Julie, 262, 270
Cross, James, 126
Cross Navigation and Shipping Company, 175
Currie, Richard, 193

D

Da Costa, Mathieu, 96, 111, 281
Davis, Angela, 248, 255
Davis, Bill, 109
dawn, 112
"Death of Joy Gardner, The" (Zephaniah), 150
de Bolas, Juan, 80, 95, 187
de Champlain, Samuel, 110–11
Declaration of Rights of the Negro Peoples of the World, 164, 166, 295
decolonization, 129, 146, 182, 272, 275
Decordova, Christine, 212, 243
Dei, George, 269
demonstrators, 18–19, 40, 42, 45, 48–52, 55, 57–58, 253–54, 274
de Serras, Juan, 80, 95, 187
Desmond, Viola, 61, 110, 117
Deverell, Rita Shelton, 16, 271n41
discrimination, 45n8, 50–51, 57, 77, 96, 110, 113, 115, 117, 136, 139, 179, 205, 249, 282, 286, 288
Dixon, George, 113, 119
Domestic Worker Program, 106
Donaldson, Lester, 56, 57n11, 142
Don Jail, 251
Douglas, Rosie, 96
Douglass, Frederick, 174–75
Du Bois, W. B., 172, 228
dub poetry, 148, 150

E

Edelweiss Park, 176
education, 21, 24, 47, 86–87, 89, 95, 112–13, 123, 128, 136, 138–39, 141–42, 177–78, 204, 208–11, 217–18, 223, 230–31, 253–54, 269, 271, 283, 297
Elizabeth II (Queen), 36, 85, 183
Ellington, Duke, 119
Employment Equity Act, 125
"Equal Rights" (Tosh), 80n14
Ethiopian Orthodox Tewahedo Church (EOTC), 89n20
Ethiopian Zion Coptic Church, 89n20
eugenics, 38, 46
Evans, Michael, 57, 233–34
Expo 67, *124*

F

Fair Accommodation Practices Act, 113
Fair Employment Practices Act, 113
festivals, 107
First Nations people, 95, 123, 301, 303–5
"Five Nights of Bleeding" (Johnson), 150
Fontaine, Dominique, 262, 270
Forni, Silvia, 16, 262–64, 307–8
Forsythe, Dennis, 89
François, Marcellus, 151
Fredericks, Kennedy, 96
freedom, 23, 31–32, 61, 65, 83–85, 88, 93, 96, 110–13, 115, 125, 146, 162, 182–83, 187–95, 200, 205, 208, 240, 248–49, 252, 255–57, 267, 269, 274–75, 281, 292, 296, 300
freedom fighters, 83, 115, 193–94, 255, 274
Front de liberation du Quebec (FLQ), 126
Fugitive Slave Act, 115

G

Gandhi, 175
Garvey, Marcus Mosiah, 19, 61, 83, 89, 131, 145, 161–63, 165–72, 174–76, 178–80, 182–83, 186, 195, 212, 214, 230, 240, 243–44, 255, 290, 293, 295–98
Garveyism, 90, 174, 179, 183
Garvey movement, 175, 179
Gemmel, Jack, 258
George, Dudley, 304
Ghana, 16, 25, 32, 84, 159–61, 163, 171, 173–74, 176–77, 179, 181–82, 184, 186, 202–4, 206, 212, 214–16, 219, 224–26, 228–30, 233–34, 243, 255, 257, 269, 293, 295–98
Ghana National Museum, 171
Ghana's 2019 Year of Return, 25
Golden Stool, 174
Goodin, Wendal, 96
Gordon, Henry, 90n22
Grandma Rowe. *See* Rowe, Geraldine
Gran' Market, 83
Grant, Yvonne, 16, 258
Griffith, D. W., 48n10
Group of Seven (G7), 122n28
Guevara, Ernesto "Che," 233–34, 279
Gzowski, Peter, 206

H

Hampton, Fred, 279
Harewood, Adrian, 264
Hawkins, Yusef, 45, 142
Head, Harold, 146
Bushman's Brew, 146
Hemphill, Davis, 261
Henson, Josiah, 96, 111, 113, 281
The Life of Josiah Henson, Formerly a Slave, Now an Inhabitant of Canada, 111
Here We Are Here, 270
Hibbert, Fredrick "Toots," 90n22
Hill, Daniel, 30n3
Hill, Lawrence, 112
The Book of Negroes, 112
History of Jamaica (Long), 85
Homecoming Screening, 194
Hoover, J. Edgar, 179
Howard, Robert, 47
Howell, Leonard P., 89n21
Hughes, Langston, 32, 164, 170
humanitarians, 115

I

immigrants, 22, 76, 93, 98–99, 101, 106, 109, 115–16, 123–24, 128
imperialism, 36, 38, 43, 80, 126, 169, 252, 274
British, 36, 80, 274
race-based, 38
Indian Act, 124, 301–2, 305
Indian Residential Schools Settlement Agreement, 303
Indians, 89, 95–96, 106, 108, 124, 179, 301–2
indigenous people, 24, 95, 97, 111, 118, 123–25, 142, 271, 281, 292, 300–305
industrialization, 38
injustice, 18, 24, 36, 39, 79–80, 85, 117–18, 120, 135, 139, 144, 174, 192, 232–33, 249, 253–54, 259, 269, 272, 286, 288
International Convention of the Negro Peoples of the World, 164
International Day for the Elimination of Racial Discrimination, 50
International Decade for People of African Descent, 25
International Dub Poetry Festival, 148
internship, 308
Into the Heart of Africa, 18, 41–42, 45, 48–49, 144, 209, 252, 261–63, 265, 273–75, 287–88, 306
Issac, Jennifer, 50, 250

J

Jackson, George L., 151
Jamaica, 79–81, 83–86, 88
Jamaica Labour Party (JLP), 88
"Jamaica: A look at the Social and Cultural Reality," 217
Jamaican Independence Festival Song Competition, 90
James, Gary, 43
James, Howard, 212
Japan, 122n28
Jenkins, Fergie, 138
Jenner, Bruce, 125
Jerome, Harry, 113, 138
Jim Crow, 77, 116, 172

John, Rodney, 96
John Crow, 64
Johnson, Albert, 57, 209
Johnson, Devon, 36, 39, 50, 52, 57–58. *See also* Akyeaw, Yaw
Johnson, Kwasi Johnson
"Five Nights of Bleeding," 150
Johnson, Linton Kwasi, 148, 150
Johnson, Ruby, 259
Jones, Denise, 107n24
Jonkonnu, 83

K

Kafale, Nene Kwesi, 212
Karuhanga, Jessica, 270
kente cloth, 20, 31, 79, 183, 186, 212, 280
Kerr, John, 257, 260
King, Mackenzie, 115
King, Martin Luther, Jr., 61, 77–78, 102, 135, 174, 179, 206, 248, 255
King, Rodney, 142, 151, 251, 286
Klein, Martin, 209
Korkori (wife), 216, 233–34, 240–42
Koromantse, 181
Ku Klux Klan, 172
Kwame (Oji's travel companion), 33, 61, 159–61, 163, 179, 186, 195, 214–15, 248, 255, 297

L

Laporte, Pierre, 126
La Rose, John, 147
Last Poets, 147
Lawrence, Raymond, 151, 286
Lawrence, Stephen, 152n33
Laws, Dudley, 61, 61n12, 96, 255
Lewis, Ray, 113, 138
Lewis, Stephen, 286
Liberty Hall, 164, 171, 297
Liburd, Sean, 201, 231
Life of Josiah Henson, Formerly a Slave, Now an Inhabitant of Canada, The (Henson), 111
Loku, Andrew, 142
Long, Edward, 85
Long Shadows: Truth, Lies and History (Paris), 23
Louis, Joe, 119
Louis Riel Day, 118
L'Ouverture, Toussaint, 190, 192
Love Africa Project, 215, 231, 295
Lovell, Lana, 264
Lumsden, Frank, 195

M

Macdonald, John A., 118, 273, 302, 302n51, 302
Machel, Samora, 240, 256
Made in Africa Awards Movement, 227–28
Mahama, John Dramani, 228
Malcolm X, 102, 135, 140, 159, 161, 173, 179, 240, 248, 255, 257, 297
Maltby, David B., 130, 217
Mancala. *See* Oware

Mandela, Nelson, 45, 58, 61
Mandhane, Renu, 303n52
Manley, Michael, 86–89, 109, 180
Manley, Rachael, 87
Manley's Project Land Lease, 87
Maplehurst Correctional Centre, 251
Marley, Bob, 80n14, 82, 163
"Talkin' Blues," 82
Maroons, 80, 96, 114, 119, 154, 184, 187–95, 200, 273, 300
Maroons, Accompong, 193
Maroons, Jamaican, 114, 119, 187, 190–91, 193
Maroons, Trelawny, 192
Marshall, Clem, 43
Martí, José, 234
Martin, M., 36, 39
Martin, Trayvon, 141
Mathias, Nathaniel, 90n22
Mathieu, Saje, 285, 285n46
Maxwell, Denise, 212
McCormack, Bill, 56
McKenzie, Sandra, 50, 52, 258
McNeill, John, 47, 261
"Mi Bibini" (Brother Oji), 17, 21
Militant Rap Party, 143
Minister Faust (poet), 15, 143, 150
Miss Lou. *See* Bennett-Coverley, Louise
Mohawks, 95, 304
Montague, Kenneth, 262
Montreal Summer Olympic, 125
Morant Bay Rebellion, 80, 85
Morgan, Henry, 84
Moriba, Geraldine, 263–64, 307
Mossop, Douglas, 96
Mother Africa's Children First International Association, 145
Mother Africa's Children Photographic Reproductions International (MACPRI), 130–31, 145–46, 153, 155, 159, 195, 201, 203, 206, 208, 211–12, 214, 217, 226, 228–30, 233, 235, 243–44, 295–98
Mother Africa's Children Primarily, 145
"Mother God," 32, 217, 219–20
multiculturalism, 109, 127, 130, 269, 281, 287
Munroe, Michelle, 212, 240
Museum of Modern Art (MoMA), 48
museums, 18–19, 39, 48, 116, 171, 211, 261–65, 269, 272–75, 306

N

Nanjing Massacre, 122
nation-language, 88
Negro Factories Corporation, 165, 175
Negro World, 166, 174–75, 297
Neil, Marlon, 56–57, 142
neocolonialism, 38, 217
New Age Promotion, 153, 206
Night of the Ancestors, 195
Nkombe, Joma Nyakorema, 58
North Preston, 114, 122–23

O

Of Africa, 262, 269, 308
"Offspring" (Brother Oji), 232
Oji, Adisa Sadiki (*see also* Brother Oji), 24, 31, 36, 39, 50–51, 71–72, 128–30, 166, 219–20, 264, 293
Oji, Genevieve Aryee. *See* Korkori (wife)
Oji, Naa Joomo, 241
Oji, Naa Shika Isaga, 241
Oji, Nana Akpaabe Adessa, 241
Oji, RA Ndemelle, 9, 241
Oka, 304
Oliver, Donald, 30
Ontario Black History Society (OBHS), 30
Ontario Court of Justice, 36, 60
Ontario Place, 128
Ontario Public Service (OPS), 45n8
Opoku, Kofi Asare, 176
oppression, 22, 39, 47, 58, 71–72, 78, 80, 82–83, 115, 124, 129, 141, 148–50, 165, 170, 188, 191, 223, 248–49, 253, 267, 269, 271–72, 274–75, 284, 286–90
O'Ree, Willie, 138
Oware, 122, 171, 195, 224–27, 233, 235, 245, 265
Oware Canada, 224, 226

P

Packieman (uncle), 194, 196, 234, 243, 245
Pan-African Congress, 77
Pan-Africanism, 173, 181, 183, 190, 248
Parchment, Elizabeth, 44
Paris, Erna, 23
Long Shadows: Truth, Lies and History, 23
Partitioning of Africa, 38, 169
Pearson, Lester B., 109
Penn, William, 84
People's National Party (PNP), 86
"Peoples of West Africa," 217
performer-poets, 139, 143
Persistent Poverty: Underdevelopment in Plantation Economies of the Third World (Beckford), 190
Peterson, Oscar, 138, 281
Philip, M. NourbeSe, 146, 270
photography, 130–31, 173, 211, 217–18, 223
poetry collective, 141, 144, 153, 155
Poitier, Sydney, 240, 256
Port Royal, 84, 111
Prude, Daniel, 142

Q

Quarrie, Donald, 126
Queen Nanny: Legendary Maroon Chieftainess, 195, 223

R

racial discrimination, 50–51, 57, 96, 110, 136, 282
racial disparity, 287
racial oppression, 39, 83, 287
racial superiority, 36–37, 124

racism, 15, 18–19, 22–24, 36–39, 43, 45, 48, 51, 58, 77, 86, 112, 115, 117–20, 122–24, 127–28, 130, 135–36, 138–39, 141–42, 147, 151–52, 161, 172, 175, 207–8, 210, 229–30, 249, 254–56, 263–64, 269, 271, 273–75, 282–88, 290–92, 303, 306, 310
anti-Black, 23, 45, 48, 58, 77, 115, 118, 128, 135, 138, 142, 208, 210, 274–75, 283, 286–87
institutionalized, 48, 124, 229, 249, 271, 283
legalized, 112
Racist Ontario Museum, 18, 41, 264
Rahimi, Dan, 15, 262, 265–66, 268–70
Ramsay, Jim, 257, 260
Rastafarianism, 89
Rastafarian movement, 89
reconciliation effort, 24, 246, 263–69, 271, 275–76, 292, 303–6
Registre, Quilem, 142
reservation system, 301
residential schools, 230, 292, 302–3
re-socialization, 302
revolution, joining, 310
"Revolution Will Not Be Televised, The" (Scott-Heron), 147
Rico, Ras, 50–52, 209–10, 250, 258, 263–64, 306
Ridge Pen, 64, 66–69, 76–77, 81, 87, 129, 186, 193–96, 201, 233, 243, 245
Riel, Louis, 96, 118, 301
riots, race, 115
Roach, Charles, 43–44, 96, 146, 255
Rodney, Walter, 188, 209, 248
ROM 2, *257*
ROM 11, *41, 50, 58, 60, 104, 144, 151, 210, 250, 252, 253, 254, 264, 265, 270, 274, 275, 295*
ROM administration, 44
Rowe, Alfred, 64, 66–67, 71, 73, 187, 193, 240, 243
Rowe, Caroline, 188
Rowe, Clifton. *See* Packieman (uncle)
Rowe, Edward, 67
Rowe, Geraldine, 66–67, 69, 72, 98, 240
Rowe, Ivan, 66
Rowe, Joseph, 67
Rowe, Louis, 66
Rowe, Mann O., 187–88
Rowe, Matilda, 187
Royal Ontario Museum (ROM), 15–16, 18–19, 23, 34, 40–55, 57–61, 104, 131, 144, 151–52, 159, 200, 209–11, 230, 246, 250–54, 257–76, 283–84, 295, 304, 306–9
Ruck, Calvin Woodrow, 117n27
The Black Battalion 1916–1920: Canada's Best Kept Military Secret, 117n27
Rushton, Philippe, 45
Ryerson, Egerton, 230n39
Ryerson Anti-Apartheid Movement, 50, 210

S

Sadlier, Rosemary, 15, 30, 282
Salkey, Andrew, 147
Sam (cousin), 69
Sankofa, 25, 214, 214n38, 216, 281
Sankofa Kingdom Enterprise, 226
Scott-Heron, Gil, 147
"The Revolution Will Not Be Televised," 147
"Whitey On the Moon," 147
Scramble for Africa, 38, 169
Seaga, Edward, 88
Sealy, Joseph Maurice, 119

Seasonal Agricultural Worker Program, 114
Seaview Memorial Park, 120
Selassie, Haile, 89
Seven Grandfather Teachings, 305
Shadd, May Ann, 282n45
Sharpe, Sam, 61, 80
Sharpton, Al, 45
Simba, Muchoki, 153, 212, 259
Sime, Elias, 309
Simon, Mary, 292n50
Sister Amuna (poet), 151
Sixties Scoop, 303
slavery, 36–37, 39, 85, 110–11, 114, 122, 127, 144, 169, 188, 192, 204, 251–52, 266–68, 271–72, 274, 282, 288, 291, 293
American, 111, 114
human, 37n5, 37
Slavery Abolition Act, 111, 192
Spinks brothers, 126
Spooky, D. J., 48
Stowe, Harriet Beecher, 111
Uncle Tom's Cabin, 111
Student's Administrative Council (SAC), 207

T

Taylor, E. B., 177
tenement yard, 82n16
Thomas, Linda, 43
Three Finger Jack, 80
Tightrope, 309
Timbucktu, 141
Timbuktu, 144
Toots and the Maytals, 90, 90n22
Toronto Dub Poets' Collective, 152
Tosh, Peter, 80n14
"Equal Rights," 80n14
Treaty 13, *96*
Treaty of Paris, 300
Treaty of Tordesillas, 38n6
Tricksy, 64, 66
Trudeau, Justin, 292n50
Trudeau, Pierre Elliot, 109, 125–26
Tubman, Harriet, 96, 115, 231, 248
Ture, Kwame, 33, 61, 248–49
Tutu, Osei, 174

U

Ujamaa, 205, 211, 211n37, 212, 231–32, 280
Ujima, 211n37, 280
Uncle Tom's Cabin (Stowe), 111
Underground Railroad, 96, 112–16, 119, 252, 282
United Fruit Company, 175
United Nations General Assembly, 77
Universal Negro Improvement Association (UNIA), 19, 89, 162, 164
University of Aberdeen, 272
University of Toronto Students' Union (UTSU), 207

V

Venables, Robert, 84
von Bismarck, Otto, 38

W

Wade-Lawson, Michael, 56, 142
Wailer, Bunny, 80n14
Walcott, Ekua, 212
Walker, C. J., 179
Wallace, George, 78
War & Mir (Faust), 143
War Measures Act, 126
wa Thiong'o, Ngũgĩ, 208, 223
Westside Cipher, 212
White, Portia, 119
white man's burden, 38
"Whitey On the Moon" (Scott-Heron), 147
Whitmore, Donna, 100, 205, 240
Williams, Eric, 188n35, 291
Capitalism and Slavery, 291
Wilson, Delroy, 86n19
Woodson, Carter G., 30n3
Wright, Daunte, 142n32

X

xenophobia, 36

Y

Yafeu, Kwabena, 50
Yaw (Kofi's cousin), 50, 52, 57–58, 161, 170–71, 210, 214, 240, 250–51, 254, 257–59, 263–64, 295, 298
Young, Cuyler, 43, 47, 261–62
Young Poets of the Revolution, 15, 124, 131, 139–43, 145–46, 149–56, 206, 208, 244
Yvonne (Caribbean Corner proprietor), 16, 108, 258–59

Z

Zephaniah, Benjamin, 148, 150
"The Death of Joy Gardner," 150
Zimmerman, George, 141

[Created with **TExtract** / www.Texyz.com]

CPSIA information can be obtained
at www.ICGtesting.com
Printed in the USA
LVHW070419160622
721415LV00002B/13